AGAINST THE DEAD HAND

AGAINST THE DEAD HAND

DEAD HAND

The Uncertain Struggle
for Global Capitalism

BRINK LINDSEY

JOHN WILEY & SONS, INC.

Published by John Wiley & Sons, Inc, New York
Published simultaneously in Canada.

This publication is designed to provide accurate and authoritative information in regard to the subject matter covered. It is sold with the understanding that the publisher is not engaged in rendering professional services. If professional advice or other expert assistance is required, the services of a competent professional person should be sought.

Library of Congress Cataloging-in-Publication Data:

Lindsey, Brink.
    Against the dead hand : the uncertain struggle for global capitalism / Brink Lindsey.
      p.   cm.
    Includes bibliographical references and index.
    ISBN 0-471-44277-1 (cloth : alk. paper)
      1. International economic relations. 2. Globalization. 3. Capitalism. 4. Economic policy. I. Title.

HF1359 L555 2002
337—dc21   2002026960

Printed in the United States of America

10 9 8 7 6 5 4 3 2 1

For Matthew, Michael, and Jack

Contents

PREFACE   ix

1.   The Weight of the Past   1

2.   The Industrial Counterrevolution   16

3.   Centralization versus Uncertainty   38

4.   From World Economy to World War   61

5.   Twilight of the Idols   86

6.   The Dead Hand   119

7.   Hollow Capitalism   137

8.   The Rule of Lawlessness   162

9.   Unpeaceful Coexistence   189

10. Recasting the Safety Net   215

11. Liberalization by Fits and Starts   244

EPILOGUE   271

NOTES   275

REFERENCES   303

INDEX   321

Preface

In the popular view, globalization is an immensely powerful, almost irresistible force in contemporary affairs. It is commonly portrayed as a kind of genie that, having somehow escaped from the bottle, now bends the whole world to its will. National governments in particular have supposedly lost much of their sovereignty to globalization's new imperium.

This view of things transcends ideological divisions. Both friends and foes of globalization portray it as the more-or-less unchecked triumph of markets over governments—of economic forces over political power. Whether the victory is to be celebrated or mourned is, of course, hotly disputed, but not whether it has in fact occurred.

This book takes a contrarian position. In it, I argue that the popular image of globalization amounts to a gross distortion of reality. What that image lacks, most fundamentally, is any sense of historical context. This book sets out to address that deficiency; it attempts to reconnect globalization with the past from which it has arisen.

When the swirl of contemporary events is placed in proper context, it becomes clear that globalization is not some demonic force unloosed upon the world. Rather, it has been a deliberately chosen response to the worldwide failures of central planning and top-down control. Over the past couple of decades, governments around the planet have been confronted with serious economic ills—both acute crises and chronic underperformance—that were caused by decades of dysfunctional anti-market policies. They have reacted to those ills by removing government controls over economic life and expanding the scope of market competition. In particular, one result of the general liberalization has been the reduction of barriers to international trade and investment. Most dramatically, vast populations that were previously cut off from the rest of the world—in the Soviet bloc, China,

India, and many other developing countries—have opened up and rejoined the international market economy. As a result, it has become possible, for the first time in the better part of a century, to speak of a truly global division of labor.

It is not the case, then, that globalization has been forcing governments to adopt market-friendly policies against their will. On the contrary, the breakdown of failed collectivist policies, and decisions by governments faced with that breakdown to explore market-friendly alternatives, are the preconditions that have made globalization possible. The popular understanding of globalization, shared by cheerleaders and doomsayers alike, thus has the main direction of historical causation precisely backwards.

But if globalization arose out of a break with the collectivist past, that break has not been a clean one. For all the crowing on one side and teeth-gnashing on the other, the triumph of markets is nowhere in sight. The world is only just beginning to overcome a century-long infatuation with state-dominated economic development; market competition continues to be hindered by a wretched excess of top-down controls, and at the same time undermined by a lack of supporting institutional infrastructure. The invisible hand of markets may be on the rise, but the dead hand of the old collectivist dream still exerts a powerful influence.

Furthermore, the advance of markets has occurred more by default than by anything else. There have been exceptions, but most of the national leaders who have instituted pro-market reforms have done so, not because of any ideological commitment to economic liberalism, but out of sheer pragmatism—in other words, for lack of any plausibly viable alternative. Consequently, reforms have all too often been half-hearted, and therefore tentative and incomplete.

The present episode of globalization is thus best understood as a transitional era—a turbulent but hopeful interregnum between the dashed hopes of centralized control and the full promise of economic freedom. During this period, elements of past and future strain against each other, and the tensions sometimes erupt in spectacular upheavals. The financial crises that have upended East Asia, Russia, and Latin America in recent years are testaments to the instability of the present state of affairs.

As director of the Center for Trade Policy Studies at the Cato Institute, I monitor international trade and investment policies in the United States and elsewhere and make recommendations as to how those policies can be improved. My job therefore puts me squarely in the middle of the current furor over globalization: the North American Free Trade Agreement, the World Trade Organization, and the like are the subjects I deal with for a living. And, prior to assuming my present position with the Cato Institute, I served as an international trade lawyer for a number of years, representing mostly East Asian companies that exported goods to the United States. That experience, which entailed spending three or four months a year in various spots along the Pacific Rim, gave me a more direct and personal exposure to the dynamism and disappointments of life in the global economy.

In my professional capacity, I have confronted again and again the historical myopia that afflicts the public debate over globalization. Both sides blithely assume that free markets are in the saddle and riding the world. It is therefore all too easy for opponents of market-oriented policies to blame them for all the world's harshness and heartache. The influence of the past on present-day conditions is too often unacknowledged; the miserable failures that preceded pro-market reforms are too often forgotten; the continuing harm inflicted by remaining anti-market policies is too often ignored. The prevailing misconceptions about globalization thus contribute to the controversy surrounding it—thereby increasing the likelihood that the advance of desperately needed economic liberalization will be slowed or even reversed.

I have written this book in an effort to set the record straight—to tell the story of globalization properly and to offer a clear-eyed assessment of its progress and prospects. In undertaking this task, I have had to stray far beyond my professional expertise in law and public policy and delve into the realms of history, economics, sociology, and political science. While I have done my best to get the details right, I have no doubt that specialists will wince occasionally at my forays into their disciplines. I beg their indulgence and defend myself on the ground that a large canvas calls for broad strokes—and the past, present, and future of the world economy is a very large canvas indeed. My hope is that getting the big picture right will excuse any minor lapses on details.

I owe a debt of gratitude to many people. First of all, Ed Crane, president of the Cato Institute, was unfailingly supportive from the very start. Without his confidence in me and his generosity in providing me with the time and resources I needed, this book would not have been possible. Let me also acknowledge at the outset Matt Holt, my editor at John Wiley & Sons, for believing in my work and helping me through all the twists and turns of the publishing process.

In doing the research for this book I traveled to various, far-flung parts of the globe, and was aided along the way by a number of people who helped me plan itineraries, schedule interviews, and get to out-of-the-way places. I would like to single out in particular Byeong-Ho Gong, Nohyung Park, Jeff McDonald, Tomas Larsson, Pornprom Karnchanachari, Chuck Holmes, Barun Mitra, Jal Khambata, Gerardo Bongiovanni, and Fernando Bach. Virginia Postrel, David Frum, Doug Irwin, Razeen Sally, David Boaz, Tom Palmer, Ian Vásquez, David Henderson, and José Piñera were kind enough to review various preliminary drafts. The end product benefited greatly from their helpful comments and criticisms; of course, I absolve them from all responsibility for any errors that remain. Scott Lincicome, my research assistant, was invaluable in tracking down sources, checking citations and endnotes, and compiling the list of references.

My wife Debbie deserves a medal for her superhuman exertions at home while I was even more distracted than usual. And finally, let me give a verbal hug to my three sons: Matthew, Michael, and Jack. This book is dedicated to them—and to the messy, tragic, wonderful world that they and all our children will inherit from us.

AGAINST THE DEAD HAND

1

The Weight of the Past

Near Gorky Park, on the banks of the Moskva River, lies the Graveyard of Fallen Monuments. It is located on the grounds of the New Tretyakov Gallery—a lifeless, white hulk of a building that houses the premier collection of paintings from the school of Soviet Socialist Realism. Stroll the museum's uncrowded exhibits and you will see such forgotten masterpieces as Yefim Cheptsov's *Meeting of the Village Communist Cell,* Arkady Platsov's *Tractor Drivers' Supper,* and Pyotor Kotov's *Building the Kuznetsk Metal Works Blast Furnace.* Walk outside, turn left, and you enter the graveyard.

Scattered over a few acres are the toppled icons of the Soviet faith. The star of the collection is the towering statue of Felix Dzerzhinsky, founder of the Soviet secret police, which stood in Lubyanka Square in front of KGB headquarters until it was hauled down after the failed coup of 1991. Statues and busts of Lenin can be found aplenty, and there is even a red marble statue of Stalin—his face partially shattered, staring impassively over a gruesome jumble of stacked stone heads penned in concrete-and-barbed-wire cages.

When I visited it in 1999, toward the end of a warm July afternoon, the graveyard hosted a thin crowd of visitors. Little groups walked quietly along its concrete paths, in and out of small groves of trees; couples sat on park benches in the overgrown, unmowed grass. There was a refreshment stand in one corner, near the museum. A few people sat at umbrella tables; canned gin and tonic was their drink of choice.

In the Graveyard of Fallen Monuments, the soaring ambitions and ruthless power of the Soviet era have been reduced to kitsch. But the mocking spirit of the place wrestles with a deep and heavy sense of gloom. In the hushed stillness and lengthening shadows, the cruel gazes of the fallen leaders still cast a pall—still chill the soul with their inhuman, all-too-human arrogance. The past, though dead, still haunts.

And so it is throughout all of Moscow. The smirk of disillusionment is everywhere in evidence. You can buy McLenin T-shirts in the Arbat or Prime Nostalgia cigarettes in any train station (your choice of Lenin or Stalin on the pack); you can sit in a karaoke bar on Tverskaya and listen to young people singing revolutionary anthems as a comedy routine; you can gaze out at the Kremlin wall over a burger and potato skins from the T.G.I. Friday's just outside Red Square. And yet Lenin still lies in his tomb, the great Stalinist Gothic towers loom on the skyline, a large statue of Marx glowers in Revolutionary Square, and the metro escalators plunge into weird phantasmagorias of socialist triumphalism. Moscow itself is one large Graveyard of Fallen Monuments.

The grip of the failed past is palpable in the former world capital of the Communist revolution, but it can be felt to a greater or lesser extent in every corner of the planet. For Soviet-style communism was but an extreme manifestation of a much broader vision that animated much of the history of the 20th century: the dream of centralized, top-down control over the course of economic development. That dream has now expired in universal failure. It died in the United States and Western Europe during the stagflation of the 1970s. It died in China when Deng Xiaoping declared that "it doesn't matter if the cat is black or white, so long as it catches mice." It died in Latin America during the debt crisis and lost decade of the 1980s. It died in the Soviet Empire with the collapse of the Berlin Wall. And it died in East Asia with the bursting of the Japanese bubble and the financial crisis of 1997–98.

The death of that misbegotten dream, more than any other single factor, has been responsible for the process conveniently summarized by the catchword "globalization."[1] After all, there was really no possibility of anything like a truly global economy as long as large parts of the globe explicitly renounced participation in a worldwide division of labor. But over the past couple of decades, barriers to the free movement of goods, services, and capital have teetered and fallen, and companies, investors, and consumers have rushed to fill the breach. As a result, a larger share of world economic activity is now exposed to foreign participation and competition than at any other time in human history.

The liberalization of international transactions is only one aspect of a larger pattern of reform. As faith in government controls has dissipated, markets have been given wider play, not only in shaping economic relations between nations, but in shaping them within nations as well. The willingness to subject domestic economic actors to foreign competition has gone hand in hand with the willingness to embrace competition at home. Trade and investment liberalization are thus of a piece with a broad array of market-oriented policies: in particular, the privatization of state-owned industries; commitment to a monetary policy of price stability; elimination of price and entry controls that sustained domestic monopolies and oligopolies; the resurrection of labor markets; the reform of punitive tax systems; and the overhaul of financial institutions to make the allocation of capital more responsive to market returns.

However, the rolling worldwide disenchantment with centralized control has not left market forces with a clear field on which to operate—far from it. The move toward more liberal policies has occurred amidst the ruins of the old order, and so has had to contend with grossly deformed conditions. The transition, as a consequence, has been wrenching and often brutally painful. And the transition is far from complete. The world economy is littered still with the wreckage of discredited systems; everywhere that wreckage constrains the present and obscures the future. Although life has left the old regime, the dead hand of its accumulated institutions, mindsets, and vested interests continues to weigh heavily upon the world.

⚬⚬⚬

Most popular accounts of globalization have focused on its novelties. It is an understandable preoccupation: The world economy today is buzzing with the new and unprecedented. Companies scatter their production facilities around the globe: research and development here, components manufacturing there and there, and final assembly and testing somewhere else entirely. "Hot money" sloshes around the world at the click of a mouse. Mind-boggling sums flicker on the computer screens of foreign exchange traders. And, in a world where information moves at the speed of light and capital follows just behind, national policymakers must take heed of events and reactions abroad as never before.

But today's world economy is not all glitter and dazzle. The past still bulks large and casts long shadows. Consequently, any picture of globalization that ignores or misunderstands its larger historical context is at best incomplete, and at worst distorted and misleading.

Both the cheerleaders and the critics of globalization are fond of highlighting the constraints that international competitive pressures impose on national-level political decisions. But their analysis usually misreads how and why those constraints have arisen and, consequently, fails to grasp globalization's true significance. Both sides tend to interpret the present situation as the ascendancy of newly invigorated economic forces over political power, but that view misses the mark. Unfortunately, this shared misconception redounds to the benefit of the anti-globalization cause, for it masks the deep and fundamental weakness of that camp's position.

The friends of globalization, it must be admitted, started all the hype about the powerlessness of governments in the new world economy. Typical in this regard are the breathless titles of two books by management guru Kenichi Ohmae: *The Borderless World* and *The End of the Nation State.* Journalist Thomas Friedman is another prominent exponent of this point of view. In his celebrated book *The Lexus and the Olive Tree,* he writes of the "golden straitjacket" that forces governments to pursue market-friendly policies—or else face the wrath of the "electronic herd" of international investors.

Friedman, like many others, argues that this new state of affairs is due to revolutionary breakthroughs in telecommunications and information technology. An inexhaustible source of catchy metaphors, he identifies "Microchip Immune Deficiency Syndrome," or "MIDS," as "the defining political disease of the globalization era." According to Friedman:

> Countries and companies with MIDS tend to be those run on Cold War corporate models—where one or a few people at the top hold all the information and make all the decisions, and all the people in the middle and the bottom simply carry out those decisions. . . . The only known cure for countries and companies with MIDS is . . . the democratization of decisionmaking and information flows, and the deconcentration of power, in ways that allow more people in your country or company to share knowledge, experiment and innovate faster.[2]

Meanwhile, the critics of globalization have taken all the hype and turned it on its head. They see the world as careening out of control. Economic forces, they claim, have broken their traditional bonds and now run riot around the globe. Like their opposite numbers, the critics tag the computer revolution as the chief culprit for this turn of events. But in their view, the new potency of markets represents, not a "golden straitjacket," but a mad and immiserizing "race to the bottom." In the press of unchecked international competition, overwhelmed governments are gutting social protections to keep footloose capital from fleeing. Control must be regained if disaster is to be averted.

Arthur Schlesinger, Jr., an elder guardian of the embattled old order, captures this familiar refrain in particularly vivid terms:

> The computer turns the untrammeled market into a global juggernaut crashing across frontiers, enfeebling national powers of taxation and regulation, undercutting national management of interest rates and exchange rates, widening disparities of wealth both within and between nations, dragging down labor standards, degrading the environment, denying nations the shaping of their own economic destiny, accountable to no one, creating a world economy without a world polity.[3]

It is true that international economic integration has reduced the freedom of action available to national policymakers, and that the Internet and other technological marvels have sped that integration. Even the most cursory glance at world events, however, suffices to show that much of the rhetoric from both sides has been ludicrously overblown. Governments continue to assume a massive and enormously influential presence in economic life. Throughout much of Western Europe, government spending as a percentage of national income still exceeds 50 percent. Federal taxes in the United States have claimed a higher share of gross output in recent years than at any time since World War II. Chinese state-owned enterprises continue to employ some 80 million people. Government subsidies in India amount to 14 percent of gross domestic product. The state oil monopoly remains enshrined in the Mexican constitution.[4]

The plain fact is that market pressures—even souped-up, Internet-driven market pressures—exert only modest and occasional discipline on national policies. To borrow Friedman's metaphor, the "golden straitjacket" is a loose-fitting garment indeed: In other words, the past remains very much with us. The defunct ideas of centralized control exert a waning but still-formidable influence on the shape of the world economy.

By exaggerating the triumph of markets over government, the friends of globalization play into the hands of their opponents. If the present world situation represents the unchallenged reign of market forces, then that reign has much to answer for. After all, the world today is a very messy place. Those hostile to markets pursue this opening with gusto. The Asian financial crisis, the collapse of Russia, chronically high unemployment in Europe—all these and other legacies of the delusional belief in centralization and top-down control are laid at the doorstep of global capitalism. This shift of blame gains unearned plausibility from all the overstatements of markets' supposedly irresistible power.

Critics of globalization take advantage of their rivals' triumphalist rhetoric in other ways as well. One of their oft-repeated charges is that the world today is in the clutches of ideological extremism—a blind and dangerous faith in laissez-faire that ignores vital social needs. "What is wrong with the Global Economy is what is wrong with our politics," contends right-wing economic nationalist Pat Buchanan. "It is rooted in the myth of Economic Man. It elevates economics above all else." Buchanan argues, "To worship the market is a form of idolatry no less than worshiping the state. The market should be made to work for man, not the other way around."[5]

Financier George Soros has taken a similar tack. In *The Crisis of Global Capitalism,* Soros rails against something he calls "market fundamentalism," or the belief that "the common interest is served by allowing everyone to look out for his or her own interests and that attempts to protect the common interest by collective decision making distort the market mechanism." Soros goes so far as to claim that "market fundamentalism is today a greater threat to open society than any totalitarian ideology."[6]

A number of anti-globalization writers have argued that the current market "idolatry" has ominous historical precedents in the early part of the 20th century. Then as now, they argue, economic forces had slipped all proper constraints; then as now, the ideology of laissez-faire ran roughshod over social needs. The consequences in the past were tragic: The excesses of unchecked markets, with their brutality and volatility, ultimately triggered the catastrophes of totalitarianism, depression, and war. Today, the resurgence of utopian faith in markets threatens a new cycle of disasters.

William Greider adopts this line in his book *One World, Ready or Not.* In particular, Greider cites the historical analysis of Karl Polanyi, author of the 1944 book *The Great Transformation.* Polanyi argued that the catastrophes of his time could ultimately be traced back to the evils of laissez-faire. "[T]he origins of the cataclysm," he wrote, "lay in the utopian endeavor of economic liberalism to set up a self-regulating market system."[7] Greider contends that we are once again on the road to ruin:

> Today, there is the same widespread conviction that the marketplace can sort out large public problems for us far better than any mere mortals could. This faith has attained almost religious certitude, at least among some governing elites, but, as Polanyi explained, it is the ideology that led the early twentieth century into the massive suffering of global depression and the rise of violent fascism.[8]

Greider is by no means alone these days in resurrecting Karl Polanyi: He has emerged in recent years as a kind of patron saint of globalization's critics. George Soros notes his intellectual debt in his acknowledgments at the beginning of *The Crisis of Global Capitalism*. Dani Rodrik, of Harvard University and author of *Has Globalization Gone Too Far?*, refers to him frequently. John Gray, a professor at the London School of Economics who wrote *False Dawn: The Delusions of Global Capitalism,* titled his first chapter "From the Great Transformation to the global free market."

The arguments of Polanyi and his latter-day disciples are completely untenable. First of all, their reading of history is an almost perfect inversion of the truth. The tragedies of the 20th century stemmed not from an overreliance on markets, but from a pervasive loss of faith in them. It was the mistaken belief in the promise of central planning that led to ruinous economic policies around the world; it was that same mistaken belief that lent legitimacy to the hideous tyrannies of totalitarian communism and fascism.

As to the supposed ascendancy of "market fundamentalism" in the present, where are the governments today that toe a strict laissez-faire line? Where even are the opposition parties of any size that do so? Scour the planet and you will be hard pressed to find a single political movement of significance anywhere that advocates anything remotely resembling minimal-state libertarianism.

Certainly the world has moved in leaps and bounds toward more market-oriented policies in recent years, but look who has led the charge—in China, Deng Xiaoping, a committed Communist; in India, P. V. Narasimha Rao, a product of the Congress Party that instituted Soviet-style central planning there; in Argentina, Carlos Menem, a Peronist; in Peru, Alberto Fujimori, an ideological cipher. Yes, there have been reformers who made their case in ideological terms (Ronald Reagan, Margaret Thatcher, Vaclav Klaus) but they have been exceptional. By and large, the worldwide rediscovery of markets has been guided by pragmatism, a rejection of the failed dogma of centralized control in favor of something, anything, that works. This is a time of idol smashing, not of setting up new gods.

The only place one can find the unchecked and unchallenged domination of market forces is in the fevered prose of writers. Here again, the rhetorical excesses of globalization's promoters boomerang. Because of all the loose talk about the end of the nation state and so forth, members of the anti-market camp are able to pass themselves off as defenders against wild-eyed zealotry. In fact, however, the anti-market forces are the ones in thrall to ideology; they cannot shake the now-defunct faith in centralization.

The "golden straitjacket" and "race to the bottom" schools not only exaggerate the constraints imposed by international competitive pressures, they also fail to see the fundamental reasons why those constraints are tightening. Yes, it is true that technological advances and the growing internationalization of economic activity have enabled market signals to transmit faster and more accurately than ever before. But that fact leaves a deeper question unanswered: Why are governments increasingly deciding to pay attention to market signals?

The usual answer is that the microchip and the Internet have allowed businesses to pick up and move wherever they want, and this mobility gives them the leverage to play national governments against each other. Consider, however, the situation in the developing nations, whose dependence on capital from richer countries makes them especially susceptible these days to pressures from foreign investors. Since when did attracting foreign investors become an economically irresistible proposition for countries of the old Third World? A generation ago those countries spurned foreign investment as neocolonialist; in fact, they often nationalized existing investments and booted the foreigners out. If that attitude still prevailed today, the intervening technological advances would make no difference at all. The truly important change is that many developing-country governments now care about whether their policies are investor-friendly. And why do they care? Because they now realize that investor-hostile policies are self-defeating—that their old development models of "import substitution" and enforced self-sufficiency were disastrously wrongheaded.

However appealing the notion that the two great trends of recent times—the information revolution and globalization—really boil down to the same thing, the spread of more market-oriented policies cannot be explained by crude technological determinism. How computerized was China when Deng Xiaoping decollectivized agriculture and created the coastal, special economic zones? What did the microchip have to do with Margaret Thatcher's decision to face down the coal miners' union? The Internet was still an obscure Pentagon initiative when the "Chicago boys" transformed Chile's economy and New Zealand's Labour government scuttled protectionism and committed the central bank to price stability.

Adversaries of market-oriented reforms benefit from the popular view that globalization is, at root, a matter of technology. That view allows them to evade responsibility for the failures that created the need for reform in the first place. Anti-market critics can pretend that recent events constitute an external assault on state controls rather than a response to those controls' internal collapse. They can pretend that all was going well before the microchip loosed the globalization genie from the bottle. But that pretense is shattered by a proper understanding of globalization's past.

Globalization is not a simplistic technological imperative. In fact, it is not primarily an economic phenomenon at all. When viewed in the larger historical perspective, it must be understood fundamentally as a political event. Globalization, in the broader view, stands revealed as but one consequence of the death and repudiation of the old ideal of central planning and top-down control. In particular, the greatest recent gains in international economic integration (the ones that have allowed us to talk sensibly of a truly global economy) have come with the demise of communism and various state-dominated systems in developing countries. Those earthshaking political transformations unraveled state controls in both the domestic and international spheres; consequently, they have brought billions of the world's population into the fold of a now planetwide division of labor.

The popular view of globalization has things topsy-turvy. Globalization, the conventional wisdom holds, undermines sovereignty. In fact, however, the more powerful currents of historical causation flow in the opposite direction. It is the retreat of the state that has allowed international market relationships to regain a foothold. This retreat was provoked, not by the impingement of blind economic forces or by transports of libertarian enthusiasm, but by disillusionment. The dream died because it failed: It failed morally in the horrors of its totalitarian variants; and it failed economically by miring billions in grinding poverty and subjecting billions more to unnecessary hardships. Globalization is the fitful, haunted awakening from that dream.

The purpose of this book is to bring globalization to terms with its past. I examine the rise and fall of the old order, whose collapse cleared the way for our current era of worldwide commerce. What were the animating beliefs and defining institutions of the old state-dominated era? What propelled its rise and triggered its demise? What made it incompatible with a global division of labor?

I then survey the lingering presence of the past in today's world economy. To what extent do anti-market policies still impede and distort economic growth? How does the uneasy coexistence of the old and the new create instability? What are the prospects for continued market-oriented reforms in the face of rearguard resistance?

The story of the current episode of globalization has its roots in a prior, failed episode that occurred a century ago. In the decades prior to World War I, the Industrial Revolution made possible a level of international economic integration that rivaled, and in some respects exceeded, our present situation. In that first world economy, unlike in our own, technology was indeed the driving force. Although political conditions grew progressively more hostile, plummeting transportation costs and radically improved communications unleashed worldwide movements of goods, services, capital, and people on an historically unprecedented scale.

But politics, in the end, won out. The spectacular wealth creation of the Industrial Revolution, made possible by the decentralized trial and error of market competition, was widely misinterpreted at that time and afterwards as a triumph of top-down control and central planning. People believed that the giant new industrial enterprises demonstrated the superiority of consolidation and technocratic control over the haphazard wastefulness of market competition. They concluded that the logic of industrialization compelled an extension of the top-down rationality of the factory to the whole of society—in other words, it compelled social engineering.

This tragic error gave rise to a social phenomenon that may be described as the Industrial Counterrevolution: an assault on the principles that brought modern technological society into being and are true to its fullest promise. The belief in technocratic control, especially in vesting that control in the state, began to gain momentum around 1880 and grew increasingly popular with the passing years. Aside from the damage that belief wrought within national boundaries, its fundamental incompatibility with the liberal international order that developed during the 19th century meant that one of them had to give way. It was the latter that yielded.

As collectivist movements gained momentum at the end of the 19th century, the liberal, cosmopolitan vision of free trade and peace gave way to the dark and dangerous vision of a "struggle for existence" among nations. Although many socialists professed to be internationalists, there was a natural association between the embrace of central planning and the rejection of international markets—an association that won out over time. On a deeper level, collectivism and nationalism both offered the comforts of group solidarity at a time of profound social tumult and stress. It was therefore unsurprising that the two waxed in tandem.

Thus, while technology widened the scope of the international division of labor, politics pushed toward protectionism, imperialism, and militarism. In the end, those destructive forces were overwhelming, and World War I was the tragic result. After the war, attempts were made to rebuild the old system. But the economic shock waves of inflation and debt that reverberated after the war, and the new political realities of social democracy and totalitarianism, rendered a return to antebellum stability impossible. Finally, the Great Depression and the protectionist spasms it provoked rang the death knell of the old liberal order. Indeed, for a dark time it appeared that any future international order would be totalitarian.

In the years following World War II, there was a partial move, led by the United States, Western Europe, and later Japan, back toward a liberal international order. But much of the world remained outside this reborn international economy: The Communist nations and most of the so-called Third World pursued economic policies of autarky and isolation. For the bulk of the world's population, the ascendancy of the Industrial Counterrevolution continued to squelch participation in an international division of labor.

Only in the past couple of decades has the counterrevolutionary momentum exhausted itself in disillusionment and failure. And, as overweening state control has receded—with the opening of China, the dissolution of the Soviet bloc, and the abandonment by many developing countries of "import substitution"—market connections have been reestablished. The death of the dream of centralized control has marked the rebirth of globalization.

While the belief in central planning has lost its utopian fire, its effects are still very much with us. We live today in the midst of an ongoing and uncertain struggle between the revitalization of markets and the dead hand of the Industrial Counterrevolution. Call it the invisible hand versus the dead hand. That struggle strains and distorts market and social development and gives rise to occasional, crippling instability. Globalization is, consequently, an uncertain and uneven process, and subject to sudden and traumatic reverses and dislocations. Critics of globalization blame the distortions and volatility on free markets run amok; in fact, however, these problems are overwhelmingly due to the continued bulking presence of anti-market policies and institutions.

The ascendancy of market forces in today's world economy has been grossly overstated—by both partisans and critics of globalization. Centralized control over economic production remains a widespread and deeply entrenched phenomenon. In many countries of the former Communist bloc, state-owned enterprises still dominate the economy; in others, nominal privatization has been undermined by the persistence of massive subsidies, otherwise known as a "soft budget constraint." In the rest of the world, controls on prices and government ownership of productive assets—the most blatant forms of top-down interference with market competition—are still surprisingly common. They are pervasive in Africa, the Middle East, and South Asia. Meanwhile, suppression of competition continues to disfigure particular industrial sectors around the world: energy, transportation, agriculture, and telecommunications, to name a few prominent examples. In the international sector, protectionism and conflicting national regulatory structures continue to pose formidable obstacles to cross-border competition.

The dead hand reaches to the very core of the capitalist market order—namely, the institutions that direct the flow of capital from savers to investors. Around the globe, those institutions are to a greater or lesser extent characterized by over-centralization and perverse incentives. Decentralized access to capital through bond and equity markets remains pitifully underdeveloped in most countries, not only because of direct regulatory inhibitions, but also because of inadequate legal protection of investors. Consequently, banks generally play the leading role in allocating capital—a role that remains heavily politicized, with uniformly dolorous consequences. In the former Communist bloc, banks are often little more than slush funds for moribund state-owned enterprises. In developing countries, interest-rate controls and high reserve requirements limit the flow of funds into the banking system, while political interference with lending decisions ensures that scarce funds are often wasted. Distortions caused by the promise of government bailouts plague even the banking sectors of the advanced nations, as evidenced by the U.S. savings-and-loan disaster and the catastrophic bursting of the Japanese "bubble economy."

The struggle between the dead hand and the invisible hand cannot be reduced to a conflict between government *per se* and markets. Governments are not merely doing too much; they are simultaneously doing too much *and* too little. At the root of so many problems in developing and transition economies is the failure of governments to provide reliable security for property and contract rights. That failure must be acknowledged as one of the bitter legacies of the Industrial Counterrevolution. Collectivist economic policies created bloated public sectors that served as breeding grounds for corruption. Meanwhile, grandiose top-down development schemes diverted attention away from the mundane but crucial work of building workable market institutions. The consequences of neglect have been dire: The lack of stability and congruence in expectations regarding the present and future disposition of property has seriously undermined the ability to make long-term investments and construct intricate divisions of labor.

The false dichotomy between government and market also crops up with respect to the issue of "safety nets" and "social cohesion." Critics of globalization argue that competitive pressures are undermining social protections against hardship and dislocation. But there is no necessary conflict between open markets and sound "safety net" programs. Indeed, as globalization makes countries richer, authentic safety nets become more affordable, not less.

Present-day welfare programs are menaced, not by any external threat, but by their own internal contradictions. Those programs, born of the top-down vision of the Industrial Counterrevolution, have become manifestly dysfunctional. In particular, the aging populations of the rich countries have turned their public pension systems into fiscal time bombs. The treasuries of many developing countries also groan under the burden of excessive transfer payments—which too often benefit the relatively affluent at the expense of those most in need of aid.

Meanwhile, much of what passes for social policy is nothing more than naked interference with the market process. Subsidies for failing state-owned enterprises, tenacious protectionism, limitations on labor mobility—all are routinely defended as necessary for "social cohesion." This is a fraud, and a cruel one. Policies that hobble competitive wealth creation in the name of alleviating hardship merely compound the problem they supposedly address.

There is no social cohesion in economic stagnation or in a corrupt scramble for ever-dwindling spoils. Enlightened social policy begins with the principle that assistance should try to help people cope with change, not prevent change from happening.

Globalization is thus a far messier affair than the prevailing caricature of markets *über alles*. It consists, rather, of an uneasy coexistence between markets and the remnants of the collectivist dream, with the former hindered and diverted at every turn by the latter. The mixture of expanding competition and resistant centralization is a combustible one, sometimes exploding in cataclysmic fashion. The great international financial meltdowns of the 1990s in Mexico, East Asia, and Russia are cases in point. The opponents of liberalization blame those episodes on excessive reliance on markets, but the reverse is actually much closer to the truth.

Admittedly, none of these crises would have occurred if international capital flows had not been liberalized. But liberalization, by itself, was not the problem. Improved access to foreign capital is profoundly beneficial for struggling transition and developing economies; without that access, poor countries would be condemned to fund future growth entirely from their own limited resources. Disaster struck because capital liberalization was not matched by market-oriented reforms on other fronts. In particular, the combination of artificially pegged exchange rates and backward, politicized financial sectors proved catastrophic. The lesson from these debacles: Globalization isn't a parlor game. It is a hard and uncertain struggle against tenacious resistance.

―――――

What is the outlook for the ongoing conflict between the invisible hand and the dead hand? Will liberalization continue to gain ground? Or has the worldwide reform of the past couple of decades been a kind of Prague spring, to be crushed sooner or later by a reassertion of anti-market policies in the form of capital controls, protectionism, re-nationalizations, and the like?

By characterizing the anti-market forces as the dead hand, I have already given some clue to my answer: I believe that the long-term advantage lies with the liberal cause. Because the collectivist, top-down ideal is moribund, there is at present only one viable model of economic development—the liberal model of markets and competition. Consequently, the ongoing struggle is not one between rival ideologies, but between what *is* and what *works*. Those terms of battle consign defenders of the dead hand to a perpetual rearguard action.

Vested interests and sheer inertia will render existing dirigiste policies difficult to dislodge. Consequently, there will be few easy victories. However, as dysfunctional controls and restrictions cause either acute crises and breakdowns or chronic underperformance relative to more open countries, national political leaders will find themselves recurrently under extreme pressure to act. At such points, leaders must move toward either liberalization or ever more heavy-handed interventionism. The current intellectual climate strongly favors the former alternative.

The economic crises of the past couple of years illustrate this dynamic. For the most part economic collapse has accelerated the process of pro-market reform. There have been exceptions (Russia, in the short term at least) but by and large the dominant political response in the crisis-affected countries has been in a liberal direction. What real choice is there?

There is little cause, however, for liberal triumphalism. So-called reforms will all too often turn out to be weak half-measures, debilitated by compromise. At the same time, the sheer poverty and underdevelopment of most of the world afford enormous opportunities for higher-than-Western "catch up" growth rates, even when public policies are far from optimal. The ongoing availability of catch-up growth, and the legitimacy it confers upon even deeply flawed policies, will weaken the incentives for comprehensive reform.

Liberalization's advances, then, will come in fits and starts. Crisis, reform, euphoria, disillusionment, and crisis and reform again—such is the dialectic of the invisible hand against the dead hand.

2

The Industrial
Counterrevolution

*I*t is October 15, 2000, and Boston, like other American cities, is abuzz with
the annual Muster Day festivities. Throughout the city, 45-year-old veterans
and 21-year-old inductees, accompanied by friends and family, head to industrial army offices for the formal ceremonies. Meanwhile, thousands throng the broad,
tree-lined avenues of downtown to view the great parade, while the city's sprawling,
wooded parks are scenes of picnics and concerts and speeches and rallies.

Out in the suburbs, smaller celebrations can be found in nearly every public
square. In one typical get-together, several families have gathered in their neighborhood green for games and a cookout. The guests of honor include one neighborhood
man who was mustered out today and two young women from down the block who
were just inducted. The veteran's breast pocket is adorned, not only with his gold industrial insignia, but also with all the medals and ribbons earned during his years of
service; the two inductees proudly sport their simple iron badges of third-grade rank.

As the late afternoon sun breaks momentarily through the clouds, the modest
beauty of this simple patriotic ritual hits home. The reds, yellows, and oranges of the
peaking autumn foliage ignite to their full, fleeting perfection, while the splashing arcs
of the square's central fountain shimmer and sparkle. Framing the square, the stately
columned facades of the dining hall, laundry, and distribution center cast bold, sharp
shadows. And off in the distance, the great domes and pinnacles of downtown, visible
through a break in the trees, take on a golden glow.

As afternoon turns to evening, people begin to head home and a gentle rain starts to fall. The sidewalk covering unfurls automatically, and everyone stays dry and comfortable. An older man, holding the hand of his young grandson, explains that a long time ago people carried personal rain screens called umbrellas, which then dripped water on everyone around them. "Do you think there's a lesson to this story?" the grandfather asks. "Yes," the little boy replies quickly, as if he has heard similar questions many times before, "in the age of individualism everybody had to fend for himself, but now in the modern age we all take care of each other."

〰〰〰

This strange Boston is obviously not the one of contemporary reality. It is instead a city of unfulfilled prophecy. The previous vignette attempts to capture the Boston imagined over a century ago by Edward Bellamy, author of the best-selling *Looking Backward: 2000–1887*.[1] To understand our world today, and especially to sort through all the controversies that swirl around the buzzword "globalization," there is no better place to begin than by examining Bellamy's now-obscure forecast, and why it did not and could not come to pass.

Looking Backward tells the story of one Julian West, a well-to-do young Bostonian who battles chronic insomnia through the services of a mesmerist. When West is placed in a trance on the night of May 30, 1887, circumstances conspire to leave him in a state of suspended animation until a chance discovery finally leads to his reawakening—on September 10, 2000. He discovers that he has not changed at all, but that the world has been transformed.

Gone are the roiling labor troubles, the business crashes, and the dark forebodings of impending social collapse. Gone are the scourges of hunger and want. West is reborn in a world reborn—where total centralization of economic decision-making in the hands of the state has created an earthly paradise.

This radical change occurred, not through violent revolution, but as a natural outgrowth of the consolidation of economic decision-making by big business—a process already well underway at the time West lapsed into his long, hypnotic trance. Doctor Leete, who discovers and revives West and acts as his guide through future shock, explains the origins of the new social order as follows:

The movement toward the conduct of business by larger and larger aggregations of capital, the tendency toward monopolies, which had been so desperately and vainly resisted, was recognized at last, in its true significance, as a process which only needed to complete its logical evolution to open a golden future to humanity.

> Early in the last century the evolution was completed by the final consolidation of the entire capital of the nation. The industry and commerce of the country, ceasing to be conducted by a set of irresponsible corporations and syndicates of private persons at their caprice and for their profit, were entrusted to a single syndicate representing the people, to be conducted in the common interest for the common profit. The nation, that is to say, organized as the one great business corporation in which all other corporations were absorbed; it became the only capitalist in the place of all other capitalists, the sole employer, the final monopoly in which all previous and lesser monopolies were swallowed up, a monopoly in the profits and economies of which all citizens shared. The epoch of trusts had ended in The Great Trust.[2]

Under the new system, the national economy is organized as one great industrial army, at the pinnacle of which the President of the United States serves as general-in-chief. Service in the army is compulsory for all able-bodied men and women between the ages of 21 and 45 (although doctors, teachers, and artists serve outside the army). The demand for particular jobs is matched to the available supply by adjustments in the daily working hours (more arduous, less attractive jobs have shorter hours); there is, however, no distinction between jobs as to wages, and, indeed, no system of wages at all. Rather, every citizen of the country, regardless of age or occupation, receives the same income. Nonpecuniary incentives prevail instead: Workers are motivated to do their best, not by higher wages, but by the social status that attends higher rank and other awards and prizes presented in recognition of special merit and achievement.

Meanwhile, all commerce has been replaced by a system of direct distribution. Every ward of Boston has one store, which offers exactly the same merchandise as every other store in the country—namely, every product produced or imported by the United States. These stores have no stock, only samples; shoppers go there and place orders, which are then filled and delivered from central warehouses. The prices of the goods (set generally according to labor content, but with some adjustment for scarcity in the case of non-staples) are then deducted from the purchaser's credit card (which is renewed each year with his or her per capita share of the national product).

Aside from its beneficent social consequences—namely, the elimination of poverty, class conflict, lawyers, politicians, and virtually all crime—the nationalization of economic life has ushered in a general prosperity unimaginable in the bygone "age of individualism." And the fountainhead of this plenty is the vastly superior productivity of central planning as compared to private enterprise. As Doctor Leete explains:

> The effectiveness of the working force of a nation, under the myriad-headed leadership of private capital, even if the leaders were not mutual enemies, as compared with that which it attains under a single head, may be likened to the military efficiency of a mob, or a horde of barbarians with a thousand petty chiefs, as compared with that of a disciplined army under one general—such a fighting machine, for example, as the German army in the time of Von Moltke.[3]

According to Doctor Leete, nationalization eliminates the "four great wastes" that were endemic to the old market system: "first, the waste by mistaken undertakings; second, the waste from the competition and mutual hostility of those engaged in industry; third, the waste by periodical gluts and crises, with the consequent interruptions of industry; fourth, the waste from idle capital and labor, at all times."[4]

The advantages of scale and central control permeate social life in 21st century Boston. Housework has been practically eliminated thanks to public laundries and kitchens; orchestral performances and Sunday morning sermons are piped into the home over telephone wires; even the inconvenience of bad weather has been removed by public sidewalk coverings that roll into position whenever needed. When West marvels at this last invention, Edith Leete (Doctor Leete's daughter, with whom West falls in love) responds:

> The private umbrella is Father's favorite figure to illustrate the old way in which everybody lived for himself and his family. There is a nineteenth-century painting at the art gallery representing a crowd of people in the rain, each one holding his umbrella over himself and his wife, and giving his neighbors the drippings, which he claims must have been meant by the artist as a satire on his times.[5]

Although now largely forgotten, Edward Bellamy's vision of a future collectivist utopia caused a sensation in its day. Published in 1888, *Looking Backward* quickly sold hundreds of thousands of copies—a publishing phenomenon unrivaled in the United States since *Uncle Tom's Cabin*. Hundreds of "Bellamy clubs" sprang up around the country; the burgeoning Populist movement absorbed much of Bellamy's vision.[6] Years later, Progressive icons John Dewey and Charles Beard, independently rating the most influential books since 1885, both put *Looking Backward* in second place, trailing only Karl Marx's *Das Kapital*.[7]

Bellamy's book made such an impact because it crystallized and dramatized a powerful new idea that, in one form or another, was taking hold of the world and remaking it in its image. That idea, reduced to its bare essence, was that the economic revolution of industrialization both enabled and required a revolution in social organization—namely, the eclipse, whether partial or total, of markets and competition by centralized, top-down control.

The intellectual and political movements spawned by this idea emerged in the last quarter of the 19th century and utterly dominated the first three-quarters of the 20th. This hundred-year historical episode, though composed of diverse and widely varying elements, possesses enough coherence to merit a name, and the one I suggest is the Industrial Counterrevolution.[8]

The Industrial Counterrevolution was protean, and in its many guises captured minds of almost every persuasion. It transcended the conventional left-right political spectrum: Both progressives who welcomed the social transformations wrought by industrialization and conservatives who feared them were united in their calls for a larger state with expanded powers. The Industrial Counterrevolution swept up reformers and revolutionaries, the religious and the anticlerical, social activists and big businessmen, workers and capitalists. The political forms that bore its imprint were many and varied: the welfare and regulatory state; the mixed economy of social democracy; the business-led associative state; Keynesian fine-tuning; the Galbraithean new industrial state; the developmental states of the Third World; and the totalitarian states, whether communist, fascist, or Nazi.

Let me be clear here at the outset: I do not seek to minimize the real and sometimes enormous differences among the various political forms that I have bundled together under a common name. Any contention that all these forms boil down to basically the same thing would be a crude, reductionist distortion of a rich and complex historical reality; in particular, any claim that democratic and totalitarian forms were in any way equivalent would be morally imbecilic.

Rather, my point is simply that all of these political forms share a common intellectual ancestry. The Industrial Counterrevolution is properly understood as a family of intellectual and political movements. Just as parents may have children who are very different from one another, in both their practical achievements and their moral character, so did the embrace of centralization result in a diverse multiplicity of offspring. But the differences among those offspring are in no way slighted by recognizing that all the progeny have something real and important in common.

The name "Industrial Counterrevolution" is fitting on two levels. First of all, as a matter of historical development, the movements grouped together under this common heading were both inspired by and reacting against the economic and social transformations effected by industrialization. In the United States and Europe, the centralizing impulse first began to register during the 1870s, just as modern technological society was bursting onto the scene. And, in later-developing countries, the ideologies of centralization almost invariably supplied the matrix for modernization.

Second, in analytical terms, the common intellectual thread that runs through all of these movements—namely, the rejection or demotion of market competition in favor of top-down control—represents a direct assault on the principles of social order that gave rise to industrialization and are truest to its full promise. Of course, the partisans of the Counterrevolution thought quite the opposite: They believed that their political programs and industrialization rode together on the same great wave of history.

The Industrial Counterrevolution was an historical phenomenon of world-spanning scope and epochal significance. To do it justice would require a colossal feat of scholarship—a feat that far exceeds the project of this book and the capacities of its author. Here I can, at best, sketch out a few points of interest, points that give some hint of the basic character of this phenomenon, how it arose, and how it shaped and continues to shape the challenges that confront the global economy today.

⟫⟫⟫⟫⟫⟫⟫⟫⟫

The idea at the core of the Industrial Counterrevolution was as much an answer to prayers as it was an empirical hypothesis. Its appeal penetrated far deeper than reason, tapping into deep longings in the human psyche for meaning and belonging at a time of unprecedented tumult and stress.

Consider the broader historical context in which industrialization occurred. Kings had been knocked from their thrones or else made subservient to parliaments; nobles had been stripped of rank and power; science had displaced the earth from the center of the Universe, dragged humanity into the animal kingdom, and cast a pall of doubt over the most cherished religious beliefs. As if these assaults on age-old verities were not enough, the *coup de grace* was then applied: the eruption of mechanized, urbanized society. Now the natural, easy rhythms of country life gave way to the clanging, clock-driven tempo of the city and the factory; new technologies of miraculous power and demonic destructiveness burst forth; vast riches were heaped up in the midst of brutal hardship and want; new social classes thrust up and struggled for position.

It is unsurprising that many people felt lost—dizzy and adrift in a surging flux without landmarks or firm ground. The deepest thinkers of the 19th century identified this anomie as the spiritual crisis of the age: Friedrich Nietzsche proclaimed the death of God while Max Weber wrote of society's "disenchantment." But it was Karl Marx, the greatest of the prophets of the Industrial Counterrevolution, who traced most clearly the connection between this spiritual crisis and the economic upheavals of his day. As he and Friedrich Engels wrote in this breathtaking passage from *The Communist Manifesto*:

> Constant revolutionising of production, uninterrupted disturbance of all social conditions, everlasting uncertainty and agitation distinguish the bourgeois epoch from all earlier ones. All fixed, fast-frozen relationships, with their train of ancient and venerable prejudices and opinions, are swept away, all new-formed ones become antiquated before they can ossify. All that is solid melts into air, all that is holy is profaned. . . .[9]

The great successes registered by the various movements of the Industrial Counterrevolution, especially the more radical ones, were due in no small part to the fact that they offered an apparent antidote to the jarring, jangling uncertainty of a world where "all that is solid melts into air." In particular, they offered a model of social organization that reconstituted, at the national or global level, the simplicity, certainty, and solidarity of village life.

Robert Nisbet, in his seminal *The Quest for Community*, identified the rise of collectivism in modern times as an effort to recreate through the state the lost sense of community that had obtained in the premodern world. "The greatest appeal of the totalitarian party, Marxist or other," wrote Nisbet, "lies in its capacity to provide a sense of moral coherence and communal membership to those who have become, to one degree or another, victims of the sense of exclusion from the ordinary channels of belonging in society."[10]

Elsewhere, Nisbet described how the specific conditions of the 19th century gave rise to the longing for political community:

> The nineteenth century has been called the Century of Great Hope. Innumerable historians have characterized its dominant qualities in the words of progress, democracy, freedom, and the liberation of reason from the shackles of superstition and ignorance. There is no need to quarrel with any of these characterizations. The nineteenth century was each and all of them. But it was

something else, too, something that touched upon and, in one way or another, involved all of these moral values, something that we are only now beginning to understand clearly.

It was the century of the emergence of the political masses: masses created in widening areas by the processes of social destruction bound up with the increasing penetration of political power into all areas of society; masses created by the impact of a factory system that, in the essentials of its discipline, frequently resembled the military State itself; masses devoid, increasingly, of any hope for relief from the established, traditional institutions of society—family, church, and class.

Between the State and the masses there developed a bond, an affinity, which however expressed—in nationalism, unitary democracy, or in Marxian socialism—made the political community the most luminous of all visions. In it lay salvation from economic misery and oppression. In it lay a new kind of liberty, equality, and fraternity. In it lay right and justice. And in it, above all else, lay community.[11]

Although the promise of reintegration into a larger whole was clearly most pronounced in the case of totalitarian movements, it was present as well in less radical programs of centralization. As against the "chaos" and "anarchy" of the market order, a central state with expanded fiscal and regulatory powers offered the reassurance that somebody was "in charge." In particular, the nationalization or regulation of previously autonomous private enterprises reasserted the primacy of the group that had always held sway in earlier times.

Note also that, though the focus here has been on the rise of centralizing movements in 19th century Europe and North America, the same analysis applies with even greater force to later-industrializing countries outside of the North Atlantic world. There the experiences of initial modernization were, if anything, even more vertiginous. Social changes were often accelerated by the confrontation, all at once, with Western innovations that had taken decades or centuries to develop originally. Moreover, these changes were experienced, not as a homegrown development, but as a real or figurative conquest by foreign powers—thus heightening the sense of loss of control. Ideologies that upheld premodern, precolonial social values were sure to find a ready audience.

Although the Industrial Counterrevolution was, at bottom, reactionary in the values it celebrated, it went far beyond simple nostalgia or defense of embattled vested interests. It is true that some of the "right wing" or "conservative" counterrevolutionary movements (for example, Bismarckian state socialism in Germany, or Tory democracy in Britain) did explicitly call for the use of state power to strike a balance between modernity and the preindustrial social order. Even these movements, though, were not purely reactionary—not by any means. They accepted industrialization as inevitable (if not particularly welcome) and allied themselves with economic progress; they promised not only to safeguard preindustrial interests, but also to improve the efficiency of industry and the lot of industrial workers. Meanwhile, "left wing" or "progressive" movements, from Marxian revolutionaries to Third World nationalists to Keynesian pump-primers, embraced the new industrial economy unreservedly.[12]

The genius of the Industrial Counterrevolution lay, not in making any compromise between progress and reaction, but in co-opting the products of progress and putting them in the service of reactionary values. The key to this legerdemain was the empirical hypothesis that I have identified as the unifying idea of all the centralizing movements: namely, that the logic of industrialization pushes inexorably toward the consolidation of economic decision-making.

With this theory of how the world works, adherents of top-down control were able to square the circle and embrace both progress and nostalgia at once. Whatever the specific details of their programs, whether conservative or unabashedly technocratic, the centralizers built their mass appeal on a vision of "back to the future"—the realization of the full benefits of science and technology through a return to archaic social values.

Although the left and right wings of the Industrial Counterrevolution clashed, often with cataclysmic violence, together they seized the mantle of progress away from proponents of liberalism. Their contending visions of progress were all grounded in the traditional *Gemeinschaft* values of the village, and thus were vastly more comforting and appealing than the liberal vision of perpetual disharmony and uncertainty. Liberalism, in short order, became an impotent anachronism.

The idea that centralization was progressive did not triumph simply because people wished it were so. Of course, conviction came more readily to those large constituencies predisposed to believe it. But during the hundred-year reign of this idea, even many of those who resisted its implications nonetheless accepted the truth of it. The empirical hypothesis that launched the Industrial Counterrevolution gained general adherence, not merely because it was so convenient, but because it was so eminently plausible.

At the midpoint of the 19th century, liberalism was indisputably the politics of progress. Representative democracy, the rule of law, free markets at home, free trade abroad—these were the waves of the future. Forward-thinking reformers around the world embraced the liberal program.

It was no coincidence that the ascendancy of liberal ideals occurred at the time that British power and influence reigned supreme. Britain was, after all, the birthplace of liberalism and its chief exemplar. In particular, her unilateral adoption of free trade—most notably with the abolition of the Corn Laws in 1846—was a dramatic demonstration of her commitment to liberal economic principles. In the intellectual sphere, the great British social philosophers, Smith, Hume, Ricardo, and Mill, made powerful theoretical cases for the safeguarding of individual liberty as the chief business of government.

At the same time, Britain was the richest and mightiest nation on earth: She was both the workshop of the world and the ruler of the waves, and her empire was vast and growing. It was fitting when, in 1861, the geographical zero meridian was drawn through a suburb of London, for at that time Britain truly was the center of the world.

Liberalism's fortunes rose with those of its chief host and defender. British preeminence gave the theoretical justifications for liberal policies the stamp of worldly success—indeed, of world dominance. Britain was the example that the world wanted to follow, and that example was a liberal one.

In the last quarter of the 19th century, however, British preeminence began to come into question. Two fast-rising nations, the recently unified Germany and the recently reunified United States, became the new economic powerhouses. American and German firms grabbed leadership in new technologies and new industries; their shares of world industrial production and exports climbed steadily as those of British firms eroded. As Britain fell into relative, if not absolute, decline, the United States and Germany came to be seen as the new proving grounds of the future—and the apparent outlines of this future were decidedly not liberal.

Although industrialization began in Britain in the mid–18th century, the modern mass-production economy first emerged in recognizable form in the United States during the decades between the Civil War and World

War I. Some economic historians call this advent the "second Industrial Revolution," but I think it makes more sense to say simply that the Industrial Revolution became an integrated whole. What had been separate strands of economic development, such as new energy sources, new production techniques, and breakthroughs in transportation and communications, were now woven together in new organizational forms to produce a wealth-creating capacity of unprecedented scale, complexity, and power. Moreover, it was at the time of this great confluence that the scientific method was systematically integrated into economic life for the first time; technological and organizational innovation became normal, routine, and ubiquitous. The whole of these interrelated advances was greater than the sum of the parts: It was nothing less than a new kind of economic order.[13]

Of course, important aspects of this process were occurring in Europe, but it was in Gilded-Age America that the new economic order first came together and developed most rapidly. And virtually all contemporaries of this flowering of the Industrial Revolution saw it as a triumph of centralization and top-down control.

When we survey today's business environment, the benefits of competition are obvious and uncontroversial; likewise with the dangers of excessive size. We look at the bubbling ferment of Silicon Valley and see dynamism, not wasteful duplication; by the same token, we frequently dismiss giant enterprises as "dinosaurs"—lumbering, dimwitted, and unable to keep up with their smaller, nimbler rivals.

This conventional wisdom is actually of very recent vintage. It was, after all, only a decade or so ago that noted experts were bemoaning the "chronic entrepreneurialism" of Silicon Valley and predicting that giant Japanese corporations would soon reduce it to a backwater.[14] We should therefore not be too surprised that, at the very dawn of the Machine Age, the virtues of competition and decentralization were easily missed.

Indeed, the leading observers of the American Industrial Revolution were struck by one overwhelming fact: Business enterprises were simultaneously much larger and much more productive than anything ever seen before. The great new industrial firms employed thousands of people scattered across a continent, they processed enormous flows of inputs and materials, and they managed highly intricate distribution chains for their final products. Military campaigns were the only form of human endeavor that rivaled these new firms in their complexity. Like military campaigns, these companies were run by line-and-staff officers (known as managers) whose chain of command led ultimately to a single commander-in-chief (known as the owner).

It was understandable, then, that people at that time routinely associated size and bureaucratic organization with efficiency. Edward Bellamy, in *Looking Backward,* was utterly typical when he stated this association as a basic law of economics: "[A]s a means of producing wealth, capital had been proved efficient in proportion to its consolidation."[15]

If consolidation was the key to productivity in the new industrial economy, it followed that the continued division of industries into rival competitive units was an anachronism. Bellamy, again, summarized this thinking with characteristic force and eloquence:

> Within each of these [firms] the strictest organization of industry was insisted on; the separate gangs worked under a single central authority. No interference and no duplicating of work were permitted. Each had his allotted task, and none were idle. By what hiatus in the logical faculty, by what lost link of reasoning, account, then, for the failure to recognize the necessity of applying the same principle to the organization of the national industries as a whole, to see that if lack of organization could impair the efficiency of a shop, it must have effects as much more disastrous in disabling the industries of the nation at large as the latter are vaster in volume and more complex in the relationship of their parts.[16]

Bellamy, however, was optimistic: He believed that the natural course of industrial development was steadily squeezing competition out of the system.

The great iconoclastic economist Thorstein Veblen—himself influenced by Bellamy, and, with Bellamy, a major influence on Progressives and New Dealers—arrived at basically the same conclusions. "[T]he modern industrial system," he wrote in *The Theory of Business Enterprise,* "is a concatenation of processes which has much of the character of a single, comprehensive, balanced mechanical process." However, he argued, "the pecuniary interests of the business men . . . are not necessarily best served by an unbroken maintenance of the industrial balance."[17]

Veblen believed that the continuation of business rivalry in an industrial economy caused "chronic derangement, duplication, and misdirected growth." He applauded the increasing concentration of market structure and hoped it would lead to full-fledged monopolization:

> So long as related industrial units are under different business managements, they are, by the nature of the case, at cross-purposes, and business consolidation remedies this untoward feature of the industrial system by eliminating the pecuniary element from the interstices of the system as far as may be. . . . The

heroic role of the captain of industry is that of a deliverer from an excess of business management. It is a casting out of business men by the chief of business men.[18]

Interestingly, many American business leaders held similar views. The popular picture of the Progressive Era is that of a fierce contest between a nascent Big Government and a resistant Big Business—the "trustbusters" against the "robber barons." Although interests obviously clashed, what is striking in retrospect is the degree to which the leaders of the new large enterprises actually welcomed government control of their industries. They were as convinced as Bellamy and Veblen that competition was an out-of-date notion.[19]

For example, Judge Elbert Gary, the first chairman of the board of U.S. Steel, was famous for holding weekly dinners with other steel executives for the purpose of setting prices. Gary defended this "cooperative plan," arguing that "the law does not compel competition; it only prohibits an agreement not to compete."[20] If such "friendly association" did run afoul of the antitrust law, Gary had another idea:

> I would be very glad if we had some place we could go, to a responsible governmental authority, and say to them, "Here are our facts and figures, here is our property, here our cost of production: now you tell us what we have the right to do and what prices we have the right to charge."[21]

George W. Perkins, J. P. Morgan's chief lieutenant, made this blanket condemnation of competition in 1913:

> I do not believe that competition is any longer the life of trade. . . . I have long believed that cooperation through large industrial units properly supervised and regulated by the Federal Government, is the only method of eliminating the abuses from which labor has suffered under the competitive method. I believe in *cooperation and organization* in industry. I believe in this for both *labor and capital . . . under strict regulation and control of the Federal Government* in order that they may give the public the maximum amount of good and the minimum amount of evil.[22]

Business leaders like Gary and Perkins stoutly opposed the outright expropriation advocated by Bellamy and other socialists. Instead they pushed for a more moderate course of extinguishing competition through regulation—either government regulation or the self-regulation of industrial cartels. Both sides, though, agreed that competition had to be suppressed; they differed merely as to how far the centralization of economic decision-making should be carried.

In any event, it was not in the regulation (much less nationalization) of industry that America stood as a model for the Industrial Counterrevolution. In those terms the United States was something of a laggard—to the persistent disappointment of American reformers who looked with longing at the more "advanced" nations of Europe. Rather, it was at the level of the individual business enterprise that the American experience captured the world's imagination. In their development of mass production and distribution, America's giant corporations were world leaders, and in their supreme inventiveness and phenomenal productivity they appeared to offer a glimpse of the prosperity that a well-organized *society* could achieve.

Today it is odd to think of American big business as an inspiration for collectivists, rather than their nemesis. But it was. Consider these glowing words from Joseph Stalin, the most brutal of totalitarian centralizers:

> American efficiency is that indomitable force which neither knows nor recognizes obstacles; which continues on a task once started until it is finished, even if it is a minor task; and without which serious constructive work is inconceivable. . . . The combination of the Russian revolutionary sweep with American efficiency is the essence of Leninism. . . .[23]

In this regard, perhaps the most important American intellectual contribution to the rise of the Industrial Counterrevolution was that of Frederick Winslow Taylor, the father of "scientific management." Although Taylor focused exclusively on the internal organization of companies, not on issues of the larger economy, advocates of broader social change seized upon his vision of how industrial enterprises were and ought to be run as a template for their efforts.

The goal of "scientific management," in Taylor's conception, was to raise the productivity of the industrial workplace through the systematization and centralization of knowledge. In the early decades of industrialization, factory work was done according to the craft system; jobs were "trades," and their secrets and rules of thumb were passed down, slowly and grudgingly, from master to apprentice. The owners and managers, meanwhile, were largely in the dark. How work was to be divided, what procedures to follow, what tools to use, and what pace was appropriate—all of these decisions were made by the workers themselves (or less idyllically, by their often brutal and domineering shop foremen).

Taylor rejected what was, in effect, the persistence of the medieval guild system in the midst of the amazing new technologies of the age. He urged managers to pierce the veil of shop floor secrecy by "the deliberate gathering in on the part of those on management's side of all the great mass of traditional knowledge, which in the past has been in the heads of the workmen, and in the physical skill and knack of the workmen."[24] Through systematic observation and experimentation (including Taylor's notorious time-and-motion studies), management could learn "the one best way" to perform each and every workplace task and coordinate it with all the others.

In the scientifically managed firm, Taylor taught, "All possible brain work should be removed from the shop and centered in the planning or laying-out department."[25] Managers would prepare detailed instruction cards, plan the use of and set the machinery, and coordinate generally who did what when and in what order. The jobs of the workers, meanwhile, would reduce to rote routine. The role of workers in Taylor's system was "to do what they are told to do promptly and without asking questions or making suggestions."[26]

What an unblinking vision of absolute top-down control! Unsurprisingly, it provoked great controversy: Labor leaders like Samuel Gompers accused Taylor (with good reason) of treating workers like mere machines. In the end, though, Taylor's "scientific management" was well suited to the temper of the times. Taylor became an international symbol of American efficiency and industrial might: His writings were translated into dozens of languages, and "Taylor Societies" sprang up everywhere.

Meanwhile, his ideas about corporate management were readily applied to the larger arena of social policy. One of Taylor's more noteworthy pupils was none other than Vladimir Lenin. In a speech made during the spring of 1918, Lenin declared:

> The possibility of building socialism will be determined precisely by our success in combining the Soviet government and the Soviet organization of administration with modern achievements of capitalism. We must organize in Russia the study and teaching of the Taylor system and systematically try it out and adapt it to our purposes.[27]

While America offered a model for the larger possibilities that centralization promised, Germany was at the cutting edge of their realization. Germany boasted not only the economic dynamism of rapid industrialization and technological leadership but also—from the centralizing perspective at least—unparalleled social and intellectual dynamism. If the United States was where the Industrial Revolution first demonstrated its full power, Germany was where the Industrial Counterrevolution first came into its own.

The great Nobel Prize-winning economist and social philosopher F. A. Hayek, whose name comes up again and again throughout this book, described what he called "the road to serfdom" as a turn away from the English example and toward the German one:

> For over two hundred years English ideas had been spreading eastward. The rule of freedom which had been achieved in England seemed destined to spread throughout the world. By about 1870 the reign of these ideas had probably reached its easternmost expansion. From then onward it began to retreat, and a different set of ideas, not really new but very old, began to advance from the East. England lost her intellectual leadership in the political and social sphere and became an importer of ideas. For the next sixty years Germany became the center from which the ideas destined to govern the world in the twentieth century spread east and west. . . . Although most of the new ideas, and particularly socialism, did not originate in Germany, it was in Germany that they were perfected and during the last quarter of the nineteenth and the first quarter of the twentieth century that they reached their fullest development.[28]

In surveying the spread of German ideas, the obvious starting place is Karl Marx. It is unnecessary to belabor the extent of his ultimate influence; a quick glance at a world map from some time before 1989 recalls the enormous sweep of territories and populations that until recently were governed in his name. A few comments are in order, though, about the nature of his influence.

It most certainly did not lie in any elucidation of how socialism was supposed to operate in practice. On that subject Marx had virtually nothing to say; indeed, he rebuked others' attempts in that direction as "utopian" and "unscientific." As a result, the details of socialism as an actual historical phenomenon—the specific policies enacted in the name of socialism, whether under avowedly Marxist governments or otherwise—owe little to anything Marx himself wrote.

Marx's great contribution—the one that places him at the summit of all the theorists of the Industrial Counterrevolution—was his attempt to show, not how socialism would work, but why it was inevitable. Marx purported to discover the mainsprings of human history, the scientific laws under which it unfolded. And the operation of those laws, according to Marx, moved events relentlessly and ineluctably toward their ultimate fulfillment in capitalism's overthrow by the oppressed proletariat.

With his philosophy of dialectical materialism, Marx did more than any other single thinker to identify collectivism with the march of progress. Many others advanced the notion that industrialization and competitive markets were somehow at odds; Marx took that notion and integrated it into a comprehensive vision of social development, a vision that combined great analytical sophistication with white-hot moral passion. In so doing Marx imparted, not only to "scientific socialism" but also to all the movements of the Industrial Counterrevolution, an almost irresistible intellectual momentum.

Fittingly, it was in Karl Marx's German homeland that this momentum of ideas first infused itself into a mass political movement. In 1863 the dashing agitator Ferdinand Lassalle formed the General German Workers' Union, whereupon he sent a copy of its rules to Prussian Minister President Bismarck with this audacious boast: "Herewith I send your Excellency the constitution of my realm, for which you will perhaps envy me."[29] Lassalle did not live to realize his vast personal ambitions; he was shot dead in a duel the very next year. However, the working-class organization he founded survived him. Meanwhile, Marx's own International Working Men's Association, established in London in 1864, took firm root in Germany in 1868, when Marx's associates August Bebel and Wilhelm Liebknecht took the reins of the formerly liberal-oriented Union of Workers' Associations and embraced the socialist program of the International. In 1875 the Marxists and Lassalleans joined forces and created the German Social Democratic Party—the same party that Gerhard Schroeder heads today.

The Social Democrats quickly became a powerful force in German politics. In the 1877 Reichstag elections they won 500,000 votes and 12 seats. The party survived active repression under the Socialist Law of 1879 and ultimately triumphed over that law's author: In the elections of 1890 the party garnered 1.4 million votes and won 35 Reichstag seats, an outcome that spelled the fall of Bismarck and the end of the Socialist Law. By the eve of World War I the Social Democrats had become the largest single party in the Reichstag.[30]

During this period the newly unified Germany moved quickly to the forefront of nations that were embracing collectivist policies. But the Social Democrats, despite their growing strength, played no direct role in these developments, as they were excluded from any role in the government. In Germany, the first and crucial moves toward collectivism were made, not by the political left, but by the right—in the form of Otto von Bismarck's "state socialism."

Bismarck's social priorities, of course, were at the farthest possible remove from those of the Marxists. He wanted no part of any workers' paradise; his goal was to preserve the Hohenzollern monarchy and the power of the feudal Junker aristocracy. But though unswerving in his ends, Bismarck was always flexible as to means. And it was his calculation that a bold expansion of state control over economic life could serve to maintain the traditional order.

Bismarck believed that the emerging industrial working class, if courted appropriately, was a potentially staunch ally of the aristocracy against the liberal middle class. Consider, in that regard, his reasoning for supporting universal male suffrage:

> At the moment of decision the masses will stand on the side of kingship, regardless of whether the latter happens to follow a liberal or a conservative tendency. . . . In a country with monarchical traditions and loyal sentiments the general suffrage, by eliminating the influences of the liberal bourgeois classes, will also lead to monarchical elections.[31]

A turn toward collectivism, he concluded, was needed to cement the alliance.

And so, in 1879, Bismarck severed his links with the National Liberal Party by repudiating his prior free-trade policies and supporting tariff increases for both industrial and agricultural products. The so-called "iron and rye" tariff united workers in heavy industry and the great landowners under the shelter of government protection. And while one hand offered the carrot, the other wielded the stick: At the same time he was abandoning free trade, Bismarck pushed through the repressive Socialist Law in an (ultimately unsuccessful) effort to crush the Social Democrats. Thus did Bismarck hope to drive the working class away from revolutionary socialism and into the arms of the Reich.

The move toward protectionism inaugurated a policy course that came to be known as state socialism. In particular, during the 1880s Bismarck instituted compulsory, state-provided "social insurance" for sickness, workplace accidents, and old age. Bismarck did not shy away from the socialist label. As he stated in 1882, "Many measures which we have adopted to the great blessing of the country are Socialistic, and the State will have to accustom itself to a little more Socialism yet."[32]

At the same time Bismarck pursued a much wider role for the state in commercial enterprise. Under his leadership the Prussian state nationalized virtually all the railroads—a goal Bismarck had long entertained for military as well as social reasons.[33] Railroads were merely the most visible element of a large and growing state-owned sector that came to include mining, utilities, telegraphy, and banking. As sociologist Ralf Dahrendorf describes the situation, "At what should, in terms of the English model, have been the heyday of private enterprise and liberal social and political patterns, the state was, in Germany, the largest single entrepreneur."[34]

In Imperial Germany state socialism was not merely official government policy, it was also the reigning intellectual orthodoxy. The German economics profession was dominated by the so-called *Kathedersozialisten,* or "socialists of the chair," who derided laissez-faire as *"Manchestertum"* and urged an expansive program of statist social reform. The two most prominent voices of this group were Gustav Schmoller and Adolf Wagner.

Schmoller, a professor at the prestigious University of Berlin, was the longtime leader of the influential Association for Social Policy. Founded in 1872, the Association became a clearinghouse for proposals to address all aspects of the "social question." Its members had varied priorities and approaches, but they were united in their disdain for market competition on moral and social grounds. "We are convinced that the unchecked reign of partially antagonistic and unequal individual interests cannot guarantee the common welfare," stated Schmoller in his opening address at the Association's initial meeting.[35]

Wagner, also at the University of Berlin, pursued a political career as well as an academic one. He served as a deputy to the Prussian state parliament, a member of the Prussian House of Lords, and a leader of the Christian Social Party. He was the author of the eponymous "Wagner's law," according to which the progress of civilization necessitated ever-expanding state control over economic life.[36] Wagner was an unabashed statist; he called for an expansion of government controls "not for the sake of one-sided eudaemonism, not for the sake of the individual or individuals, but for the sake of the whole, for the sake of the nation."[37]

Liberalism had never enjoyed better than a tenuous foothold in German political life. By the time Bismarck left office in 1890, it had been, not just defeated, but utterly demoralized. Meanwhile, in those countries where economic liberalism had been most firmly established—the United States and Britain—the ideas and policies of German state socialism, with their allure heightened by German industrial and military might, helped to turn the intellectual tide toward collectivism.

Many Americans absorbed German influences by first-hand experiences of travel and study abroad. Edward Bellamy, for one, visited Germany as a young man; his discovery of the miserable conditions of the German working class inflamed his social conscience. Recall as well Bellamy's less tenderhearted evocation of von Moltke, the great chief of the Prussian general staff, in his discussion of the superior efficiency of central planning.

The young American economics profession organized itself along German lines and with German-style goals. The American Economics Association was founded in 1885 in direct imitation of Schmoller's Association for Social Policy. Like its German counterpart, the new organization sought to challenge liberal economic doctrines. As its platform read:

> We regard the state as an educational and ethical agency whose positive aid is an indispensable condition of human progress. While we recognize the necessity of individual initiative in industrial life, we hold that the doctrine of *laissez-faire* is unsafe in politics and unsound in morals; and that it suggests an inadequate explanation of the relations between the state and its citizens.[38]

Five of the AEA's six original officers had studied in Germany, as had 20 of its first 26 presidents. Thus did German influence permeate what became part of the American intellectual establishment.

Progressive Era reformers explicitly touted the German model. To cite just one striking example, as late as 1916, on the verge of U.S. entry into World War I, Theodore Roosevelt was still citing the German example as worthy of emulation:

> [T]his country has more to learn from Germany than from any other nation—and this as regards fealty to non-utilitarian ideals, no less than as regards the essentials of social and industrial efficiency, of that species of socialized governmental action which is absolutely necessary for individual protection and general well-being under the conditions of modern industrialism.[39]

Germany-as-enemy would soon replace Germany-as-teacher in the American mind, but not before a strong dose of German-style collectivism had been injected into the political culture.

Meanwhile, Britain's absorption of German influence was tinged from the start with darker considerations of economic and military rivalry. Beginning around 1870, Britain began to experience what is called "relative decline." This does not mean that Britain stopped growing, only that other countries began growing faster. Consequently, Britain's relative position in world markets started to slip and then give way. In 1870, Britain accounted for an estimated 31.8 percent of world industrial output; by 1913 its share had dropped precipitously to 14.0 percent. Britain's hold on export markets likewise loosened: from 41.1 percent of the world's manufactured exports in 1880 to 29.9 percent in 1913. Britain lost much of this ground to the United

States. However, on the European continent, its chief challenger was Imperial Germany. German firms accounted for 19.3 percent of the world's manufactured exports in 1880; by 1913, that figure rose to 26.5 percent.[40]

Of course, to some extent this relative decline was natural and inevitable. Britain had led the world into industrialization, and so enjoyed for a time a near-exclusive claim on its wealth-creating powers. Other countries were bound to follow; Britain could not have expected or even wanted otherwise. More troubling, though, was the fact that British firms were not faring well in many of the new science-based industries that had propelled the Industrial Revolution to the next level of development. As the 20th century got underway, British firms were completely dominated by German rivals in such high-tech industries as synthetic dyes, optical glass, and sophisticated electrical goods.[41]

Even more troubling was the way in which Germany's growing economic might was feeding its military aspirations and capabilities. In 1898, under the direction of Admiral Alfred von Tirpitz, Germany began an ambitious program of naval expansion—a direct challenge to Britain's previously unquestioned naval supremacy. What ensued was a fierce arms race as Britain strove to maintain its traditional "two-power standard"—that is, to ensure that the British fleet could match the combined power of the world's next two largest navies.

In this charged atmosphere British partisans of the Industrial Counterrevolution gained political traction through a campaign for "national efficiency." Propelled by British military bungling in the Boer War, an ideologically eclectic coalition of imperialists, protectionists, business leaders, and Fabian socialists joined forces to decry British liberal complacency in the face of an increasingly fast-moving, competitive, and hostile world. "Efficiency" became a ubiquitous buzzword during the years leading up to World War I, and Germany—with its strong army and compulsory military service, its state-controlled educational system and scientific and technological dynamism, its large public sector and protected and cartelized private industries, and its state-provided social insurance—loomed large as both inspiration and threat. As historian G. R. Searle notes:

> If one were to sum up its meaning in a single sentence, one might describe the "National Efficiency" ideology as an attempt to discredit the habits, beliefs and institutions that put the British at a handicap in their competition with foreigners and to commend instead a social organization that more closely followed the *German* model.[42]

Under the spell of the national efficiency movement, the "New Liberal" government of Herbert Asquith, led by David Lloyd George at the Exchequer and a young Winston Churchill at the Board of Trade, broke with the old Gladstonian liberal orthodoxy and pursued German-style social policies. Between 1908 and 1911 they pushed through minimum wage legislation, old age pensions, progressive land and income taxation, and compulsory sickness and unemployment insurance. The debt to Germany was explicit. As Churchill wrote in 1908 of the New Liberal program, "Thrust a big slice of Bismarckianism over the whole underside of our industrial system and await the consequences whatever they may be with a good conscience."[43]

That such a statement could be made—that a British liberal, of all people, could endorse Bismarck, of all people—is eloquent testimony to the overwhelming intellectual momentum the Industrial Counterrevolution had amassed by the outset of the 20th century. Even to those who would have preferred otherwise, centralization and top-down control appeared to be the marching orders of progress—on the factory floor and in society at large. The evident direction of history was as plain as the rise and decline of nations: The centralizers, America and Germany, were gaining the world while Britain, the old liberal bastion, was losing its grip. In the new century, like it or not, the centralizers would inherit the earth.

3

Centralization versus Uncertainty

The Industrial Revolution represented a quantum leap in the complexity of economic life. A bewildering variety of new industries and occupations arose. Production techniques became vastly more complicated as mechanization developed and spread. Mass distribution and marketing spun sprawling, intricate webs that connected producers and customers. Countless organizational innovations were devised to manage successfully the high-volume, high-speed flows of inputs and goods through the proliferating new production and distribution systems. In short, industrialization entailed a dramatic elaboration of the division of labor, the result of which was to expand the horizons of achievable prosperity beyond all prior imaginings.

The Industrial Counterrevolution pushed in precisely the opposite direction. It reordered society in drastically simplified fashion, substituting crude, top-down command structures for the coordinated and mutually adjusting creativity, know-how, and on-the-spot judgments of millions of human beings. Its tragic effect, consequently, was to retard the spreading division of intellectual labor that the new economy encouraged. Just as Taylor argued that, in the factory, "all possible brain work should be removed from the shop" and vested in the planning department, so the partisans of centralization withdrew brain work from society at large and vested it in a central bureaucratic command post.

In recent years scientists have greatly expanded our understanding of a broad range of phenomena known as complex systems. From ant colonies to ecosystems, from hurricanes to spiral galaxies, their common denominator is order that emerges from the interactions and mutual adjustments of large numbers of elements.[1] The market economy is just such a complex system—though its complexity is immeasurably embellished by the fact that its constituent elements are human beings with minds and plans and preferences of their own.

The partisans of the Industrial Counterrevolution, though, did not see market competition in anything like these terms. They saw complexity and order as diametrically opposed; consequently, they dismissed the intricate and sophisticated institutional arrangements of the marketplace as "chaos" and "anarchy." In their view, order existed only by design—and the simpler the design, the more elegant and "rational" the order.

Edward Bellamy, for one, was quite explicit in his belief that simplification was the path to utopia. In describing the process that led up to wholesale nationalization, Doctor Leete explains:

> It had come to be recognized as an axiom that the larger the business the simpler the principles that can be applied to it; that, as the machine is truer than the hand, so the system, which in a great concern does the work of the master's eye in a small business, turns out more accurate results. Thus it came about that, thanks to the corporations themselves, when it was proposed that the nation should assume their functions, the suggestion implied nothing which seemed impracticable even to the timid.[2]

The failure to grasp and appreciate the complex order of market competition was the fundamental intellectual error that propelled the Industrial Counterrevolution. The nature of that error is captured well by one of the catch phrases spawned by the Counterrevolution: "social engineering."

The phrase was originally taken quite literally. Dazzled by the new mechanical marvels springing up around them, the partisans of social engineering saw the new industrial economy as, fundamentally, a technical achievement; they dismissed as irrelevant or even obstructive the market order that had made such marvels possible. In their view, engineers were the Atlas of the new industrial economy. Businessmen, at best, were simply along for the ride, and, at worst, hampered economic development with their considerations of profit and loss. Herbert Hoover—who as Secretary of Commerce and then President promoted sweeping centralization of the economy under the rule of trade associations, and who first attained fame as the "Great Engineer"—typified this viewpoint when he wrote in 1909: "[The] engineering profession generally rises yearly in dignity and importance as the rest of the world learns more of where the real brains of industrial progress are. The time will come when people will ask, not who paid for a thing, but who built it."[3]

If the industrial economy was really just an engineering feat, then it only made sense that engineers should run it—on engineering principles. As journalist Stuart Chase wrote in *Harper's* in 1931, "Plato once called for philosopher kings. To-day the greatest need in all the bewildered world is for philosopher engineers." In a similar vein, the *Study Course* of an organization with the delightful name of Technocracy, Inc. intoned fatuously, "The stoking of a bunsen burner, the stoking of a boiler, the stoking of the people of a nation, are all one problem."[4]

The original inspiration for the concept of social engineering was to apply the rationality of the centralized factory to the running of society as a whole. Even when the concept was used more figuratively, its basic logic remained intact. According to that logic, economic welfare is maximized when control is vested in a technocratic elite that is insulated from traditional market signals of profit and loss. By pursuing that logic, the votaries of social engineering thought they were putting economic affairs, at long last, on a truly rational basis. In fact, they were imposing on those affairs a tragically dysfunctional dumbing-down.

The advocates of centralization condemned market competition as wasteful and primitive, or at best dismissed it as irrelevant to the central challenges of economic development. They regarded considerations of profit and loss as distractions from the great and ameliorative project of developing and applying socially useful knowledge for the betterment of living standards. In fact, the competitive system they rejected is a marvelously subtle and sophisticated social order whose greatest virtues are its fertility in developing and facility in applying useful knowledge.

The amount of information that can be used effectively within the decentralized framework of the market system is enormously greater than that which can be deployed under central planning. F. A. Hayek was one of the first to recognize this fact. Although it is fashionable today to declare that this is an information age and that we live in a knowledge-based economy,

Hayek understood decades ago that wealth creation is essentially a process of finding and using information. He also understood that the fluctuating prices of a competitive market system convey and coordinate enormous volumes of information:

> It is worth contemplating for a moment a very simple and commonplace instance of the action of the price system to see what precisely it accomplishes. Assume that somewhere in the world a new opportunity for the use of some raw material, say, tin, has arisen, or that one of the sources of supply of tin has been eliminated. It does not matter for our purpose—and it is significant that it does not matter—which of these two causes has made tin more scarce. All that the users of tin need to know is that some of the tin they used to consume is now more profitably employed elsewhere and that, in consequence, they must economize tin. There is no need for the great majority of them even to know where the more urgent need has arisen, or in favor of what other needs they ought to husband the supply. If only some of them know directly of the new demand, and switch resources over to it, and if the people who are aware of the new gap thus created in turn fill it from still other sources, the effect will rapidly spread throughout the whole economic system and influence not only all the uses of tin but also those of its substitutes and the substitutes of these substitutes, the supply of all things made of tin, and their substitutes, and so on; and all this without the great majority of those instrumental in bringing about these substitutions knowing anything at all about the original cause of these changes. The whole acts as one market, not because any of its members survey the whole field, but because their limited individual fields of vision sufficiently overlap so that through many intermediaries the relevant information is communicated to all.[5]

Thus, the price system is able to coordinate large amounts of dispersed information held locally by various economic actors. Furthermore, it allows other actors to make use of that information without ever directly becoming aware of what they are doing, and without the intercession of any central guiding authority. "The most significant fact about this system," noted Hayek, "is the economy of knowledge with which it operates, or how little the individual participants need to know in order to be able to take the right action."[6]

The market order, far from being a wasteful diversion from the real economic task of applying useful information, is in fact superbly well adapted to accomplish that very task. While collectivists saw central planning as more rational and scientific, in reality it is a woefully crude substitute for the market process.

The inferior capacity of central planning to coordinate useful information runs deeper than the inherent difficulties and unwieldiness of channeling the necessary information through the "central processing unit" of a government agency. The fundamental problem is that much of the necessary information dispersed throughout society is of a kind that, by its nature, cannot be transmitted to the central planner. It is local and ephemeral knowledge that, if it is to be used at all, must be used at once by those who possess it. Hayek explained:

> Today it is almost heresy to suggest that scientific knowledge is not the sum of all knowledge. But a little reflection will show that there is beyond question a body of very important but unorganized knowledge which cannot possibly be called scientific in the sense of knowledge of general rules: the knowledge of the particular circumstances of time and place. It is with respect to this that practically every individual has some advantage over all others because he possesses unique information of which beneficial use might be made, but of which use can be made only if the decisions depending upon it are left to him or are made with his active cooperation. We need to remember only how much we have to learn in any occupation after we have completed our theoretical training, how big a part of our working life we spend learning particular jobs, and how valuable an asset in all walks of life is knowledge of people, of local conditions, and of special circumstances. To know of and put to use a machine not fully employed, or somebody's skill which could be better utilized, or to be aware of a surplus stock which can be drawn upon during an interruption of supplies, is socially quite as useful as the knowledge of better alternative techniques.[7]

Most fundamentally, the market system is superbly well adapted to make use of fleeting, ephemeral information dispersed among consumers—namely, the knowledge of their own relative preferences. This knowledge, for the most part, is not articulable in advance of its being put to use; it reveals itself in individuals' decisions to buy or not to buy particular goods at particular prices. The transmission of that knowledge through markets determines the relative prices of consumer goods and, by extension, producer goods; those relative prices in turn direct the overall structure of production.

Thus, the market order, by making use of dispersed information that can only be applied locally, achieves through a decentralized process of mutual adjustments of millions of different actors a much richer and more robust "knowledge economy" than any system forced to rely on central planning and top-down control. Collectivists failed to see this because they held a drastically oversimplified view of what comprises socially useful knowledge. They saw the productive powers of the new industrial techniques and believed that the abstract knowledge of those techniques was the key to wealth. A disinterested clique of experts, they thought, could wield this knowledge to create general prosperity.

The collectivists' error lay in ignoring the humbler and more mundane bits of dispersed knowledge that are ultimately critical to the successful utilization of the new techniques. By failing to recognize both the enormous utility of this kind of information and the market's irreplaceability in making use of it, they urged the replacement of supposedly "wasteful" competition with a system whose squandering of the wealth-creating potential of the new production techniques was wasteful in the prodigal extreme.

———※※※———

The market order's superiority in applying socially useful information is most apparent when it is contrasted with the attempt to push top-down control to its logical extreme: the complete abolition of markets in favor of pure central planning. That extreme was depicted in Bellamy's utopian fantasy, but it is only in the realm of fantasy that it can exist. In reality, the complete abolition of markets cannot be reconciled with an industrial economy.

The project of eliminating markets *in toto* founders ultimately on what the economist Ludwig von Mises (who was Hayek's intellectual mentor) termed the impossibility of "economic calculation" in the absence of market prices. Socialists like Bellamy believed that economic calculation—the evaluation of alternatives in terms of market values and costs, in terms of profit and loss—was no longer necessary; they believed that such pecuniary considerations could be ignored altogether and that decisions about what to produce and how to produce it could be made on purely technical and objective grounds. In other words, they believed that economics could be reduced to engineering.

But this is impossible. Consider the manager of a single factory who tries to run the plant's operations with maximum "efficiency" according to objective technical criteria. Which criteria does the manager use? Should he strive to maximize efficiency in terms of energy usage? Labor hours per unit of output? Waste of raw materials? Defective products? It is impossible to maximize everything; gains with respect to one criterion invariably come at the expense of performance with respect to others. How does he measure the relative "efficiency" of various alternative tradeoffs?

There is no answer to the manager's dilemma without recourse to those pecuniary considerations that the socialists so despised. The only form of efficiency that is relevant to the welfare of people is economic efficiency: the maximization of the differential between output value and input costs. This differential is calculable only in terms of market prices. It turns out that economics is irreducible, and economics presupposes the existence of market prices.

The manager's position is hopeless when all he is trying to do is manufacture a single product. Imagine his predicament when he is charged with planning all production activities within his country! What is the "efficient" amount of steel to produce? What is the "efficient" allocation of that amount to automobiles? To airplanes? To lawnmowers? To girders for office buildings? To nails? To bailing wire? How do all these amounts change when a major new steelmaking technology is developed? The unanswerable questions can be multiplied *ad infinitum* for every product that is made or can be made.

Socialists imagined that there exists an objective measure of intrinsic value, a measure separate from money prices, that could be used to guide economic calculation by central planners. Typically, they believed that the "true" value of every good was equal to the amount of labor required to produce it. The concept of intrinsic value, however, turns out to be a will-o'-the-wisp. The production horizons of a modern industrial economy far exceed the limited confines of basic human needs; beyond those confines there are only subjective wants and desires. And only the decentralized market system is capable of responding to those wants and desires in any kind of coherent fashion.

The market system creates a coherent order by integrating those subjective preferences into price signals that then guide all economic activity through a fantastically intricate process of mutual adjustment. The political process can vary the intensity of the signals in specific instances—for example, by taxing or subsidizing particular activities, or redistributing wealth or income among individuals. But such interventions presuppose an underlying order of market-signaled activity; they are no substitute for it.[8]

When the political process does attempt to replace the market order altogether, the only possible result is chaos. Such was the experience of the young Soviet Union.[9] Soon after seizing power, the new Bolshevik regime, led by Vladimir Lenin, launched an ambitious effort to effect the radical transformation to a full-fledged central planning system. In early 1918, Lenin (according to his closest lieutenant, Leon Trotsky) repeatedly declared, "In six months we will have built socialism."[10] Industries were nationalized. Private trade was prohibited. The use of money was actively undermined. Compulsory labor, including government requisitioning of "surplus" grain, was instituted.

An enthusiastic report on the new experiment, written in 1920 and published by the Communist International, declared, "All enterprises and all branches of industry are considered as one enterprise . . . ." According to that report, all factories reported directly or indirectly to the Supreme Economic Council and received from it their operating instructions. Raw materials were assigned directly to plants, either by the Supreme Economic Council or by local planning boards. Central authorities supplied plants with capital and workers with rations. Producer goods were distributed to industries by the Supreme Economic Council's "utilization department," while consumer goods were distributed by the Council in cooperation with the Commissariat for Food.[11] All in all, the arrangements were similar to those that Edward Bellamy imagined for the United States at the dawn of the 21st century.

The results of the experiment were catastrophic. Industrial production collapsed. Food shortages in the towns and cities steadily worsened. Peasant rebellions against grain requisitioning erupted into a full-scale national revolt. In early 1921, worker uprisings broke out in Petrograd; the situation was so bad that Red Army soldiers there were not given boots lest they leave their barracks and join the workers.[12] Finally, a mutiny by sailors in Kronstadt—whom Trotsky in 1917 had called the "pride and glory of the revolution"—forced Lenin to relent. After crushing the Kronstadt rebellion, he announced in March 1921 the "New Economic Policy": The policy restored small businesses to private ownership, permitted private trade to resume, reopened trade with foreign countries, reformed the currency, and ended grain requisitioning.

While the industrial economy began to recover immediately, the worst effects of the failed experiment were yet to come. The damage inflicted on the rural sector by grain requisitioning and peasant resistance caused the outbreak of a general famine in 1921–22. Official Soviet statistics put the death toll in excess of five million.[13]

After the fact the episode was referred to as "war communism"—as if the attempt to build utopia in one stroke had really been a series of emergency measures brought about by the ongoing civil war. Whatever they called it, Soviet leaders were duly chastened by the experience. Where once they believed that running an industrial economy from the center was much easier and more straightforward than the "chaos" of capitalist competition, they now appreciated the mind-boggling complexities of what they had undertaken. Joseph Stalin, for example, speaking in November 1920, admitted that the task of central planning was "incomparably more complicated and more difficult" than the challenges of operating within a market system. Trotsky, speaking a month later, elaborated:

> All this is easily said, but even in a small farm . . . , in which there are various agricultural branches represented, it is necessary to preserve certain propor-tions; to regulate our vast, far-flung, disorganized economic life so that the var-ious boards should maintain the necessary cross-connections and feed each other, so to speak—for example when it is necessary to build workers' houses, one board should give so many nails as the other gives planks and the third building materials—to achieve such proportionality, such internal correspon-dence, that is a difficult task which the Soviet power has yet to achieve.[14]

After a few years' breathing space, Stalin abandoned the NEP and em-barked again upon collectivizing the Soviet economy. The cost in human lives and suffering was tremendous, but never did Stalin or his successors succeed in constructing a fully centralized system. Small-scale private agri-culture remained necessary to feed the nation. Money prices, even if they bore no real relation to market value, were still used. Individual industrial enterprises continued to operate with considerable autonomy. Extensive black markets emerged and kept the system from falling apart. In short, a de-centralized system of mutual adjustments remained; all that the Soviet ex-perimenters had accomplished was to divorce those adjustments from the goal of serving people's real wants and desires.[15]

〜〜〜〜〜

Only the most radical movements of the Industrial Counterrevolution attempted to do away with the market order completely. More common were efforts to replace market competition in piecemeal fashion—through nationalization of "key" industries, regulation of price and entry, and redis-tribution through taxes and subsidies.

With such piecemeal interventions, the macro-level coordinating func-tions of the market order remain more or less intact—less, to the extent that the distortion and blockage of market signals (for example, through price controls) become pervasive. But the deeper and more far-reaching dysfunc-tion caused by interventionist policies lies in their suppression of competi-tion within particular (nationalized, regulated, or subsidized) sectors. The effect of this suppression is the marked diminution of society's ability to add to the stock of useful knowledge.

This is because the productive superiority of the competitive market order goes beyond the effective use it makes of existing knowledge. It is in the development of new, socially useful knowledge that competition makes its greatest contribution to wealth creation.

In the first place, competition counteracts the natural tendency of organizations to grow conservative and rigid. For any organization, change is disruptive; it upends established ways of doing things and threatens those who are successful under the status quo. Furthermore, for any organization that achieves some initial success, many in the organization will quite naturally regard that success as vindication of the established way of doing things. It is entirely predictable and natural, therefore, that as organizations age they tend to grow sclerotic.

Competition pushes organizations in the other direction. Loss of position relative to rivals provides objective evidence of the need for change; it shows that the old ways need revision or wholesale replacement. The prospect of failure, or of new gains, offers a tonic for complacency. The existence of competition, incessant and unremitting, gives organizations a reason to buck their natural tendencies and swim upstream in search of new ideas and new ways of doing things. Even with competition, it remains notoriously difficult for established firms to maintain their edge over time; without competition, however, stagnation becomes almost inevitable.

Competition's fertility is not just a matter of providing proper incentives. Even if a central planning agency were staffed by people of such public-spirited zeal that they never lost their restless desire for improvement, the lack of competition would still be crippling. The problem is that, as fallible human beings, they would not recognize the merits of many new good ideas that were brought to their attention. And when other avenues to pursue those meritorious but neglected ideas are closed off by the system of centralized control, it follows that those ideas would never get pursued.

In imagining the desirability of a centrally planned economy, or of top-down control of particular industries or broader economic functions, the opponents of competition failed to grasp the problem of uncertainty. They either assumed that the knowledge necessary to create and spread prosperity was already at hand, or that it would be generated more or less automatically from known sources. They never came to terms with the possibility that at any given time there exists, dispersed throughout society, critical knowledge that planners can never obtain, or that the future course of economic progress is radically unpredictable.

The failure to appreciate the problem of uncertainty was especially apparent when partisans of centralization gazed toward the future. Hayek, with characteristic acuity, saw his adversaries' blind spot clearly:

> Indeed, there are few points on which the assumptions made (usually only implicitly) by the "planners" differ from those of their opponents as much as with regard to the significance and frequency of changes which will make substantial alterations of production plans necessary. Of course, if detailed economic plans could be laid down for fairly long periods in advance and then closely adhered to, so that no further economic decisions of importance would be required, the task of drawing up a comprehensive plan governing all economic activity would be much less formidable.[16]

Nowhere was the collectivist assumption of a static, unchanging future more glaringly explicit than in Lenin's utopian blueprint *The State and Revolution*. Written just before the October Revolution while Lenin was hiding in Finland, this pamphlet lays out the Bolshevik vision of Russia's (and the world's) coming metamorphosis. Once the triumph of the proletariat was complete, management of the economy would be a matter of clerical routine:

> The accounting and control in this respect have been *simplified* by capitalism to the extreme and reduced to the extraordinarily simple operations—which any literate person can perform—of supervising and recording, of knowing the basic rules of arithmetic and of issuing the appropriate receipts. . . . When the state is reduced in the greatest part of its functions to such accounting and control by the workers themselves, it will cease to be a "political state" and the "public functions will lose their political character and be transformed into simple administrative functions". . . . The whole of society will have become a single office and a single factory with equality of labour and equality of pay.[17]

The belief that the future would be stable and predictable was by no means confined to Bolshevik revolutionaries. Indeed, it was commonplace among American capitalists. The mantra of Frederick Taylor's "scientific management"—the pursuit, in every aspect of business operation, of "the one best way"—betrayed precisely the same kind of thinking. Achieving industrial efficiency was a one-shot proposition; once accomplished, all that remained was to go through the prescribed motions, repeatedly and without variation.

As America's large business enterprises lost their novelty and became established figures on the economic scene, their managers increasingly saw themselves as caretakers, not creators. Speaking in 1926, Walter S. Gifford, president of AT&T, stated in typical fashion that the old "pioneering" days of business, with their "captains of industry," were over; the new era called for "statesmen of industry." "Their task," he argued, "is less to carve out a place for their business than it is to carry forward a highly organized undertaking already established. They must conserve what has been built, and steadily add to it." [18]

Three decades later, William Whyte gave the "statesman of industry" a new name: the "Organization Man." His highly influential book by that name surveyed a business culture in which conformity and conservatism had emerged as the signal corporate virtues. Interviewing new recruits at big corporations, he found their attitudes about the challenges of economic life not far removed from Lenin's view of things:

> From company to company, trainees express the same impatience. All the great ideas, they explain, have already been discovered and not only in physics and chemistry but in practical fields like engineering. The basic creative work is done, so the man you need—for every kind of job—is a practical, team-player fellow who will do a good shirtsleeves job. "I would sacrifice brilliance," one trainee said, "for human understanding every time." [19]

Today we think of the economist Joseph Schumpeter primarily for his celebration of the role of the entrepreneur in fomenting "creative destruction." We forget that he believed that the future lay, not with the entrepreneur, but with the Organization Man. "Can capitalism survive?" he asked in *Capitalism, Socialism and Democracy*. "No. I do not think it can." [20]

Schumpeter, along with Bellamy and Veblen, believed that the bureaucratization of economic life by the large industrial enterprises was paving the way for full-fledged socialism:

> Since capitalist enterprise, by its very achievements, tends to automatize progress, we conclude that it tends to make itself superfluous—to break to pieces under the pressure of its own success. The perfectly bureaucratized giant industrial unit not only ousts the small or medium-sized firm and "expropriates" its owners, but in the end it also ousts the entrepreneur and expropriates the bourgeoisie as a class. . . . The true pacemakers of socialism were not the intellectuals or agitators who preached it but the Vanderbilts, Carnegies and Rockefellers. [21]

At the heart of this bloodless revolution, in Schumpeter's analysis, was the fact that, in the large enterprises, "innovation itself is being reduced to routine." "Technological progress," he argued, "is increasingly becoming the business of teams of trained specialists who turn out what is required and make it work in predictable ways." [22] In this new world of automatic and predictable progress, central planners would assume the control over allocating resources once held by capitalist entrepreneurs.

Contemporaries of Schumpeter, the Keynesian "stagnationists," took a very different approach. Contrary to Schumpeter, they feared that technological progress was grinding to a halt; Keynes himself wrote of the "decreasing response of nature to human effort."[23] As innovation ebbed, population growth slowed, and the geographic frontier closed, the modern economy was sliding into "secular stagnation."[24] Under these circumstances, the stagnationists believed that full employment could be maintained only by progressively larger doses of government spending to compensate for the shortfall in private investment. Along these lines, Keynes recommended "a somewhat comprehensive socialisation of investment" at the end of his *General Theory*.[25] Keynesians were not necessarily opposed to competition at the microeconomic level; they simply believed that such competition was of declining importance to the health of "mature" economies. That health now depended on control of the macroeconomic commanding heights by a technocratic elite.

John Kenneth Galbraith saw the triumph of the Organization Man combined with Keynesian demand management to produce "the new industrial state." Though a harsh critic of its failure to address certain social needs adequately, Galbraith believed that the new industrial state had decisively conquered unpredictability by replacing blind market forces with a forward-looking "planning system" or "technostructure." In this respect he believed that the role of large corporations in the U.S. economy paralleled that of central planners in Soviet-style systems:

> In the Soviet Union and the Soviet-type economies prices are extensively managed by the state. Production is not in response to market demand but given by the overall plan. In the Western economies markets are dominated by great firms. These establish prices and seek to ensure a demand for what they have to sell. The enemies of the market are thus highly visible, although rarely in social matters has there been such a case of mistaken identity. They are not socialists. The enemies, in both cases, are advanced technology, the specialization and organization of men and process that this requires and the resulting commitment of time and capital. These make the market work badly when the need is for greatly enhanced reliability—when planning is essential. The modern large Western corporation and the modern apparatus of socialist planning are variant accommodations to the same need.[26]

Galbraith wrote with the wolf at the door. *The New Industrial State* was published in 1967; just a few years later the supposedly invincible planning system was collapsing under the unanticipated stresses of stagflation. Meanwhile, the gales of creative destruction began to buffet the technostructure and soon set the whole edifice tottering; the challenges of intensified competition at home and abroad required creativity, not caretaking, and the Organization Man's day was over.

But I am getting ahead of the story. The point to be made here is that the partisans of the Industrial Counterrevolution were blindsided by events precisely because they discounted the very possibility that the future could be unpredictable. In their view, implicitly or explicitly, the future was one of either uneventful routine or automatic, bureaucratized progress.

Hayek dispensed with such thinking in a single phrase: "The mind can never foresee its own advance."[27] The future is inevitably and irreducibly unpredictable, for the simple reason that we cannot now know what still remains to be known.

Hayek then drew the connection between the fact of uncertainty, about both the present and the future, and the need for competition as a response to that fact:

> [W]herever the use of competition can be rationally justified, it is on the ground that we do *not* know in advance the facts that determine the actions of competitors. In sports or in examinations, no less than in the award of government contracts or of prizes for poetry, it would clearly be pointless to arrange for competition, if we were certain beforehand who would do best. . . .

> [C]ompetition is valuable *only* because, and so far as, its results are unpredictable and on the whole different from those which anyone has, or could have, deliberately aimed at.[28]

"[C]ompetition," said Hayek, "is important as a process of exploration in which prospectors search for unused opportunities that, when discovered, can also be used by others."[29]

Competition increases the chances for successful discoveries by multiplying the number of experiments that are conducted. Economic historians Nathan Rosenberg and L. E. Birdzell, Jr. conclude that the market order's openness to unpredictable new ideas is crucial to its phenomenal productivity:

> The difficulty of predicting the success or failure of proposals for innovation is twofold. Until a product or service has actually been produced, there is uncertainty about its technological feasibility, its cost, or both. There is also uncertainty about the consumer's response. The two are related, since the consumer's response depends in part on what the cost turns out to be. The relatively short history of the computer industry is an example of the unpredictability of both cost and the consumer's response.

> The Western method of dealing with these uncertainties is basically statistical. Western economies authorize a large number of enterprises, as well as

individuals who might form new enterprises, to make decisions to accept or reject proposals for innovation, their own or others'. The rejection of a meritorious proposal by a half-dozen decision-making centers is presumably less probable than its rejection by only one. The system is thus biased toward the acceptance of proposals, but with the cautionary qualification that the costs of unsuccessful programs are borne by the decision maker, and all the rewards go to the programs which succeed.[30]

As Rosenberg and Birdzell make clear, the market system thrives, not only because it encourages new ideas, but also because of how it rewards good ideas and punishes bad ones. Entrepreneurs who successfully develop and apply new good ideas are rewarded with profits. Those profits perform vital signaling functions: They encourage the original entrepreneur to expand operations, while at the same time they lure new competitors into the market. In other words, profits are the signal that leads to the propagation of good ideas throughout the economy by attracting additional resources that will be devoted to applying those ideas. Meanwhile, entrepreneurs whose ideas fail are stuck with losses. Losses, likewise, act as signals: They drive entrepreneurs to contract their operations or else fold completely. Accordingly, losses are the means for reducing the resources devoted to less successful ideas. The profit-and-loss system thus creates feedback loops that constantly push the rearrangement of resources to concentrate them on applying the best ideas for creating value.

To use a biological metaphor, the market system may be compared to the evolutionary process of natural selection. The market system accelerates the evolution of useful new ideas in a two-step process: First, it increases the number of "mutations" by decentralizing investment decisions; second, it then applies to those mutations the ruthless selection pressures of profit and loss.

※※※※

Competition provides enormous social benefits, but that does not mean there is no place for centralization. Indeed, the benefits of the market order are realized only through an intricate interplay between centralization and competition. First, in a modern economy there is a vital, if limited, role for localized centralization within the market system in the form of large business enterprises. Second, the market system itself exists within a larger political order defined and enforced by the centralized coercion of government.

Collectivists asserted the superiority of a "planned economy" over the market system, but in fact the market system is intricately planned. Within each "planning unit" or business enterprise, there is a systematic and often elaborate effort to anticipate and prepare for market developments. In other words, there is an intensive internal process of developing and evaluating new ideas (for new products, or new production methods) before the winners of this internal competition are put to the external market test.

The existence of large, sophisticated "planning units" within the market order (in other words, business firms) demonstrates that centralized control of economic decision-making, at the proper level, does serve a vital function. It is a function that was created by the coming of mass production, and which first emerged in late-19th century America. The partisans of the Industrial Counterrevolution, however, were unable to see the limits to which that function is subject. As a result, they misinterpreted the rise of large industrial enterprises as the wave of a future that could never be.

Given the irreplaceable information-processing capabilities of the market order, the question arises as to why large firms exist at all. If markets are so efficient at allocating resources to their most productive uses, why are they replaced at the enterprise level by the centralized, administrative allocation of resources? After all, it would be possible, in theory, to recreate the coordination of activities that is achieved under one big corporation's roof through a web of ad hoc contractual arrangements.

The Nobel Prize-winning economist Ronald Coase pioneered the understanding of this basic but critical issue in his 1937 article, "The Theory of the Firm." Coase recognized that firms represent the supercession of the normal market method of allocating resources—the price system—by centralized control. He concluded that corporations supercede markets because it is sometimes less costly to organize production administratively:

> The main reason why it is profitable to establish a firm would seem to be that there is a cost of using the price mechanism. The most obvious cost of "organizing" production through the price mechanism is that of discovering what the relevant prices are. This cost may be reduced but it will not be eliminated by the emergence of specialists who will sell this information. The costs of negotiating and concluding a separate contract for each exchange transaction which takes place on a market must also be taken into account.[31]

In other words, firms exist because they reduce the "transaction costs" of coordinating a particular economic activity through marketplace relations.[32]

Putting Coase and Hayek together, the organizational structure of a modern market economy reflects the interplay between transaction costs, on the one hand, and what might be called "hierarchy costs" on the other—the costs of ignoring dispersed information not available to the decision-makers in the organizational hierarchy. Firms grow in size and scope to the extent that reductions in transaction costs outweigh the loss of access to outside information.

To look at the matter from the perspective of creating value rather than containing costs, the boundaries between firms and markets are set according to the relative value of applying specific, available information versus openness to unknown information. Centralized control maximizes the faithful execution of known purposes. When the objective is to carry out some activity precisely according to a prearranged plan, there is no place for flexibility or experimentation. Looseness of organizational structure simply increases the chances that people will work at cross-purposes. What are needed instead are carefully defined responsibilities and clear lines of authority to reduce the transaction costs of coordinating implementation of the plan.

On the other hand, as we have already seen, centralized control flounders in the face of uncertainty. When an activity requires access to dispersed information, concentrating decision-making at the center undermines chances for success. And, when an activity requires nimble responsiveness to change and new ideas, rigidity and strict discipline are counterproductive. In these situations, decentralization, flexibility, and experimentation are vital. This truth applies, not only to the larger overall economy, but to the individual enterprise as well.[33]

The tradeoffs between transaction costs and hierarchy costs—between doing known things well and being ready for the unknown—are thus pervasive in the economic realm. At the level of society as a whole, the overwhelming significance of uncertainty—and thus the tremendous weight of hierarchy costs—is what Hayek identified as the fundamental and decisive economic argument in favor of a competitive market system. Meanwhile, as Coase showed, the presence of transaction costs makes the case for centralization of decision-making at the enterprise level. These same tradeoffs reach further down and influence not only the size and scope of firms but their internal structure as well. Within every organization, there is a never-ending tension between the need to exercise control in the name of promoting efficiency, and the need to relax control in the name of promoting creativity. The proper balance differs by industry and by company, and for a given company differs over time.

These tradeoffs may be pervasive today, but their significance is a relative novelty. Specifically, they are a legacy of industrialization. Prior to the Industrial Revolution, the knowledge embodied in production techniques was so rudimentary that the scope for large-scale enterprise was marginal; the overwhelming bulk of economic production could be managed by the individual farmer or artisan or merchant. The discovery of new, complex production techniques—ones that required the cooperation of large numbers of people and the careful and precise coordination of materials and equipment—changed all that. Centralized control within the market order was the organizational response to the new technological dispensation.

Alfred Chandler is the leading chronicler of the organizational consequences of industrialization. As he notes in his masterpiece *The Visible Hand:*

> The multiunit business enterprise, it must always be kept in mind, is a modern phenomenon. It did not exist in the United States in 1840. At that time the volume of economic activity was not yet large enough to make administrative coordination more productive and, therefore, more profitable than market coordination. . . . Until coal provided a cheap and flexible source of energy and until the railroad made possible fast, regular all-weather transportation, the processes of production and distribution continued to be managed in much the same way as they had been for half a millennium. All these processes, including transportation and finance, were carried out by small personally owned and managed firms.[34]

According to Chandler, large, centrally managed enterprises arose in large part to capture "economies of speed"—the reductions in unit costs through "high volume throughput" in production and "high stock-turn" in distribution:

> By integrating mass production with mass distribution, a single enterprise carried out the many transactions and processes involved in making and selling a line of products. The visible hand of managerial direction had replaced the invisible hand of market forces in coordinating the flow of goods from the suppliers of raw and semifinished materials to the retailer and ultimate customer. The internalizing of these activities and the transactions between them reduced transaction and information costs. More important, a firm was able to coordinate supply more closely with demand, to use its working force and capital equipment more intensively, and thus to lower its unit costs.[35]

Chandler's historical narrative fits perfectly within the analytical frameworks devised by Coase and Hayek. Although Chandler distinguishes between reducing transaction costs and improving coordination of material and product flows, they are really the same thing. With new, complex production techniques that required intricate choreography and precise timing, coordination exclusively through market transactions was obviously unworkable; the transaction costs of making the necessary arrangements continually on an ad hoc basis (in particular, the costs of lost time) would wreck the whole enterprise.[36] Centralization of control within the confines of a single multifunction firm was therefore the appropriate answer to the problem. In other words, the value of the specific knowledge imbedded in the new mass production techniques outweighed any loss of access to other information, and so centralization made sense.

Centralization, however, did not sweep the field; the heavy burden of associated hierarchy costs kept it within definite limits. Chandler is clear on this point. He states, "[I]n those sectors and industries where technology did not bring a sharp increase in output and where markets remained small and specialized, administrative coordination was rarely more profitable than market coordination."[37]

Meanwhile, all firms, large and small, remained creatures of the larger market order. The leaps in technological and organizational knowledge that constituted the Industrial Revolution allowed a new kind of order to emerge: the consciously designed, centrally managed order of the large business enterprise. But however impressive that achievement, the new kind of corporate order was extremely simple compared to the larger system within which it was nestled. The centralized control of the business enterprise dealt merely with applying specific knowledge (such as certain production techniques, or a certain entrepreneurial vision) with reasonable effectiveness. The larger, ambient market order, however, continued to handle problems of unimaginably greater complexity: namely, determining the relative value of different bodies of knowledge and coordinating them with the tacit knowledge of millions of consumers, thus allowing coherent planning at the enterprise level and achieving overall coherence throughout the system as whole.

Just as business enterprises operate within the larger economic order of the market, so the market system itself is situated within a larger political order. It is a crude mistake to equate free markets with the mere absence of government. On the contrary, markets only function properly by virtue of institutions created and maintained by government.

Most fundamentally, markets rely on the elaboration and enforcement of basic property and contract rights. When property titles are insecure, and contracts are not reliably enforceable, the large-scale, long-term investments on which so much of wealth creation in modern society depends are discouraged and underdeveloped. Also, specialized rules for sophisticated commercial dealings must be structured properly if the wealth-creating power of competition is to fulfill its potential. Poorly designed rules on such matters as intellectual property, corporate governance, and bankruptcy can exert a significant drag on market performance.

A sound legal framework for the market order includes a considerable amount of regulatory activity typically associated with "activist" government. Thus, safeguarding persons and property from harm is sometimes better accomplished by preventive health and safety regulation than by waiting for harm to occur and then assigning liability. Also, in areas where property rights are inherently difficult to define clearly (for example, with respect to air quality), enforcement of standards by regulatory agencies can be the best or even the only practicable approach. In the commercial sphere, requirements to disclose financial information can prevent fraud and boost investor confidence. And restrictions on collusion and monopoly can help to preserve competitive vitality.

The smooth functioning of the competitive market system thus requires the vigorous exercise of government powers. But securing this great public good does not necessarily exhaust the efforts of government in a liberal polity. Government may promote other public goods as well—for example, care for the needy, education, conservation of the natural and cultural heritage, promotion of scientific research, and the construction of "safety nets" to ease dislocations caused by economic fluctuations and structural change.

In a free society, a vibrant independent sector—neither profit-oriented nor governmental—will arise to provide these and other public goods. But because the independent sector provides social benefits regardless of the beneficiaries' ability or willingness to pay for them, it can encounter significant free-rider problems. Accordingly, it is possible for government, through its taxing and regulatory powers, to support and supplement private efforts and thereby ensure that public goods are provided more comprehensively and systematically.

It is true that, in assuming such responsibilities, government does impinge, at least marginally, upon voluntary, private activity in favor of collective decision-making. But it must be remembered that the legal framework within which voluntary, private activity is made possible is itself a public good created by virtue of political action. That framework may be the primary political value in a liberal society, but it does not have to be the exclusive one.

It may be useful here to recall the importance of uncertainty in gauging the tradeoffs between centralization and competition. Competition merits the central role in organizing society because of its fertility in overcoming uncertainty. But when uncertainty recedes, the case for competition weakens while that for centralization improves.

The case for competitive markets rests ultimately on their ability to further certain broadly shared public values—in particular, the creation of prosperity as measured by the subjective preferences of the members of a given society. That goal is certain enough, and thus is a public good potentially achievable by political action. The means to achieve that goal, however, are radically uncertain: No centralized decision-making body can know what to produce and how to produce it in order to achieve prosperity. Consequently, the public good of pursuing prosperity is best achieved by creating an institutional framework within which competitive experimentation and discovery can overcome uncertainty. Government interventions within that framework—subsidizing particular industries or controlling prices—are highly likely to be self-defeating.

But when the outcomes of the competitive process do not jibe with other broadly shared public values—such as compassion for the unfortunate, the pursuit of knowledge, or the protection of the national heritage—government action can be justified. Uncertainty has dissipated, since the objective is not coordinating subjective preferences known only to particular individuals but rather coordinating public values known generally throughout society.

In light of the above, it is clear that the recognition of competition's central importance does not entail any fixed or narrow limits on the breadth of concerns addressed by public policy. F. A. Hayek, competition's greatest defender in modern times, never failed to make this point:

> It is important not to confuse opposition against . . . planning with a dogmatic laissez faire attitude. The liberal argument is in favor of making the best possible use of the forces of competition as a means of co-ordinating human efforts, not an argument for leaving things just as they are. . . . It does not deny, but even emphasizes, that, in order that competition should work beneficially, a carefully thought-out legal framework is required and that neither the existing nor the past legal rules are free from grave defects. Nor does it deny that, where it is impossible to create the conditions necessary to make competition effective, we must resort to other methods of guiding economic activity.[38]

A vitally important caveat is in order here. Notwithstanding the fact that government regulations and spending programs *can be* beneficial, it most certainly does not follow that they *will be* beneficial just because their officially avowed purpose is the promotion of some widely agreed-upon public good. The fact that certain limited government regulations can be justified in the name of protecting health and safety does not mean that all regulations claiming that justification are worthwhile. The fact that education is an almost universally accepted public good does not mean that all government intrusions into that field are appropriate. On the contrary, in the United States today—and this is a country far less plagued by over-centralization than most others in the world—the vast bulk of government regulations and spending programs are deeply and hopelessly flawed. In virtually every phase of social affairs, the public good would be well served by a dramatic diminution of government's involvement. The proper scope of government policy may be broad, but severely strict theoretical and practical limitations on government's effectiveness dictate that the actual instrumentalities of government policy should be as modest as possible.

As the Industrial Counterrevolution unfolded, however, the crucial distinction between ends and means was seldom clearly understood. Too often the political contest between the partisans of sweeping centralization and the defenders of competition was interpreted as a dispute over *whether* government had a role in addressing issues of public concern rather than *how* that role was best played. The leaders of the centralizing movements portrayed themselves as public-spirited advocates of "activist" government and their opponents as crabbed and small-minded defenders of the status quo. It was in those terms that the debate was usually framed and, needless to say, such terms favored the steady progress of centralization.

As to their choice of means, the advocates of collectivism simply assumed that centralized control was a panacea. Here their confusion was fundamental. From the facts that centralization had a growing role within the market order (in the form of large business enterprises), and that centralization was needed to assemble the institutional framework of the market order (as well as supplement that order by promoting particular noncommercial public values), collectivists leaped to the utterly unwarranted conclusion that centralization should, in whole or in part, supplant the market order itself.

Consequently, the partisans of the Industrial Counterrevolution led a campaign to unloose centralization from its proper limits and make it, rather than competition, the major organizing principle of economic life.

Centralization would no longer undergird or supplement competition, but would supplant it.

It was a disastrous course of action. The hypertrophy of centralization tortured the logic of industrialization and deranged economic development. In particular—and of particular relevance for this study of globalization and its discontents—it undermined and ultimately destroyed the international economic order that arose in the wake of the Industrial Revolution. What we call globalization today is in large part really just the process of recovery from that awful collapse.

4

From World Economy to World War

At 7:30 A.M. on July 1, 1916, the whistles blew for the first attack in the Allied offensive on the Somme. After seven continuous days of punishing artillery bombardment, intended to demolish the German front lines, British and French soldiers climbed up the ladders, out of the trenches, and into No-Man's-Land. In successive waves spaced 50 yards or so apart and stretched out over a 25-mile front, infantrymen lumbering under 60-pound packs set off to cover the half-mile to the German trenches.

But the artillery barrage, however apocalyptically ferocious, had failed to do its job. The German forces, hidden deep in armored emplacements, were still intact. And so were their machine guns. And so were the thick belts of barbed wire in front of their trenches. As soon as the shelling stopped, the German troops clambered out of their dug-outs and mounted their machine guns. Once in position, they saw their targets spread out before them like in a shooting gallery.

The slaughter was obscene in its mechanical efficiency. "The machine-gunner is best thought of," writes military historian John Keegan, "as a sort of machine-minder, whose principal task was to feed ammunition belts into the breech, . . . top up the fluid in the cooling jacket, and traverse the gun from left to right and back again." Following this simple routine "would keep in the air a stream of bullets so dense that no one could walk upright across the front of the machine-gunner's position without being hit."[1] And never before had this new industrialized killing technique found a more plentiful supply of raw material.

An Irish sergeant described the bloodbath. "I could see, away to my left and right, long lines of men. Then I heard the 'patter, patter' of machine-guns in the distance. By the time I'd gone another ten yards there seemed to be only a few men left around me; by the time I had gone twenty yards, I seemed to be on my own. Then I was hit myself." Signalers viewing the attack from behind an earthen mound watched in horror as "our comrades move forward in an attempt to cross No-Man's-Land, only to be mown down like meadow grass."[2]

The body count that day was higher than on any other day of World War I: some 60,000 British casualties alone. By the time the battle ended, inconclusively, in November, combined British, French, and German casualties exceeded one million men. A German soldier, Ernst Jünger, gave his verdict: "Here chivalry disappeared for always. Like all noble and personal feelings it had to give way to the new tempo of battle and to the rule of the machine. Here the new Europe revealed itself for the first time in combat."[3]

But if the battlefield was defiled by the coming of the Machine Age, so much worse was the defilement of the Machine Age by the coming of the Great War. As epitomized by the horrors of the Somme campaign, the descent of the world into total war represented the utter perversion of the Industrial Revolution: An historical phenomenon that promised the progressive deliverance of humanity from misery and want had been turned against itself to produce misery on an unprecedented scale. The techniques of mass production had become those of mass destruction.

The Great War marked the cataclysmic eruption of the broader perversion of the Industrial Revolution that I have called the Industrial Counterrevolution. For World War I was the first of the great collectivist tragedies of the 20th century, and the mother of all those that followed. Its origins lay in the abandonment of the liberal faith in markets and competition—and their corollaries in international relations of interdependence and peaceful cooperation. And its consequences were woeful in the extreme: totalitarianism, the Great Depression, and another, even more savage, world war.

But what, really, does any of this have to do with the problems facing the current global economy? The answer is that these problems cannot be clearly understood without first grasping that the present wave of globalization is actually the resumption and continuation of a much older phenomenon.

Beginning in the final decades of the 19th century, globalization—triggered by the technological breakthroughs of the Industrial Revolution—was a powerful force in world affairs. But its progress was interrupted, its achievements demolished, in the disastrous years between the outbreak of World War I and the close of World War II. A partial reconstruction of a functioning international order was achieved thereafter, but a truly global economy reemerged only in the past couple of decades. And, even still, the legacy of the former collapse—and the ideas and movements that caused it—lives on to distort and frustrate the world's economic development.

———

"Globalization" may be a relatively new buzzword, but the underlying concept is an old one. The truth is that globalization, by any other name, was in full swing a century ago. Indeed, its progress was remarkably advanced, even by contemporary standards.

In 1913, merchandise trade as a percentage of gross output totaled an estimated 11.9 percent for the industrialized countries. That level of export performance was not matched again in those nations until sometime in the 1970s. Meanwhile, the volume of international capital flows relative to total output attained heights during the early 20th century that have not yet been approached in the present day. For example, capital flows out of Great Britain rose as high as 9 percent of the gross domestic product in that earlier time; by contrast, the seemingly staggering current account surpluses of Japan and Germany during the 1980s never surpassed 5 percent of GDP. It is fair to say that much of the growth of the international economy since World War II has simply recapitulated the achievements of the era prior to World War I.[4]

The first world economy was made possible by the breathtaking technological breakthroughs of the Industrial Revolution. Most obviously, new forms of transportation toppled the age-old tyranny of distance. For inland transport, the significance of the railroad is difficult to overestimate. Before its advent, a journey from New York to Chicago in 1830 took three weeks; just one generation later, in 1857, that same trip took only two days. The second half of the 19th century witnessed an explosion of railroad construction around the world. Great Britain's railway mileage more than tripled, from 6,621 miles in 1850 to 23,387 miles in 1910; over the same period, mileage in Germany grew nearly tenfold from 3,637 miles to 36,152 miles;

the United States, astonishingly, experienced a nearly thirtyfold increase, from 9,021 miles in 1850 to 249,902 miles in 1910. The railroads knitted together countries into truly integrated national markets and so facilitated the penetration of foreign goods from port cities into the interior.[5]

Meanwhile, the steamship was the technological key to uniting those national markets into a global whole. Although the steamship was first developed early in the 19th century, further innovations in subsequent decades—the screw propeller, steel hulls, the compound engine—transformed what had been primarily a river vessel into cheap and reliable ocean transport. The effect on freight costs was nothing short of spectacular: An index of freight rates along Atlantic export routes fell by 70 percent in real terms between 1840 and 1910.[6]

The Industrial Revolution's burst of technological creativity thus demolished the natural barriers to trade posed by geography. At the same time, it created entirely new possibilities for beneficial international exchange. In the "core" of the new global economy, the factories of the North Atlantic industrializing countries pumped out an ever-widening stream of manufactured goods desired around the world. Those factories, in turn, relied upon access to cheap natural resources and raw materials. And in the less advanced "periphery" of Asia, Africa, and Latin America, new technologies allowed those natural resources and raw materials to be grown or extracted more cheaply than ever before.

So arose the initial grand bargain on which the first global division of labor was based: The core specialized in manufacturing, while the periphery specialized in primary products. For Great Britain, the first industrial power, manufactured goods constituted roughly three-quarters of its exports. The sprawling continental United States, on the other hand, straddled both core and periphery. The urbanized East took industrialization to a new level and carried America past Great Britain in economic development. The American West, meanwhile, followed the path of other temperate "regions of European settlement" (Canada, Australia, New Zealand, and Argentina) and specialized in the production of grains, meats, leather, wool, and other high-value agricultural products. Finally, the American South followed to some extent the tropical pattern of development, which focused on such products as rubber, coffee, cotton, sugar, vegetable oil, and other low-value goods.[7]

While far-flung foreign trade is as old as human history, this was something new. No longer was such commerce a marginal matter, limited to a few high-value luxuries. Now, for the first time, specialization of production on a worldwide scale was a central element of economic life in all the countries that participated. Between 1870 and 1913, exports as a percentage of national income doubled in India and Indonesia, and more than tripled in Thailand and China. Japan's transformation was especially dramatic. After Commodore Perry's black ships arrived in 1858, Japan turned from almost total isolation to free trade. In a mere 15 years, its export share multiplied an astonishing 70 times to 7 percent of gross domestic output.[8]

But it was not to last. Just as the Industrial Revolution created the first world economy, so the Industrial Counterrevolution eventually destroyed it. In the waning years of the 19th century, at precisely the same time that surging international trade and investment were fashioning a market-mediated global economic order, the revolt against market competition was attacking that order at its very foundations. The advanced countries, while disseminating new technologies, new institutions, and new modernizing cultures around the world, were themselves succumbing to atavism. Protectionism, nationalism, imperialism, militarism—these were the dark forces unleashed by the Industrial Counterrevolution in the international arena. Those dark forces, struggling and straining and gaining strength just under the surface of an apparently pacific and progressive Europe, ultimately exploded in the cataclysm of World War I. From that awful conflict the first world economy never recovered. The tragedies that followed—totalitarianism, the Great Depression, and World War II—completed the descent into fire and chaos that began with the guns of August.

At the midpoint of the 19th century, a very different future appeared to be on the horizon. At that time the liberal creed of cosmopolitanism, free trade, and peace promised to define the shape of things to come. Great Britain, as in so much else, led the way. In the decades after Waterloo, it made gradual but significant progress in dismantling its protectionist policies. Seizing this political opening, a pair of textile manufacturers, Richard Cobden and John Bright, led their country to bolder action. They organized the Manchester-based Anti-Corn Law League into a national mass movement of middle-class urban interests against the landed elite. Their seven-year campaign achieved victory in 1846 with the repeal of the Corn Laws and the elimination of all duties on imported grains.

Cobden and Bright's movement achieved what their intellectual mentor,

Adam Smith, had dismissed as impossible. Smith, of course, made the groundbreaking theoretical case for free trade in *The Wealth of Nations,* but he doubted that his argument could ever carry the day. "To expect, indeed, that the freedom of trade should ever be entirely restored in Great Britain," he wrote, "is as absurd as to expect that an Oceana or Utopia should ever be established in it. Not only the prejudices of the public, but what is much more unconquerable, the private interests of many individuals, irresistibly oppose it."[9] Seven decades later, the impossible had come to pass.

From its testing ground in Great Britain, free trade began to spread into continental Europe. The major breakthrough, again featuring Richard Cobden, was the Cobden-Chevalier treaty of 1860 between Great Britain and France. A flurry of European trade agreements followed. Building on its tradition of the *Zollverein,* the newly unified Germany steadily pursued a liberal trade policy. By the mid-1870s average tariffs on manufactured goods had fallen to between 9 and 12 percent on the continent—compared to effective rates of 50 percent or more at the close of the Napoleonic Wars.[10]

The liberal champions of free trade did not view their cause solely or even primarily as a commercial matter. In their view, free trade carried profound implications for the whole field of international relations. Free trade, they believed, could pave the way toward a new and modern form of international order—one that would replace the pointless and destructive dynastic struggles foisted upon the people by kings and aristocracies. Peaceful cooperation among nations, not mere economic efficiency, was the grand prize for which they strove.

Cobden outlined this larger vision in a speech in Manchester on the eve of the Corn Laws' repeal:

> I believe that the physical gain will be the smallest gain to humanity from the success of this principle. I look farther; I see in the Free-trade principle that which will act on the moral world as the principle of gravitation in the universe,—drawing men together, thrusting aside the antagonism of race, and creed, and language, and uniting us in the bonds of eternal peace. I have looked even farther. I have speculated, and probably dreamt, in the dim future—ay, a thousand years hence—I have speculated on what the effect of the triumph of this principle may be. I believe that the effect will be to change the face of the world, so as to introduce a system of government entirely distinct from that which now prevails. I believe that the desire and the motive for large and mighty empires; for gigantic armies and great navies—for those materials which are used for the destruction of life and the desolation of the rewards of labour—will die away; I believe that such things will cease to be necessary, or

to be used when man becomes one family, and freely exchanges the fruits of
his labour with his brother man.[11]

Cobden and his fellow Victorian free traders are often faulted for their
naïve faith in the healing powers of commerce. And indeed, some in that camp
did fall prey to the facile assumption that major wars were no longer possible
in the new global economy. But Cobden himself, as the above passage makes
clear, was under no illusions as to the difficulty of subduing the powers of destruction. He saw the task as a monumental and centuries-long project.

However tempered by realism, though, the Cobdenite vision of the future was clearly optimistic. Though the challenges ahead were still daunting,
the remaking of the world had begun. The sterile futility of conflict among
nations was slowly but surely giving way to interdependence, peace, and
prosperity—with commerce the steam-powered engine of that beneficent
change.

〜〜〜〜

The free traders' sunny cosmopolitanism all too quickly gave way to a
very different vision of the international scene. As the Industrial Counterrevolution began to gather momentum, the prospect of a world at peace
started to recede. A new prospect, dark and menacing, came in its stead to
the fore—one of rival nations, rival races, pitted in fundamental and irre-
solvable conflict, and engaged in a grim and merciless struggle for supremacy or submission. This radical and ruinous shift of perspective did not
merely coincide with the spreading enthusiasm for centralization and top-
down control; rather, the two developments were interconnected and
mutually reinforcing.[12]

It must be remembered, of course, that the term "Industrial Counterrevolution" is a broad and sweeping generalization. This movement included a vast and messy tangle of different viewpoints and agendas; on the
moral scale, it spanned the range from the most high-minded nobility to
the most shocking and hideous evil. The blame for the great cataclysms of
the 20th century is not equally shared, and doling it out indiscriminately
would constitute a gross historical injustice. Many who shared the age's faith
in centralization were resolutely opposed to the destructive demons that
were hatched by that faith; many struggled with great courage and heroism
to uphold the humane values of Western civilization in the face of the dark
onslaught. For their efforts they deserve our undying gratitude.

However, it is still valid to say that the Industrial Counterrevolution, taken as a whole, was responsible for the shift in worldview that led, first to the Great War, and then to all the horrors that followed. In support of that conclusion, I attempt here to retrace the intellectual and historical links that connected the ideas of centralization to their terrible consequences.

First, the momentum of the Industrial Counterrevolution pushed inexorably toward expanding the power of the national state. This was true despite the fact that the most potent and influential of all the counterrevolutionary movements—Marxist socialism—was deeply internationalist in orientation. Marx himself was thoroughly cosmopolitan: He conceived of the coming socialist revolution and the workers' paradise it would establish as worldwide phenomena that would overwhelm dynastic, national, and racial distinctions as thoroughly as they did the historically fundamental distinctions of class. He had no interest in augmenting the strength of current states, which he condemned as tools of capitalist oppression.

Recall, however, that Marx's great contribution to the Industrial Counterrevolution was a powerful theoretical and historical conception of *why* collectivism was inevitable. As to *how* collectivism would actually work in practice, Marx had little to say and even less influence over the ultimate course of events. For the fact is that the worldwide proletarian uprising never came. And in the absence of that hoped-for event, the overwhelming drive toward centralization that Marx did so much to engender fastened itself upon the instrumentality at hand—the national state.

Consider, for example, the fate of the German Social Democrats. Their original leaders were orthodox Marxists who preached international revolution, not domestic statism. Over time, though, electoral success spoiled the Social Democrats' doctrinal purity. In the 1890s, after their stunning gains in the Reichstag had precipitated Bismarck's fall and the repeal of the Socialist Law, new leaders like Georg Vollmar and Eduard Bernstein pushed the party toward "revisionism," or support for gradual reform and cooperation with the existing state. The domestication of the Social Democrats culminated in August 1914, when every single party member in the Reichstag voted in favor of war credits for the Kaiser's army.

Meanwhile, many of the other emerging centralizing movements embraced an expanded national state from the outset. Edward Bellamy, for one, called his philosophy "nationalism" to distinguish it from Marxist-style socialism. In Great Britain, the Fabians advocated incremental reform and a political strategy of "permeation," or working through established political parties. And in Germany, the "state socialists" were unabashed in their devotion to the national state. Characteristic in this regard was Gustav Schmoller, who proclaimed the state to be "the most sublime ethical institution in history."[13]

Furthermore, the growing enthusiasm for national economic planning was fundamentally at odds with the new international division of labor. After all, if centralized decision-making is more efficient than markets, why allow international markets to persist? Inflows and outflows of goods and capital, if unregulated, will only disrupt the best-laid plans of the national authorities. What good is it to set minimum wages in a particular industry if the workers who are supposed to benefit then lose their jobs because of competition from cheaper foreign goods? Or, what if the authorities seek to encourage downstream processing industries, but the domestic producers of the raw inputs prefer exporting them at a high price to selling them cheaply at home?

A new collectivist case for protectionism thus began to emerge. If a nation's economic life is to come under central control, that control must extend to the nation's connections with the outside world. In outlining his vision for a "nationalist" utopia, Edward Bellamy was quite clear on this point:

> A nation simply does not import what its government does not think requisite for the general interest. Each nation has a bureau of foreign exchange, which manages its trading. For example, the American bureau, estimating such and such quantities of French goods necessary to America for a given year, sends the order to the French bureau, which in turn sends its order to our bureau. The same is done mutually by all the nations.[14]

George Bernard Shaw, a Fabian pamphleteer as well as a playwright, took a similar view. In *Fabianism and the Fiscal Question,* he wrote that if protectionism means "the deliberate interference of the State with trade" and "the subordination of commercial enterprise to national ends, Socialism has no quarrel with it." On the contrary, Shaw asserted, socialism must be considered "ultra-Protectionist."[15] And in Germany, the state socialists waged a blistering attack on free trade as a part of their larger campaign against laissez-faire and "*Manchestertum.*"

It is true that many partisans of centralization, especially on the Left, resisted the protectionist logic of their position. Free trade appealed to their internationalist sympathies; also, a low-tariff policy was generally associated with cheap bread and thus was widely considered to be favorable to the working class (how times have changed!). The momentum of centralization, though, generally prevailed over tradition and class interests. In the end, the fortunes of collectivism and protectionism rose together. In the middle of the 19th century, enlightened opinion was almost uniformly in favor of free trade; by the end of the century protectionism had once again become intellectually respectable.

With that renewed respectability came a significant retreat from free trade in actual practice. In Germany, the breakthrough came in 1879 with Bismarck's "iron and rye" tariff. In France, the Meline Tariff raised duties to the equivalent of 10 to 15 percent for agricultural goods and over 25 percent for industrial products. Tariffs also climbed in Sweden, Italy, and Spain during the 1880s and '90s. In the United States, tariff rates rose during the Civil War and stayed high for the rest of the century; they got a further boost with the McKinley Tariff of 1890. In Latin America, rates of protection ascended steadily during the final quarter of the 19th century. Tariffs in Russia were punishingly high and never came down.[16]

The direct impact of resurgent protectionism on the new world economy should not be overestimated. Average tariff rates rose, but were still relatively modest on the eve of World War I: under 10 percent in France, Germany, and Great Britain; between 10 and 20 percent in Italy; between 20 and 30 percent in the United States; and between 20 and 40 percent in Russia and Latin America. Meanwhile, such nontariff barriers as quotas or exchange controls were barely in evidence.[17] Protectionist measures did slow the pace of globalization (and blocked it for certain regions and sectors), but did not stop it. Despite increasing obstacles, the internationalization of economic life flourished in the decades before World War I.

Nevertheless, the drift toward protectionism did contribute to a new international atmosphere of conflict and tension. In Bellamy's utopia, national planners could somehow control their imports and exports without so much as a cross word from abroad. But in reality, restrictions on trade inevitably set nations against each other. When governments interfere with the ability of their citizens to do business with the citizens of other nations, they must expect such acts to be seen abroad as provocative. They are, after all, reducing the prosperity that other countries might otherwise enjoy. High tariffs in one country throttle export industries abroad; embargoes deprive other nations of needed raw materials, products, and capital. These restrictions can be matters of life and death if the dependence on foreign products or markets is great enough.

The implications of trade barriers for international relations are thus enormous. In a world of free trade, citizens of one country can exploit the benefits of a broader division of labor through peaceful commerce. But in a world where severe trade restrictions are endemic, such benefits can be attained only through warfare—through defeat of the foreign sovereignty that blocks access to the desired products or markets. Free trade makes war economically irrational; protectionism, carried far enough, makes it pay.[18]

These grim implications were abundantly clear in the circumstances of the late 19th century. The enriching possibilities of international specialization had never been greater, and were increasing daily due to incessant technological breakthroughs. At the same time, however, countries were beginning to close their borders. While the current level of protectionism was still within reasonable limits, it was widely believed that barriers would only increase with time. Making matters worse, the great powers of the core were rapidly consolidating political control over the periphery in a mad rush of imperial land grabs. The world appeared to be fracturing into great imperial blocs, each one more or less closed off from the others. It seemed as though the countries that controlled these blocs would reign supreme; those without enough territory to combine self-sufficiency with prosperity would be doomed.[19]

Under these conditions the Cobdenite cosmopolitan vision looked hopelessly outmoded. Expanding opportunities for a far-flung division of labor were not ushering in an age of peace; on the contrary, they were propelling nations toward inevitable and bloody conflict. What had wrought this dreadful turn of events? It was the expectation that countries would find it in their interest to close their economies to the outside world. And what created that expectation? It was the growing sense that national economic planning was the wave of the future. The drive toward centralization had thus transformed the legacy of the Industrial Revolution from that of world peace to one of a world at war. It is indeed fitting to call this transformation an Industrial Counterrevolution in international affairs.[20]

The Industrial Counterrevolution thus supplied a rationale for aggressive nationalism, imperialism, and militarism—the forces that eventually exploded in World War I. But the connection between centralization and the forces of destruction ran deeper than any rational considerations. As I argued earlier, the faith in central control grew out of deeper impulses—namely, a profound sense of disorientation as all the traditional verities of agrarian civilization came into doubt. Calls for central planning responded to that disorientation by promising to reconstitute the cohesiveness of village life through political action. While upholding essentially reactionary values, the Industrial Counterrevolution also embraced the promise of science and technology that industrialization offered. It managed to straddle both progress and nostalgia by claiming that the logic of industrialization required the centralization of economic decision-making. In other words, it offered a beguiling program of "back to the future."

The dark new vision of international conflict responded to the same deep-seated yearnings for meaning and belonging that proponents of central planning exploited. After all, there is no more potent promoter of solidarity than uniting against a common enemy. Collectivism held considerable appeal when its object was prosperity; that appeal took on an especially raw intensity, though, when its object was war. And by positing that military prowess was necessary for economic success, the Industrial Counterrevolution, in the realm of international affairs, merged these two objects into one.

Here again, the Counterrevolution captured the spirit of the age with a vision of "back to the future." Economic nationalism played to the deep-seated, primitive, and brutal imperatives of loyalty to the tribe, but it then cloaked this atavism in the garb of science and progress. The most advanced nations, in this view, were the most tightly organized. Only they could achieve the internal coordination needed to realize the full benefits of industrialization; only they had the discipline to repel external threats. The embellishment of Darwinian rhetoric was often added. In the collectivized world of the future, nations would be pitted in a struggle for existence, and only the fittest (that is, the most centralized) would survive.

The result was that collectivism and militarism became mutually reinforcing. Aggressive nationalism was needed to secure and safeguard the full blessings of collectivism; at the same time, collectivization was needed to render the nation fit for military conflict. From this basic feedback loop issued the great tragedies of dictatorship and total war.

The links that connected the dreams of central planning and the nightmares of the 20th century were forged, to a greater or lesser extent, by many of the disparate movements of the Industrial Counterrevolution. But those who pursued this fatal logic most explicitly and consistently, and to greatest historical effect, were the state socialists of Imperial Germany. The Bismarckian program brought together and integrated all the necessary elements: collectivism in domestic affairs, protectionism in commercial policy, and aggressive nationalism and militarism in matters of state. William Dawson, a sympathetic English observer of the German scene, distilled the essence of the new Reich into a single sentence: "As State Socialism is the protest of Collectivism against Individualism, so it is the protest of Nationality against Cosmopolitanism."[21]

The leading theorists of state socialism, the so-called *Kathedersozialisten,* were fervent supporters of belligerent nationalism. Gustav Schmoller, perhaps their brightest light, was emphatic in his rejection of the Cobdenite vision. For him, the international sphere was inevitably and properly a zone of never-ending conflict:

> All small and large civilized states have a natural tendency to extend their borders, to reach seas and large rivers, to acquire trading posts and colonies in other parts of the world. And there they constantly come into contact with foreign nations, with whom they must, quite frequently, fight. Economic development and national expansion, progress in trade and an enhancement of power are in most cases inextricably connected. . . .[22]

Adolf Wagner, another prominent voice, was even more truculent. Wagner asserted that the "decisive fact" in international relations was "the principle of power, of force, the right of power, the right of conquest." Weaker nations, he contended, would meet "the fate of all lower organisms in the Darwinian struggle for existence."[23]

Schmoller and Wagner called upon Germany to steel itself for the coming struggle of nations. To that end, they were ardent supporters of a protectionist trade policy. Wagner, in particular, stressed the need for the protection of German agriculture in the name of national security. First, dependence on foreign food supplies could be crippling in the event of war; furthermore, protectionism would preserve the large peasantry that supplied the backbone of a strong army.[24]

The two scholars also urged an aggressive program of territorial expansion. Germany needed more space to ensure a high standard of living in an age of vast and autarkic empires—and to settle the country's rapidly increasing population. Schmoller called for creating a German country with 20 to 30 million inhabitants in southern Brazil. Wagner, in a similar vein, dismissed "idle pretensions like the American Monroe Doctrine" as an obstacle to German colonization. In addition to overseas adventures, Schmoller and Wagner foresaw a dominant German role in European affairs. Both expressed the view that German hegemony should extend throughout what came to be referred to in pan-German circles as *Mitteleuropa.*[25]

To assume its rightful station, Germany would have to rely ultimately on its military prowess. Schmoller wrote that "the high standard of living of the English worker would be unthinkable without Great Britain's sea power" and that Germany should follow her example by building a strong navy. Wagner, for his part, called military power "the first and most important of all national, and may I add, of all economic necessities." The army, he claimed, was "a truly productive institution" because of "the connection between national might, security, honor and economic development and prosperity."[26]

The writings of these renowned professors served as a blueprint for Germany's disastrous course toward war. They and others like them fostered the intellectual climate in which Germany's leaders made the fateful decisions that crushed liberalism domestically and heightened tensions internationally. They stoked the strident and reckless nationalism that intoxicated the German people and had them spoiling for war. They saw and made the connection between collectivism at home and belligerence abroad.[27]

And they provoked imitators. I have already addressed how the German example and threat served to promote collectivist domestic policies in Great Britain under the banner of "national efficiency." The German influence extended in similar fashion to British attitudes about international affairs. For the "national efficiency" push for social reform was inextricably connected with a newly assertive imperialism.

The connections ran in both directions. On the one hand, social reforms to benefit the working class were touted as strengthening the Empire. Lord Rosebery, a Liberal imperialist and leading spokesman of the "national efficiency" cause, argued that "[a]n Empire such as ours requires as its first condition an imperial race—a race vigorous and industrious and intrepid." But, he continued, "in the rookeries and slums which still survive, an imperial race cannot be reared." Meanwhile, the Empire was defended as an essential support for working class living standards. Nobody put this case more bluntly than Joseph Chamberlain, the great champion of the protectionist "tariff reform" movement: "If tomorrow it were possible, as some people apparently desire, to reduce by a stroke of the pen the British Empire to the dimensions of the United Kingdom, half at least of our population would be starved."[28]

And so in Britain, as in Germany, collectivism at home went hand in hand with an expansionist foreign policy. The Cobdenite vision of peaceful coexistence and non-intervention yielded to one of great empires locked in a "struggle for existence"—a phrase that Joseph Chamberlain employed repeatedly in his speeches. The British Empire—which had been acquired, in the famous phrase, in "a fit of absence of mind"—now came to be seen as a prized asset, or even a life-or-death necessity. And its health demanded the centralization of economic decision-making. In other words, the conditions of external competition required the suppression of competition internally.

Britain, unlike Germany, did not succumb to economic nationalism. Chamberlain led a well-organized campaign to convert the Empire into a vast, protectionist trading bloc, and for a time it appeared he would succeed. In the end, though, he lost the campaign for working class support to the New Liberals, who combined imperialism and social reform with continued allegiance to free trade. The election of 1906, a sweeping victory for the Liberals, effectively squelched the tariff reformers.

Their near-success, though, was enough to stoke fears abroad that the British Empire would soon be closed to outsiders. This prospect contributed to Germany's spiraling economic nationalism and militarism, which in turn provoked an accelerating British military buildup. As Winston Churchill remarked about that buildup, "The Admiralty had demanded six ships: the economists offered four and we finally compromised on eight." [29] As Britain and Germany armed to the teeth, it became increasingly likely that some chance event would spark a major confrontation. On June 28, 1914, the assassination of Archduke Franz Ferdinand and his wife in Sarajevo ignited that spark.

It is customary to view World War I as a tragic accident—a senseless war about nothing in particular, at least nothing that makes any sense to us now; a war that nobody wanted but into which all were dragged by a ruinous system of entangling alliances. It is true that the outbreak of war at that particular time did hinge on a maddening and heartbreaking sequence of contingencies. But at a deeper level, the war was no accident. It was a product of the ideas of the Industrial Counterrevolution—ideas of centralization that merged into statism, ideas of statism that merged into aggressive nationalism, ideas of nationalism that merged into plans for military conquest. [30]

The Germans certainly understood this at the time. German intellectuals, who developed and pursued the ideas of the Industrial Counterrevolution more consistently and ruthlessly than anyone else, were very clear on what their countrymen were fighting for. When war came they welcomed it: It would give the Fatherland a glorious victory in the struggle of nations; it would give the German *Volk* their coveted "place in the sun." And it would also vindicate the German way, the *Sonderweg* of collectivism and martial spirit, as superior to the narrow individualism and shallow commercialism of the British.

Professor Johann Plenge, an authority on Marx and Hegel, captured this thinking in his wartime book *1789 and 1914: The Symbolic Years in the History of the Political Mind*. According to Plenge, the outbreak of the war signaled a new "German revolution" that would repudiate the liberal ideals unleashed on Europe by the French Revolution. The outmoded "ideas of 1789," wrote Plenge, were nothing but "shopkeepers' ideals, pure and simple, which served solely to provide individuals with particular benefits." The new order, animated by the "ideas of 1914," would "exert all the powers of the state in concerted opposition to the revolution of destructive liberation of the eighteenth century."[31]

Paul Lensch, a Social Democratic (!) member of the Reichstag, sounded similar themes in the 1917 book, *Three Years of World Revolution*. Interestingly, he identified Bismarck's conversion to protectionism in 1879 as the crucial turning point in world history:

> The result of Bismarck's decision of the year 1879 was that Germany took on the role of the revolutionary; that is to say, of a state whose position in relation to the rest of the world is that of a representative of a higher and more advanced economic system. Having realized this, we should perceive that in the present World Revolution Germany represents the revolutionary, and her greatest antagonist, England, the counter-revolutionary side.[32]

Nobody defined the "ideas of 1914" with more brutal directness than Werner Sombart, who inherited Adolf Wagner's chair at the University of Berlin. Sombart, who started out as a Marxist and ended his life as a Nazi (an intellectual journey that was by no means uncommon), saw the war as a contest between *Händler und Helden*—merchants and heroes. The war, he wrote in 1915, "is necessary in order to prevent the heroic outlook from falling prey to the forces of evil, to the narrow, abject spirit of commerce."[33]

These apologists of German militarism proved prophetic, albeit not in the way they expected. They were right that the war would lead to the triumph of the "ideas of 1914"—the ideas of collectivism and aggressive nationalism. But the triumph did not come through victories of the Kaiser's army. That army was defeated, the Kaiser himself abdicated, and the German Reich collapsed. Far from winning its place in the sun, Germany was devastated, humiliated, chopped up, and required to pay reparations.

Yet the triumph of the "German Revolution" (or, as I have called it, the

Industrial Counterrevolution) came anyway. The war and its aftermath dramatically accelerated the centralizing momentum that had been building steadily for decades. A quarter-century after Sarajevo, the forces of centralization had made such sweeping gains that the only serious question was whether the ongoing consolidation of state power knew any limits at all. Given the rise of totalitarianism, the smart money was on *no*.

Wartime economic controls provided the template for all subsequent experiments in central planning. The length and intense severity of the conflict led to an unprecedented expansion of government power in the economic realm. Nationalization of mines and railroads; state control over food production and consumption; mobilization of industrial production; labor drafts—such were the techniques of total war. The partisans of centralization were quick to grasp the peacetime applications of those techniques.

Lenin, for one, saw the German war economy, which he called "state monopoly capitalism," as "a complete material preparation for socialism, the threshold of socialism, a rung on the ladder of history between which and the rung called socialism there are no intermediate rungs."[34] Writing in 1916, he declared that the time was ripe for revolution:

> The war has reaffirmed clearly enough and in a very practical way . . . that modern capitalist society, particularly in the advanced countries, has fully matured for the transition to socialism. If, for instance, Germany can direct the economic life of 66 million people from a single, central institution . . . then the same can be done, in the interests of nine-tenths of the population, by the non-propertied masses if their struggle is directed by class-conscious workers. . . .[35]

The chaos of Russia's military collapse afforded him the chance to put the lessons of the German example to immediate use. Indeed, the German government sent him back to Russia in a special sealed train—injected, in Churchill's memorable phrase, "like a plague bacillus."[36] The infection took hold and the Soviet Union was born.

In the United States, the great lurch toward collectivism during Franklin Roosevelt's New Deal owed an enormous debt to wartime precedents. The National Industrial Recovery Act, with its sweeping cartelization of industry under "fair competition codes," revived the business-led planning regime of the old War Industries Board; one of the proposals that led to its enactment had called explicitly for a "Peace Industries Board." The National Recovery Administration's first director, General Hugh Johnson, was a veteran of the WIB. In similar fashion, the production and price controls of the Agricultural Adjustment Act represented an expansion of Herbert Hoover's

Federal Farm Board, which in turn hearkened back to the controls administered by Hoover when he served as wartime "Food Czar." The AAA's first director was another WIB man, George Peek. The Reconstruction Finance Corporation, begun by Hoover and expanded by Roosevelt, was modeled on the War Finance Corporation and staffed by many former WFC officers. The Tennessee Valley Authority grew out of a government nitrate and power project at Muscle Shoals. And so on and so on. According to historian William Leuchtenburg, "[T]here was scarcely a New Deal act or agency that did not owe something to the experience of World War I."[37]

The Great War furnished the partisans of centralization with powerful technocratic tools and expertise. It thus heightened collectivism's *intellectual* appeal by bringing central planning out of the realm of theory and into the real world. At the same time, the war also greatly increased collectivism's *emotional* appeal by supplying the intoxicating emotional experience of all-embracing national unity. In the disordered and often bleak years that followed, the centralizing cause profited greatly from its offer of a return to wartime solidarity.

Nowhere did nostalgia for the trenches lead to more horrific consequences than in Germany. "National Socialism is, in its truest meaning, the domain of the front," claimed Gottfried Feder, an original member of the party. Such rhetoric proved disastrously persuasive. On March 31, 1933, newly installed Chancellor Hitler and aging President Hindenburg met at the historic Garnisonkirche in Potsdam and shook hands publicly for the first time. In his sermon, the pastor proclaimed that this symbolic union of the Prussian old guard and the Nazi new order marked a "rebirth of the 'spirit of 1914.'"[38] How terribly right he was.

Militaristic metaphors were by no means confined to totalitarian movements. Consider these passages from Franklin Roosevelt's first inaugural address:

> [W]e must move as a trained and loyal army willing to sacrifice for the good of a common discipline. . . . [T]he larger purposes will bind upon us all as a sacred obligation with a unity of duty hitherto evoked only in time of armed strife. . . . I assume unhesitatingly the leadership of this great army of our people. . . . I shall ask the Congress for . . . broad executive power to wage a war against the emergency as great as the power that would be given me if we were in fact invaded by a foreign foe.[39]

In a similar vein, General Hugh Johnson urged citizens to do their patriotic duty and patronize only those businesses that displayed the NRA Blue Eagle, claiming, "Those who are not with us are against us. . . . The way to show that you are part of this great army of the New Deal is to insist on this symbol of solidarity." [40]

World War I thus provided both means and motive for the collectivist spasm that followed. It also provided the opportunity: the economic and social chaos of the Great War's aftermath. The war subjected the emerging global market order to tumultuous stresses and strains—ones that would ultimately lead to the worldwide implosion of the Great Depression. Just as central planning was gaining ground as both a practical and a romantic alternative to the status quo, the market system tottered and collapsed. Collectivism and aggressive nationalism filled the breach.

The outbreak of hostilities in 1914 caused an abrupt and traumatic disruption of international economic ties: naval blockades; submarine warfare against merchant shipping; suspension of the gold standard; exchange controls; emergency tariffs, quotas, and export restrictions. The global division of labor quickly disintegrated, often with tragic results. The effects of the British blockade of the Central Powers were especially severe. Germans were forced to eat their dogs and cats (the latter came to be known as "roof rabbits") as well as bread made from potato peels and sawdust. Civilian deaths by starvation climbed to hundreds of thousands per year. [41]

After the war, attempts to restore the international economy had to contend with profoundly disturbed and unstable conditions. Governments had run up enormous debts to finance the war effort: Great Britain's public debt nearly quadrupled between 1914 and 1919, while Germany's rose over tenfold. [42] When governments reached their borrowing limits, they turned to the printing press and indulged in more or less rampant inflation. Fiscal pressures did not relax with the armistice: Reconstruction of areas devastated by the fighting, relief efforts for the destitute, and new benefits demanded by returning veterans all heaped additional burdens on already strained treasuries. And, for Germany, crippling reparation obligations inflicted yet further hardships.

A number of central European countries—Austria, Hungary, Poland, and Germany—ultimately succumbed to runaway hyperinflation. The figures from the German case are incomprehensibly extreme: Prices in 1923 reached a peak of 1.26 *trillion* times higher than their pre-war levels. [43] Monetary stability was eventually restored, but too late for the struggling middle classes. They had already been effectively pauperized by the destruction of their life savings.

Patterns of production and trade had been scrambled by the war and re-scrambled by the peace. Industrial production had been diverted to war needs on a massive scale; demobilization meant another round of jarring and disruptive changes in the allocation of resources. Trade flows were altered by the war: European suppliers lost Latin American markets to American exporters and lost Asian markets to the Japanese. The dismemberment of the Habsburg Empire, combined with the protectionist policies of the successor countries, further disrupted the prewar division of labor. The United States compounded the woes of European exporters by enacting the highly protectionist Fordney-McCumber Tariff of 1922. In general, tariff rates crept upward during the 1920s. Average duty rates in Germany climbed from 8.4 percent before the war to 15 percent in the mid-1920s, while in France rates rose from 8.0 percent to 16 percent, and Spanish rates shot from 13.4 percent to 30 percent.[44]

Postwar leaders sought to calm their roiled economies by returning to the international gold standard that had prevailed in the decades before the war. Slowly but surely over the first half of the 1920s, Humpty Dumpty was reassembled. But in the distorted and volatile conditions of the time, returning to a system of fixed exchange rates was fraught with peril. The reconstituted gold standard was plagued from the outset by serious imbalances. Great Britain, in a misconceived effort to boost confidence in the integrity of the system, reentered at the prewar conversion rate. As a result it experienced severe contractionary pressures (and resulting high unemployment) throughout the '20s. However, this austerity still did not prevent chronic balance of payment difficulties. Other European countries, their export markets compromised by shifts in competitiveness and rising protectionism, likewise ran large current account deficits. Meanwhile, France's currency was seriously undervalued, and so France heightened problems elsewhere in Europe by draining world gold reserves. For a number of years the United States counteracted these imbalances via large-scale lending. But the system was a house of cards—one jolt could send it tumbling.

The jolt came in 1928 and '29. The U.S. Federal Reserve Board, concerned about speculative excesses in the rollicking stock market boom, decided to yank the punch bowl away from the party. Despite the absence of inflation, it raised its discount rate repeatedly to constrict the money supply. As interest rates rose, American capital that had been heading overseas returned home. To stanch the outflow of their reserves, other countries were forced to tighten monetary policy in turn, sending one after another into recession. Germany and Brazil fell in 1928, and Argentina, Canada, and Poland followed in early 1929. U.S. exports began to slump, then industrial production, then—on Black Tuesday, October 29, 1929—the stock market. Coming on the heels of a sharp drop in already depressed farm prices, the stock market crash led into a sharp economic contraction.[45]

What followed was a colossal and tragic blunder by U.S. monetary authorities. In the face of a sharp downturn that called for expansionary policy, the Fed proceeded to starve the economy of the money it needed to function. Typically, business slumps provoke a rush to liquidity; as asset values fall and future prospects darken, people tend to build up their money balances as a buffer against insecurity. That process intensifies when bank failures cause people to fear that money balances in the form of bank deposits may be lost; those fears can provoke a mad dash out of the banking system and into currency—in other words, bank runs. The central bank can counteract these destructive tendencies by increasing the money supply and so satisfying the rising demand. Such a response is in keeping with the most basic logic of markets: A rise in demand prompts a shift in resources to accommodate that demand with increased supply.

But the Fed moved perversely in exactly the opposite direction. Despite a sustained and accelerated increase in the demand for money (the price level fell 11 percent between 1929 and 1931, and another 15 percent between 1931 and 1933), and despite successive waves of bank failures in 1930, 1931, and 1933, the Fed allowed the money supply to contract—transaction money (M_1) shrank by an astonishing 27 percent between 1929 and 1933.[46]

The result was a catastrophe. Real gross domestic product fell more than 30 percent between 1929 and 1933; industrial production plummeted over 50 percent. Unemployment climbed as high as one in four, and one third of those who still had jobs saw their hours reduced. By the time Franklin Roosevelt declared a bank holiday on March 5, 1933, the banking system was in ruins—demand deposits had fallen by 36 percent from their 1929 level. The stock market, meanwhile, had dropped 80 percent from its pre-crash high.[47]

Shock waves from the U.S. collapse leveled Europe. Fidelity to the gold standard required other countries to mimic the Fed's contractionary policy in order to stop the hemorrhaging of gold reserves. Thus did Europe follow the Fed into the abyss: The longer countries defended their fixed exchange rates rather than their domestic price level, the more severe and protracted their economic trauma.[48] Eventually, the gold standard collapsed as countries abandoned it in order to reflate their economies, but by then enormous damage had already been done.

The volatility of the 1920s and the cataclysm of the 1930s opened the way for collectivists of all stripes to gain power and put their ideas into practice. In corrupt and inflation-ridden Italy, Benito Mussolini and his black-shirted *fascisti* staged their 1922 march on Rome. In sluggish and strike-plagued Great Britain, the rapidly growing Labour Party promised "a new social order, based not on fighting but on fraternity; not on the competitive struggle for the means of bare life, but on a deliberately planned co-operation in production and distribution"; the first Labour government was formed in 1924.[49] In the United States, Herbert Hoover won a landslide in 1928 with his vision of a cartelized business commonwealth; four years later, in the depths of the depression, he was ousted in favor of the even more aggressive statism of Franklin Roosevelt. And in Germany during the late '20s and early '30s, votes for the Nazi Party rose in eerie parallel with the unemployment rate. Of course, these various movements differed wildly in both their programs and their moral standing; their common denominator, though, was a rejection of economic liberalism.

The Great Depression was widely seen as final proof that the day of the market economy had come and gone. "[T]he laissez faire economy which worked admirably in earlier and simpler industrial life must be replaced by a philosophy of planned national economy"—so said the president of the U.S. Chamber of Commerce, Henry Harriman, in 1933.[50] That a person holding that position could utter such a statement is compelling evidence indeed of collectivism's grip on the popular imagination at that time. It seemed clear that the age of national planning had arrived. Whether the planners would be pro-business or pro-labor, democratic or totalitarian, communist or fascist—those momentous issues remained unsettled. The fate of economic liberalism, though, was sealed. Rexford Tugwell—Columbia University professor, New Dealer at the Agriculture Department, and a man who found things to admire in both Italian fascism and Soviet communism—gave voice to the general verdict: "The jig is up. The cat is out of the bag. There is no invisible hand. There never was. . . . [W]e must now supply a real and visible guiding hand to do the task which that mythical, nonexistent, invisible agency was supposed to perform, but never did."[51]

As collectivism waxed, the global economy waned. The spreading and deepening depression triggered a chain reaction of heightened protectionism.[52] Countries seized upon the expedient of trade barriers to halt deflationary pressures, arrest mounting unemployment, and defend their battered currencies against depreciating exchange rates abroad. In the end, though, the spiraling escalation of "beggar thy neighbor" policies achieved nothing but deeper misery for all. The United States helped to blaze the trail toward ruin with the infamous Smoot-Hawley Tariff of 1930: The average rate on dutiable imports climbed to a punishing 60 percent. In 1932, Great Britain abandoned its historic free-trade stance and adopted a high general tariff and a so-called "imperial preference" for colonies and Commonwealth countries.

Tariff hikes, though, were not the worst of it. Starting with Germany in 1931, countries began to impose exchange controls; by the end of that year such controls had spread throughout much of Central and Eastern Europe, as well as South America and the Middle East. Import quotas, clearing agreements, and state trading monopolies proliferated and international trade became completely politicized. The immediate effect was international economic freefall: World exports in 1933 were only a third of their 1929 value.[53]

Afterward, trade flows began to recover slowly as the worst of the slump passed. But the fundamental nature of that trade had been altered. The old multilateral system of nondiscriminatory trade under the "most favored nation" clause had given way to a confused tangle of bilateral and regional accommodations. In Central and Eastern Europe, where exchange controls prevailed, trade degenerated into state-to-state barter arrangements. As Germany prepared for war, autarky became an explicit policy goal: Hitler launched a concerted drive toward self-sufficiency in strategic materials with the 1936 Four Year Plan.

And so, in the "low, dishonest decade" of the 1930s, the grim prophecies of the Bismarckian state socialists were, by all appearances, fulfilled. Liberalism had been vanquished, domestically and internationally. "Wagner's law" of increasing state power was working its inexorable logic on the world; the struggle of nations had asserted itself and put Cobdenite cosmopolitanism to ruin. The world that was foreseen had arrived.

In the late 19th century, the mere intimations of such a world had sufficed to loose the destructive forces of nationalism and militarism. Now, its ascendancy imbued those same forces with an added and toxic virulence. Thus, in Germany, came the transition from state socialism to national socialism. All of the elements of the Nazi program had been present in the nationalist ideology of Imperial Germany—the Nazis merely developed that ideology to a brutalized and degenerate extreme. Even Nazi anti-Semitism

was nothing new. Adolf Wagner had served as president of the Christian Social Party, the first avowedly anti-Semitic party in Germany. It is the Jews,
wrote Wagner, "through whom our Fatherland has been more and more
economically, socially and morally corrupted." [54]

The Nazi state was animated by one central goal: to prevail in the
struggle of nations. As the economist Ludwig von Mises wrote in 1944, "The
essential point in the plans of the German National Socialist Workers' Party
is the conquest of *Lebensraum* for the Germans, i.e., a territory so large and
rich in natural resources that they could live in economic self-sufficiency at
a standard not lower than that of any other nation." [55] Sharing this goal and
allying with Germany were two other highly collectivized predator-states,
Italy and Japan, whose economic and military power was not yet matched
by the extent of territory under their control. Italy sought a new Roman
Empire, while Japan envisioned a "Greater East Asia Co-Prosperity Sphere."
According to Mussolini, a former Marxist, these rising powers were "proletarian nations," exploited by existing political boundaries. The time had
come to expropriate the expropriators.

As the world plunged once again into war, James Burnham diagnosed the
conflict as the latest phase in what he called "the managerial revolution." In
his influential 1941 book by that title, he predicted, "The war of 1914 was the
last great war of capitalist society; the war of 1939 is the first great war of managerial society." [56] Burnham, a former Communist, had come to believe that,
while capitalism was obviously dying, the socialist vision of a classless society
was a pipe dream. The new social order that was taking shape was another
class-based society, but this time the dominant class was, not the bourgeoisie,
but the professional managers—the technocratic elite that runs modern industrial society. Burnham believed that all the major collectivist movements,
however much they opposed each other, were in fact variations on a common
theme—namely, furthering the interests of the rising managerial class:

> The ideologies expressing the social role and interests and aspirations of the
> managers . . . have not yet been fully worked out, any more than were the
> bourgeois ideologies in the period of transition to capitalism. They are already
> approximated, however, from several different but similar directions, by, for
> example: Leninism-Stalinism; fascism-nazism; and, at a more primitive level, by
> New Dealism and such less influential American ideologies as "technocracy." [57]

Burnham grasped that the triumph of managerial central planning in a
world of sovereign states meant that existing political boundaries could not be
sustained:

Experience has shown that the existence of a large number of sovereign nations . . . is incompatible with contemporary economic and social needs. The
system simply does not work. . . . The complex division of labor, the flow of
trade and raw materials made possible and demanded by modern technology,
were strangled in the network of diverse tariffs, laws, currencies, passports,
boundary restrictions, bureaucracies, and independent armies. It has been clear
for some while that these were going to be smashed; the only problem was
who was going to do it and how and when. Now it is being done under the
prime initial impulse of Germany.[58]

In Burnham's view, then, the outbreak of World War II was an entirely
predictable development in the ongoing evolution of managerial society. He
writes, "The comparatively large number of sovereign nations under capitalism is being replaced by a comparatively small number of great nations, or
'super-states,' which will divide the world among them."[59] Identifying the
United States, Germany, and Japan as the likely cores of those super-states,
he believed that future conflicts among them were inevitable:

No one of the three central areas is able to conquer definitely the other central areas, and therefore no one state power can in fact rule the world. This will
not, however, prevent the struggle from taking place. And, besides, there *will*
be periodically decided just how much of the world will fall within the spheres
of each of the super-states.[60]

Many years later, Alfred Chandler paid tribute to Burnham by subtitling
The Visible Hand, his magisterial account of the rise of large corporations,
"The Managerial Revolution in American Business." No doubt Chandler
intended only a superficial allusion to Burnham's notion of a rising managerial class. But in fact the connections between the two books are deep and
profound. For it was the emergence of giant industrial enterprises—or,
more precisely, the fundamental misunderstanding of that phenomenon—
that first ignited the belief that the future belonged to centralization and top-
down control. As the Industrial Revolution progressed, so too did the ideas
that would turn that revolution against itself—the ideas of the "managerial
revolution," or the Industrial Counterrevolution. The end result of those
ideas revealed itself in the world that Burnham thought lay before him: a
world where the Industrial Revolution's promise of a worldwide division of
labor led instead to unceasing global carnage.

5

Twilight of the Idols

Unter den Linden is a haunted avenue—haunted by the ghosts of the Industrial Counterrevolution. As I walked along Berlin's most famous boulevard on a brilliant April morning in 1999, ghosts of history and personal memory crowded my thoughts at every step.

From its origin at the Brandenburg Gate, the street presents a prospect of stately but derivative Baroque and neoclassical architecture—a bid by the arriviste Hohenzollern state to assume the proper trappings of a great power. From the very first glance, the scene evokes the days of imperial glory, those fateful days when liberalism was crushed and the dark forces of centralization gathered strength. Looking over one's shoulder back through the Brandenburg Gate, the Siegessäule—the victory column that celebrates Bismarck's triumphs—thrusts upward in the distance.

Down the street past Friedrichstrasse, across from Humboldt University, is the unassuming Bebelplatz—a scene of horror and the promise of worse to come. On the night of May 11, 1933, under the direction of Nazi propaganda minister Joseph Goebbels, the square blazed with a bonfire of thousands of "un-German" books. Today, in the middle of Bebelplatz, there is an inconspicuous but emotionally powerful memorial of the event. Set in the ground is a pane of glass, through which one peers into what looks like some kind of spectral, underworld library. The inscription bears the chillingly prophetic words of Heinrich Heine: "Where they start by burning books, they'll end by burning people."

Down the way on the left-hand side is the Neue Wache, which looks like a Roman temple and originally housed the royal guard. During the Weimar Republic it was made into a shrine for the dead of World War I, but today it serves as a memorial of the even more terrible destruction of World War II. Inside, the tombs of an unknown soldier and an unknown concentration camp victim rest in eerie, mournful silence.

Past the Schlossbrücke, the street's name changes to Karl-Liebknecht-Strasse, and the character of the city changes as well. At this point the East German authorities stopped their reconstruction of bombed-out ruins to realize instead their ghastly vision of a gleaming socialist future. Standing on the site of the old Imperial Palace is what was the Palast der Republik, a grotesque expanse of bronzed and mirrored windows that once was the East German parliament building. Because of a serious asbestos problem, it now stands empty and unusable. Looming to the east is the giant television tower, the signature symbol of Communist-era Berlin and a kind of latter-day counterpart to the Bismarckian Siegessäule. Before it lies the drab Marx-Engels Forum, a dreary little park in the middle of which stand the squat but massive figures of the two great scientific socialists. They look eastward, toward Moscow, impassive in the face of the surrounding indignities—a nearby Radisson Hotel and a clutch of commercial billboards.

Crammed along this single street are reminders, frozen in stone and steel, of all the great calamities of the 20th century: the world wars, first and second; the totalitarian empires, fascist and communist. Now, happily, they are all only memories. As I strolled along, the lime trees that give Unter den Linden its name were bursting forth with the delicate and hopeful foliage of spring; all around the gangly, waving arms of construction cranes were beckoning the rise of a new Berlin.

The last time I had visited this city was as a college student in the summer of 1982. Back then the Counterrevolution was still alive and well. In the Soviet Empire, of which Berlin was a major provincial capital, the gleaming socialist future had settled into a tarnished and repressive present; but that present seemed durable enough—as solid and unshakable as the wall that clove Berlin in two. On the western side of the wall, most Berliners were sufficiently convinced of communism's permanence that they had lost heart in resisting it. At the time the controversy over the emplacement of Pershing missles in Europe was at its height, and West Berlin was a hotbed of opposition. I remember the graffiti scrawled all over Kreuzberg, denouncing the United States in general and "President Ray-Gun" in particular.

One night in June I had gone club-hopping with a group of German and American students. Around 4 A.M. it began to get light outside, and we decided to go watch the sun rise over the wall. We parked our van in a residential area that was then cut in two, and were treated to the golden dawn of a beautiful summer day. The eeriness of the scene has always stayed with me: the jarring contrast between the peaceful loveliness of the sunrise and the bleak, blank ugliness of the wall; the birds, mocking us, darting back and forth between east and west; a young East German guard, just about our age, in a watch tower on the "death strip," inspecting us through binoculars.

When I returned, 17 years later, everything had changed. Checkpoint Charlie, through which I once passed, is no more, though the famous sign that warns "YOU ARE NOW LEAVING THE AMERICAN SECTOR" still stands. The Soviet sentinels at their war memorial near the Brandenburg Gate—gone. The goose-stepping East German guard in front of the Neue Wache—gone. It is difficult to find intact stretches of the wall anymore; most of it has been torn down and pulverized into souvenirs. Berlin is now a city reunified, the restored capital of a country reunified. Once the symbol of the world's Cold War division, now its wholeness proclaims a world reunified.

As in Berlin, so has everything changed all around the planet. The Soviet Union is gone, China has enjoyed two decades of spectacular market-based wealth creation, and throughout the old Third World, governments now court the multinational corporations they formerly denounced and demonized. The Industrial Counterrevolution, which once seemed so overwhelming and irresistible, has sputtered and collapsed. As a result, the global division of labor interrupted by World War I and its collectivist aftermath has now reasserted itself—indeed, on a scale and to a degree of intricacy unparalleled in history.

What happened? Why has there been such a dramatic worldwide shift toward market-oriented policies—not only in the former Communist bloc and Third World, but in the industrialized democracies as well? And, in light of collectivism's global implosion, how did centralization perform as well as it did as long as it did?

∼∼∼∼∼∼∼

World War II and its aftermath did not bring the global triumph of centralized regimentation that James Burnham had predicted. Instead, the Industrial Counterrevolution, or what Burnham called the "managerial revolution," suffered a major and unexpected setback. After decades of steadily building intellectual and political momentum, on the cusp of total victory, it stalled and, indeed, retreated in—of all places—the most economically advanced countries. When the smoke cleared from the most violent and disruptive convulsion in all of human history—two binges of worldwide slaughter, a global economic cataclysm, and the rise of monstrous and predatory tyrannies—the basic liberal principle of market competition survived intact in those nations at the forefront of economic progress. The radical agenda of full-blown collectivist planning had been decisively repulsed.

Yes, the market economies of the postwar "free world" bore the heavy and deforming imprint of collectivist ideology. But economic freedom was not snuffed out; on the contrary, it regained ground previously lost to price controls, rationing, and centralized direction of labor and investment. And, of crucial importance, market competition was restored at the international level. The calamitous descent into autarky during the 1930s was reversed, and the advanced countries gradually reopened the flows of goods, services, and capital across national borders.

F. A. Hayek, prescient as ever, anticipated the reasons for economic liberalism's partial comeback. In his famous 1944 warning, *The Road to Serfdom*, Hayek attacked the still-prevalent belief that comprehensive central planning is compatible with popular government and a full measure of individual freedom—if only it is done by the right people. Such thinking, he argued, was a dangerous illusion. According to Hayek, it was no accident that the regimes that had pursued economic centralization to its furthest limits were also barbarous despotisms. "There are strong reasons for believing," he wrote, "that what to us appear the worst features of the existing totalitarian systems are not accidental by-products but phenomena which totalitarianism is certain sooner or later to produce."[1]

The basic problem is that collectivism taken to its practical limits (that is, the maximum possible substitution of bureaucratic administration for the market price mechanism) requires centralized decision-making on a scale that far exceeds the capacity of democratic institutions to manage. Consequently, once nations embark upon comprehensive planning, the only alternative to paralysis is dictatorship. Only absolute power, unconstrained by democratic procedures or any need to obtain the consent of the governed, is capable of keeping up with the workload to any minimally acceptable degree. "[S]ocialism can be put into practice only by methods which most socialists disapprove," wrote Hayek, with characteristic generosity to his opponents. Over time, therefore, the continued pursuit of planning will likely bring to power leaders without any scruples or moral inhibitions about employing those methods. "Just as the democratic statesman who sets out to plan economic life will soon be confronted with the alternative of either assuming dictatorial powers or abandoning his plans," he concluded, "so the totalitarian dictator would soon have to choose between disregard of ordinary morals and failure."[2]

It was the unavoidability of Hayek's stark alternative—planning or freedom—that ultimately doomed the more extreme manifestations of the Industrial Counterrevolution in the advanced countries. The broad liberal tradition of democracy and personal freedom, on its heels during the 1930s, reasserted itself in the 1940s. Most obviously, the military might of the Allied democracies helped to smash the fascist powers; after the war, it then restored liberal institutions to Western Europe and Japan, and protected them afterward from the threat of Soviet expansion. The clash with fascist totalitarianism in World War II, and then with communist totalitarianism in the Cold War, reaffirmed in what became known as "the West" the moral superiority of liberal values, and strengthened opposition to anything that smacked of totalitarian ideology at home. In this changed environment, the quest to eradicate market competition—a quest that a mere decade before had seemed so near its prize—was quickly and unceremoniously called off.

In the United States, where liberal traditions had remained the strongest, the high-water mark of the peacetime suppression of market competition came and passed early, in the 1933–35 reign of the National Recovery Administration. Under the sign of the NRA's blue eagle, industries rushed toward government-sponsored cartelization with price-fixing "fair competition" codes; 557 basic and 189 supplementary codes, covering some 95 percent of industrial workers, were ultimately approved. Subjection to and compliance with the codes were supported by a massive government propaganda campaign that vilified "shirkers and slackers" as virtual traitors.

But just as it seemed the triumph over markets was at hand, the grand experiment failed ingloriously. The NRA quickly alienated almost everybody: The general public had been promised jobs but got only higher prices; labor leaders felt their organizing efforts were being frustrated by the new cartels; small businesses objected that their larger rivals were using the codes to crush competition; and big business wearied of all the red tape and bureaucratic meddling. The vibrancy of American democracy, it turned out, rendered radical centralization unworkable. No single plan could reconcile and harmonize the varied and competing interests of American society, and none of those interests was willing to roll over and play dead for the sake of the plan. Consequently, the NRA was soon paralyzed by intractable internal conflicts. When a unanimous Supreme Court struck it down as unconstitutional in 1935, virtually nobody objected.[3]

After Pearl Harbor, Americans did submit to radical centralization in the form of wartime economic controls—but only as a temporary military expedient. On August 18, 1945, President Harry Truman ordered his administration "to move as rapidly as possible without endangering the stability of the economy toward the removal of price, wage, production, and other controls and toward the restoration of collective bargaining and the free market." By the end of 1945 many of the wartime agencies had closed their doors, and by 1946 virtually all price controls had been lifted. That year nine million soldiers returned to civilian life, and the great American postwar boom was on.[4]

In Great Britain, it took a postwar planning debacle to break the anti-market fever. The socialist government of Clement Attlee, swept into power at the end of the war, ignored Hayek's warning and pushed ahead with the conversion of wartime controls into peacetime central planning. "[I]n matters of economic planning," Attlee declared flatly in 1946, "we agree with Soviet Russia."[5] That a Western politician could say such a thing seems shocking today—and indeed would have seemed nearly as shocking just a few years later.

After enduring the horrors of a war for national survival, the British people were now subjected to the shabby, dreary banality of economic madness. Shortages of consumer goods and production bottlenecks were commonplace; the quality of goods deteriorated markedly. One massive blunder brought the whole economy to a standstill: In February 1947, a coal shortage forced the cutoff of electricity to about two-thirds of British industry for a period of some three weeks. In August of that year, a balance-of-payments crisis forced the government to announce a new austerity plan, including the slashing of food imports. Meanwhile, labor shortages in vital industries led the government to institute industrial conscription: Workers changing jobs could now be dispatched to whatever employment the Ministry of Labor determined would best serve the national interest. Here, in this final step, the "road to serfdom" ceased to be a metaphor and become instead an accurate description.[6]

Even ardent socialists rebelled. Most notably, George Orwell—who in fact had written favorably about Hayek's book—now authored his own towering classic of anti-utopian literature (*1984* was simply an inversion of 1948, the year the book was published). In the end, the planners relented. In 1948 Harold Wilson, then president of the Board of Trade, announced a "bonfire of controls"; though it proved to be a slow-burning flame, over the following years market mechanisms were gradually restored. The portion of consumer spending controlled by rationing declined from 31 percent in 1948 to 10 percent in 1951; industrial raw materials subject to administrative allocation comprised 81 percent of total value in 1948, fell to 41 percent by 1951, then dropped precipitously after the Korean War; price controls covered 49 percent of consumer spending in 1949, 21 percent in 1953, and only 10 percent by 1958.[7]

During the darkest hours of German history, the seeds of liberal renewal were being planted by a small band of dissident academics—seeds that would eventually burst forth in the postwar *Wirtschaftswunder*. The collapse of the German economy during the Great Depression, and the collapse of German civilization during the Nazi period, prompted the so-called "ordoliberals"—including Walter Eucken, Franz Bohm, Wilhelm Röpke, and Alexander Rüstow—to attempt to recover and restate the lost German liberal tradition. At the center of their thinking was hostility toward arbitrary power and the identification of competition as the antidote to power. In their conception, a properly designed and maintained competitive market order was the only reliable foundation for a free society, for it restrained both private accretions of power (in the form of monopolies and cartels) and public accretions (in the form of an interventionist or totalitarian state).[8]

After the war, the ordoliberal movement found its historical moment when one of its members, the economist Ludwig Erhard, was tapped to serve as General Lucius Clay's director of economic administration for the American and British occupation zones (later West Germany). In June 1948, Erhard, acting on his own authority and without consulting Clay, eliminated in one stroke virtually all the Nazi-era price and other controls that were strangling economic recovery. So began the heralded German "miracle." Later, as economics minister of the new Federal Republic of Germany under Chancellor Konrad Adenauer, Erhard led a team of ordoliberal economists in fashioning what came to be known as the German "social market economy."[9]

I do not wish for a moment to minimize the many and gross violations of liberal economic principles that persisted and flourished in the postwar democracies. A spate of nationalizations created huge state-owned industrial sectors in many countries: in Great Britain, for example, the government took over coal, iron and steel, electricity, gas, telecommunications, airlines, and railroads and other inland transport. Even when state ownership was avoided, price and entry regulations stifled competition in a wide range of industries. In the United States, regulation was the favored method of government control: Railroads, trucking, airlines, utilities, telephony, and broadcasting were all subject to intrusive bureaucratic oversight. Agriculture everywhere was swathed in production limits, price supports, and subsidies. State ownership of banks, interest-rate controls, and tight restrictions on capital markets blocked financial-sector development. Compulsory unionism and corporatist wage-setting arrangements suppressed labor markets and perpetuated restrictive work rules. "Indicative planning" distorted resource allocation through taxes, subsidies, and public-sector investment, while Keynesian "fine tuning" unleashed chronic inflation in the name of "demand management." And enormous bureaucratic social welfare programs channeled an ever-increasing share of national income through the government budget.

But underneath this towering edifice of interventionism, the liberal market order survived. The price system was preserved, albeit with distortions. The fundamental legal protections of property and contract, though circumscribed by collectivist policies, continued to operate. Freedom to choose one's occupation and to spend one's income according to individual preferences was restored. Private enterprise was not eliminated. The right to start new businesses and introduce new products without government permission persisted. And competition among enterprises revived, and over time intensified.

The Industrial Counterrevolution had stopped short. The original dream of a rationally designed and centrally administered economy—Edward Bellamy's fantasy of a world without markets, without competition—gave way to the much more modest ambitions of the "mixed economy" and "welfare state." The market order had faced the threat of annihilation and endured. The foundation was laid for its future expansion.

In particular, the liberal revival led to the reconstruction of an international trading system. The United States, whose protectionist policies of the 1920s and early '30s had helped to precipitate the meltdown of the Great Depression, now sought to redeem itself. Beginning in 1934 with the passage of the Reciprocal Trade Agreements Act, the United States under Secretary of State Cordell Hull negotiated dozens of bilateral tariff-cutting agreements; by 1947 average duty levels on U.S. imports had fallen by a third. In October 1947, U.S.-led negotiations resulted in a new multilateral trade agreement: the General Agreement on Tariffs and Trade, or GATT. The GATT, initially composed of 23 countries representing some 80 percent of world trade, memorialized such important principles as "most favored nation" (a tariff cut granted to the exports of any member country must be extended to all member countries) and "national treatment" (national regulations must apply the same standards to domestic and foreign goods), and imposed a general rule against quantitative import restrictions (honored in the breach, admittedly, for some years to follow). The GATT also provided for occasional "rounds" of tariff-cutting negotiations. The United States led the way in the initial round, reducing overall duty levels by over 20 percent.[10]

The GATT's tariff-cutting was of limited use, though, so long as exchange controls and import quotas were still in effect. Although postwar European leaders were committed in principle to restoring convertible currencies, serious balance-of-payments problems that were brought about by overvalued fixed exchange rates prevented them from acting immediately. Beginning in the late 1940s and continuing through the '50s, controls were gradually dismantled—first on intra-European trade, then generally. In Great Britain, 91 percent of imports had been subject to restrictions in 1949; by 1958 the figure was down to 10 percent. On December 31, 1958, convertibility on the current account was restored throughout Western Europe.[11]

Conventional wisdom credits the "Bretton Woods" international monetary arrangements (agreed to in Bretton Woods, New Hampshire in July 1944) with laying the foundation for the postwar resurgence of trade. Actually, the new system—exchange rates pegged to a gold-backed dollar, with the International Monetary Fund providing liquidity to support the exchange-rate pegs—did much to retard the advance of trade. As with all pegged-rate regimes, it was prone to recurrent balance-of-payments crises, which then prompted governments to defend their currencies with trade restrictions. In particular, the long delay in resuming convertible currencies—over 13 years from the end of the war—was due to the chronic "dollar shortage" caused by grossly overvalued exchange rates. Had European currencies been allowed to depreciate and find their free-market levels, there would have been no balance-of-payments crises and no need to maintain exchange controls and import quotas for so long. After the resumption of currency convertibility, continuing instability provoked repeated, panicky resorts to import surcharges and capital controls, until the whole misbegotten mess finally collapsed in August 1971. In short, while the Bretton Woods system was certainly an improvement over the chaos of the 1930s, the growth of the international economy would have been far better served by adopting freely floating exchange rates from the start.[12]

In spite of the occasional monetary crises, barriers to trade continued to fall overall, and the international market economy flourished accordingly. In 1958, West Germany, France, Italy, Belgium, the Netherlands, and Luxembourg signed the Treaty of Rome and created the Common Market. In 1960, Great Britain, Norway, Sweden, Denmark, and Switzerland proceeded with their own European Free Trade Area. The GATT, meanwhile, after stalling in the 1950s, regained momentum with the bold Kennedy Round of talks (1962–1967). International flows of goods and services quickly became torrents: By 1973, world exports as a percentage of the gross domestic product had roughly regained the level last seen in 1913.[13] And while the North Atlantic was the original center of the new liberal trading order, the Pacific Rim was rising quickly: First Japan, then the "four tigers" of Hong Kong, South Korea, Taiwan, and Singapore burst onto the scene as export powerhouses.

As with the restoration of domestic market economies, the recreation of an international market economy was guided more by political than economic considerations. The rise of fascism and the carnage of World War II had made all too clear the monsters that could hatch from economic chaos, and the failure to restore international economic order after World War I was widely blamed for the chaos that ensued. In his memoirs, Cordell Hull recognized that his trade-agreements program had started too late to avert disaster:

> [B]y the time the Trade Agreements Act was passed, Hitler had been in power a year and a half and was furiously arming, Mussolini had been in power nearly twelve years and was planning the Ethiopian War, and Japan had been in Manchuria nearly three years and was getting ready to withdraw from the naval limitations treaty. These nations had no use for the liberal commerce of trade agreements, for they were already transforming their commerce to the needs of war. If, as I urged in my speeches during the First World War, something like the Trade Agreements Act could have been passed instead of the Fordney-McCumber Act of 1922 and other nations had seen fit to follow suit at once, the story might have been different.[14]

Postwar leaders were resolved not to repeat the mistakes of the past. At a terrible cost, they had rediscovered the long-neglected wisdom of Cobdenite liberalism—that free trade is vital to the preservation of peace.

The postwar liberal trading order, however promising, was nonetheless incomplete. Still far out of reach was the truly global division of labor that obtained prior to World War I. The problem was as simple as it was profound: The great majority of the world's population now lived under regimes that flatly rejected the whole notion of an international market economy.

After World War II, the leading edge of the Industrial Counterrevolution shifted from the advanced countries to the less developed world. At the vanguard stood the Soviet Union, the totalitarian superpower, and its Communist satellites in Eastern Europe. China and India, the world's most populous countries, pursued divergent political paths, but both embraced Soviet-style central planning. And throughout Latin America, Africa, and Asia, a bubbling stew of imported and homegrown ideologies shared the common denominator of devotion to state-dominated economic development.

Why was the lure of radical centralization so strong in economically backward regions of the planet? The strength of the centralizing momentum in those areas was, of course, completely at odds with Marxist dogma. Socialist revolution was supposed to be the final stage of economic development, the culmination of history; its earliest sparks should have ignited in those countries where the bourgeois epoch had already unfolded. Yet, the first Marxist revolution had occurred, not in Great Britain or the United States, but in relatively primitive Russia; now it was in the former colonial possessions that collectivist fires were raging the hottest.

When the nature of collectivism is properly understood, the course of developments that so confounded Marxist expectations becomes much less mysterious. For in truth collectivism was a reactionary force, not a progressive one—an Industrial Counterrevolution, not the fulfillment of industrialism's promise. Consequently, it is not especially surprising that the forces of reaction were especially potent in the world's economic backwaters.

As I addressed in Chapter 2, the appeal of the Industrial Counterrevolution was at bottom a spiritual one. The coming of technological, urban society was the most deep-seated and sweeping transformation of human affairs in all of recorded history. Ways of life that had persisted for thousands of years were suddenly wiped away; the beliefs and institutions that had grown out of and adapted to traditional agricultural society now came under withering assault. Such rapid and radical change could not help but exact a heavy psychological toll; it was easy to feel lost in a world where, in Marx's felicitous phrase, "all that is solid melts into air." Amidst the spiritual turmoil and disorientation, collectivism promised deliverance—a return to the age-old verities of village life and the sense of community and rootedness that had been lost in industrialization. The agent of deliverance would be the centralizing state; its means, the nationalization of economic life.

The spiritual trauma of modernization was particularly acute in the non-Western world. In Europe and North America, industrialization, however wrenching and disruptive, was nonetheless the organic outgrowth of centuries of social development. In other parts of the globe, modernization came from outside—from foreign interlopers and invaders. As a result, it came without any of the cultural preconditioning that had occurred in the West. Furthermore, while in the West industrialization was experienced as a great (if problematic) civilizational achievement, elsewhere modernity came as a humiliation—a shocking realization that the local culture was hopelessly backward compared to that of the new foreign masters. Feelings of helplessness and loss of control were therefore all the more intense. Consequently, in the non-Western context, collectivist ideologies were especially enticing. They offered, not only spiritual redemption, but worldly redemption as well: a restoration of group solidarity, this time at the level of the new nation-state, and the opportunity to catch up with the West through accelerated economic development.[15]

The relative backwardness of non-Western countries not only increased the attraction to collectivism, it also reduced the level of resistance. First of all, those countries had no preexisting industrial economies to be disrupted and deranged by centralized control. As a result, the progress of industrialization could not suffer by comparison with what had gone before; collectivism, meanwhile, could claim credit for constructing impressive-looking industrial bases (however dysfunctional) from scratch.

More important, because preindustrial societies had relatively simple divisions of labor, they generally lacked the rich diversity of competing power centers that is the hallmark of liberal civil society and the economic foundation of political liberty. Political underdevelopment, exacerbated by economic underdevelopment, was crucial to the rapid spread of radical collectivism throughout the non-Western world. It was all too easy in these new and immature polities for small, cohesive groups of ideological zealots, or just plain ruthless opportunists, to grab power and impose their collectivizing schemes. Democratic institutions and traditions had saved the advanced countries from the onslaught of collectivist extremism. That line of defense was unavailable to the rest of the world, with predictably dismal consequences.

The Industrial Counterrevolution had begun as an effort to push the boundaries of economic development—to accelerate progress on the economic frontier by reorganizing society according to the supposedly centralizing logic of industrialization. In the postwar world, the fundamental character of the Industrial Counterrevolution changed: Its center of gravity had now moved to the underdeveloped world, and its primary focus turned to catching up with the market-based economies of the West.

It was the Soviet Union that forged the new alliance between collectivism and economic backwardness. For centuries Russia had been a kind of Eurasian Third World: a vast economic and political hinterland, torn between envying the West's material success and rejecting its perceived spiritual corruption. Given its longstanding but ambiguous ties to the West, Russia proved a fertile breeding ground for the collectivist contagion. Although the success of the Russian Revolution was puzzling from an orthodox Marxist perspective, in retrospect Russia's receptiveness to radical centralization made perfect sense.

Lenin was the prototype for all the Third World revolutionaries to come: westernized yet anti-Western, seized by the vision of a collectivist forced march to modernity. In the words of historian Theodore von Laue:

> Vladimir Ilich Ulianov, a radical revolutionary from a privileged family, a well-educated political exile living in western Europe but revealingly self-named "Lenin" after the easternmost Siberian river, the Lena, dreamed of anti-Western world revolution. . . . He envisioned a global counterrevolution to the Western outreach led by its victims—victims half admiring the Western model and half rejecting it—by universalizing its message of freedom, equality, and universal fellowship. Revolutionary Russia's allies were to come from all the colonial and semi-colonial lands.[16]

What Lenin began, Stalin brought to fruition. He led the forced march with complete and utter ruthlessness, and in the process transformed Russia from backwater to superpower. From humiliating defeat by the Kaiser's armies to triumph over Hitler, from loss of territory at the end of World War I to mastery of half of Europe (including half of Germany) at the end of World War II—Stalin's brutal industrialization drive had achieved nothing less than a miracle. Now the world's second-largest economic power, with a huge and formidable conventional army and a growing nuclear arsenal, the

Soviet Union had raised itself up to the verge of global dominance. In the name of Marxist internationalism, Stalin had given Russian nationalism the fulfillment of its wildest dreams—and provided a blueprint for Third World nationalists to follow at home.

Bled dry by two world wars, and disabused by those terrible conflicts of the old lust for territorial gain, the colonial powers lost the will to maintain the empires they had created. And so the decades after World War II saw the rise and triumph of anticolonial independence movements around the world, and the entrance of dozens of new members into the community of nations. Throughout the emerging Third World, leaders followed the Soviet example of collectivized nation-building, often explicitly. "[T]he Soviet Revolution had advanced human society by a great leap," wrote Jawaharlal Nehru from prison during World War II, "and had lit a bright flame which could not be smothered and . . . laid the foundation for a new civilization toward which the world could advance."[17] In 1947 India would win its independence, and, under Nehru's leadership, plunge into mimicry of Stalinist planning. In the years that followed, Nehru would be accompanied by Mao in China, Nasser in Egypt, Sukarno in Indonesia, Nkrumah in Ghana, and many others—all eager to mobilize and modernize their people through the agency of the centralizing state.

In his autobiography, published in 1957 just as Ghana was gaining its independence, Kwame Nkrumah sounded the theme that reverberated all across the underdeveloped world at the time—the pressing need to accelerate progress:

> All dependent territories are backward in education, in agriculture and in industry. The economic independence that should follow and maintain political independence demands . . . a total mobilisation of brain and manpower resources. What other countries have taken three hundred years or more to achieve, a once dependent territory must try to accomplish in a generation if it is to survive.[18]

Collectivism, Nkrumah and his fellow Third World leaders believed, would provide the needed shortcut to modernity. "Capitalism is too complicated a system for a newly independent nation," Nkrumah admitted revealingly. "Hence the need for a socialistic society."[19] On this point, Nkrumah was merely echoing what Lenin had recognized decades earlier. "What is to a great extent automatic in a politically free country," wrote Lenin, "must in Russia be done deliberately and systematically by our organizations."[20]

The Third World pursuit of state-dominated economic development was guided by two basic hypotheses, each as influential as it was untethered to reality. First was the assertion of a so-called "vicious circle of poverty"; second was the belief that market-based relationships between developing and advanced countries necessarily exploited the former for the latter's benefit. One provided intellectual support for top-down control at home; the other justified the extension of central planning to the international sphere.

The concept of the vicious circle of poverty was central to the new discipline of "development economics" that sprang up after World War II. One of the concept's most prominent exponents, the economist Ragnar Nurske, wrote flippantly that it "can be summed up in the trite proposition: 'a country is poor because it is poor.' "[21] In particular, it was alleged that low levels of income inhibited the saving needed to fund investment, and that without investment and capital accumulation there could be no improvement in income levels. Hence poor countries, without some heroic intervention from above, were forever trapped in desperate want.

Central planning, the votaries of development economics concluded, was necessary to break the vicious circle. Gunnar Myrdal, a leading light of the discipline (and, amusingly, a co-winner of the 1974 Nobel prize in economics—along with F. A. Hayek), expressed the prevailing consensus:

> The . . . idea that large-scale state intervention, coordinated in a plan, is needed to bring about economic development follows as an inference from the realization that these countries have long remained in a state of relative stagnation, while the Western world has for many generations developed rapidly. A strong, induced impetus is needed to end that stagnation and bring about economic progress, which apparently is not coming spontaneously, or at least not rapidly enough.[22]

Myrdal was unabashedly paternalistic in his conception of the role of planning "in this Rip van Winkle world, among people still drowsy with the slumber of centuries."[23] That conception, he wrote, "envisages a government and its entourage as the active subject in planning, and the rest of the people as the relatively passive objects of the policies emerging from planning."[24]

Here again was what Hayek called the "fatal conceit" of central planning, now applied to the particular circumstances of the world's poorest nations. Once again it was assumed that economic advancement turns on the faithful application of an existing body of technical knowledge. All that is needed to usher in a golden age of growth and prosperity is to grant the elite that possesses the necessary knowledge the plenary power to apply it—or, in other words, to force the rest of us to do as we're told.

In truth, the justification for all the grandiose schemes of development planning was manifest nonsense. "Indeed, if the notion of the vicious circle of poverty were valid," wrote Peter Bauer, the great dissident in development economics, "mankind would still be living in the Old Stone Age."[25] The existence of rich countries (and the fact that they were not always rich) disproves any claim that poverty is inescapable. As to the belief that special circumstances rendered non-Western countries incapable of saving and investing, Bauer was contemptuous:

> It is difficult to see how development economists could have entertained this notion if they had recognized how millions of poor producers in the Third World had in the aggregate made massive investments in agriculture. . . . If there had been a vicious circle of poverty, these poor people had failed to notice it. Millions of acres of cultivated land under cash crops such as rubber, cocoa, and coffee, as well as foodstuffs for domestic markets, testify not only to Third World peoples' economic responsiveness and readiness to take the long view but also to the vacuousness of the idea of the vicious circle of poverty.[26]

The other great intellectual prop for Third World statism was the idea that eventually came to be known as "dependency theory"—namely, the belief that the operation of international markets served only to make rich countries richer and poor countries poorer. Here was an alternative and supplemental explanation of Third World poverty: Not only are underdeveloped countries economically inept, but such potential for growth that they do possess is being systematically looted by the advanced nations and their multinational corporations. Escape from poverty is possible, in this view, only if poor countries reject participation in international markets and strive instead for national or collective self-sufficiency.

Dependency theory had its roots in Lenin's ingenious interpretation of imperialism as capitalism's highest and final stage of development. According to Lenin, the expansion of world markets and accompanying rush for empire had elevated capitalist exploitation to a new, global scale. By opening up new territories for the export of capital, capitalism had entered a parasitic stage in which the advanced countries grew increasingly dependent on the profits they extracted from their colonial possessions. This globalization of exploitation gave the bourgeois epoch in those advanced countries a temporary lease on life by co-opting exploited workers at home with the booty pillaged from abroad. "Imperialism," wrote Lenin, "which means the partitioning of the world, and the exploitation of other countries . . . , which means high monopoly profits for a handful of very rich countries, makes it economically possible to bribe the upper strata of the proletariat. . . ."[27] In the end, though, conflicts among the imperial powers, and between the subjected peoples of colonial and semi-colonial lands and those powers, would bring the whole rotten system to its inevitable demise.

With his theory of imperialism, Lenin was killing two birds with one stone. First, he was salvaging Marxism by explaining why the working classes in the advanced countries were not rising up against their capitalist oppressors, but instead were becoming increasingly "bourgeois" themselves. The answer, according to Lenin, lay in the profits being drained by international financial capital from the resource-rich economic hinterland. Next, and ultimately more important, Lenin was making a case for the central role of less developed countries—such as his own—in the revolutionary struggle. In Lenin's conception, Bolshevik victory in Russia could be the trigger for a worldwide revolution of exploited peoples—both the "internal" proletariat of the rich countries and the "external" proletariat of the underdeveloped regions—and the final collapse of capitalism everywhere.

Of course it was all a fantasy, but sufficiently engaging nonetheless to propel Lenin and his Bolsheviks to power. What followed, in the decades after World War II, was the spread of that fantasy throughout most of the underdeveloped world, and the transmutation of Marxist theory from a prophecy of developments at the economic frontier into an ideology of Third World liberation. Peter Bauer summarized the metamorphosis:

> First, that the underdeveloped world is not only desperately poor but stagnant or even retrogressing; this notion is the current version of the doctrine of the ever-increasing misery of the proletariat. Second, that the exploitation of underdeveloped by developed countries is a major cause of this poverty; this is the current version of the doctrine of the exploitation of the proletariat. Third, that political independence or freedom is meaningless without economic independence; this is an extension of the suggestion that political freedom and representative government are meaningless under capitalism. Fourth, that comprehensive development planning is indispensable for economic advance in underdeveloped countries and especially for the industrialisation required for material progress. Though reflecting Marxism-Leninism less directly, this last point nevertheless owes much to the recognition of the political possibilities of economic planning (as exemplified in Soviet experience), and also to the emphasis on the industrial proletariat in communist literature and strategy.[28]

The spread of the Leninist vision led to the general refusal of less developed countries, after the chaos of 1914–45 abated, to join the reconstructed international market economy. Virtually all the dominant Third World ideologies, whether or not explicitly Marxist, asserted an inherent economic conflict between rich and poor countries. Accordingly, strict state controls on international transactions would be necessary to prevent further exploitation by the West.

Raúl Prebisch was the leading theorist of Latin America's turn toward isolationist "import substitution" policies. The intellectual godfather of the highly influential United Nations Economic Commission for Latin America (ECLA), Prebisch rejected as anachronistic the liberal belief in the mutual advantageousness of trade. "In Latin America," he declared boldly in 1950, "reality is undermining the out-dated schema of the international division of labour."[29] Prebisch observed that the old liberal international economic order consisted of a "center" (the industrialized nations) and a "periphery" (the underdeveloped world); the periphery provided raw materials in exchange for manufactured goods from the center. But that exchange, he argued, was inherently unequal and only getting worse. The terms of trade between rich and poor countries were steadily deteriorating from the latter's standpoint; in other words, a given volume of poor-country exports was, over time, buying a progressively shrinking volume of imports.

"Thus there exists an obvious disequilibrium," wrote Prebisch, "a fact which, whatever its explanation or justification, destroys the basic premise underlying the schema of the international division of labor."[30] The international market economy was not mutually advantageous; it was a zero-sum game in which the rich countries profited at the poor countries' expense. Continued participation by the periphery in unregulated market relationships with the center was a hopeless dead end.

Prebisch's and ECLA's solution, adopted almost universally by poor countries after World War II, was to eschew the supposedly false promise of export-led growth in favor of "import substitution." Imports would be restricted to necessities that were impossible to produce locally; under the guidance of development planning and powered by public investment in state-owned enterprises, home-grown industrialization, with production aimed at the home market, would lead the way out of stagnation and into prosperity.

Prebisch's diagnosis of the problems confronting poor countries was spectacularly misguided. The assertion of inexorably deteriorating terms of trade for traditional primary-product exports could not withstand empirical scrutiny; furthermore, the bland assumption that poor countries could not develop new export industries (for example, labor-intensive manufacturing) was obviously mistaken. As events unfolded, though, the "export pessimism" that propelled so many poor countries into import-substitution policies turned out to be a self-fulfilling prophecy. Overvalued exchange rates, protectionism's increase in the profitability of domestic production relative to that of export production, protectionism's stimulation of domestic demand for potentially exportable goods, and the costliness or unavailability of foreign inputs needed to support export production—all of these factors resulted in the steady dwindling of poor countries' export prospects.

Meanwhile, the payoff from homegrown industrialization proved meager. Only 13 years after his manifesto for economic self-sufficiency, Raúl Prebisch offered this disillusioned assessment of the consequences of taking his advice:

> [T]he proliferation of industries of every kind in a closed market has deprived the Latin American countries of the advantages of specialization and economies of scale, and owing to the protection afforded by excessive tariff duties and restrictions, a healthy form of internal competition has failed to develop, to the detriment of efficient production.[31]

One is tempted to ask: And this was a surprise?

During the 1960s Latin America began groping for alternatives. Regional protectionism was one path: Bolivia, Chile, Colombia, Ecuador, and Peru banded together to create the Andean Pact, and were later joined by Venezuela. Other countries—notably Brazil, Mexico, and Colombia—launched major export subsidy programs. But regions of monopolistic sloth proved little improvement over their national building blocks, and subsidized exports of subsidized production did not provide the hoped-for engine of growth.

Confronted with the disappointments of past policies, true believers in the Leninist vision came up with "dependency theory"—a radicalized version of Prebisch's analysis that claimed autarky must be combined with comprehensive central planning.[32] The problem with ECLA's import-substitution paradigm was that it was too timid. "In spite of their critical nature," wrote leading *dependencistas* Fernando Henrique Cardoso and Enzo Faletto in 1976, "ECLA economic theories and critiques were not based on an analysis of social process, did not call attention to imperialist relationships among countries, and did not take into account the asymmetric relations between classes."[33] Import substitution had succeeded in building up national industries, but those industries were too often controlled by the local bourgeoisie or, even worse, foreign multinational corporations. The only true escape from economic subservience was to press on further along the collectivist path. In the words of

Samir Amin, a prominent African dependency theorist, "It is not by accident that every serious attempt by the periphery to free itself from the political domination of the center has led to conflicts that suggest the need to consider a socialist way forward." [34]

The 1960s and '70s saw theory translated into action as many developing countries lurched toward ever-greater government involvement in economic affairs. State-owned enterprises multiplied rapidly throughout the Third World, and so did expropriations of foreign investors. Takeovers of U.S. firms, which had averaged less than one per year between 1946 and 1960, jumped to 15.8 per year in 1967–71 and then 28.5 per year in 1972–73. [35] At the international level, the U.N. General Assembly became a hotbed of agitation for a "new international economic order"—shorthand for a grab bag of schemes that included massive official wealth transfers from rich to poor countries and the organization of international commodity cartels in mimicry of OPEC's example. According to partisans of the "NIEO," it was time for the West to pay back all the riches it had stolen. Tanzanian leader Julius Nyerere summarized the view during a 1975 state visit to Great Britain:

> In one world, as in one state, when I am rich because you are poor, and I am poor because you are rich, the transfer of wealth from the rich to the poor is a matter of right; it is not an appropriate matter for charity. . . . If the rich countries go on getting richer and richer at the expense of the poor, the poor of the world must demand a change, in the same way as the proletariat in the rich countries demanded change in the past. [36]

It should be noted in passing that while Nyerere was blaming the West for Third World poverty, his own *ujaama* policy of forced rural collectivization was wrecking Tanzania's agriculture and plunging the country into new depths of misery.

The ultimate fate of dependency theory is best captured in the subsequent career of one of its principal exponents, Fernando Henrique Cardoso. Without ever explicitly renouncing his former views, he went on—first as Brazil's finance minister, and since 1995 as its president—to pursue the "neoliberal" agenda: stabilizing the inflation-wracked currency, privatizing state-owned enterprises, and reducing trade barriers. Having begun, though by no means completed, the dismantling of his country's inglorious statist legacy, the one-time apologist for Castro and Allende now follows in the footsteps of Pinochet's "Chicago boys." In *Macbeth* it was said of the treasonous Thane of Cawdor that "nothing in his life became him like the leaving it"; the same may be said of Cardoso's life as a *dependencista*.

There was one region of the non-Western world where the international market economy was viewed increasingly as an opportunity, not a threat. Along the Pacific Rim, a growing number of economies began pursuing their own distinctive path toward economic development—neither Soviet-style totalitarian communism, nor the Western model of regulatory welfare states, nor the Third World orthodoxy of strength through autarky. Instead they followed the trail blazed by Japan—that curious exception to the conventional categories, the only non-Western member of the Western club.

Japan pioneered a hybrid type of economic system dubbed by its admirers the "capitalist developmental state." Far better than most of the rest of the world, it succeeded in establishing a fundamentally market-friendly environment: civil peace, relatively stable money, low taxes, tolerable security for private property, and a political culture in which commercial success was encouraged and valued. At the same time, though, the government took a strongly interventionist approach toward controlling the allocation of capital to new investments and new industries—through preferential finance, trade barriers, direct subsidies, tax breaks, regulatory restrictions, promotion of cartels, and regular consultations between government and industry.

Japan's spectacular postwar economic rise attracted imitators: first the "four tigers"—South Korea, Taiwan, Hong Kong, and Singapore—and later the Southeast Asian nations of Thailand, Malaysia, and Indonesia. Admittedly, the other economies of the "Asian miracle" varied considerably in their fidelity to Japan's example. Korea and Taiwan followed it fairly closely; Hong Kong, by contrast, was much more uniformly liberal, doing little or nothing in the way of industrial policy. The Southeast Asian economies, led by Singapore, welcomed foreign direct investment, while Japan and Korea shunned it. With regard to industrial policy, venality and corruption played a much greater role in Indonesia and Thailand than any coherent economic strategy did, while in Malaysia, racial considerations (namely, promotion of the indigenous Malay population) predominated. Overall, though, it is fair to generalize about an "East Asian model" that combined pro-market fundamentals with an activist industrial policy.

One critical element of that fundamental pro-market orientation was the elimination of barriers to exports. Again, details varied. Hong Kong encouraged its international sector most directly—through unilateral free trade. The rest of the region maintained more or less protectionist policies for their domestic producers; however, they compensated with general pro-export policies—cheap exchange rates, tax breaks, duty exemptions for imported components, and so forth. As a result, exporters, at least, operated in the equivalent of a free-trade environment.[37]

By facilitating the development of export sectors, Japan and its Pacific Rim protégés defied intellectual fashion. Yet while the rest of the non-Western world stumbled down one blind alley after another, these economies discovered the true short cut to prosperity. By importing Western mass-production technology and applying their native resources of entrepreneurial talent and cheap labor, the East Asian economies developed new areas of comparative advantage—first in labor-intensive light manufacturing, and later in more capital-intensive production. Their competitive edge as low-cost producers, combined with the relative openness of rich-country markets, allowed their new and highly productive industries to grow far faster than domestic demand; meanwhile, the rapid wealth creation of the export sectors rippled through the domestic economies and stimulated accelerated growth at home. The results were nothing short of breathtaking. At the start of South Korea's export push in the early 1960s, the country's economic prospects compared unfavorably to those of West Africa; by the 1990s, within a single generation, income per head was close to southern European levels.

East Asia's combination of competition and interventionism gave the region a dual role in the economic policy debates of the 1980s and '90s. Compared to the Soviet-style command economies, or inflationary and isolationist Latin America, East Asia was clearly market-oriented. And so, during the 1980s, when the Communist bloc was sinking into ruin and Latin America was lashed by its debt crisis, the glittering performance of the Pacific Rim gave powerful testimony to the benefits of market competition. On the other hand, East Asian industrial policies and the clubby ties among industries, banks, and governments offered a sharp contrast to the relatively hands-off policy in the United States regarding the promotion of particular industries. As U.S. economic preeminence appeared to fade before the Japanese challenge, and the "four tigers" and Southeast Asia were surging up to join Japan, the partisans of centralized control had a powerful argument that excessive reliance on market forces was a recipe for economic decline.

Hence this ironic twist: East Asia's rise had utterly confounded all of the most cherished prejudices of the true believers in state-led economic development, yet in the end, the East Asian model became the last great refuge for those very same true believers. Champions of the East Asian "capitalist developmental state" argued that the economies of the Pacific Rim had combined markets and central planning to achieve the best of both worlds. In this combination, market mechanisms were a useful way of administering given economic structures, but the task of economic architecture—of choosing and designing those basic structures—remained the preserve of a small technocratic elite. Journalist James Fallows explained approvingly:

> The Asian-style system deeply mistrusts markets. It sees competition as a useful tool for keeping companies on their toes but not as a way to resolve any of the big questions of life—how a society should be run, in what direction its economy should unfold.[38]

Competition had a part to play, it was now conceded, but the leading role was still held by the state. By directing resources toward promising new industries with high-growth potential, the central planners in capitalist development states could outperform the hit-or-miss results of uncoordinated markets.

What the advocates of Asian-style planning did not realize was that its best days were already behind it, and disasters were lurking just around the bend. When Japan emerged as the darling of planning advocates, it was already well on its way down the arc from miracle to decline. The high point of "Japan, Inc." ended nearly three decades ago, though general realization of that fact is only a few years old. After the early 1970s, particular industries continued to develop impressively and even lead the world to new levels of achievement, but the economic system as a whole grew progressively dysfunctional.[39]

For a quarter-century or so, from the outbreak of the Korean War until the Arab oil embargo, Japan, Inc. enjoyed its golden age. During those years the country built and consolidated its distinctive system of heavy-handed government control. At the center of the system was the Ministry of International Trade and Industry, which worked closely with business leaders to set investment and export targets. In particular, MITI promoted breakneck "investment races" that led repeatedly to excess capacity and downturns; MITI would then organize "recession cartels" in which companies scaled back proportionally to preserve their market shares. In this way Japanese industry acquired the habit of seeing market share, not market returns, as the chief measure of business success.[40]

MITI's authority to steer economic development was buttressed by the systematic suppression of financial market forces. The Ministry of Finance rationed scarce domestic credit and blocked the inflow of foreign funds. A bond cartel determined when corporations could issue debt securities. Run by the banks, the cartel prevented the bond market from offering any serious competition to the banking system.[41] The bank-led corporate groups, or *keiretsu,* cemented their long-term relationships (and fended off potential takeovers) with an elaborate web of cross-shareholding. The equity market, as a consequence, was largely frozen.

Centralized control went hand in hand with spectacular economic progress: Annual growth in real GDP averaged a gaudy 9.3 percent from 1956 to 1973.[42] But, as it must, the shooting star eventually fell to earth. Rapid productivity gains from industrialization petered out as manufacturing's share of total output peaked and then began to decline. Many industries attained rough technological parity with the West, thus exhausting their catch-up potential. A steady supply of surplus rural labor had kept wages low and costs competitive; as remaining farm employment dwindled, the supply ran out and costs began to climb.

Struggling against these forces of economic gravity, a few Japanese industries—notably automobiles, consumer electronics, and semiconductors—achieved new heights of productivity. Overhauling the manufacturing process with such innovations as continuous improvement and just-in-time inventory, they triumphed in world markets during the 1970s and '80s, perpetuating and augmenting Japan's reputation as an economic superstar.[43] However, the dazzling performance of these export powerhouses obscured the deteriorating condition of the rest of the Japanese economy. Resource- and labor-intensive industries experienced chronic excess capacity—a problem exacerbated by MITI's policy of encouraging "recession cartels." And low productivity in the uncompetitive and overregulated service sector increasingly hindered overall growth. Japan developed into a deformed "dual economy"—a vibrant and dynamic international sector that all the world envied and feared, and a much larger, but largely stagnant, domestic sector that the world all but ignored.

Japan's international sector progressively freed itself from the grip of centralized control. By the mid-1960s, sustained growth abated capital scarcity and ended the Ministry of Finance's credit rationing. Furthermore, as export-oriented industries grew, their own internally generated cash flow made them less dependent on external financing of any kind. Beginning in the 1980s, liberalization of capital flows allowed Japan's export giants to bypass the domestic banking system and tap directly into foreign equity and bond markets for needed financing.

While outside observers continued to credit MITI with masterminding Japan's export successes, the fact is that the main focus of Japan, Inc. shifted from promoting sunrise industries to nursing declining sectors. MITI had little to offer industries at the economic frontier, and dwindling leverage over them.[44] The dark side of the dual economy, however, grew increasingly dependent on protection from the accountability of competition.

The Japanese capitalist developmental state reached a critical juncture in the mid-1980s as the yen roughly doubled in value versus the dollar in the space of two years. The strong yen, or *endaka,* put the squeeze on export industries and prompted an exodus of manufacturing capacity out of Japan. The one prop of economic vitality, the international sector, was slipping away. It was at this time that Japanese authorities should have realized that the jig was up: The postwar economic structures had plainly outlived their usefulness and were in need of fundamental overhaul. Instead, the Bank of Japan slashed interest rates and the country indulged in one last feverish bout of false prosperity. Banks and their affiliated finance companies, the *jusen,* poured money into a booming real estate sector; soaring stock values fueled a wild investment spree.[45]

In 1990 the bubble finally burst. Within a few years, the sad state into which the Japanese economy had fallen was, at last, undeniable. And after a few years more, the outbreak of the Asian financial crisis revealed deep structural flaws in economies up and down the Pacific Rim. The East Asian model was dead. And with its demise, not a single viable model of central planning was left on this earth.

———※———

The crackup of the East Asian model was the last in a series of calamities that ended the Industrial Counterrevolution as a living movement. The crisis began in the 1970s, though at the time the collectivist cause appeared to be gathering new momentum. Notwithstanding the steady deterioration in the Soviet bloc's economic performance, the communist model continued to claim new adherents—in Southeast Asia, Africa, and Central America. Throughout the Third World, the failures of development planning were leading to ever more strident denunciations of capitalist exploitation, culminating in the mass delusion of the NIEO movement. And in the advanced countries, stagflation and a self-imposed energy crisis led many to believe that what remained of the market economy was not long for this world.

Just as the Industrial Counterrevolution seemed poised to make bold new advances, it experienced instead a worldwide catastrophic reversal.[46] In the advanced countries, the stagflation of the 1970s led to a double revolution in economic policymaking during the 1980s. With the pretensions of Keynesian fine-tuning decisively shattered, price stability replaced full employment as the polestar of monetary policy. At the same time, support for the postwar "mixed economy" suddenly unraveled: In country after country and industry after industry, state-owned enterprises were sold off and price-and-entry regulations were scrapped.

In August 1982, Mexico announced to the world that it was unable to service its foreign loans. That news was the trigger for a massive debt crisis that quickly consumed Latin America and much of the developing world. The 1970s had witnessed an orgy of Third World borrowing from Western banks: In Latin America alone, long-term foreign debt skyrocketed from $45.2 billion in 1975 to $176.4 billion in 1982.[47] Now the bill was due, but the borrowed money had been squandered in statist misadventures. The cutoff of foreign capital inflicted agonizing withdrawal pains on the debtor countries; in Latin America, the 1980s became known as the "lost decade." Out of this misery, though, came a fundamental reorientation of many Latin American economies: from rampant inflation to stable money, from state ownership to privatization, and from import substitution to trade liberalization. The *dependencistas* had given way to the "neoliberals."

Foreign borrowing caught up with India in the summer of 1991. Faced with a balance-of-payments crisis, the new government of P. V. Narasimha Rao launched a sharp break with four decades of Soviet-style central planning. It moved swiftly to dethrone the "Permit Raj"—the suffocating accumulation of controls and licenses that blanketed the industrial economy and presumed to govern almost every investment and production decision. In the international sphere, the Rao government began to cut tariffs, eliminate import licenses, and open up to foreign investment. The Gandhian ideal of *swadeshi,* or self-reliance, was increasingly honored in the breach.

Most dramatic of all, of course, was the sudden and utterly unexpected collapse of communism. In little more than a decade, from the late 1970s to the early 1990s, what had been a world-historical force of the first order all but vanished from the face of the earth. The end began in China after Mao's death in 1976. Under the leadership of Deng Xiaoping, the country embarked on a new course that came to be known, euphemistically, as

"socialism with Chinese characteristics." Starting in 1978 with the decollec-
tivization of agriculture under the "household responsibility system," and
then with the creation of the first "special economic zones" on the southern
coast in 1980, what was really happening was the gradual abandonment of the
command economy. In the Soviet Union, Mikhail Gorbachev assumed
power in 1985 and began his famous reforms of *glasnost* and *perestroika*. Although Gorbachev intended to revitalize the Soviet system, he instead ended
up destroying it: In 1989–90 the empire in Eastern Europe broke away, and
on Christmas Day of 1991 the Soviet Union itself ceased to exist.

The combined effect of these startling events—along with the more recent implosion of the East Asian model discussed earlier—has been nothing
less than the death of the Industrial Counterrevolution. This is not to say that
collectivism has vanished from the scene, or that the principles of economic
liberalism now reign triumphant—far from it. But collectivism's intellectual
vitality is defunct; it has lost the ability to inspire, to frame the debate, to set
the agenda for policy change. A century's bitter experience has now established beyond all serious debate that, as a general rule, centralized control
does not deliver the goods: It does not yield the widely shared abundance
that its partisans promised. The overwhelming consensus of informed opinion today recognizes that market competition, once so widely despised, is in
fact the indispensable foundation of prosperity. Consequently, the Intellectual Counterrevolution, for so long the wave of the future, has lost its alliance with progress. Hostility to markets remains, and remains formidable,
but only as a force of reaction.

The consequences of the Industrial Counterrevolution's downfall have
been many and far-reaching. Few, though, have been more significant, or
more visible, than the resumption of a global division of labor. With the fall
of the Soviet Empire, the opening of China, and the move away from import substitution by much of the developing world, the liberal trading system of the advanced countries and the Pacific Rim moved swiftly to embrace those formerly sealed-off regions. While globalization—depicted as
some demiurge born of information technology—is often credited with or
blamed for the recent worldwide spread of markets, the great tide of history
has actually been moving in the opposite direction: It is the collapse of anti-
market ideology that has allowed globalization to resume its course.

〰〰〰

The ultimate explanation for the demise of the Industrial Counterrevolution is straightforward. It was based on fundamental errors, and thus was doomed to fail. Failures accumulated and proliferated until the gap between promise and accomplishment became unsustainably large. When that happened, the Industrial Counterrevolution lost its legitimacy, and surrendered the mantle of heaven.

That explanation ascribes central importance to the power of ideas in driving historical change. Accordingly, it raises several tough questions. First, it assumes that the political process has some capacity, however minimal, for recognizing and correcting errors. What is the nature of that capacity? Second, if collectivism was doomed to fail, why did so many years have to go by before those failures finally dragged it down?

I will postpone tackling the first question until the final chapter of this book. There I will set forth my reasons for believing that political institutions create a weak but functional mechanism for learning from mistakes. That mechanism provides the basis for hope that, in the long run, bad ideas are eventually rejected—and thus that liberalism's progress will continue. Here, though, I want to address the other side of the coin: not why the errors of the Industrial Counterrevolution eventually came to light, but why they eluded detection for so long.

First of all, many dysfunctions caused by over-centralization take time to reveal themselves, and may even create the temporary appearance of success. Inflation is an obvious example. Its initial effect is the euphoria of a boom, and each additional burst of monetary stimulus above prevailing inflationary expectations extends the euphoria. It can take many years before inflationary expectations become so deeply engrained that further money creation no longer brings the illusion of prosperity; by that time, the accumulated distortions in relative prices have seriously compromised the economy's ability to produce genuine sustained growth. The final result is runaway inflation and chronic stagnation—the dreaded stagflation. But that endgame may arrive decades after the first surrender to inflationary temptation.

Governments can likewise maintain the appearance of success, for a while, by borrowing. The Third World debt crisis of the 1980s and the Asian financial crisis of the 1990s were both preceded by massive runups of indebtedness. As long as the money is rolling in, life on borrowed time can be sweet. But when the bill comes due, all the problems that were temporarily masked still remain, and now are compounded by a heavy and sometimes crippling burden of debt.

Errors in the allocation of capital are seldom immediately obvious. An increase in investment, however misdirected it might be, almost always conveys the impression of economic vitality. Employment surges, as do GDP figures, and the investment expenditures ripple through the economy. Accordingly, central planning schemes that presume to outguess capital markets can appear to succeed so long as they keep mobilizing new pools of savings to fund their investment projects. Many years may elapse before the errors of malinvestment manifest themselves in widespread unprofitability. White elephants, like the real-life kind, have long gestation periods.

The lag between bad policies and bad outcomes is often extended by the presence of certain cultural values—values that incline people to behave in ways conducive to wealth creation regardless of the pecuniary incentives created by government policies. Prominent among such values are a strong work ethic, high levels of trust that allow people to work cooperatively with relative strangers, a general orientation toward worldly success, entrepreneurial habits of mind, and widespread aptitude in scientific and technological endeavors. Such values can overcome—at least partially or temporarily—the suppression or absence of market institutions and feedback mechanisms.[48]

For instance, the anti-work incentives of some collectivist social welfare programs may not register until those programs have been in operation for a generation or more. A preexisting culture that stigmatizes joblessness or dependency will trump the signals conveyed by, say, lavish unemployment benefits. Over time, though, the culture is likely to adapt to the new institutions, and employment then deteriorates accordingly. To take another example, high levels of trust—commonly found in particular ethnic minorities—can allow a lively business sector to develop and thrive (up to a certain point, at least) even without a well-developed legal infrastructure. The Chinese business networks throughout Southeast Asia are an obvious illustration of the point.

Actually, collectivist movements can, at times, generate their own cultural bonds that, for as long as they endure, help to mitigate the problems caused by the policies produced. In particular, ideological enthusiasm can elicit hard work and selfless dedication against the current of dysfunctional pecuniary incentives. The Soviet command economy functioned far better when the dream of an attainable socialist paradise still seemed plausible—first, because Soviet managers had internalized incentives to do their best; and second, because the Soviet leadership was sufficiently fanatical that it was willing to use terror to combat slacking. As revolutionary ardor succumbed to disillusioned cynicism, Soviet managers became willing to do whatever they could get away with, while the leadership grew too dispirited to crack down. Only when the culture of true believers finally dissipated did the full perversity of the command economy's institutional design reveal itself.

In this same regard, consider the various industrial policies of the East Asian miracle economies. Regardless of their effectiveness as strictly economic measures, their existence sent a strong cultural signal: The government was committed to fostering economic growth and, to that end, a pro-business environment. That signal doubtless contributed positively to the development of the strong entrepreneurial cultures that now grace the region. In other words, the cultural effect of industrial policy gave a boost to economic dynamism that was wholly separate from the actual substance of the measures taken.[49]

Collectivism's errors thus take time to surface, and can be obscured to some extent by other factors. Furthermore, collectivism tends to make relatively fewer errors at the outset of its reign. To understand why, it is necessary to revisit the fundamental tradeoffs between centralization and competition I addressed back in Chapter 2. Centralization maximizes the faithful application of specific known information; competition, by contrast, maximizes receptivity to the new and unknown. Accordingly, when what to do and how to do it are relatively clear-cut, centralized decision-making can work well; on the other hand, when the proper course is uncertain, the discovery process of competition is irreplaceable.

In countries well removed from the frontiers of economic development, opportunities for rapid productivity growth abound. This is the well-known advantage of backwardness: Less developed countries can post impressively high "catch-up" growth rates for the simple reason that they are starting from such a relatively low base. In particular, they can borrow existing technologies and organizational techniques from the more advanced countries. Under these circumstances, it is possible for centralized control to function with reasonable effectiveness, because uncertainty is at a low ebb. Obviously profitable investment opportunities are plentiful, while capital is extremely scarce relative to its availability in more advanced countries. Selecting good investments from the many available possibilities is not terribly difficult despite the lack of guidance from market signals. Surrounded by low-hanging fruit, even the blind can pick their fill—for a while.

Japan's postwar miracle and subsequent malaise illustrate the considerable potential and ultimate limitations of centrally managed catch-up growth. Japan combined a generally market-friendly environment with the substantial substitution of bureaucratic guidance for capital markets; in addition, its export orientation subjected investments in tradable sectors to the stringent discipline of world product markets. This policy mix allowed Japan to rise from a smoldering ruin after World War II to technological parity with the United States by the 1970s. At that point, however, the suppression of market mechanisms for allocating capital became increasingly problematic. The easy pickings of surefire investments were exhausted; at the same time, the accumulation of capital meant that more money was now chasing a dwindling number of obviously profitable opportunities. And as nontradable service industries waxed in economic importance, export orientation did less to compensate for the lack of financial market signals. Japan, Inc. fell victim to its own success: Like a star athlete with a heart defect, it moved closer to tragedy with every victory.

Even countries without many of Japan's advantages have still managed catch-up growth that far exceeded what their economies could have generated internally. Latin America, for example, enjoyed a temporary boom with import substitution during the 1950s. But macroeconomic and political instability, combined with isolation from international markets, imposed constraints on growth that quickly began to tug performance downward. In Southeast Asia, more Japan-like conditions have allowed greater and more durable vitality. Still, because countries like Thailand and Indonesia lack many of the social capabilities that Japan has developed, including good physical infrastructure and a large pool of highly skilled workers, they have not been able to push all the way to the technological frontier. Consequently, they experienced limits to catch-up growth much more quickly than Japan did—as the Asian financial crisis and its aftermath have made devastatingly clear.

For an extreme example of limited but nonetheless impressive catch-up growth, consider the Soviet industrialization drive under Stalin. From the perspective of ordinary Soviet citizens, communism was an unmitigated catastrophe from the beginning; living standards remained abysmal relative to the West for the whole life of the regime. However, from the perspective of the Soviet state, the command economy worked wonders (for a time). A nation defeated and dismembered in World War I rose a quarter-century later to exact revenge on Germany and assert itself as a world power. Admittedly, this feat was accomplished by appropriating the whole capital stock of the nation and ruthlessly diverting resources away from supplying consumer wants—but still it was accomplished. When the goal was clear (build up an industrial base capable of supporting total war) and the necessary technology already existed, the Stalinist system was able to catch up with other world powers. Thereafter, however, it floundered.

Besides the exhaustion of easy catch-up opportunities, there is another dimension to collectivism's tendency toward declining performance over time. Competition's greatest advantage over central planning lies in its superior ability to promote innovation. That advantage becomes apparent, though, only with the passage of time. Central planning might be capable of negotiating a one-shot catch-up drive, thus creating the appearance of dynamism. But sustaining, over the long term, a continuous process of marginal improvements, mixed with occasional bursts of "creative destruction," is a different matter altogether. Centralization can contend in sprints, but in the marathon competition has no equal.

The Soviet Union's post-Stalin sclerosis is an especially dramatic case in point. Stalin did succeed in constructing a formidable industrial base, but one that was incapable of ongoing internal improvement. As Yegor Gaidar, who later served as Boris Yeltsin's acting prime minister, observed in 1993:

> After the first stage of industrialization . . . no industry in Russia had its resources distributed to other industries; production would not cease because there was no demand for the products, or because there was a more efficient way to produce them. . . . This type of economy could be dynamic and could have a high level of growth, but only until its resources were needed to create a new industry.[50]

Without competition to prod incumbent producers and give chances to new ones, the Soviet economy began to deteriorate almost from the moment of its inception. For a while, extraordinarily high investment rates succeeded in compensating for the miserably low productivity of investment, but the law of diminishing returns eventually won out and growth ground to a halt.

Even assuming that central planners can overcome systemic resistance to innovation, the fact is that the increasing complexity of market economies becomes harder and harder for planners to mimic. In Chapter 1 I criticize the simplistic view that information technology is the primary driving force behind the spread of markets. That said, there is a subtle but real connection between technological progress, broadly defined, and the recent progress of economic liberty. The economic structures of the early industrial era were very crude by contemporary standards: There were fewer products, longer product cycles, simpler production technologies and processes, less complicated organizational charts, and so forth. In short, there was much less specialization, much less complexity. As the economy's moving parts have multiplied over time, the task of centralized control has grown ever more unmanageable. The performance gap between competition and centralization has thus widened with every breakthrough of the market's discovery process.[51]

For all the reasons discussed above, it took many decades before the failures of collectivism achieved the critical mass needed to break the Industrial Counterrevolution's bewitching spell. Of course there were always dissenting voices—none more deeply insightful than Hayek's—but their criticism of a vision that so many wanted so desperately to be true too often fell on deaf ears. Because reason lost the battle, it fell to experience to win the war. The price of victory, though, was terrible.

And the victory won so far remains distressingly incomplete. Errors recognized are not the same as errors corrected: As the remaining chapters of this book make clear, correcting the errors of the Industrial Counterrevolution has only just begun. The twilight of the collectivist idols will linger on for many years to come.

6

The Dead Hand

The world seems to be spinning faster these days: "Internet time" sets the pace for an accelerated age. Companies and whole industries balloon out of thin air; products dash from the drawing board to obsolescence; vast fortunes zip around the planet with the click of a mouse. The incessant barrage of ringing cell phones, buzzing pagers, and announcements of "you've got mail" keeps us breathlessly up to the minute in our business and personal lives, while CNN camera crews bring history into our living rooms in real time. It is all too easy, under these manic, now-obsessed conditions, to imagine that the musty old past no longer matters.

But it does. For a hundred years the partisans of the Industrial Counterrevolution worked to reshape the world in accordance with their vision. Some of them pursued their aims with a violent ferocity unmatched in human history: Tens of millions fell victim to war, famine, and terror. During the centralizing century, a sprawling, towering edifice of error was built up, expanded, and renovated. Powerful interests grew up dependent on it. Faith in its strength and rightness and inevitability trained and retrained deep-seated habits of thought. No country on earth was untouched.

Over the past couple of decades the dream of centrally controlled economic development has faded, and the edifice that it inspired has crumbled and fallen. But an historical force with the reach and intensity of the Industrial Counterrevolution does not simply vanish without a trace in such a short space of time. The dead hand of its surviving institutions, vested interests, and mindsets is still a powerful shaper of events. Social and economic conditions around the world remain badly deformed and disfigured as a result of excessive centralization, and the legacy of past mistakes and misdeeds will continue to darken prospects for improvement for years and years to come.

In *The Lexus and the Olive Tree,* Thomas Friedman uses the falling of the Berlin Wall as a metaphor for the larger demise of the Industrial Counterrevolution. "The Berlin Wall didn't just fall in Berlin," he writes. "It fell East and West, and North and South, and it hit both countries and companies, and hit them all at roughly the same time. . . . And it is the fall of all those walls all over the world that made this era of globalization and integration possible."[1]

Friedman's metaphor is apt—as far as it goes. But what he neglects to mention is that the rubble from all those fallen walls still lies scattered everywhere.

───※※※───

In 1932, in the depths of the Great Depression, 20-year-old John Scott dropped out of the University of Wisconsin and headed off to the Soviet Union. "Something seemed to be wrong with America," he wrote in his memoirs. "I decided to go to Russia to work, study, and to lend a hand in the construction of a society which seemed to be at least one step ahead of the American."[2]

Scott worked for the next five years in the giant new steel mill at Magnitogorsk—one of the great symbols of the Soviets' breakneck industrialization drive. "In Magnitogorsk I was precipitated into a battle," Scott wrote. "I was deployed on the iron and steel front."[3] Begun in 1929, Magnitogorsk was modeled after U.S. Steel's Gary Works, the largest and most advanced steel mill in the world. Despite appalling conditions, it arose from the remote Ural steppe in just a few short years—a testament to the audacity and brutal determination of a new social order. "Money was spent like water, men froze, hungered, and suffered," Scott recounted, "but the construction work went on with a disregard for individuals and a mass heroism seldom paralleled in history."[4] The payoff came in World War II, when half the tanks of the Soviet Red Army were made from Magnitogorsk steel.

Today, the romance of blast furnaces and five-year plans is long dead. The Soviet Union, the country into whose service John Scott enlisted, has ceased to exist. But Magnitogorsk is still there, still making steel. The Industrial Counterrevolution has been put to rout, but the dead hand of its influence still holds Magnitogorsk in its grip.

Magnitogorsk, when I visited in the summer of 1999, was an assault on the senses. When you stood on the west bank of the Ural River, at the foot of a colossal statue of two brawny, sword-wielding socialist heroes, the immense sprawl of the mill on the other side of the river extended across your entire field of vision. Belching out of the smokestacks that morning were plumes of orange, black, and blue-gray smoke; by late afternoon the winds had swirled them into a monochrome smear of brown. Driving around the huge, hulking works, past dingy and decrepit worker housing and out to the old iron ore deposit, your eyes and throat quickly began burning from exposure to the fouled air. And yet things used to be much worse: In recent years a number of the original, filthy open hearths have been replaced with more modern, cleaner furnaces. "In the old days," said Yelena Sherbakova, a retired mill worker, "the snow used to be black when it fell."[5]

The mill has struggled to make its way in the new, postcommunist world. Domestic demand for steel has fallen by more than 70 percent since 1990; consequently, Magnitogorsk has had to turn to foreign markets to survive. Built, though, to be far away from potential invaders, it is equally remote from potential customers: The nearest port is 1,200 miles away, so transportation costs are a major problem. Meanwhile, the Asian crisis and protectionism in the European Union and the United States have posed further obstacles. Despite everything, though, the mill now manages to export some 60 percent of its production.

Magnitogorsk has been officially privatized, but its ownership structure and finances remain murky. It reported profits in 1999, but what that means when some 40 percent of its domestic sales were barter transactions is far from clear. My own experience testifies to the lack of transparency at the mill: The firm's management refused to talk to my brother-in-law, then the Moscow correspondent for Cox newspapers, and me on the ground that we might be "spies."

Magnitogorsk has plowed billions of dollars into modernizing its facilities. Old open-hearth furnaces were replaced with modern converter shops, and a new hot-rolling mill was constructed. Labor policies at the mill, though, remain a holdover from the Soviet era. Although total output has plummeted from 16 million tons in the late 1980s to less than nine million tons, the work force has only contracted from 65,000 to 55,000. Workers are paid half in cash, half in credits at company-approved stores. Companies honor the workers' plastic cards in exchange for free electricity from the steel plant's generator and other barter goods. Faik Mukhametzianov, chairman of the local *Duma* (or city council), found these arrangements unexceptionable. "In America you use credit cards all the time," he said.[6] I tried to explain that credit cards in the United States are used to expand purchasers' options, not restrict them, but the point was lost in translation.

Magnitogorsk's awkward straddle of its Stalinist past and the globalized present typifies the predicament of the postcommunist "transition economies." In particular, the industrial sectors of those economies remain grotesquely distorted by the legacy of command and control. The transition to truly market-based industry is far from complete.

The most basic step along that path is the transfer of ownership from government to private hands. While great progress has been made in Central Europe, privatization of state-owned industries has lagged badly in southeastern Europe and much of the former Soviet Union. As of 1999, Albania, Azerbaijan, Belarus, Bosnia, Tajikistan, Turkmenistan, and Ukraine had privatized less than 25 percent of large-scale industrial assets; meanwhile, in Armenia, Bulgaria, Croatia, Macedonia, Kazakhstan, Kyrgyzstan, Latvia, Lithuania, Moldova, Romania, and Uzbekistan, privatization of industrial assets still had not passed the 50 percent mark.[7] And lagging privatization generally means lagging restructuring. For example, a World Bank study found that only 12 percent of Romanian industrial firms were privatized by 1995, as compared to 93 percent of such firms in the Czech Republic; more than coincidentally, only 24 percent of Romanian industrial enterprises were profitable that year, as opposed to 73 percent in the Czech Republic.[8] Such abysmal performance is possible year after year because of what economists daintily term a "soft budget constraint"—in other words, some combination of subsidies and a general failure to protect creditors' and investors' rights that allows firms to sustain losses indefinitely.

Privatization alone is no guarantee that real market-oriented restructuring will occur. The experience of Russia is sad testimony to that fact. Between 1992 and 1996, Russia sold off or gave away over 100,000 state-owned enterprises; the private sector now accounts for roughly 90 percent of industrial production.[9] Yet few of the anticipated benefits of privatization have occurred. Consultants at McKinsey studied ten major Russian industries in 1999 and found that their average labor productivity was a shockingly low 18 percent of U.S. levels. They concluded that some 25 percent of Russia's Soviet-era industrial assets are obsolete and should be scrapped.[10]

Why has Russia's experience with privatization been so disappointing? First of all, the new owners are not all that new. "Insiders," or Soviet-era managers and employees, grabbed up the bulk of industrial assets, taking an estimated 50 to 60 percent of all the outstanding shares of privatized companies.[11] It would be difficult to imagine a less promising industrial elite than the group of people who presided over communism's final economic collapse. Those people gained their positions of authority, after all, by their ability to derive as little output as possible from as many inputs as possible, while appropriating as much of the waste as possible for personal gain.

For the most part they have kept up with their old tricks in their new capacity as "capitalists." Very little restructuring—investing in new equipment, changing product lines to meet demand, laying off excess workers—has been undertaken. One survey catalogued 69 different "restructuring activities" and measured how many of them were being performed by a large sample of privatized Russian firms. The average score was 20, and no company scored more than 42.[12] Rather than overhauling their enterprises to maximize their long-term value, insiders have generally gone instead for the quick kill of asset-stripping. Much of this scavenged wealth now resides in offshore bank accounts: Estimates of capital flight vary widely, but $50 billion—roughly half the country's annual GDP—is a good educated guess.[13]

The problems of Russia's privatized enterprises run deeper than the identity of their owners. In a well-functioning market system, even holdovers from the *nomenklatura* would face the alternative of making a profit or being replaced by those who can. But, of course, this is the nub of the matter, for Russia does not have a well-functioning market system or anything like it. Most critically, massive explicit and implicit subsidies work to perpetuate the Communist-era soft budget constraint.

The federal and regional governments continue to prop up moribund industrial enterprises with outright grants and soft loans. According to a World Bank study, such explicit subsidies have been as high as 8 to 10 percent of GDP in recent years. But those figures, grim as they are, do not begin to tell the whole story. Russia's bizarre "nonpayments system" has added another thick layer of insulation from market accountability. Arrears in the payment of taxes, wages, and debts to suppliers ballooned from 15 percent at year-end 1994 to 40 percent at the end of 1998. And those payments that were being made were increasingly in nonmonetary form—most notably, barter. By 1998, the percentage of total enterprise sales with noncash settlements had risen to an astounding 50 to 70 percent. For the utility monopolies—Gazprom (gas) and RAO UES (electricity)—noncash settlements exceeded 85 percent in the crisis year of 1998. The heavy use of barter and other offsets masks significant underpayments. The same World Bank study previously mentioned estimated that implicit subsidies to the non-energy enterprise sector from nonpayment or underpayment of taxes and utilities totaled from 7.4 to 11.9 percent of GDP in 1996–97.[14]

The continued existence of the soft budget constraint has dulled the normal market incentives to raise productivity. Many Soviet-era enterprises are little better than economic zombies—the unburied dead of a failed but not fully abandoned system. Consider, for example, the Russian steel industry. Magnitogorsk, for all its problems, is actually one of the strongest performers; it has worked hard to modernize its facilities and seek out export markets. By contrast, a hundred or so small steel mills are completely hopeless: Though they account for about a third of the industry's total employment, they manage to produce only 7 percent of its output.[15]

The costs of the soft budget constraint are not confined to the resources squandered by zombie enterprises. The subsidies that sustain those ailing firms also impede the efforts of market-oriented competitors, whether new or privatized, to invest and grow. Consultants at McKinsey found that, contrary to normal market logic, the most productive enterprises in Russia are frequently the least profitable. The answer to this riddle lies in the fact that the weakest firms receive the biggest subsidies.[16] As a result, high-productivity companies cannot gain market share at the expense of their wealth-destroying rivals; indeed, all too often they find it difficult to hold their own against firms that may be woefully mismanaged but whose tax rates and energy bills are a fraction of their own. Under these conditions, it is unsurprising that the restructuring of the Russian economy has sputtered so badly.

In contrast to the generally disappointing performance of the old Soviet Empire, China has thus far navigated its transition from communism with a remarkable and sustained surge of economic growth. Since reforms began in 1978, China's GDP has roughly quadrupled. That explosion of wealth has been fueled by a booming non-state sector as well as rapid integration into the international economy. State-owned enterprises accounted for 80 percent of total output in 1978; that figure has now fallen to below 30 percent.

Meanwhile, international trade as a percentage of GDP has skyrocketed from 10 percent in 1978 to some 36 percent in the late 1990s; in addition, China was the leading destination of foreign direct investment in the developing world throughout the 1990s.[17] The effect of China's reforms on human welfare can scarcely be overstated: An estimated 160 million people have been delivered from officially defined poverty.[18]

But China's economic outlook has been dimming in recent years. The official growth rate, while still strong, has dropped from double digits to the 7 to 8 percent range. The drop would have been even sharper but for furious "pump priming" spending by the government. Such spending has occasioned a rapid run-up of government debt: The budget deficit in 2000 rose to an estimated $31 billion, or quadruple the 1998 figure.[19]

It is the unresolved legacy of communism that now clouds China's future. Up until the past few years, China's reform strategy was one of "growing out of the plan"—in other words, opening up and encouraging the nonstate sector rather than privatizing state assets. The marked decline in the state sector's share of GDP reflected the rapid growth of other parts of the economy, not any serious overhaul of the Maoist industrial base. Indeed, despite their declining contribution to overall output, state-owned firms continued to absorb enormous amounts of resources. Between 1978 and 1995 employment in state-owned enterprises actually rose by 50 percent—from 75 million to 113 million. State-owned firms accounted for nearly 60 percent of total investment in fixed assets in 1995 and soaked up more than three-quarters of total bank credit.[20]

In the second half of the 1990s, the neglected and festering problems of the state sector could no longer be ignored. By 1995 roughly half of the 75,000 state-owned enterprises were either teetering on the edge of insolvency or had already crossed the line. The ratio of liabilities to assets for the sector as a whole had climbed to 85 percent—the equivalent of a debt-equity ratio of over 500 percent.[21] What had become a giant zombie economy was sustained only by massive subsidies in the form of "policy loans" from the state-owned financial sector, which served only to shift the burden of mounting losses onto the banking system. About 40 percent of total outstanding loans are now nonperforming.[22]

In recent years the Chinese government has at last begun to grapple seriously with its ailing state sector. It has restructured or shut down many loss-making firms and cut employment dramatically: State-owned firms laid off over 20 million workers during 1998–99.[23] Entry into the World

Trade Organization and the associated drop in trade barriers should catalyze further restructuring as state-owned enterprises are subject to unprecedented levels of competition. But let there be no mistake: A "soft landing" from communism to a bona fide market economy is by no means assured. Under the best of circumstances, China faces many years of wrenching change and dislocation before the zombie economy is vanquished. An acute economic crisis in the not-too-distant future remains a distinct possibility—along with the social and political upheavals that such crises all too often set in motion.

<p style="text-align:center">~~~~~~~</p>

The stigmata of centralization are most apparent in the former Communist bloc, but they may be found almost everywhere. Despite two decades of market-oriented reforms, government controls over economic production remain depressingly commonplace and onerous. Yes, there has been an unmistakable movement away from collectivism and in the direction of liberalization. Most obvious is the switch from nationalization to privatization: Over 100 countries have made some movement toward privatizing state enterprises over the past couple of decades. And furthermore, it is true that particular countries have succeeded in effecting dramatic and thoroughgoing market-oriented reforms. Outside the postcommunist world, New Zealand and Chile have probably traveled the farthest; here in the United States, the deregulation of airlines, railroads, trucking, oil, natural gas, and telecommunications has liberated enormous productive energies from bureaucratic suppression. But in the global view, the cold, hard fact is that the widely talked-about "triumph of markets" has been grossly overstated.

Most obviously, government ownership of commercial enterprises is still widespread. The privatization movement, although truly impressive, has been broader than it has been deep. Consider, in this regard, the findings of the Economic Freedom of the World project, a rigorous and thoughtful effort to track and quantify global trends in economic policy. The role of state-owned enterprises (SOEs) is one of the criteria by which the project evaluates countries' overall fidelity to market-economy principles. On this particular criterion, a country is assigned a maximum score of 10 when only a few SOEs remain. At the other end of the spectrum, a score of 4 indicates "a substantial number of SOEs operated in many sectors, including manufacturing"; a score of 2 is given when "numerous SOEs operated in many sectors, including retail sales"; the bottom score of 0 means that "the economy was dominated by SOEs."[24]

The 2000 *Economic Freedom of the World* report found that as of 1996–97, 24 countries out of 123 surveyed earned the lowest possible score of 0, another 23 countries received a score of 2, and 27 countries earned a 4.[25] Thus, in a total of 74 countries, accounting for 67 percent of the world's population, state-owned enterprises continue to play a leading role in economic life. And it should be noted that some of the world's most regimented economies—including Cuba, North Korea, Vietnam, Cambodia, Laos, Libya, Iraq, Yugoslavia, and a number of the former Soviet republics—were not even included in the survey for lack of reliable data.

Only moderately less depressing are the same report's findings on price controls, which are perhaps the most blatant form of government interference with the transmission of market signals. On this item, as well as the previous one, countries are graded on a 0 to 10 rating scale. Countries that have no price controls or marketing boards earn a perfect score of 10. On the illiberal side of the scale, countries receive a rating of 4 "when price controls were levied on energy, agriculture, and many other stable products that are widely purchased by households"; countries garner a score of 2 "when price controls applied to a significant number of products in both agriculture and manufacturing"; and the lowest score of 0 means that "there was widespread use of price controls throughout various sectors of the economy."[26] The report found that as of 1997, nine countries scored a 0, 15 countries received a 2, and 30 countries earned a 4.[27] Those 54 countries contain 39 percent of the world's population. And here again, the same caveat applies: Many of the world's most illiberal regimes were not included in the analysis.

Statist controls on economic production are by no means evenly distributed throughout the global economy. They are concentrated geographically, not only in the former Communist bloc, but also in Africa, the Middle East, and South Asia. Also, there are particular industrial sectors that, around the world, have proved especially resistant to the introduction of market competition.

The energy sector is one where government control remains the norm. Oil production, of course, is still dominated by state-owned enterprises in the Middle East, Mexico, Venezuela, Nigeria, and Indonesia. Oil refining also remains heavily shielded from competition. A World Bank survey of 57 developing countries with oil refining industries found that only 16 of them, or 28 percent, had engaged in any privatization of state assets, while only 13 countries, or 23 percent, had allowed any new private investment. In the electrical power industry, there has been a surge of new independent power producers, but privatization of existing state assets has lagged. The same

World Bank survey found that only 24 developing countries out of 115 surveyed (21 percent) had privatized any generation facilities, and only 21 countries (18 percent) had moved to privatize distribution assets.[28]

Government ownership and anticompetitive regulation are likewise rampant in the transportation field. National air carriers still abound: In Western Europe alone, Aer Lingus, Air France, Alitalia, Iberia, Olympic Airways, and SAS continue to have at least 50 percent government ownership. Price controls and entry restrictions are still common. Similarly, government ownership of railroads remains the norm. In Europe, most rail systems are 100 percent state-owned; meanwhile, a recent World Bank report on developing countries' rail systems found only 14 countries that had allowed any private participation in the rail sector.[29] In ocean transport, widespread antitrust immunity for ocean liners and outright monopolization of port services have resulted in enfeebled or nonexistent competition. A recent World Bank study concluded that, for goods carried into the United States, ocean liner charges could be reduced by 31.7 percent if port services were liberalized and carrier cartels were broken up.[30]

The systematic suppression of market forces continues to prevail in agriculture. Rich countries, in particular, are profligate in supporting farmers at the expense of taxpayers and consumers. Total farm subsidies in the Organisation for Economic Co-operation and Development (OECD) averaged an estimated $349 billion during 1996–98—in other words, some 37 percent of gross farm receipts. That ratio reached 63 percent in Japan and 73 percent in Switzerland. Most of this largesse was delivered through direct interference with the market process: 67 percent of producer subsidies took the form of price supports.[31]

Traditionally, the agricultural policies of the communist and developing worlds sinned against market logic in the opposite direction—namely, by soaking farmers rather than subsidizing them. In an attempt to accelerate industrialization (and support political power bases in large urban areas) governments ruthlessly exploited the agricultural sector by imposing below-market prices through price and distribution controls and state purchasing monopolies. A policy bias against agriculture persists in many countries. In India, for example, the 700 million people who live in rural areas and depend on farming for their livelihood must contend with low administered prices for food security programs and a welter of restrictions on the processing, movement, and storage of farm products.[32]

Many members of the old Communist bloc have yet to extricate themselves from the collectivized mire. In Belarus and Kazakhstan, all agricultural land remains state-owned except for small household plots; in many other Central Asian republics there has been no privatization of farmland at all. In Russia, nominally private collective farms still hold some 80 percent of all agricultural land. These testaments to the Soviet-era faith in gigantism are absurdly oversized by Western standards: They average nearly 20,000 acres, compared to only 500 acres for the typical American farm. Yet continuing subsidies and the absence of workable bankruptcy procedures have blocked their breakup. Further complicating matters, Russia still has no national land code and thus no agricultural land market to speak of.[33]

The same dead hand that stunts the preindustrial sector also reaches the postindustrial. Although the recent technological upheavals in telecommunications are too familiar to need repetition, what is less well known is the extent to which stultifying regulatory structures continue to block the development and spread of the digital revolution. Yes, there has been great progress, but every inch of it has been won against the press of a powerful, countervailing inertia. Thus far in the justly celebrated Information Age, the dead hand of centralized control still works with considerable effectiveness to choke the flows of information.

In the industry traditionally known as telephony, the old incumbent monopolies maintain their dominance. Among the advanced countries that belong to the OECD, those incumbents held 81 percent of the total market in 1997 and over 100 percent of total profits (all the new entrants into the industry, taken as a whole, suffered a combined loss). And even in the advanced countries, most of the incumbents remain creatures of the state: 17 out of 29 in the OECD still have majority government ownership. While the old monopolies have lost market share in the long-distance and mobile telecommunications markets, they continue to control the crucial "local loop." In the OECD, new entrants provided only a trifling 0.9 percent of local access lines as of 1997. Accordingly, switched networks with direct access to the consumer remain shielded from effective competition.[34]

It is true that cellular telephony, which has been growing by leaps and bounds, does bypass the monopolized local loop. At the present time, however, mobile technology does not really compete head-to-head with the traditional network: It is more of a complement to than substitute for regular telephone service. The lack of direct competitive challenge is due, in part, to the current state of cellular technology, but regulatory obstacles bear much of the blame. Centralized control over spectrum allocation has stunted the growth of wireless communications by restricting the number of entrants. As a result, in 25 of the 29 OECD countries, the two largest mobile telephony operators (or the single operator in monopoly jurisdictions) accounted for at least 80 percent of the cellular market in 1997.[35]

The persistence of the old state-owned monopoly system is even more pronounced in the developing world. According to a World Bank study, as of 1998, only 42 of the more than 100 developing countries that were surveyed allowed any private participation in long distance service, and, of those, only 12 countries permitted any form of competition. As to local service, only 15 countries allowed any kind of competition between private new entrants and incumbent operators. Private operators offered mobile service in 94 countries, but in 66 of those countries the market was either a monopoly or duopoly and closed to additional entrants.[36]

Meanwhile, the industry traditionally known as broadcasting also bears the heavy imprint of centralization. The growth of cable and satellite networks has challenged the old stronghold: Subscription fees for these alternatives to broadcast fare now account for 32 percent of television market revenues in the OECD.[37] Nonetheless, broadcasters are still a formidable presence—a presence defined by anti-market regulatory and fiscal policies. Broadcasting spectrum remains subject to public licensing and all manner of content regulations. Public funding accounts for over 15 percent of total television revenues in the OECD and is as high as 40 to 60 percent in a number of countries. There are no private nationwide broadcasters at all in Austria, Belgium, Denmark, Iceland, Ireland, Korea, the Netherlands, Poland, and Switzerland.[38]

I have referred to the industries "traditionally known as" telephony and broadcasting because the technological revolution of digitalization (and in particular the rise of the Internet) is promoting the convergence of previously distinctive services into new and unprecedented syntheses. But while technological progress pushes toward convergence, regulatory inertia acts to preserve old and outmoded industry structures. In particular, the continued dominance of the old telephone monopolies is a serious drag on the spread of the Internet. There is a strong correlation between a country's telephone lines per capita and its Internet hosts per capita, which merely illustrates the fairly obvious point that the vigor of Internet activity depends upon the quality and price-competitiveness of the underlying telecommunications infrastructure. The World Wide Web will never live up to the full promise of its name so long as uncontested telecom monopolies around the world continue to get away with offering shoddy service at inflated prices.

—————

The international sector also remains choked with obstacles to competition. Despite dramatic progress in liberalization, the notion of a "borderless world" is today little more than a pipe dream. National boundaries matter less than in the past, but they continue to constitute significant barriers to the effective transmission of market signals.

Overall levels of protectionism are still quite high throughout the old Third World. Tariff rates average 13.3 percent in developing countries, as compared to 2.6 percent in the advanced industrialized nations.[39] That average figure conceals wide variations among countries and in the treatment of different products. Many poorer countries remain heavily shielded from outside competition: Average tariffs reach 18 percent in Thailand, 22 percent in Bangladesh, 23.5 percent in Nigeria, 27 percent in Egypt, and 35 percent in India.[40] Furthermore, "tariff dispersion"—high and low rates that diverge sharply from the mean—is a continuing problem. Such variability exacerbates the distortions caused by trade barriers and yields effective rates of protection far in excess of nominal duty rates. Tariff peaks on food and clothing in particular are especially common: Tariffs in developing countries average 18 percent on agricultural products and 21 percent on textiles and apparel.[41]

In service industries, protectionism takes the form not of customs duties but rather regulatory barriers to entry—in particular, limits on foreign ownership of service-providing firms. Such restrictions on competition remain pandemic in the less advanced nations. Consider, for example, the extreme modesty of the World Trade Organization's General Agreement on Trade in Services, or GATS. The GATS, negotiated during the Uruguay Round of trade talks and concluded in 1994, represents the first attempt to set any international rules on services trade. Rather than imposing uniform obligations on all signatories, the GATS includes widely varying commitments by different countries with respect to the broad range of service sectors. Typically countries committed, not to reduce existing barriers, but simply to maintain current practice; quite frequently commitments were actually below the current level of practice.

Even so, despite the very loose constraint that making a commitment entailed, many developing countries declined to offer *any* commitments in many sectors. For example, 73 percent of developing-country WTO members made no commitments regarding market access for or nondiscriminatory treatment of foreign-owned law firms; 83 percent promised nothing regarding foreign-owned retailers. In voice telephony, over 50 percent of developing countries made no commitment at all.[42]

While trade barriers are low on average in the advanced industrialized countries, pockets of protectionism continue to hamper cross-border competition in key sectors. Look, for example, at the situation in the United States, which is rightfully considered among the most open economies on earth. Despite that fortunate status, substantial restrictions on foreign goods and services remain in effect. Food and clothing are particular problem areas. Import quotas on textiles and apparel are due to be phased out by 2005, but high tariffs still persist: Duty rates average 10.6 percent for broadwoven fabrics, 11.9 percent for knit fabrics, and 13.2 percent for apparel. Tariffs for imports above set quantitative limits are prohibitive for many food items: 170 percent for cheese, 137 percent for butter, 130 percent for sugar, 350 percent for tobacco, 131.8 percent for shelled peanuts, and a mere 26.4 percent for beef.

In addition, high tariff walls still stand for an arbitrary grab bag of products: 13.9 percent on average for luggage and handbags, 9.3 percent for nonrubber footwear, 7.4 percent for glassware, 9.8 percent for china tableware, and 7.4 percent for ball and roller bearings. Also, the so-called "trade remedy" laws (the antidumping and countervailing duty laws and the Section 201 "safeguard" provision) allow the imposition of punishingly high trade barriers against targeted products and countries. Meanwhile, in services, the Jones Act prohibits foreign-owned or foreign-built ships from carrying freight between U.S. ports; restrictions on foreign ownership of airlines and broadcasters remain in force as well.[43]

Fortunately, American trade barriers are too few and far between to impose a serious drag on the country's overall economic prospects. To be sure, they distort outcomes at the level of the affected sectors, and they impose real and significant losses on downstream industries and consumers. But from the bird's eye view that surveys the entirety of a $10 trillion economy, they are barely visible at all.

From the perspective of some countries whose exports are blocked, however, vestigial U.S. protectionism looms very large indeed. The stupendous rise of East Asia over the course of a generation has shown how development of export industries can trigger and then accelerate the transformation from mass poverty to mass affluence. But export-oriented growth depends on access to rich-country markets. Today, many poor and struggling economies find their most promising export opportunities thwarted by America's (and other advanced countries') remaining trade restrictions. It is hypocrisy heaped upon cruelty for American trade officials to urge *les misérables* to open their markets while keeping U.S. markets closed to their most competitive products—whether they be sugar from the Caribbean, clothing from China, or steel from Russia.

Which brings us back full circle to Magnitogorsk. For that beleaguered mill struggles not only against the legacy of the hideously oppressive Soviet version of the Industrial Counterrevolution. It struggles as well against the retreating rearguard of the milder, but still disfiguring, American version.

The steel industry has played a leading role in all the phases of the American Industrial Counterrevolution—from rise and ascendancy to decline and current senescence. A century ago, Frederick Winslow Taylor developed his system of "scientific management" and the "one best way" during his 12 years as an engineer at Midvale Steel. Elbert Gary, the first president of U.S. Steel and host of the infamous price-fixing gatherings known as "Gary dinners," was an early and ardent apostle of industrial "cooperation"—or, in other words, cartelization. In this vein, steel executives later embraced Franklin Roosevelt's National Industrial Recovery Act of 1933. As Robert Lamont, president of the American Iron and Steel Institute, explained, "The lip service which we have been so ready to render to the ideal of cooperation . . . will now be supplemented by a very real cooperation and standards enforced by law. The selfish and often ruthless minority will now be compelled to conform to a code of fair and ethical practices. . . ."[44]

The connections that bound the steel industry to the government ran in both directions. At the same time that the industry tried to co-opt government power to squelch competition, the government asserted authority over the industry to promote its own ends, most notably, war-making. During World War I, War Industries Board Chairman Bernard Baruch dictated prices to the steel industry on pain of nationalization. During World War II, military requirements necessitated a major capacity expansion; the industry resisted, fearing a return to recessionary conditions after the war and the burden of more excess capacity. As a result, the government took matters into its own hands: It built 29 new integrated plants solely with government funds and then transferred them to private companies; it then constructed another 20 plants as joint ventures with private firms. [45] During the Korean War, President Truman went so far as to order the seizure of the entire steel industry to head off a nationwide strike; the Supreme Court, though, voided the order. Despite being foiled in that power grab, Truman did successfully browbeat the industry into undertaking a massive capacity expansion during the 1950s.

That decade marked the zenith of the American Industrial Counterrevolution, and the steel industry of the time was in every way its creature. Within the companies raged a kind of cold war between Taylorist managers and adversarial labor unions. Between the companies prevailed lazy price coordination and sluggish aversion to innovation. And investment decisions had become thoroughly politicized. Yet, because the rest of the world still lay in ruins, steel executives could imagine themselves farsighted statesmen of industry.

Postwar reconstruction and the reemergence of international competition soon provided the fall to which such hubris inevitably leads. To satisfy Washington on the cheap, American mills continued to use already obsolete open-hearth technology when expanding capacity; Japanese and European mills, meanwhile, were installing new basic oxygen furnaces and becoming the low-cost producers. By the mid-1960s American producers finally began to play catch-up, but foreign rivals leaped even further ahead with early adoption of continuous casting. At the same time, a ruinous cycle of paralyzing labor strikes and out-of-control wage increases further worsened the uncompetitiveness of the U.S. industry's cost structure. By 1982, average steel wages were 95 percent above the average for all U.S. manufacturing industries. [46]

Unsurprisingly, foreign steel steadily expanded its share of the U.S. market: Imports climbed from four million tons in 1959 to 18 million in 1971. [47] This intensifying competitive challenge could have provoked Big Steel to realize that it needed a major shakeup in its traditional ways of doing business. But counterrevolutionary inertia proved too strong, and instead U.S. steel mills blamed everybody but themselves—their "unfair" foreign competitors in particular. Rather than responding constructively and creatively to its embattled situation, the industry sank into dependence on political fixes. In 1969, the first "voluntary restraint agreement" imposed import quotas on foreign steel, and so commenced an addiction to protectionism and subsidies now in its fourth decade. Quotas, "trigger price mechanisms," antidumping duties, pension subsidies, special tax breaks—such were Big Steel's substitutes for market-based restructuring.

The result was a long, slow, and painful decline for a once dominant industry. Imports continued to gain market share, approaching 30 percent by the mid-1980s before renewed trade barriers offered temporary relief.[48] But the more serious competitive threat to Big Steel came from domestic rivals: the new, high-tech, largely nonunionized "mini-mills." With the vastly superior productivity of their electric arc furnace technology, the mini-mills steadily expanded their product range at the integrated mills' expense. Their share of U.S. steel production has risen from around 20 percent in the mid-1970s to nearly 50 percent today.

Now a shadow of its former self—steel employment has collapsed from almost 450,000 in 1980 to under 200,000 today—Big Steel remains stuck in the counterrevolutionary past. It continues to lash out at "unfair" competition rather than scrutinizing its own shortcomings—witness the latest spasm of accusations in the wake of the Asian financial crisis. The sudden and utterly unexpected collapse of high-flying Pacific Rim economies precipitated a worldwide steel glut: Capacity once geared to serve Asia's torrid expansion now flooded a shrunken market. Predictably, the healthy U.S. economy absorbed much of the overproduction, and prices fell sharply. Although similar import surges occurred for many other products, and although the U.S. industry's share of world steel production actually rose during the surge, Big Steel immediately proclaimed a life-or-death "steel crisis" and demanded political intervention. The results of its massive "Stand Up for Steel" lobbying campaign were mixed. Legislation to set across-the-board quotas on steel imports failed in the Senate, but a $1 billion special loan guarantee subsidy was approved. In addition, a rash of antidumping complaints by the industry succeeded in stifling foreign competition in a number of key sectors.

Whatever breathing space the industry won proved fleeting. In 2000, the slowing U.S. economy precipitated yet another industry "crisis" as marginal producers like Wheeling-Pittsburgh and LTV declared bankruptcy. Big Steel mounted a new lobbying campaign against "unfair" imports, and steel spokespersons continued to pretend that all the industry's problems are somebody else's fault. The Bush administration responded to Big Steel's pressure tactics with a major new investigation of imports under the Section 201 safeguard law.

Meanwhile, Russian steel mills were especially hard hit by the U.S. industry's protectionist rampage. U.S. imports of Russian steel plummeted from $1.4 billion in 1998 to $381 million in 1999 as a result of special "suspension agreements" to fix maximum quantities and minimum prices. Mills like Magnitogorsk were caught in a brutal pincer movement: First Asian markets evaporated because of the financial crisis, and then the protectionist reaction to that crisis in the United States (as well as the European Union) slammed the door on rich-country markets.

The U.S. steel industry's failure to break free from the centralizing past thus has international consequences. Its retrograde actions make escape from the past more difficult abroad as well. The interlinked fates of the American and Russian steel industries, both caught still in the dark shadows of the Industrial Counterrevolution, offer a sober counterpoint to the naïve triumphalism too often heard from the partisans of globalization. For in the present era, markets are not the only global phenomenon: The dead hand of the statist past also has a worldwide reach.

7

Hollow Capitalism

I n early 1999, a large banner billowed in front of Korea First Bank's
headquarters in Seoul. On it was the announcement: "We are a safe
bank now. We have foreign capital." Korea First, one of the country's top commercial banks, had made the fatal mistake of lending heavily to Hanbo Steel, Sammi Steel, and Kia Motors—three weak players in
glutted markets. As first Hanbo, then Sammi, and then Kia all went bust
during the course of 1997, Korea First found itself dragged down by bad
loans; with nowhere else to turn, it was nationalized at the end of the
year. Now, the government had arranged to sell a majority stake in the
bank to Newbridge Capital, a U.S. investment fund that buys companies
for eventual resale.[1]

For those who believed that East Asia was the proving ground for a new
and superior economic system, the fate of Korea First Bank captures in
miniature the devastating repudiation that events ultimately dealt them. Korea First was a leading institution in what was considered to be a model financial system—one driven, not by narrow calculations of short-term profit,
but by a long-term national economic strategy. By contrast, a firm like
Newbridge Capital, one that buys and sells companies for profit, represented
all that was supposedly wrong with the addled, rate-of-return-obsessed free-
for-all of American capital markets. Yet obliviousness to market returns had
led Korea First to disaster. And sensitivity to them had brought Newbridge
Capital to the rescue.

Only a few years before, champions of the East Asian economic model had argued that government-directed industrial policy was the key to the surging growth rates up and down the Pacific Rim. And Asian-style centralized control depended crucially upon an appropriately structured financial sector. Specifically, highly developed and liquid capital markets were anathema. Their decentralized nature would put resources in the hands of unsanctioned outsiders, while their transparency would generate strong, clear price signals in direct competition with top-down directives. Banks were far preferable as sources of financing. In a bank-dominated financial system, funding for new investments must flow through relatively few chokepoints. Also, the lack of public information about the value of loan portfolios insulates decisions about credit allocation from market pressures. Accordingly, control over a bank-heavy system is much easier to gain and then maintain.

East Asian financial sectors were generally well suited to serve as instruments of top-down control. There were exceptions: Hong Kong and Singapore were open to foreign financial institutions and encouraged the development of local capital markets, while Taiwan had a thriving informal "curb" market that broadened access to financing. But throughout much of the region, a host of interventionist policies favored banks over market-based financing. Limits on entry (including, especially, entry by foreign institutions) and controls on interest rates for deposits inflated bank profits, while deposit insurance and "too large to fail" policies gave banks cover in hard times. Meanwhile, restrictive regulations often hindered the issuance of bonds and the public listing of stocks.

And not only did governments move affirmatively to suppress direct financing; just as critically, they failed to perform those functions that underpin capital-market development. They did not protect creditors' rights by providing efficient bankruptcy proceedings, nor did they safeguard the rights of minority shareholders in corporate governance. Furthermore, they did not require companies to make adequate disclosure of their financial condition in accordance with sound accounting practices. In short, investors enjoyed few legal protections, and arm's-length market transactions were therefore highly risky.

As a result, bank lending overshadowed equity and bond markets in most of East Asia. And the banks themselves were heavily politicized. Outright state ownership of banks was common in the region, and "directed credit" policies and informal government "guidance" strongly influenced the lending policies of even nominally private banks. Banks thus served as a leading tool of government industrial policy, funneling household savings into favored industries in accordance with bureaucratic oversight. Pressure also came from the borrowers' side, as politically connected companies flexed their muscles to obtain needed financing.

Even when political influence was not impinging directly on banking operations, capital allocation still deviated sharply from what would have occurred if market forces had been given free play. With banks subsidized and shielded from competition, and with capital markets stunted, the institutional environment for funding new investments was both highly centralized and thickly insulated from market signals. Banks often lent without any serious analysis of the projected returns of the investments they were financing. In many countries banks were either owned or dominated by large conglomerates that used them as empire-building slush funds. Business and personal relationships, not market criteria, generally determined who got access to capital. As a result, members of the "old boys' network" could count on ready financing no matter how misconceived their investment plans. Outsiders, no matter how promising their ideas, were too often frozen out.

For a glimpse at just how blithely indifferent to market forces East Asian banks could be, consider Tom Horton's autopsy work on Korea First Bank. Horton, a principal with Ernst & Young Kenneth Leventhal, represented Newbridge Capital in its purchase of the failed bank. Over the years he had seen his share of slipshod banking practices; after all, he served as a senior vice president with the Resolution Trust Corporation during the bailout of the infamous U.S. savings-and-loan debacle. But Korea First was in a league of its own.

"When I was at Korea First," Horton told me, "I sat in on their credit committee meetings and I asked them how many loans they ever denied. They all looked at each other, and after a pause they said their rejection rate was about 1 percent. Can you believe it? That's because they were lending everything to the big *chaebol* [conglomerates]—at Korea First about 90 percent of the loans were to 10 *chaebol*. And a $100 million loan would be just two pieces of paper—the loan itself and a security agreement with cross-guarantees from the rest of the *chaebol*. That's all you had. I told the people at Korea First that, in the States, we would have enormous documents with all kinds of covenants and conditions. Not in Korea, they said—we trust the *chaebol*."

"You have to understand," Horton said, "that banks in Korea weren't looked on as an investment that was supposed to make a lot of money. Banks were seen as a social tool to help the *chaebol* and then they were supposed to create the wealth. And it worked, too—at least for a while."[2]

Financial developments in the United States provided a stark contrast. For at the same time that East Asia's surging growth was spawning new theories of technocratic control, controversy was swirling around the alleged excesses of a newly unbuttoned Wall Street. In particular, the headline-grabbing spectacles of high-stakes corporate takeover battles helped to tag the 1980s as the "decade of greed." The colorful lexicon of those takeover contests—raiders, greenmail, white knights, golden parachutes, and poison pills—made clear that America's corporate and financial establishment was under attack.

The booming market for corporate control was merely one prominent aspect of a larger shift in American finance. High-yield bonds and venture capital firms made money available to outsiders shunned by traditional sources of financing. Deregulation of brokerage commissions and the growth of discount brokerages promoted wider stock ownership; 401(k) plans and the rise of mutual funds accelerated the trend. The emergence of large investment funds created powerful institutional investors that demanded high returns from the companies they owned. In all of these different ways, control over investment was being decentralized. And as a result, corporate managers were being forced to pay more attention to creating value for investors.

Leading commentators decried the destabilizing influence that financial-market innovations were having on American business. Robert Reich, who later served as Bill Clinton's Secretary of Labor, dismissed "paper entrepreneurialism" as empty and ultimately destructive:

> All this rearranging of industrial assets and people in turn has made it more difficult for American enterprise to undertake basic change. It has enforced short-term thinking, discouraged genuine innovation, and consumed the careers of some of our most talented citizens.[3]

Champions of the East Asian model argued that excessive competition in financial markets was a major reason why U.S. companies were losing ground to Japanese rivals in one critical industry after another. American firms, hobbled by the "myopia" and "short-termism" of a Wall Street obsessed with quarterly earnings, could not afford to make the strategic investments in technology or market share that pay off only in the long run. Japanese companies, by contrast, were blessed with plentiful supplies of no-questions-asked "patient capital."

Japanese triumphalism reached its most shrill with the notorious *The Japan That Can Say "No,"* a collaboration between Sony Chairman Akio Morita and nationalist maverick politician Shintaro Ishihara. The book provoked furious controversy with its suggestion (made by Ishihara) that Japan could change the Cold War military balance by withholding semiconductors from the United States and supplying them instead to the Soviet Union. In one of his contributions, Morita identified the short-term focus of American financial markets as the U.S. economy's Achilles' heel:

> [W]e Japanese plan and develop our business strategies ten years ahead. When I asked an American money trader "how far ahead do you plan . . . one week?" the reply was "no, no . . . ten minutes." He was moving money through a computer, targeting the fate of that transaction ten minutes later. . . . At that rate, you may well never be able to compete with us.[4]

Admirers of the Japanese system on this side of the Pacific echoed this analysis. "Japan is dynamic," explained Chalmers Johnson, a leading advocate of the East Asian model, "because its managers devote themselves to competing with other companies at home and abroad, without having to serve the parasitic interests of shareholders. . . ."[5] Clyde Prestowitz, author of *Trading Places: How We Are Giving Our Future to Japan and How to Reclaim It,* agreed. "The greatest single weakness of U.S. industry in competing with Japan is lack not of management effort but rather of financial staying power," he wrote. "Our capital is both too expensive and too impatient."[6]

⫘⫘⫘

What a difference a decade can make. During the 1990s, the United States, far from succumbing (as widely expected) to terminal decline, experienced instead a stupendous burst of wealth creation and economic dynamism. Even more surprising, America's ebullient economic performance was obviously and undeniably linked to its uniquely decentralized and market-driven financial system. While the stock-market bloodletting and general economic slowdown that began in 2000 have been sobering, no one can doubt that the U.S. economy made tremendous strides during the boom of the 1990s—or that deep and liquid capital markets were a vital ingredient of the advances that were made.

Throughout the '90s, the roaring stock market fed off of the democratization of stock ownership through mutual funds, discount brokerages, and 401(k) plans. The explosion of high-tech startups and the resulting Internet revolution would not have been possible without a vibrant and sophisticated venture capital community and over-the-counter markets like the NASDAQ that welcomed promising (if risky) new listings. Many of the major names in the development of the information economy—MCI, Telecommunications, Inc., McCaw Cellular, and CNN, to name a few—were weaned on Michael Milken's reviled high-yield "junk" bonds. And among established members of the Fortune 500, a wave of wrenching but productivity-enhancing restructuring (also known as "downsizing," "outsourcing," or "re-engineering") was encouraged by the active market in mergers and acquisitions, by financial innovations like leveraged buyouts, and by newly assertive institutional investors that insisted upon competitive returns.

Meanwhile, the high-flying economies of the Pacific Rim suffered catastrophic nosedives. First came the bursting of Japan's "bubble economy" in 1990, and the subsequent (and still continuing) years of torpor and drift. Following Japan's slow-motion collapse was the all-too-sudden 1997–98 Asian financial crisis, as economies throughout the region—but most especially Thailand, South Korea, Malaysia, and Indonesia—endured crashes as brutal as they were unexpected. While many factors played a role in these reversals, and analysts continue to argue about the relative importance of various contributing causes, it has been established beyond serious debate that Asia's clubby and uncompetitive financial sectors bear a significant share of the blame.[7]

Specifically, Asian financial institutions broke down in the face of rising liquidity. In Japan, the dramatic appreciation of the yen after 1985 and the central bank's subsequent monetary easing left banks awash with loanable funds. For the economies that were later hardest hit by the Asian crisis, domestic credit expansion during the early 1990s was supplemented by large inflows of short-term foreign lending attracted by gaping spreads between local and foreign interest rates. In both episodes, the increase in liquidity overwhelmed the capacity of top-heavy financial systems to allocate capital properly. Malinvestment occurred on a massive scale. Total loan losses on "bubble-era" lending in Japan exceeded 10 percent of the country's annual gross output.[8] The waste in the wake of the Asian financial crisis is even more staggering: Recapitalizing the banking system is costing an estimated 50 to 60 percent of GDP in Indonesia, around 40 percent in Thailand, 15 percent in Korea, and 12 percent in Malaysia.[9] By way of comparison, the total cost of the U.S. savings-and-loan crisis during the 1980s amounted to only about 3 percent of U.S. GDP.

The combination of American resurgence and Asian reverses has reduced the partisans of Asian-style "patient capital" to embarrassed silence. Their cause, once advanced with such vigor and conviction, is now without serious defenders on either side of the Pacific. Around the world, a near universal consensus has come to prevail among those concerned with financial affairs: Centralized control over capital allocation must give way to decentralized and competitive markets.

What has occurred, then, is yet another intellectual defeat for the misbegotten ideal of centralized control. The now-discredited enthusiasm for the accommodating steadfastness of East Asian financial systems, and disdain for rambunctious and mercurial American finance, sprang from the same fundamental misunderstanding of competition that lay at the root of the Industrial Counterrevolution. The mindset that dismissed financial innovation as "paper entrepreneurialism," and castigated shareholders as "parasitic," was the very same one that spun the illusion of social engineering. It was a new expression of the old wish that economic rationality could be reduced to purely technical considerations, separate and apart from measurements of profit and loss.

A century earlier, Edward Bellamy had heaped scorn on financiers and banished them altogether from his collectivist utopia. Whoever claimed that financial institutions pumped the lifeblood of a modern economy, wrote Bellamy, "had mistaken the throbbing of an abscess for the beating of the heart."[10] In similar fashion, Thorstein Veblen had distinguished between "industry," which is motivated by the "instinct of workmanship," and "business," which is motivated by the prospect of pecuniary gain. The latter he regarded as a useless anachronism; the industrial system would come into its own, he thought, when it was run by engineers according to engineering principles.

Partisans of the capitalist developmental state adopted the same style of thinking, even if they reached less radical conclusions. Like the social engineers of old, they exalted "people who actually make things" over "paper pushers." And they believed that economic development was essentially a technical problem that could be "solved" without reference to indicators of financial performance. On that point Clyde Prestowitz's formulation was typical:

> A key objective in any economy . . . is to create an industry that produces technologically sophisticated products with high income elasticity (that is, the higher a person's income, the more one buys of those products) and a rapid growth rate (for example, VCRs). That objective . . . cannot be achieved without government intervention.[11]

What is most striking about the criteria Prestowitz used to identify "strategic" industries is the one that is missing—namely, profitability.

The preference for Asian-style financial systems was thus an outgrowth of a deep-seated hostility to finance in general. Bank-centered, relationship-based capital allocation was singled out for praise precisely because it did so *little* to impose financial considerations on the approval of new investments. The more passive and inert the financial sector, so the thinking went, the better off the larger economy. And East Asian financial institutions had been effectively neutered: They rarely exercised any independent judgment as to which of the investment projects competing for funding would maximize returns on the money they handled. Instead they served as dutiful functionaries of government industrial policy, and otherwise as uncritical backers of the privileged and powerful.

Like all of their predecessors, the defenders of East Asian social engineering failed to appreciate the fertility of markets (specifically, financial markets) in generating and applying new, socially useful knowledge. To revisit a biological metaphor I used earlier, market competition accelerates economic "evolution" in a twofold manner: first, encouraging innovative "mutations" by decentralizing investment decisions; and second, subjecting those mutations to the relentless selection pressures of profit and loss.

Well-developed and properly functioning financial markets make enormous contributions on both of these fronts. It is largely through such markets, after all, that the decentralization of investment decisions is accomplished. Without institutions to bring together people with resources and people with ideas, new ventures can be launched only by the narrow circle of people who have both. But at the same time that financial markets facilitate new investment projects, they also act as filters to screen out unpromising ventures before they are undertaken. When financial markets fail to perform this screening function or perform it poorly, product markets must bear the full burden of distinguishing between wealth-creating and wealth-wasting projects. However, the verdicts of consumers in product markets are issued only after resources have been committed, thus allowing much more waste and requiring many more wrenching adjustments than the preemptive judgments of investors.[12]

A growing body of empirical research confirms the strong connections between financial development and broader economic vitality. An influential 1993 study by Robert King of the University of Rochester and Ross Levine of the World Bank examined data from 80 countries over the period from 1960 to 1989. King and Levine found that broad measures of financial development—such as domestic credit to private enterprises as a percentage of GDP—were strong predictors of countries' subsequent economic growth rates.[13] Jeffrey Wurgler of the Yale School of Management looked more specifically at the relationship between financial development (as measured by the size of a country's credit and equity markets relative to GDP) and the allocation of capital. Studying 65 countries over a period spanning 33 years, Wurgler found that countries with more advanced financial sectors allocate capital more efficiently—that is, they increase investment more in growing industries and decrease investment more in declining industries.[14]

Other studies have focused in particular on the impact of equity markets. Asli Demirgüç-Kunt of the World Bank and Vojislav Maksimovic of the University of Maryland examined firm-level data in a 30-country sample to estimate the proportion of firms in each country that exceeded the growth rates that firms could have expected if they had lacked access to long-term financing. Their analysis shows that the proportion is higher in countries with higher stock-market turnover and better legal enforcement (a basic precondition of healthy capital markets).[15] Meanwhile, Ross Levine and Sarah Zervos of Brunel University examined 41 countries and concluded that stock market liquidity is strongly linked with growth, capital accumulation, and productivity.[16]

Cross-country comparisons, like the ones just mentioned, must always be interpreted cautiously, as huge differences among countries make it extremely difficult to ensure that all the relevant variables have been taken into account. Raghuram Rajan and Luigi Zingales of the University of Chicago avoided those pitfalls in ingenious fashion by comparing industries within the same country. Specifically, they looked at the effect of financial development on firms that by their nature depend heavily on external financing (as opposed to internally generated cash flow). Such companies, after all, should be the most direct beneficiaries of any positive impact of a larger and more sophisticated financial sector. Surveying industries in over 40 countries, they found that the more advanced a country's level of financial development (as measured by the sum of total domestic credit and stock market capitalization as a percentage of GDP), the faster industries typically dependent on external financing grew relative to other industries in the same country.[17] That result offers powerful corroborating evidence to support the findings of the more traditional cross-country studies.

~~~

With the loss of faith in Asian-style centralized finance, another great edifice of error has fallen. But recognizing a mistake is not the same thing as undoing it, and so the collapse of the Asian model should not be confused with the victory of the American one. Outside of the United States and United

Kingdom, bank-dominated finance remains the norm as sins of commission and omission conspire to keep equity and bond markets badly underdeveloped. Banking systems, meanwhile, are more or less dysfunctional virtually everywhere in the world. A dangerous mix of regulatory restrictions and special subsidies renders banks chronically vulnerable to meltdowns of mass insolvency. And in countries where banking crises have occurred, crushing burdens of unresolved bad loans can paralyze financial institutions—and the larger economies that depend on them—for years at a stretch.

The institutions that allocate capital among competing investment possibilities form the heart of any economic system. They direct the lifeblood of new resources to some companies and industries and withhold it from others; they determine which sectors of the economy will live and grow and which will recede and die. In today's world economy, the core function of capital allocation remains firmly in the grip of the Industrial Counterrevolution's dead hand. For all the facile talk about the triumph of global markets, the prevailing order today is at best a kind of hollow capitalism. Market competition has made real advances in other areas, but the fundamental principle of capitalism remains all but unapplied to capital itself.

Nowhere is the dead hand's malignant sway over finance more evident than in the wreckage caused by banking crises. Consider, for example, the dozens of unfinished office and apartment buildings that now haunt Bangkok's skyline—high-rise tombstones for the boom gone bust. To learn the story behind some of them, I visited the offices of Siam Syntech in March 1999.

As a Thai construction company, Siam Syntech was standing at ground zero when the Asian financial crisis exploded. The company, a joint venture between Singaporean contractors and a Thai steelmaking group, enjoyed meteoric growth from its creation in 1988 through the mid-1990s. It gained its listing on the Stock Exchange of Thailand faster than any other company in the construction industry, and ballooned into a conglomerate with over 30 affiliated companies and operations scattered throughout Southeast Asia. "We were doing projects without any market research into whether anybody was going to occupy all these buildings," said Jack Wild, a senior manager with the company. "People here just thought the good times were never going to end."[18]

At the time of my visit, almost two years after the "floating" (more accurately, sinking) of the baht in July 1997 that catalyzed Thailand's spectacular collapse, it was painfully clear that the good times had most definitely ended. Monthly turnover had fallen to about one-half of its $12 million peak, and three-quarters of what remained came from a new government housing project. In other words, general construction revenue had fallen by 88 percent; in corresponding fashion, Siam Syntech's general construction staff had shrunk from over 550 employees to under 70.

The normal two-way flow of funds between company and creditors had stopped at Siam Syntech. The company owed more than $200 million to financial institutions and trade creditors, but had made no payments on any of that debt for the past year. Creditors reciprocated by cutting off virtually all new financing. Still, Siam Syntech managed somehow to keep going. It leaned on joint-venture partners; it went to foreign creditors that focused on distressed borrowers; it issued post-dated checks when it could. And on many of its projects, it now relied on its customers to provide building materials. "They supply the concrete and the rebar, and we supply the labor," explained Eric Webb, a financial officer with Siam Syntech.[19]

In February 2001—nearly two years after my visit, and three years after it stopped paying interest on its loans—Siam Syntech finally appeared to be getting back on its feet. A group of investors pledged to supply $7 million in new capital for the firm in exchange for a 75 percent ownership stake. And, in the largest debt-forgiveness deal thus far in Thailand, Siam Syntech's creditors agreed to wipe away 94 percent of the firm's outstanding debt.[20]

Siam Syntech's experience has been all too widely shared—and not just in Thailand. In countries all over the world, massive volumes of bad bank loans have induced debilitating bouts of financial paralysis. Economic activity is stunted and deformed on both sides of the credit relationship—by both distressed lenders who cannot lend and distressed borrowers who cannot borrow. Banks, once they acknowledge their seriously weakened balance sheets or even insolvency, curtail or completely stop their lending as they struggle to recapitalize on their own or await a taxpayer or merger bailout. As a result, even healthy borrowers are cut off from access to credit. Meanwhile, as nonperforming loans sit on the books for year after year, neither repaid nor written off, ailing borrowers like Siam Syntech are trapped in a kind of financial limbo: They avoid the final reckoning of foreclosure and bankruptcy but cannot obtain new financing because of their past sins. The productive capacity held by those businesses atrophies without the financing to sustain ongoing new investments.

Consider the persistence of bad-debt problems in East Asia. After a chaotic 1997 and a horrendous 1998, the four hardest hit countries—Korea,

Thailand, Indonesia, and Malaysia—all returned to positive GDP growth in 1999, but a huge overhang of problem loans continued to cast a deep shadow. As of June 2000, on the eve of the third anniversary of the beginning of the crisis, the situation remained critical: In Indonesia, bad loans constituted 64 percent of the outstanding total; 35 percent of all outstanding loans were nonperforming in Thailand; in Malaysia, problem loans constituted 23 percent of the total; in Korea, 19 percent of loans were nonperforming.[21] These grim figures do not even include international borrowing from foreign banks: In Indonesia's case, foreign debt equaled about three-quarters of GDP in 1998.[22]

Despite the transfer of a significant share of these bad loans to government restructuring agencies, and despite large injections of public and private funds to rebuild lost capital, East Asian banks' balance sheets remained anemic for years after the crisis broke. As of September 2000, nonperforming loans were still five times greater than loan loss provisions in the four crisis-affected countries.[23] Such exposure prevents banks from resuming a healthy level of lending activity and thus exerts a drag on overall growth.

Meanwhile, distressed borrowers like Siam Syntech abounded up and down the Pacific Rim. The experience in Korea is instructive, because that country is widely credited with having proceeded most rapidly in cleaning up its financial mess. As of July 2000, Korea's largest *chaebol,* or conglomerates, still groaned under enormous debt burdens—despite facing strong political (as well as economic) pressure to reduce their leverage. LG reported a debt-equity ratio of 260 percent, followed by 230 percent for Hyundai, 220 percent for SK, and 194 percent for Samsung. Hyundai, in particular, came under withering fire for delays in restructuring while its financial outlook progressively deteriorated. Daewoo is the largest of the *chaebol* to collapse thus far; the dismantling of its corporate empire, however, has dragged on inconclusively.

Problems in Korea's corporate sector were not confined to the giants at the top. Analysts estimate that, well into 2000, about 25 percent of Korean manufacturing firms were not generating enough cash flow to meet their interest expenses. Many ailing borrowers were languishing in debt restructuring "workout" programs: As of March 2000 their combined assets totaled 9 percent of GDP. Even more had placed themselves under court receivership: At the end of 1999 their total assets amounted to 10.5 percent of GDP.[24]

Thus, the macroeconomic aggregates that showed a strong rebound in East Asia in 1999 and 2000 did not tell the full story. The fact is that much of the region's productive resources remained suspended in financial limbo—

avoiding death but unable to return fully to life. Until claims on those resources are subjected to a final reckoning—with losses recognized by the lenders and a shakeup in the ownership of the borrowers—the costs of past errors continue to mount to the detriment of long-term economic vitality.

For the perils of procrastination, look no farther than Japan. That country's lost decade of chronic low growth is attributable in large part to unresolved bad loans. For years after the bubble economy collapsed at the outset of the 1990s, Japanese financial institutions and policymakers took the ostrich's approach to crisis management: With heads in the sand, they hoped that reviving growth would reflate asset values and thus eliminate the source of their troubles. But the hoped-for growth never came. Finally, in 1997, the return of recession, and the collapse of Hokkaido Takushoku Bank and Yamaichi Securities, revealed a financial system on the verge of collapse. Since then, the government has staged a massive bank bailout, spending 46 trillion yen (over $400 billion) between April 1998 and July 2000 to take over failed banks, replenish capital in struggling ones, and buy up bad loans.[25]

Nevertheless, the end of Japan's bad-debt woes is nowhere in sight. Although banks have built up their reserves against possible defaults, they have been painfully slow to foreclose on problem loans, recover what they can from selling seized collateral, and write off the rest. They are still holding out hope that asset values will eventually recover and that their ultimate realized losses will be far less than their current paper losses. With interest rates hovering near zero for years, the costs of financing that hope have been relatively modest. In the meantime, however, ailing borrowers have been trapped in financial limbo, and the productive resources controlled by those businesses cannot be developed properly for lack of new financing. Especially hard hit are the construction and real estate sectors, which employ nearly 20 percent of the Japanese work force. In April 2001—more than a decade after the bubble burst—the Japanese government finally took its first official steps toward encouraging banks to write off and restructure their bad loans. The full resolution of this mess, though, is still years away.

Banking crises and their debilitating aftermath are by no means phenomena peculiar to East Asia. According to a recent World Bank analysis, 34 countries on five continents experienced major banking crises over the past two decades: Argentina, Bolivia, Brazil, Canada, Chile, Colombia,

Denmark, Ecuador, Egypt, El Salvador, Finland, Ghana, Hong Kong, India, Indonesia, Italy, Japan, Korea, Madagascar, Malaysia, Mexico, Nigeria, Norway, Peru, Philippines, Sri Lanka, Sweden, Tanzania, Thailand, Turkey, United States, Uruguay, Venezuela, and Zimbabwe. Banking crises are a plague that afflicts rich and poor countries alike. For some countries, they are a recurrent plague: 13 of those listed suffered multiple breakdowns of their banking systems during the period in question. And note that this roll call of misery understates significantly the extent of the suffering: It excludes all the former members of the Communist bloc, most of whose banking systems are severely distressed.[26]

What makes banks so prone to calamity? By their very design banks are vulnerable to sudden reversals of fortune. Their liabilities, in the form of demand deposits, are highly liquid, while their assets (loans to businesses and consumers) are much less so. Furthermore, the lending business is subject to what economists call "information asymmetries"—in other words, borrowers know more about their financial position than the banks that lend to them, and bank managers know more about the quality of their loans than do outside depositors, investors, or regulators. Given these facts, banks can make big blunders in their lending decisions, those blunders can be hidden from public view for some time, and when they finally come to light they can provoke a frantic rush to the exits by depositors.

While such vulnerabilities explain isolated bank failures, they do not sufficiently explain systemic meltdowns of much or all of a country's banking system. Those meltdowns have their origins in political interference with market signals. First, political controls on lending decisions can misdirect the flow of credit away from more profitable ventures and toward high-risk borrowers. Also, geographical restrictions on banking activity can heighten risk by frustrating diversification. Finally, a politically created atmosphere of "moral hazard"—in which banks know or assume that the government will not allow them or their borrowers to fail—can warp business judgment and lead to disastrous consequences.

It is not necessary to look to East Asia or struggling developing economies to see these factors in play. Instead, consider what happened in the United States—the most advanced and market-oriented financial market in the world—with the collapse of its savings-and-loan industry. The industry was purely a creature of public policy: The composition of both sides of the balance sheet was determined by statute and regulation. Specifically, savings-and-loans were required to lend long-term for home and commercial real estate mortgages and borrow short-term through interest-bearing time deposits. That mismatch of assets and liabilities created a critical vulnerability: If interest rates rose rapidly, S&Ls would be stuck for years with lower-yielding mortgages while paying out higher rates to depositors. In the inflationary 1970s that nightmare scenario came to pass, and by 1982 the S&L industry as a whole had a net worth of negative $70 billion.[27]

The perverse incentives of deposit insurance then compounded the problem. Owners of ailing S&Ls, with their own investments already wiped out, had a strong incentive to make increasingly risky loans. If the bets paid off, the high returns would rescue the owners' investments; if they didn't, deposit insurance would cover the losses. Meanwhile, restrictions on branching meant that S&Ls couldn't even diversify their risks; lending was concentrated geographically and thus highly exposed to the vagaries of local real estate markets. In the end, regional real estate busts during the disinflationary 1980s delivered the industry its deathblow.[28]

The same kinds of mistakes were replayed in East Asia. Lending decisions were heavily politicized in a depressing variety of ways—whether through state-owned banks, "administrative guidance" from bureaucrats, or good old-fashioned venality and corruption. Even when bankers exercised their own judgment about issuing loans, that judgment was clouded by the narcotizing belief that, in the final analysis, the government would never allow them or their major borrowers to fail. And even if all the other market distortions were eliminated, banking operations restricted to small and underdeveloped national economies were always accidents waiting to happen. On this last point, consider the fact that Thailand's total outstanding bank loans at the end of 1999 amounted to a little more than $100 billion—or around one third the market capitalization of Microsoft.[29] No nation's savings are ever safe in such a precariously undiversified portfolio.

The primary difference between Asia's banking meltdown and the S&L mess is that the former occurred on a much larger scale relative to the overall economy. S&Ls were a middling component of the larger American financial system; their collapse caused regional distress, not nationwide calamity. In East Asia, by contrast, banks dominate the financial scene. Consequently, when they went under, they dragged their countries down with them.

Notwithstanding their recent woes, East Asian financial systems actually compare favorably to those in much of the rest of the world. Or to put matters more plainly, in most countries today, the core of economic life—the allocation of capital—is even more egregiously dysfunctional than it is along the Pacific Rim. For all their flaws, East Asian banking sectors are at least large and active; in most developing countries, the banking sector has been stunted by what economists call "financial repression"—a cocktail of policies whose combined effect is to discourage financial intermediation. Especially damaging is the tandem of inflationary monetary policies and interest rate controls, which frequently results in negative real (that is, inflation-adjusted) interest rates and thus causes savers to shun the banking system. Another key element of financial repression is the requirement that banks maintain large reserves with the central bank. These interest-free loans to the government tie up resources that otherwise could be financing private productive activity. Finally, governments repress the financial sector through compulsory allocations of credit to particular sectors—whether through lending by state-owned banks, controls on private banks, or credit subsidies.

Latin America was a leading practitioner of financial repression in the decades before the debt crisis of the 1980s. Negative real interest rates were commonplace: In 1980 the average real rate for bank deposits was –0.1 percent in Mexico, –1.9 percent in Ecuador, –7.4 percent in Honduras, –16.2 percent in Peru, and –19.9 percent in Bolivia. Reserve requirements were also punishingly high. While the effective reserve requirement in the United States was only 4.6 percent in 1980, it climbed to 33.4 percent in Brazil, 45.2 percent in Colombia, and 51.4 percent in Mexico. And direct state allocation of credit to different sectors bulked very large: Approximately 80 percent of all loans were directly allocated in Brazil in 1986, as compared to 25 percent in Mexico, 30 percent in Colombia, and 40 percent in Argentina.[30]

Financial repression had the blessing of Keynesian economic orthodoxy. Demand for money, it was thought, draws savings away from physical capital, thus retarding the investments needed for growth. According to this logic—advocated in Latin America most prominently by Raúl Prebisch, the guru of import substitution—developing countries could accelerate growth by stunting their financial sectors. It was a highly convenient logic for deficit-spending populist politicians. Negative real interest rates were a boon for government borrowing; furthermore, governments were better able to raise revenues by inflating their currencies, since the demand for currency was heightened by the lack of alternative forms of liquidity.[31]

Economic analysis has now turned against financial repression, but its political temptations are abiding. According to the 2000 *Economic Freedom of the World* report, state-owned banks remain widespread: In 40 countries containing 57 percent of the world's population, state-owned banks held a clear majority of total deposits during 1997–98.[32] The same report shows that 40 countries accounting for 35 percent of the world's population still maintained significant regulation of interest rates during the period 1995–97. In 19 of those countries real interest rates were frequently or persistently negative.[33]

Even for countries that have made serious attempts to open up their financial systems, the legacy of the past continues to frustrate economic progress. In Latin America, the depth of the financial sector remains dismally underdeveloped. In Argentina, for example, bank lending to the private sector amounted to a mere 23.7 percent of GDP in 1998; in Brazil, the corresponding figure was 28.5 percent. In Mexico, where a recent banking crisis has aggravated an already poor situation, bank lending to the private sector had dropped to 17.8 percent of GDP in 1998, down from 28.9 percent in 1993. By contrast, in East Asia, where financial repression was pursued much less vigorously, the banking industry is much larger and better developed. In Malaysia, for instance, bank loans to the private sector amounted to 100.3 percent of GDP in 1997; in Thailand, the ratio was 118.7 percent.[34]

While developing countries generally throttled their banking sectors, the members of the old Communist bloc extinguished theirs altogether. The "banks" in those countries were such in name only; in reality they were mere bookkeeping operations for the incoherent calculus of central planning. Whatever they actually did, they certainly did not do what real banks do—namely, pool household savings and use them to finance commercial activity. For many of the so-called transition economies, the transition from banking in name only to real banking has made little headway.

Consider, for example, China and Russia: Both have floundered, albeit in very different ways. In both cases, though, the problems of the financial sector have been tied up inextricably with the failure to reform the old communist industrial base. In China, as addressed in the previous chapter, the state industrial sector was more or less untouched by liberalizing reforms until quite recently. As state-owned enterprises grew increasingly moribund, the Chinese banking system was saddled with the cost of keeping them afloat. Beginning in the early 1990s, China shifted away from covering industry losses directly out of the state budget. Instead, it relied on "policy loans" from state-owned banks to keep resources pumping into loss-hemorrhaging firms. Rather than being able to evolve into bona fide financial intermediaries, Chinese banks were stuck in the role of off-budget slush funds for the zombie economy.

That role proved ruinous. By 1997 the four largest state-owned banks, which dominated the country's financial system, were insolvent as a group. Nonbank financial institutions were also hit hard: For trust and investment companies, credit cooperatives, finance companies, and leasing companies, 50 percent of total assets were nonperforming by 1996. In 1998 the government began injecting public money into the banks to shore up their balance sheets, while at the same time creating public asset management companies to buy up their bad loans.

Bank bailouts, however, are mere palliatives. What is really needed is to free banks from having to prop up loss-making firms. Although restructuring of state-owned industries has finally begun, it is far from complete. In the meantime, the banking system continues to serve as lender of last resort. Thus, in 1999 total bank loans grew by 12.5 percent while GDP growth was only 7.1 percent, suggesting that credit was being extended not just to finance growth but also to cover losses. Meanwhile, as the zombies persist in sucking up resources, the most vital parts of the Chinese economy are being starved of the credit they need to develop and flourish. At the end of 1999, working capital loans to the private sector amounted to less than 1 percent of total loans outstanding.[35]

While China's banking problems grew out of maintaining a huge state-owned industrial base, in Russia it was the looting of the state sector that gave rise to a spectacularly dysfunctional financial system.[36] The collapse of the Soviet command economy in the late 1980s and early '90s saw an explosion of new private banks—1,600 of them by the time the Soviet Union dissolved at the end of 1991. Formed by Soviet bureaucrats, these banks facilitated the stripping of state industrial assets for private gain and transfer of profits overseas.

Over the following years, the banks continued to focus their efforts on making quick killings amidst economic chaos. They cashed in on hyperinflation by converting low-interest ruble deposits and government funds into dollars and then making high-interest, short-term loans to finance commodity exports; they could then exchange their dollar receipts back into depreciated rubles to cover their depositors' accounts. Beginning in 1995, a determined tight-money policy squelched runaway inflation and put an end to the banks' racket; they now used their considerable resources to buy up large chunks of Russian basic industry, including cement, steel, nickel, copper, oil, and aluminum. At the same time, increased government borrowing gave the banks one more opportunity to profit off of economic disorder: They bought up large quantities of the government's short-term, high interest-rate treasury notes, or GKOs.

What the banks did not do much of was traditional commercial banking—that is, taking deposits and making loans. In 1998 total deposits amounted to only 12 percent of GDP, while lending to the business sector came to only 11 percent of GDP. And when banks did lend, they didn't lend well. By 1996, roughly half of all their loans were overdue.

In the end, the addiction to quick-killing opportunism proved fatal. On August 17, 1998, the Russian government devalued the ruble and declared a moratorium on debt repayments. The banks, with their huge acquisitions of government debt and heavy foreign-currency borrowing, were wiped out instantly. Appropriately, they were consumed by the very economic chaos that spawned them. What survived were hundreds of smaller banks that had not invested in government debt. Whether this remnant can grow into the foundation of a viable financial sector remains to be seen.

<hr />

The problems that plague the world's banking sectors underscore the need for alternative modes of financing—notably, capital markets for bonds and equities. Bypassing centralized intermediaries, capital markets allow a multitude of investors to choose directly among companies bidding for financing. The result can be a dramatic intensification of financial competition. When capital markets are well developed and functioning properly, a much wider array of entrepreneurs is able to get funding for promising new ideas; at the same time, companies that receive funding are held to a far less forgiving standard of performance. Capital markets thus are capable of accelerating the rate of entrepreneurial innovation while at the same time ratcheting up the ruthlessness of market feedback. With more "mutations" and stronger "selection pressures," market evolution is able to move to a new level of creative power.

In particular, the need for strong capital markets becomes increasingly emphatic as a country's economy shifts away from agriculture and traditional manufacturing and toward service and high-tech industries. Banks typically favor borrowers with tangible collateral; in "new economy" industries, though, the primary firm assets are usually intellectual property and human capital. Without well-developed capital markets, including venture capital and other private equity markets, the financial system will chronically underserve new firms with bright, new ideas.

Capital markets do not simply expand the horizons of financing beyond what banks are able to provide; they also enable banks to do their jobs better. The information contained in bond and stock prices can provide valuable guidance to banks when they are making their lending decisions. Furthermore, securitization of bank assets (for example, real estate mortgages) spreads credit risk and facilitates the resolution of bad debts when lending decisions misfire. Although bankers often think of capital markets as a threat to their livelihood, the fact is that direct and indirect financing are not substitutes, but complements. In the United States, for example, the world's largest financial markets exist side by side with a large and vibrant banking sector.

Moreover, a country with a more decentralized and diversified financial system is far more resilient in the face of a banking crisis—a crucial advantage in light of the catastrophic financial paralysis that has tormented so many countries in recent years. For all its financial sophistication, the United States still endured its savings-and-loan debacle. But the consequences for the overall economy were contained by the wealth of other financial resources. In bank-dependent countries, a crisis in the sector causes a systemic breakdown in the flow of resources from savers to investors; the consequences, as we have seen, are often disastrous. When capital markets are operating properly, on the other hand, companies with good prospects can still get financing even when the banking sector is distressed.

Unfortunately, however, deep and liquid capital markets are enjoyed by only a handful of countries around the world—most prominently, the United States and United Kingdom. Even other advanced industrialized countries have relied historically on bank-centered finance; consequently, their financial markets have been relatively small and inactive. In the United States, total equity market capitalization equaled 114 percent of GDP in 1996; by comparison, the corresponding figure was 66 percent in Japan, 38 percent in France, and a mere 28 percent in Germany.[37]

And relative size is only the most obvious yardstick of comparison. More important than the size of financial markets is how open and liquid they are. The stock markets of continental Europe and Japan, however, have been dominated by insiders. An international comparison of listed companies found that, in the United States, the top five shareholders held an average of 25.4 percent of total equity; by contrast, for German firms the largest *single* shareholder averaged 55.9 percent, and for French companies the largest shareholder averaged 57.9 percent. Cross-shareholding among enterprises, which keeps shares off the market and thereby cements insider control, is also commonplace. The phenomenon is strongly associated with Japan, and with good reason: As of 1994 banks and nonfinancial firms held 52 percent of all common stock (as compared to 7 percent in the United States). But the practice is by no means limited to Japan. In Germany, such cross-shareholding also tied up 52 percent of common stock in 1996, and in France the figure was 62 percent in 1994.[38]

In the less-developed world the situation is generally no better—in fact, it is usually much worse. In Thailand, for example, total equity market capitalization is equal to only 28 percent of GDP, and the ten largest firms account for over 47 percent of total market capitalization. Equity liquidity (dollar volume of shares traded divided by market capitalization) is only 71 percent.[39] As of 1996, equity market capitalization in Korea was only 25 percent of GDP; in Brazil, the figure was 29 percent; in India, 35 percent; in Argentina, 16 percent; in Pakistan, a miserable 10 percent.[40] There are a few bright spots: In Hong Kong, Singapore, Taiwan, and Chile, for example, equity markets are relatively large and liquid. Apart from these happy exceptions, though, now that the "emerging markets" craze of the early 1990s has fizzled unceremoniously, it is clear that most of the world's stock markets are turbid, stagnant backwaters. Too often, they are just another racket for insiders to maintain their control, not the liberating tool for democratizing finance that they could and should be.

Around the world, capital markets have been systematically throttled by restrictive regulations. Take Japan, for example. For many years the issuance of bonds had to be approved by a bond cartel that consisted of the major banks. Jealous of the competition that bonds might pose to their own business, the banks made sure that bond issues were few and far between. Meanwhile, stock exchange rules made it exceptionally difficult for companies to become publicly listed: It takes an astonishing 34 years, on average, before a Japanese company can make a public offering on the Tokyo Stock Exchange.[41]

The past few years have seen a number of countries make promising but still fledgling efforts to open up their capital markets and thereby democratize access to financing. In Japan, the creation of two new startup-friendly stock markets—Nasdaq Japan and the Tokyo Stock Exchange's new offshoot, "Mothers" (Market of the High-growth and Emerging Stocks)—led to a flurry of new listings. At the same time, Japan's venture capital sector, which only a few years ago was all but nonexistent, was besieged with new entrants, including U.S.-based firms like Hambrecht & Quist, Goldman Sachs, J. H. Whitney, and Warburg.[42]

Germany has also taken steps toward greater openness. In 1997 the fusty old Frankfurt Exchange opened the Neuer Markt, or New Market, which proceeded to list more than 200 mostly high-tech companies in its first three years. Stock options, a critical tool for attracting top talent to new companies and keeping talent focused at established firms, finally became legal in 1998. The watershed hostile takeover of Mannesmann by Vodafone Air-Touch in early 2000 signaled, perhaps, the dawn of a functioning market for corporate control. And, starting in 2002, the elimination of capital gains taxes on sales by corporations of their stakes in other firms promises to prompt the unraveling of Germany's tangled web of cross-shareholdings.[43]

Although such moves are encouraging, the insider entrenchment of Japan, Inc. and "Rhenish capitalism" is not about to disappear overnight. Most of Japan's $12 trillion in household savings remains locked up in low-interest-bearing time deposits or postal savings accounts. In Germany, as of 1999, equity holdings still equaled only 22 percent of household disposable income—as compared to 82 percent in the United Kingdom.[44] Capital markets in these countries will remain undersized as long as participation by ordinary individual investors continues to be marginal. Meanwhile, the countries' new stock exchanges were badly bloodied by the collapse of the Internet stock boom. As a result, the process of opening up equity markets has encountered a serious—if temporary—setback.

And in most of the rest of the world, it is not enough simply to remove artificial restrictions and then, *voilà,* watch capital markets spring up overnight. Governments, especially those of developing and transition economies, must do more than dismantle an overlay of inhibiting regulations; they must at the same time construct an underlying infrastructure of legal rules and institutions within which capital markets can flourish. The sad tale of Michael Wansley and Kaset Thai Sugar Company gives some indication of how daunting that latter task is.[45]

Michael Wansley was a bright light in the world of international accounting. The 58-year-old Australian was a senior partner at Deloitte Touche Tohmatsu—he had made partner at age 27, the youngest ever at his firm. His achievements outside of his profession were also considerable: He had served as chairman of the Australian Red Cross and been awarded the Order of Australia for his charitable efforts. When Thailand's bad debt mess erupted, Wansley and his firm took a leading role in cleanup efforts from the outset. Wansley had been called upon to evaluate the assets of 22 of the 56 finance companies that were closed in December 1997. And in early 1999, a Thai bankruptcy court appointed him to supervise the debt restructuring of Kaset Thai and two other affiliated sugar mills. The three companies, all of which were controlled by the Siriviriyakul family, owed creditors a combined $450 million. The court-ordered restructuring was seen as a major test of Thailand's bankruptcy process.

At Kaset Thai, Wansley apparently uncovered evidence of massive fraud. According to police, factory managers had been looting the company to the tune of tens of millions of dollars and then shifting the funds to shell companies and private bank accounts. On March 10, Wansley and four colleagues headed up to the sugar mill near the small town of Takhli, about 120 miles north of Bangkok. As their black Toyota minivan approached the factory gate, a motorcycle pulled up alongside them and a gunman seated on the back shot Wansley eight times at close range. He died instantly.

Police eventually apprehended five suspects: the driver and the gunman, two midlevel factory managers, and Pradit Siriviriyakul, one of the mill's owners and the alleged mastermind of the conspiracy. The driver was quickly convicted and sentenced to life in prison, but the prosecution of the other accused plotters turned into a fiasco. A year into the murder trial, only two of some 50 planned witnesses had testified. Meanwhile, after the court had denied Pradit's request for bail seven consecutive times, a special appeals panel intervened and granted it—amid allegations that the senior judge on that panel had received a half-million dollar bribe from Pradit, and that further bribes of ten times that amount had been promised in the event the case was dropped. The senior judge in question was removed from office following a Justice Ministry investigation, but Pradit's bail was not revoked and he remained at large. As of August 2001, two-and-a-half years after Wansley's murder, it was estimated that the trial would drag on for another year before a verdict could be reached.

Meanwhile, the restructuring of Kaset Thai and its sister mills sputtered as well. After Wansley's death, his firm presented creditors with debt restructuring plans for the three companies. The proposals called for a thorough housecleaning: a near total write-off of each firm's capital and replacement of existing management. Small creditors, mostly sugar growers, opposed the plan because it effectively killed their hopes of ever being repaid. Although major creditors, including one French bank and a handful of large Thai banks, held 83 percent of Kaset Thai's outstanding debt, Thai bankruptcy law at the time (it has subsequently been changed) held that at least 50 percent of creditors must vote to approve the plan. Small creditors had the strength of numbers, and they vetoed the proposal by a vote of 2,910 to 63. Faced with this impasse, the bankruptcy court could have ordered the firms liquidated. Instead it terminated court supervision of the matter, leaving the Siriviriyakul family still in charge and creditors to try all over again to reach some accommodation.

Eventually, in June 2000, the banks settled on a much more modest deal. They agreed simply to stretch out repayment periods another ten years— no debt write-offs, no write-downs of capital. And although the banks won the right to appoint representatives to the group's management team, the Siriviriyakul family retained ultimate control.

On a crisp, brilliant Sunday afternoon in November 2000, I set out with a friend to retrace Michael Wansley's last fateful trip. Finding the sugar mill wasn't easy. It is hidden at the end of a maze of progressively deteriorating roads that snake and tangle their way off the main highway and through rice paddies, scrub brush, and sugar cane fields. Only one beaten-up, discolored sign (in Thai only, of course) offered guidance along the way. After stopping more than a few times to ask for directions, we headed down a bumpy dirt road that cut through chest-high brush on either side. Just as we began to believe we had made another wrong turn, the mill loomed into view.

Somewhere along this road, I thought, Michael Wansley was murdered. On the day I visited, though, all evidence of violence and horror was long gone. Everything was drowsily peaceful: A few hens and roosters strutted back and forth across the road, while a couple of guards lounged quietly behind the shuttered factory gate. The mill itself was closed and empty—it operates only a few months of the year, just after the sugar cane is harvested. The only break in the silence was provided, eerily, by the occasional motorcyclist buzzing up or down the road.

Along that faraway, out-of-the-way dirt road, the lie was put to all the blather about the triumph of footloose capital and the tyranny of "Anglo-Saxon" finance. The Wansley case shows vividly that—at Kaset Thai Sugar Company, at least—the dead hand of crony capitalism still clings tenaciously to power. The company's saga offers an especially egregious example of the breakdowns in investor protection that are all too common in most developing countries: the looting of minority shareholders, the lack of transparency, the unworkable bankruptcy procedures. As long as these breakdowns remain common, capital markets will continue to be deprived of the high levels of investor confidence that are an essential precondition of those markets' robust development.

In the case of Kaset Thai, supposedly all-powerful Western capital set out to challenge these breakdowns and was decisively repulsed. Despite the pressure by a French bank to put the case under court supervision, and despite the court appointment of a Big Five accounting firm to oversee restructuring, nothing much changed at Kaset Thai. The Sirivirikayul family remained in charge despite running the firm into insolvency. The criminal ransacking of the company by rogue managers was successfully covered up. And the plotters of that cover-up have so far gotten away—quite literally—with murder.

This last point is especially ominous. In a high-profile case conducted under the hot spotlight of international scrutiny, the Thai legal system proved incapable of upholding the single most rudimentary norm of any legal system—the rule against murder. Instead, the proceedings degenerated into a squalid and pathetic farce of corruption and fecklessness.

The Wansley case is not an isolated incident: It is symptomatic of a systemic failure to ensure the basic operational integrity of legal protections of person and property. As addressed in the next chapter, the consequences of this failure—in Thailand and throughout the developing and postcommunist worlds—extend far beyond problems in the financial sector. Indeed, every phase of the division of labor is implicated and undermined.

8

The Rule of Lawlessness

enry Ford's innovations in automobile production captured the
centralizing imagination of the world. The assembly line, intro-
duced at Ford's Highland Park facility in 1913, offered a dazzling
display of top-down planning's productive power. Here was a rationally designed system in which every step of the production process and the role of
every worker on the line had been specified and sequenced to achieve maximum possible efficiency. To the partisans of the Industrial Counterrevolution, it appeared that Ford had constructed a scale model of the centrally
planned economy.

In particular, Ford's methods were celebrated throughout the Soviet
Union—despite the American capitalist's strong personal antipathy toward communism. His 1922 autobiography *My Life and Work* ran through
four printings there by 1925. Soviet managers studied Ford's philosophy
of mass production alongside the teachings of Lenin. By 1927, Ford had
supplied some 85 percent of all the trucks and tractors in the Soviet Union;
the Fordson tractor inspired Fordson days and Fordson festivals in Soviet
villages.[1]

In light of this history, it is a supreme irony that in rural northern India
today, decades of mimicking Soviet-style policies have caused—of all
things—the abandonment of the mass production of automobiles. Economic
life there is so grotesquely deformed that pre-1913 production methods have
once again become economically viable.

To find this strange anachronism, I set out with a colleague and a driver one morning in February 2001 to brave India's infamous rural roads. Leaving Delhi still murky with wood and dung smoke from the previous night's home fires, we headed south down the Delhi-Agra highway and weaved our way through a chaos of cars, trucks, buses, motorcycles, three-wheeled "Vikrams," tractors, ox-carts, and camel carts. I even saw a man walking alongside the road with a bear on a leash—a traveling entertainer who worked his way from village to village. My colleague told me that this highway was actually a showpiece by Indian standards—at least it had a median strip. As we ventured onto smaller roads I quickly understood what he meant: With traffic on the two-lane roads undulating back and forth across both lanes to pass slow-moving tractors and camels or avoid potholes the size of bomb craters, dodging the oncoming traffic was like a video game come to life.

All along the way vehicles were overflowing with passengers—people sitting on top of a jeep-like "Mahindra," or standing on the floorboard of a van with the back door swinging open, or crammed into the back of a truck or camel cart. With a billion people, India has only around 40 million vehicles—two-, three-, and four-wheeled combined. It is a desperately poor country, to be sure, but in this particular respect the poverty is a matter of explicit policy. Vehicle prices are grossly inflated by punishingly high taxes: Total duties on used cars, for instance, are 180 percent. Although American, Japanese, and Korean auto companies now assemble vehicles in India, their products are well out of financial reach for most Indians.

With admirable ingenuity and initiative, rural Indians have decided to take matters into their own hands: They are now building their own automobiles. Known alternately as a "jugaad," a "maruta," or a "boogi," the vehicle offers basic, barebones transportation for Indian farmers. It has no roof, the 10 to 14 horsepower engine must be hand-cranked and maxes out around 15 miles per hour, and the driver sits on a wooden bench. But the rear compartment—a plywood bed with wood-panel sides—has plenty of room for passengers or cargo. And with a price tag of only around $1,000, it is an unbeatable bargain.

We found boogi manufacturers in the remote village of Toda Bhim in eastern Rajasthan. There were no assembly lines, no factories at all—just three small mechanic's garages spaced out along the semi-paved road that runs through the village. The mechanics buy minivan spare parts—wheels, axles, transmissions, gear boxes, and steering—from markets in Delhi; they get their engines, made to power water pumps, from Agra; and they pick up steel for the chassis and wood for the framing from Jaipur. They cut and fit the framing and weld the chassis themselves and then assemble the rest; according to the mechanic we spoke with, one shop can turn out four or five boogis a month.

Technically, these vehicles are illegal under India's Motor Vehicles Act. They are not officially registered, they have no license plates, and they are supposedly subject to seizure by the highway patrol whenever they are found. But the law is roundly ignored. In addition to the mechanics in Toda Bhim who actually make the cars, we spoke with a dealer in the nearby town of Mahwa and several satisfied customers, and none reported any problems with the police. We even saw boogis puttering along the main Delhi-Agra highway, not 60 miles from the capital city.

The production of boogis is part of India's enormous "informal sector"—unsanctioned economic activity that is nonetheless tolerated by the authorities. You don't have to venture to out-of-the-way Toda Bhim to see informal enterprise in India. Just drive around the streets of Delhi and it will confront you at every turn and traffic light. At red lights your car will be accosted by merchants hawking various wares: Boxes of tissue paper are an especially popular item, along with balloons, maps, and even toy-sized snake charmer's baskets. You'll whizz past streetside fruit and vegetable stands and—with inexplicable frequency—pyramid stacks of motorcycle helmets for sale on the curbside. You'll pass pedaling peddlers, driving bicycle carts with loads of folded cardboard boxes, or lumber, or scrap metal. On weekends, impromptu markets spring up and take over a street; one I saw specialized in second-hand clothes. And in the depressingly common garbage heaps alongside the road, you'll see scavengers rooting through the trash for things that can be recycled.

The informal sector dominates India's economic life. Only around 30 million people, or 9 percent of the labor force, work in the official, "organized" economy; everybody else, the other 91 percent, works informally. It is a breathtaking statistic: 91 percent of Indian workers operate off the books and outside the law.[2] Those 91 percent don't have the proper permits and licenses, most don't pay taxes, and few show up at all in the official economic statistics. At the same time, many are subject to incessant extortion by corrupt officials, few have any access to the courts for legal redress, and virtually none are eligible for bank loans or any other type of formal financing.

The Indian economy is thus characterized by an extreme dualism. In the organized economy, even after a decade of reforms, large-scale enterprises still groan under a crushing burden of rules, regulations, licenses, prohibitions, and taxes. Meanwhile, in the vast and sprawling shadow economy, subsistence farmers and small-scale entrepreneurs eke out their existence in the lawless void of anarchy. The Indian government is simultaneously doing far *too much* and far *too little:* On the formal sector it inflicts a gruesome excess of controls, while to the informal sector it fails to provide even the basic public good of legal protection.

These sins of commission and omission are closely interrelated. Many enterprises in the informal sector are there because they fled the onerous controls and inflated costs of the organized economy. Heavy taxes beget smuggling and avoidance; cumbersome and restrictive licensing procedures beget illicit, unlicensed enterprises; burdensome labor laws beget stunted companies that keep below the employment thresholds that trigger the laws' application.

The story of EDP Aids, an informal computer company in Delhi with ten employees, illustrates the interplay between the level of government controls and the extent of informal lawlessness. Adarsh Alreja, the founder and head of the company, told me he entered the business of manufacturing personal computers back in 1990—notwithstanding the fact that it was illegal to do so without a license. And because duties on computer parts exceeded 100 percent, he used mostly smuggled components. Despite a ridiculously low production volume by Western standards (EDP Aids never made more than about 700 PCs a year), he was able sell his computers at half the price charged for imports or by his domestic, formal competitors. Even more amazing, his profit margin was a fat 20 to 30 percent. Before 1998, Alreja estimates, some 70 to 80 percent of PCs sold in India were informally manufactured. Here again, as with the boogis in Rajasthan, the perversity of top-down controls had led to the overthrow of mass production.

But then import duties on computers and parts started to fall—down to their present level of around 25 percent. Falling duties led to declining competitiveness and profits in the informal sector: By 2001, EDP Aids' price advantage had shrunk to 8 to 10 percent, and the profit margin had dwindled to 5 percent. Consequently, the company has all but abandoned manufacturing, assembling only around 50 PCs a year. It now concentrates on service and maintenance instead. Adarsh Alreja figures that, nationwide, the informal share of the PC market has dropped to 60 percent.

The lifting of import controls has thus succeeded in causing a partial shift away from informality. In spite of this, EDP Aids, and much of the Indian computer industry, remains outside the organized economy. Why? Complying with the excise tax regime to which formal companies are subject would be impossible; the company would have to request and undergo a formal inspection before shipping each piece of merchandise. Furthermore, by staying informal, EDP Aids can avoid making social welfare deductions from workers' paychecks—and thus entice better workers with higher take-home pay. Also, as the head of an informal enterprise, Adarsh Alreja can hire and fire workers as he sees fit without any interference from India's onerous labor laws.

Informality, though, carries heavy costs. Most obviously, productivity suffers grievously because of the inability to exploit scale economies. The production of a few automobiles a month, or a few computers a day, is an absurdity in light of currently available technology. If boogis and informal computers were mass-produced, they could be made for a fraction of the current cost—and sold for a fraction of the current price. But in the informal sector, such obvious and enormous productivity gains are unattainable. Any enterprise large enough to realize them would be too big for the authorities to ignore; it would be swept into the formal sector's tangle of rules and requirements, and so would lose the cost advantages that allowed it to expand in the first place. Furthermore, growth requires capital, and the enterprises in the shadow economy have no access to formal financing. All expansion must be financed out of cash flow, or from woefully inefficient informal sources at grossly inflated interest rates. Consequently, informal enterprises are stunted by lack of resources as well as the need to avoid the heavy burdens of formality. Profligate wastefulness—and the agonizing persistence of mass poverty—is the inevitable and tragic result.

～～～～

India's informal sector is only an especially egregious example of a global phenomenon. In Latin America, for example, the sprawling *favelas* of Brazil are perhaps the most familiar face of a pervasive shadow economy. In Brazil, as well as Costa Rica, Honduras, Panama, and Venezuela, 40 percent or more of total employment is informal; in Bolivia and Paraguay the figure tops 50 percent, while roughly 65 percent of Guatemalans work outside the organized economy.[3] Meanwhile, in Southeast Asia, over 70 percent of workers in heavily rural Thailand and Indonesia operate in the informal sector. Even in urban areas, roughly half of Thai workers are informal.

Estimating the size of informal economic output is a task fraught with difficulty. How, after all, does one measure that which is officially ignored and, indeed, often strives to remain hidden? In one recent study, economists Friedrich Schneider and Dominik Enste tried, among other things, to compare official GDP statistics to estimates of GDP based on electricity consumption. There is a strong and well-established empirical relationship between electricity use and overall economic activity; accordingly, by comparing the official numbers to those predicted by power consumption, it is possible to get at least a rough idea of the size of the unofficial, or informal, economy.

Using this methodology, Schneider and Enste found that the informal sector contributes substantially to total output throughout the developing and transition economies. Here are some of their estimated ratios of shadow economy output to official GDP for select developing countries: Malaysia, 39 percent; Peru, 44 percent; Mexico, 49 percent; Philippines, 50 percent; Egypt, 68 percent; and Nigeria, 76 percent. Schneider and Enste used two different data sources to calculate average ratios of 20.9 percent and 31.6 percent for the transition economies of Central and Eastern Europe; in the former Soviet Union, the average ratio of informal output to official GDP ranged from 35.3 percent to 43.6 percent.[4]

Peruvian author and political advisor Hernando de Soto has done more than just about anybody to bring the informal sector and its workings to public attention. In his pioneering 1989 book *The Other Path,* he showed that private property and market exchange, far from being tools of oppression imposed upon the poor of Latin America, are in fact being generated spontaneously by those very poor to free themselves from unworkable collectivist policies. Large and vibrant informal economies—created by the humblest elements of society in the face of official indifference and even hostility—are proof of market competition's indispensable usefulness. But what this people's capitalism lacks, argues de Soto, and what it desperately needs in order to fulfill its wealth-creating potential, is formal recognition and legal protection.

In his latest book, *The Mystery of Capital,* de Soto attempts to measure the amount of wealth locked up in informal sectors around the developing and postcommunist worlds. To simplify the task, he and his colleagues at the

Institute for Liberty and Democracy in Lima looked only at informal real estate. In de Soto's native Peru, they estimate that 53 percent of people in urban areas and 81 percent of people in rural areas live in dwellings to which nobody has clear title. In the Philippines, the corresponding figures are 57 percent and 67 percent, respectively; in Haiti, 68 percent and 97 percent; and in Egypt, 92 percent and 83 percent.[5]

Although these informal properties are certainly modest, collectively they represent enormous treasure troves of untapped wealth. In the Philippines, for example, the estimated value of informal housing is $133 billion— or four times the total capitalization of the stock market, seven times all the deposits in commercial banks, nine times the capital of all the state-owned enterprises, and 14 times the value of all foreign direct investment. De Soto estimates that the total value of informal real estate in the world is an astonishing $9.3 trillion—20 times the total foreign direct investment in all developing and transition economies since 1989, 46 times all the World Bank loans for the past three decades, and 93 times the total official development assistance from all rich countries over the same time span.[6] Unfortunately, all of this vast potential capital remains trapped in legal limbo.

Those of us who live in rich countries are used to thinking of the "underground" economy as marginal—and indeed for us it largely is.[7] But in the poorer nations, where most of the world's population lives and works, it is a different story altogether. There, the informal sector has become a major, even dominant, presence in economic life. The disastrously dysfunctional policies of the old Third World, once trumpeted as salvation for the struggling masses, have in fact exiled great multitudes of the poor and uneducated to a kind of legal wilderness. Into that same wilderness have wandered large numbers of refugees from the collapse of communism's economic structures—and the failure to build in their stead functioning market institutions. In this wilderness there is survival, and escape from oppression, but self-sustaining economic development remains out of reach.

———〰〰〰———

It is widely but mistakenly assumed that support for free markets equals hostility toward government. Economic liberals who advocate dismantling or reforming failed collectivist policies are routinely characterized by their opponents as spoiling for anarchy.

Even someone as generally sympathetic to markets as Thomas Friedman

succumbs to this confusion. Although an enthusiastic champion of globalization, Friedman retains his allegiance to certain aspects of the collectivist
legacy—notably top-down social welfare programs in the domestic sphere
and International Monetary Fund bailouts internationally. In *The Lexus and
the Olive Tree,* he heaps contempt upon anyone who would question his particular sacred cows. "I heard mean-spirited voices," he writes, "voices un-
interested in any compromise, voices for whom the American government
was some kind of evil enemy." In particular, he lampoons the freshman congressional Republicans who swept their party to legislative power in the
elections of 1994:

> I said to myself, "Well, my freshman Republican friends, come to Africa—it's
> a freshman Republican's paradise." Yes sir, nobody in Liberia pays taxes.
> There's no gun control in Angola. There's no welfare as we know it in Bu-
> rundi and no big government to interfere in the market in Rwanda. But a lot
> of their people sure wish there were.[8]

Friedman is thrashing a straw man. Economic liberals—"free-market
ideologues" or "market fundamentalists" as they are called by those who dis-
agree with them on any particular point—are hostile only to the collectivist
hypertrophy of government, not government itself. As I addressed in Chapter 3, economic liberals recognize that strong and effective government is essential to the vitality and proper functioning of markets. Specifically, the ongoing development of a healthy market order entails the articulation of an
increasingly complex division of labor—one that unites large numbers of
people, the vast majority of whom don't know each other and, indeed, are
only dimly aware of each other, in cooperative projects that may take many
years to bear fruit. That level of social cooperation is possible only within a
framework of clear and reliable rules for acquiring, holding, and transferring
property. The great public good of market competition depends in turn
upon the public good of a well-constructed legal infrastructure—whose
construction and maintenance require the agencies of government.

But due in no small part to the Industrial Counterrevolution, most people in the world live under governments that fail to provide the necessary
legal infrastructure. The persistent influence of the dead hand can thus be
seen in the fact that contemporary governments are doing too little as well
as too much. The present-day program of economic liberalism, especially in
developing and transition economies, calls for greater government activism
in addition to greater restraint.

The existence of large informal sectors is only one symptom of a broader institutional failure. It is not just that legal systems exclude large areas of economic life; they also fail to serve well those areas they do cover. The formal sectors of poorer countries are plagued by inadequate and unreliable legal infrastructure. Unclear or conflicting definitions of rights, unreasonable costs and delays in obtaining legal relief, inadequate enforcement of legal rulings, and endemic corruption all hamper and distort economic development.

A widely cited study by economist Paulo Mauro attempts to quantify the consequences of poor legal institutions. Using indices (prepared by a private business intelligence firm) that measure bureaucracy, red tape, corruption, and judicial efficiency and integrity, the analysis points to a significant effect of inadequate legal systems on the amount of private investment, and thereby on the rate of economic growth. Specifically, an increase of one standard deviation in those indices (for example, a jump from Bangladesh's level of institutional quality to that of Uruguay's) would cause a jump in the investment rate of almost 5 percentage points, and a consequent jump in annual GDP growth by more than half a percentage point.[9]

To examine the problem of institutional failure in detail, take the case of Argentina. During the first age of globalization, it developed an immensely productive agricultural sector and rode the wave of export-led growth to become one of the wealthiest nations on earth. But as the international economy on which its fortunes rested disintegrated during the 1930s and '40s, this once liberal country succumbed to military dictatorship and Perónism—and steadily sank back into the economic backwardness from which it had earlier escaped. In the 1980s, the Industrial Counterrevolution in Argentina finally expired, not with a whimper, but with two bangs: first, the defeat in the Falklands War, which toppled the dictators and brought back democracy; and second, the debt crisis and hyperinflation that prompted, as a desperate last resort, the rediscovery of market-oriented policies.

Over the past decade or so, Argentina's pro-market reforms have been undeniably impressive—yet woefully inadequate. In the *Economic Freedom of the World* ratings, Argentina now scores well on many crucial elements of economic policy: 8.9 out of a possible score of 10 for monetary policy and price stability (up from a score of zero in 1985); 7.7 for the average rate of its import tariffs (up from 4.6 in 1985); and a perfect score of 10 for its privatization of government-owned enterprises (up from 4.0). Indeed, Argentina's overall score in the 2000 *Economic Freedom of the World* report ranked 12th out of 123 countries surveyed.[10]

But flourishing markets require more than good policies; they require

good institutions as well. And on that score, unfortunately, Argentina's reforms
have thus far accomplished virtually nothing: The country's legal and administrative infrastructure is a shambles of corruption and inefficiency.
Transparency International releases an annual index of corruption levels
around the world based on surveys of business people, academics, and risk
analysts. In 2001, Argentina ranked a dismal 57th out of 91 countries—
worse than Botswana, Namibia, Peru, Brazil, Bulgaria, and Colombia, and
on the same level as notoriously corrupt China.[11] In a similar vein, the 2000
Global Competitiveness Report, coproduced by Harvard University and the
World Economic Forum, surveyed business leaders from 4,022 firms in 59
countries for their perceptions of business conditions in those countries. Argentina ranked consistently near the bottom in the perceived quality of its
legal and administrative institutions: 40th in the frequency of irregular payments to government officials; 54th in the independence of the judiciary;
55th in litigation costs; 45th in corruption in the legal system; and 54th in
the reliability of police protection.[12]

The dilapidation of Argentina's institutional infrastructure is a continuing legacy of the Industrial Counterrevolution. Look, for example, at the crucial question of judicial independence. Prior to the descent into statism, justices of Argentina's Supreme Court enjoyed long tenures undisturbed by
political interference. Thus, at the beginning of Juan Perón's first administration Supreme Court justices averaged 12 years on the bench. Since 1960, the
average tenure has dropped below four years. Since Perón, five of 17 presidents named every member of the Court during their term; prior to Perón,
only President Mitre, the country's first constitutional president, enjoyed the
same distinction. Before Perón, it was typical for a majority of the Court to
have been appointed by presidents from the current political opposition; afterwards, that was no longer the case.[13] The Supreme Court, the supposed
bulwark of the rule of law, was reduced to a mere creature of politics.

The present era of reform has brought little improvement. President
Carlos Menem, who did so much to better Argentina's policies, persisted in
traducing the integrity of its institutions. Faced with a politically hostile
Supreme Court, Menem responded with a court-packing scheme: He expanded the Court from five to nine members and filled the new slots with
political supporters. And his transgressions did not stop there: Allegations of
corruption swirled throughout his two terms in office. Those charges finally
caught up with him on June 7, 2001, when the former president was arres-
ted for his role in an illegal arms shipments deal. Such is the sad state of

Argentina's legal system that it is unclear whether the prosecution of Menem represents the first step in a long overdue cleanup—or whether it is merely an act of revenge by his political opponents now that they are in power.

On the day of Menem's arrest I happened to be in Rosario, Argentina's second largest city. A small but noisy group of pro-Menem demonstrators temporarily tangled traffic that afternoon—compounding the transportation woes I was experiencing as I scrambled to get back to Buenos Aires on the eve of a one-day, nationwide general strike. (The strike, by the way, had been scheduled well beforehand as a protest of Argentina's long-running recession, but was totally upstaged by the stunning news of the former president's legal troubles.) Putting aside the petty personal inconveniences, I could not have picked a more fortuitous time to be in Argentina. I was there, after all, to investigate up close the effect of the country's ramshackle institutions on its economic prospects.

Especially illuminating was my visit to the northwestern province of Tucumán. During the "dirty war" of the 1970s, Tucumán served as a refuge for pro-Castro guerillas and was roiled by bloody fighting. Today it is better known as home to the world's largest producer of lemons, as well as a now-declining sugar industry, and its problems are more prosaic: bloated and corrupt bureaucracy, and a backward and unreliable legal system.

The public sector in Tucumán serves primarily to enrich politicians and fund patronage jobs; the provision of public services is but an afterthought. Out of a formal work force of some 400,000, there are nearly 80,000 provincial and municipal government employees and another 10,000 federal government workers. Elected officials are able to siphon off small fortunes for themselves: The annual salary for provincial legislators is roughly $300,000.[14] Tucumán is by no means noteworthy for such abuses. A true standout is the impoverished province of Formosa on the country's northern border. There about half of all formally employed workers are on the government payroll, and many of them show up on the job only once a month—to collect their paychecks.[15]

Such profligacy lies at the root of Argentina's latest financial crisis. Government spending as a percentage of gross domestic product climbed from 9.4 percent in 1989 to 21 percent in 2000—despite the fact that sweeping privatizations were at the same time relieving the government of significant fiscal burdens.[16] Free-spending provincial officials bear much of the blame: Operating expenses at the provincial level rose 25 percent from 1995 to 2000 even though inflation was nonexistent.[17] The spending binge has driven the country's external debt above 50 percent of GDP and led many investors to conclude that default, and resulting severe economic hardship, are virtually inevitable.

Meanwhile, as the public sector balloons uncontrollably, vital government responsibilities go unfulfilled—among them, the provision of a legal system that promptly and reliably vindicates the rights of the citizenry. As a result, the acute financial traumas that now beset Argentina are compounded by deeper, chronic ills—namely, a business environment that is profoundly hostile to investment, dynamism, and growth. In San Miguel de Tucumán, the capital of Tucumán province, I spoke with Ignacio Colombres Garmendia, the head of a major law firm in town. "The legal system is absolutely vital for our region's economic development," he complained, "but the politicians are blind to it. It's hard to see what doesn't happen because of a bad legal climate, and so nobody knows about it. But every day I see deals collapse—I see potential investors who decide not to come to Tucumán—because of the legal risks. They call and ask me about this or that legal issue, and I have to tell them, and they say 'thank you very much' and that's the end of it. 'The world is a big place,' a client told me once, 'and we don't need Tucumán.'"[18]

Colombres related numerous examples of legal dysfunction. Foreign investors in particular have suffered hardships when their rights were not protected. Phibro, a major U.S. commodities trading firm, decided to invest in the province, providing $20 million in financing to a local sugar mill secured by sugar inventory. When the mill ran into problems, workers seized the factory and refused to leave until they were paid. Phibro, a secured creditor, was prevented by the seizure from obtaining its collateral, and courts failed to order the workers to stand aside. Months went by before an accommodation was finally reached, and Phibro never came back to Tucumán. In another case, a French company won the bid to provide water service when the provincial utility was privatized. Bidders had been required to offer a very high level of service, so the French company needed to impose a significant rate hike. In the face of public complaints about the higher rates, government officials began to look for ways out of the contract, and ultimately encouraged customers to stop paying for their water service. Collection rates plummeted to 25 percent, whereupon the French company terminated service and sued the province. After two years, international arbitrators have referred the matter back to local courts.

Foreign investors do not suffer alone in Tucumán: Creditors generally face serious obstacles when attempting to collect on their debts. In particular, it takes an average of five years to foreclose on a commercial mortgage in Tucumán. Given the punishingly high interest rates that prevail now in Argentina, such delays can render even excellent collateral insufficient to cover the amount ultimately due. The net effect of a system that leaves investors and creditors so badly exposed is simple: less investment, less financing, and therefore less growth and opportunity.

The failures of the Argentine legal system cannot be chalked up to insufficient funding. Total federal, provincial, and municipal spending on the judiciary came to 0.54 percent of gross domestic product in 1993—up from 0.39 percent of GDP in 1980 with no apparent improvement in service. By contrast, total spending on federal, state, and local courts in the United States amounted to only 0.33 percent of GDP in 1993, or roughly half the level of spending in Argentina.[19] The problem lies, not in a lack of resources, but rather a lack of accountability. There is nobody in the government at any level who is responsible for ensuring the prompt and reliable administration of justice; there are no consequences for anyone in the system when the system breaks down. Under such conditions, a total disconnect between the public sector and the public good is all but inevitable.

※※※

What is the link between a country's legal system and its rate of economic growth? Good legal institutions facilitate market development by reducing transaction costs.[20] Finding partners with whom to conduct mutually beneficial exchanges, settling the terms of those exchanges, monitoring compliance with agreed-upon terms, and enforcing compliance with those terms—all of these transaction costs are obstacles that must be overcome before market activity can occur. Specifically, if such costs outweigh the benefits of particular market exchanges, those exchanges will generally not be pursued. Accordingly, the lower the transaction costs, the broader the range of potentially profitable exchange opportunities for market participants to discover and exploit.

Consider, by way of analogy, the rise of the Internet. The explosion of new businesses unleashed by the advent and expansion of the World Wide Web is the emphatic response of entrepreneurs to a dramatic fall in transaction costs. Because of Internet technology, it has suddenly become much cheaper to bring together buyers and sellers of a wide range of products. As a result, entirely new types of businesses—such as Amazon.com, eBay, and

Priceline on the business-to-consumer side, and EnronOnline on the business-to-business side—have sprung into existence to explore the vast but untested possibilities of e-commerce. Of course, how best to take advantage of the Internet's reduction of transaction costs is shrouded in uncertainty, and so it should be no surprise that the discovery process of the past few years has included many wrong turns and stumbles. For all the recent shakeouts, though, Internet technology has indisputably broadened economic horizons—and has done so by conquering previously insurmountable transaction costs.

The rules of property and contract, and the institutions that define and enforce them, may be thought of as a kind of original Internet. They roll back the tides of transaction costs to reveal vast new terrains of market opportunity—terrains that entrepreneurs can explore and then cultivate for the mutual enrichment of all. Specifically, enforceable property and contract rules dramatically expand not only the circle of people with whom dealings are possible but also the time horizons over which dealings can extend. When property rights are insecure and agreements are not legally binding, market participants will do business only with people they know and trust, or in situations where exchanges can be consummated face to face. All other possibilities are precluded by the high costs of monitoring and ensuring compliance. Good legal institutions slash those costs and thus allow a much more complex, and prosperous, division of labor than otherwise would be possible.

As the economist Mancur Olson was wise to point out, poor countries today are not struggling because of a general lack of markets:

> Those who live in low-income economies know that there are shops and market days in the villages, bazaars in the towns, and peddlers hawking their wares on the street. The number of shops and peddlers in a large, poor city such as Calcutta is almost uncountable. The largest number of markets that I have ever seen in one place was in far-from-prosperous Moscow in early 1992, where there were people buying and selling at almost every metro stop and street corner.[21]

Olson argued persuasively that underdevelopment reflects, not the absence of markets generally, but rather the absence of particular types of markets—namely, "socially contrived" or "property-rights-intensive" markets that arise and flower only with the help of appropriate, government-provided legal institutions. For example, capital-intensive industry—an essential component of Western prosperity—entails high fixed costs that must be amortized over many years. Industries of this type can never arise and develop spontaneously except where property rights are reasonably secure. Likewise, sophisticated financial markets (whose vital importance to wealth creation was reviewed in the previous chapter) are utterly dependent upon reliable contract enforcement.

In what are now the rich countries, property rights were sufficiently well defined and protected to allow industrialization and the phenomenal elevation of living standards that it provides. There have been important exceptions—notably, inadequate enforcement of creditor and investor rights has stunted the growth of capital markets everywhere outside the Anglo-Saxon countries—but overall the legal infrastructure upon which markets are based is firmly in place and has been for many decades, or, in some cases, centuries. For these fortunate countries, the great threat to markets has been an overlying burden of statist controls, not an inadequate foundation of legal institutions. It is understandable, therefore, why market critics in the advanced nations tend to think of economic liberalism as always anti-government. Those essential government activities that undergird a liberal market order are, by and large, so routine and uncontroversial that they do not figure in the ongoing debate over the role of government. In that context, economic liberals are always seen demanding less government intervention, and so develops the misconception that "the less government, the better" is the sum and substance of their position.

But the situation is altogether different for roughly five billion of the earth's six billion people. In the underdeveloped world, it is the underdevelopment of legal institutions that is especially debilitating. In a continuum from bad to worse—from corrupt officials and inadequate courts, to laws so dysfunctional that many or most people are chased into the informal sector, to the arbitrary confiscations of kleptocratic misrule, to the chaos of Hobbesian anarchy—the poorer countries are all plagued by the insufficient protection of property and contract rights. Under these conditions, most economic activity is confined to what Olson called "spontaneous" or "self-enforcing" markets—markets based on personal relationships or face-to-face contact. But those markets, however resilient and durable, cannot produce the division of labor upon which affluence depends. They are a dead end, or at best a holding pattern.

In the early 1990s—as Latin America was overcoming its debt crisis with bold liberal reforms, and the former Soviet bloc was throwing off the shackles of communism—it appeared to many friends of markets that a golden age of economic growth was at hand. International investors swooned over the prospects of "emerging markets," and pundits proclaimed the arrival of a "borderless world." Disappointing results in recent years, though, have erased that naïve optimism, and, in many quarters, have made such terms as "neoliberalism" and "privatization" into epithets. What went wrong?

In the past two chapters, and in the chapter that follows this one, I make the case that the elimination of government controls over economic life has not progressed as far as most people believe. Despite real gains over the past two decades, state-owned enterprises, price and entry controls, and other barriers to competition remain depressingly pervasive. But that is not the whole story. Removing top-down controls is a necessary condition for robust and self-sustaining economic development, but it is not a sufficient one. In addition, governments must take the affirmative steps of creating and nurturing the legal institutions that underlie market competition. The widespread failure to do so has saddled poorer countries with a growth-stunting rule of lawlessness—yet another bitter legacy of the Industrial Counterrevolution.

Nowhere is that legacy more evident today than in Africa. Although he completely misreads the implications of the fact, Thomas Friedman is correct in identifying that tragic continent as the place where the absence of government is at its most wretched. Property rights, and even basic personal safety, are miserably insecure; as a consequence, the promise of globalization is more remote there than almost any place on earth.

At its worst Africa presents a picture of unmitigated chaos. In Rwanda, a genocidal rampage by Hutu tribe members against rival Tutsis in 1994 left up to a million people dead, forced two million out of the country, and displaced yet another million internally. A civil war in Sudan has dragged on since 1983; combat, famine, and disease have claimed an estimated two million lives. In Sierra Leone, a ghastly ten-year conflict between the government and the insurgent Revolutionary United Front has featured rape, mass amputations, and ritual cannibalism; the soldiers on both sides are often children, whose induction into service can include being forced to kill their parents. Somalia, torn apart by contending warlords, has not had a central government since 1991.

Too often the alternative to chaos has been brutal tyranny. Over the course of the 1970s and '80s, the trio of Idi Amin, Milton Obote, and Tito Okello in Uganda murdered more than 800,000 people. From 1972 to 1979, the death toll under President Francisco Marcias Nguema of Equatorial Guinea came to 50,000, or one-seventh of the population.[22] Today, despotism—if less spectacularly bloodthirsty—remains a fixture of African political life. Freedom House's most recent world survey of political rights and civil liberties examined 53 African nations; it rated 21 countries as "not free," and only eight as "free."[23] Arbitrary imprisonment, extrajudicial killing, and confiscation of property are commonplace.

Repression has been accompanied by massive-scale looting. Although other examples can be cited *ad nauseam,* few regimes can match the kleptocratic heights achieved by Mobutu Sese Seko in the country formerly known as Zaire. Mobutu, who ruled from 1965 until 1997, treated the rich natural resources of his country as his own private property. He took personal control of diamond and gold mines, the marketing of cobalt and copper, and the management of Zaire's coffee plantations; some 60 percent of the government's annual revenues were lost or diverted to him and his cronies. He acquired dozens of properties around the world, including orchards and a vineyard in Portugal, a 32-room mansion in Switzerland, and a 16th century castle in Spain. He expanded the airport in his home village of Gbadolite to allow landings by the supersonic Concorde, which he frequently chartered from Air France. His Swiss bank accounts were believed to contain billions of dollars. The country, meanwhile, descended into complete and utter ruin. One chilling statistic tells the broader picture: When it gained its independence in 1960, Zaire's main roads ran 31,000 miles, only 3,700 miles of which were still passable a mere 20 years later.[24]

There is no possibility of economic development under these kinds of conditions. When predators reign, planning ahead is foolhardy; trusting anyone other than the closest intimates is a potentially fatal mistake. Economic horizons are reduced to the shortest of short terms, and entrepreneurial activity (to the extent it exists at all) lurks furtively in the shadows on the smallest of small scales.

Africa fell into the abyss under the spell of collectivism. George Ayittey, a Ghanaian-born intellectual who writes searingly of Africa's tragic postcolonial history, explains the special allure that runaway centralization held for the new African states:

> A wave of socialism swept across the continent as almost all the new African leaders succumbed to the contagious ideology. The dalliance and fascination with socialism seemed to have emerged during the struggle for political independence and freedom from colonial rule in the 1950s. Many African nationalists harbored a deep distrust and distaste for capitalism, which, with Lenin, they identified as an extension of colonialism and imperialism. Consequently, they interpreted freedom from colonial rule as freedom from capitalism as well.[25]

The result was economic, institutional, and political catastrophe. Natural-resource industries were nationalized, and agriculture was ensnared in a mad tangle of price controls and confiscatory marketing boards. Economic centralization not only stifled the discovery process of competitive markets; it also precipitated an orgy of corruption. Once national wealth was under government control, the temptation to exert that control for private enrichment proved irresistible. Meanwhile, the logic of central planning proved a handy excuse for centralization of political power, as fledgling parliamentary democracies were quickly dispatched by a rogue's gallery of military dictators and Presidents-for-life. Political violence then escalated to sickening levels: If exclusion from power meant repression or even death, and enjoyment of power meant fantastic riches, how could any other outcome be possible? And all the while, as chaos and savagery consumed the continent, the sweet perfume of socialist ideology helped to mask the stench of putrefaction.

It is the intimate connection between Africa's disastrous lack of government on the one hand and its woeful excess of statist tyranny on the other that Thomas Friedman completely fails to grasp. African governments do too little today in large part because in the past they presumed to do too much. Instead of undertaking the vital but unglamorous responsibility of building market-friendly institutions, they actively wrecked those markets that existed in pursuit of grandiose schemes of centralized control. In many cases, they destroyed in the process their societies' capacity for generating new markets—and thus for overcoming the mistakes of the past. Africa's plight is therefore not, as Friedman imagines, a rebuke to excessive enthusiasm for free markets. On the contrary, Africa today reveals the dead hand of collectivism at its most oppressive.

⌇⌇⌇⌇

The security of property and contract rights cannot be safeguarded in a vacuum. Ultimately, the quality of market institutions is inseparable from the structure of political institutions. What the rules are depends crucially on who gets to make them and how.

A country's legal framework functions to the extent that its political system succeeds in meeting two different and conflicting challenges. First, it must produce a government strong enough to enforce rules and uphold their integrity against powerful private groups that seek to hold themselves above the law. At the same time, the political system must constrain government officials from placing themselves above the law. James Madison summed up the problem over two centuries ago in the *Federalist Papers*. "In framing a government which is to be administered by men over men," he wrote, "the great difficulty lies in this: you must first enable the government to control the governed; and in the next place oblige it to control itself." [26]

There is no magic formula for meeting these challenges. Autocratic governments with blood on their hands have sometimes succeeded, while democratic governments have sometimes failed miserably. On balance, though, both theory and history point to a link between accountability to the broad public and a functional rule of law.

The most obvious threat to legal order posed by dictatorship is the absence of any institutional constraints on power. Human nature being what it is, that absence is all too often a recipe for disaster. The dolorous political history of the 20th century is packed with confirmations of Lord Acton's dictum: autocratic regimes, accountable to no one, that have preyed on their own people like wolves among sheep. Nothing is more destructive to legal order than a rogue government bent on plunder. No property is safe, no agreements can be relied upon, and, consequently, no complex division of labor is possible. Economic life remains stunted and impoverished, confined to small-scale, short-term activities that lie low and hide from the rapacious gaze of predatory government.

Even if an autocratic government is more or less able to control itself, its control over those it governs is often deceptively fragile. Dictatorships are chronically unstable because they lack any institutional mechanism for transferring power. And since the stakes of gaining or losing power are so high, transitions are frequently bloody. They can also be highly disruptive: Groups that flourished under the favor of the old regime are suddenly targeted for persecution under the new. Political instability thus translates into legal instability, which once again undermines the kind of large-scale, long-term investments upon which prosperity in a modern industrial society depends.

Finally, just because a government wields unrestricted power doesn't mean that it is firmly in the saddle. Indeed, a regime's resort to repressive measures is often an indication of how tenuous its grasp on power really is. To maintain power without broad public support, many autocratic governments find it necessary to use special subsidies and privileges to buy the allegiance of other power centers within society. The auctioning off of state favors can end up badly compromising the regime's own autonomy—thus the spectacle of a seemingly all-powerful government that, in fact, is the pawn of powerful private interests. The weak but despotic government is incapable of upholding secure and stable property rights, which now are vulnerable to the depredations of multiple predators.

Nevertheless, history does provide examples of so-called "benevolent dictatorships": regimes that, although they suppress political dissent (and sometimes brutally), exhibit decent restraint when it comes to plundering the property of their citizens, and maintain security and stability long enough to promote sustained economic growth. Indeed, many of the fastest-growing economies of recent times—Chile, Korea, Taiwan, Hong Kong, Singapore, Indonesia, Malaysia, Thailand, and China—began their ascent (and in the cases of China, Malaysia, and Singapore, continue it) by combining a lack of political rights with tolerable security for property rights.[27] Those recent success stories, concentrated as they are along the Pacific Rim, gave rise to notions of an "Asian model" of politics as well as economics— a model that supposedly demonstrated that development proceeds best without too much democracy.

Special circumstances allowed those high-performing economies to escape the usual sad destiny of autocracies. A combination of external and internal factors oriented their leaders toward promoting long-term growth instead of maximizing short-term plunder, and at the same time shielded political life from takeover by economically destructive narrow interests. For many of those economies, the threat of communism was enormously important in shaping the incentives of political leaders. In Korea and Taiwan, Southeast Asia and Chile, leaders were acutely aware of their vulnerability in the face of the communist challenge, and were therefore determined to repel that challenge with broad-based economic growth. In Taiwan and China, leaders were further chastened by past failures: Chiang Kai-Shek knew that endemic corruption had contributed to his downfall on the mainland, while Deng Xiaoping was resolved to turn China away from the mayhem of the Cultural Revolution.

At the same time that leaders in those economies were unusually disposed toward controlling themselves, many were also unusually well positioned to exert control over those they governed. Specifically, they were relatively immune from pressure and manipulation by privilege-seeking private interests. The Hong Kong colonial government, controlled from distant Great Britain, did not have to answer (at least directly) to its subjects. The Nationalist government in Taiwan was also a kind of foreign occupying power: Mandarin-speaking refugees from the mainland who dominated the Taiwanese-speaking natives. Accordingly, narrow interests in Taiwan had little access to state-granted favors. In Korea, General Park Chung-Hee launched his country's amazing economic rise by initiating a ruthless crackdown on business elites in 1962. Like countless plundering autocrats, he jailed most major business leaders and expropriated their holdings; but then, contrary to type, he agreed to release them and their property in exchange for support for a new export-led growth strategy. The power of vested interests attached to the old import-substitution policy had been shattered.

Despite their successes, the growth-friendly autocracies of recent times have had a pronounced tendency to outgrow themselves. The progress of wealth creation breeds new power centers within society, which over time grow increasingly restive about their exclusion from political decision-making. Governing cliques find themselves under mounting pressure to share power—hence the gradual process of democratization seen in Chile, Korea, Taiwan, and Thailand. Under these conditions, autocratic rule is especially vulnerable in the event of a sharp economic downturn. These regimes stake their claim to legitimacy on economic performance; when performance nosedives, that claim begins to dissolve. The 1997–98 financial crisis was thus a debacle for the Asian model of politics as well as of economics: In Indonesia, the seemingly all-powerful Suharto regime toppled in a matter of months; in Korea, the election of Kim Dae-Jung as president marked the first-ever victory by an opposition candidate; and in Thailand, a new, more democratic constitution won parliamentary approval. On the other hand, the Malaysian *reformasi* movement proved abortive, and the current regimes in Singapore and China still look secure. But now it seems that Asia's pro-growth autocrats are clinging to the past rather than defining the future.

The present era of globalization has rejoined the causes of economic liberalism and democracy under a single banner. In Latin America and, to a lesser extent, Africa and East Asia, dictatorships—benevolent and otherwise—have given way to popular rule, just as statist controls around the world have given way to markets. The association of economic and political freedom is by no means novel: In the 19th century, liberal reformers sought both to extend the franchise and remove obstacles to market competition. It was only the advent of the Industrial Counterrevolution that put the two causes at odds. Economic liberals grew suspicious of popular sovereignty in response to the rise of mass collectivist movements; at the same time, collectivists campaigned for "economic democracy" as the complement to political freedom or—more radically—as the only real democracy.

But though it appropriated the rhetoric of democracy, the Industrial Counterrevolution proved highly congenial to monstrous tyranny, as the enslavement of millions living in so-called "democratic republics" so grimly demonstrated. The belief in centralization was all too easy to carry over from economics into politics. Rationality meant top-down control, and for those who pursued this logic to its limits, it followed that both the chaos of the marketplace and the chaos of "bourgeois" democracy were equally useless anachronisms. Meanwhile, those collectivists who retained their allegiance to political freedom were often hard pressed to condemn even the most hideous crimes committed in the name of their ideology. They excused the "excesses" of "democrats in a hurry"; the centralizing tyrants mocked their naïve apologists as "useful idiots."

The combination of despotism and collectivism throughout the old Communist bloc and Third World set the stage for the present-day reunion of political and economic liberalism. Revolutionary governments used the promise of accelerated development (and, of course, terror) to substitute for the lack of a popular mandate; moreover, belief in that promise emboldened political leaders to use terror when necessary. Consequently, as disillusionment with economic centralization spread around the world, the justification for autocratic rule began to erode. At the same time that momentum for market-based liberalization was building, popular resistance to repression hardened while despots were losing the will to spill more blood. And thus the overlapping and mutually reinforcing waves that have swept the planet over the past couple of decades: political and economic reform, democracy and free markets.

The recurring historical connections between democracy and free markets are not accidental: There is a deep affinity between the two ideals. Both systems are animated by the fundamental liberal value of autonomy: The market order upholds individual autonomy against top-down control, while democracy upholds collective autonomy against any narrow ruling class. In other words, the genius of both systems is to rely on decentralized decision-making. The market holds producers accountable to consumers, while democracy requires politicians to seek the consent of voters. The market is always open to new investments and new ideas; likewise, democracy allows new political movements to spring spontaneously from any quarter of society.

Because of its decentralization of power, democracy offers the surest foundation for protecting the legal order within which market competition unfolds. Popular government offers clear advantages over autocratic rule with respect to both controlling the governed and controlling itself. Laws blessed with the mandate of popular consent are much less subject to challenge and defiance; furthermore, the peaceful transfer of power ensures that legal protections are shielded from internal convulsions. Democracy thus fortifies the legal framework with legitimacy and stability. At the same time, by holding rulers accountable to the broad public and maintaining open avenues for outsiders to challenge incumbents, popular government guards against abusive ruling cliques that would place themselves above the law. It is no coincidence that the world's most advanced market economies are also stable democracies.

But the process of democratization is strewn with pitfalls. For just as market competition needs an infrastructure of legal institutions in order to function properly, so too does democracy require proper political institutions to fulfill its promise. Democracy is more than just free elections and majority rule, just as free markets are more than the absence of government controls. When democracy is not ensconced in an appropriately supportive political culture, its forms may be present but its substance will be sorely lacking.

Democracy is supposed to mean more than broadly inclusive procedures. It is also supposed to produce broadly inclusive results. The policies of a popular government should reflect public opinion, not the back-room maneuverings of scheming cliques; they should serve the general welfare, not the grasping of narrow interests. True democracy is government of the people, by the people, and for the people. But that ideal cannot be attained—indeed, not even a recognizable approximation of that ideal can be attained—without a long and tortuous process of political development.

Countries just beginning the transition to democracy often lack even rudimentary institutions for holding selfish interests in check. In such countries, the substitution of competitive elections for autocratic rule can prove, at least initially, a hollow victory. A fundamental problem remains: As before, state power is still treated as the private possession of the rulers. Only now, power is not seized by armed might; instead it is bought and sold. In this degraded and corrupted form, democracy is a kind of commercial enterprise: Politicians invest in power by purchasing votes and doling out favors, and then reap the rewards in graft and lucrative privileges. As a result, the market order—and the great public good of growth and opportunity it provides—is doubly embattled. It is distorted and deformed from above by a tangle of special-interest quotas, licenses, subsidies, and controls, and is simultaneously undermined from below by a legal system that too frequently sides with the highest bidder.

Immature democracies are especially prone to this kind of dysfunction because of a basic rule of political organization. As the economist Mancur Olson made clear in his groundbreaking work on the subject, different types of groups in society have different capacities for organizing and asserting their interests in the political arena. Because of the "free-rider" problems associated with collective action, it is much easier to organize small groups with narrow, focused interests than large groups with broad, diffuse interests. Consequently, in countries without longstanding traditions of popular participation in political life, narrow interests that seek their own selfish gain at the expense of the general welfare have a natural head start in jockeying for power.

Nonetheless, there is hope—over time. If basic democratic rights can be maintained, the organization of interests will continue, and the laggards—the broader, more diffuse interests—will begin to catch up. Meanwhile, as economic growth proceeds, the variety of narrow interests will proliferate. As a result, the task of raiding the public trust for private gain becomes much harder. It is now necessary to overcome resistance from a growing number of conflicting narrow interests as well as the opposition of increasingly vigorous organizations that claim to speak for the public good. Moreover, public attitudes change with economic development. As more and more people move from the villages to the cities and integrate their lives into the national, and world, economy, the general interest in a growing, thriving economy becomes increasingly relevant to them. They begin to expect more from politicians than an envelope full of cash on election day; they begin to expect, and demand, good policies.[28]

Thailand's political history over the past generation provides a case in point. Until the 1970s, it was a volatile, if relatively benign, autocracy dominated by the military and royal bureaucracy. Political life was confined to members of a small ruling class; while often enlivened by coups and failed plots, it did not involve or engage the great body of a mostly rural society. The 1970s, though, saw democratic activism and the rise of political parties that represented the interests of newly powerful elements of Thai society—namely, the Bangkok business elite (mostly ethnic Chinese) and the so-called *chao po* or provincial bosses.

The *chao po* had gotten rich in resource-based industries, government contracting, and a host of illicit enterprises—jewelry smuggling, gun running, the drug trade, and prostitution. At home, they translated their wealth into influence through patronage and liberal distribution of cash. And in Bangkok, they converted their ability to deliver votes into political power—which they, in turn, used to get even richer.

As the military's political strength gradually declined, the provincial bosses became the dominant force in Thai politics. With a winning populist style, they pursued a single, simple goal—maximizing wealth and advantages for themselves and their friends. Their chief rivals were the business interests and growing middle classes of Bangkok, who tended to favor cleaner government and more professional economic management. The balance of power between the provinces and the capital turned, though, on this fundamental fact: The Bangkok metropolitan area accounts for about half of Thailand's total economic output but only about 10 percent of its population. Thus, although the urban middle classes wielded considerable influence, the provincial bosses controlled the votes.

The mismatch between metropolitan wealth and provincial power, amidst the backdrop of fading but occasionally reassertive authoritarianism, put Thai politics in a turbulent cycle of corruption, crackdown, democratic agitation, and reform. The 1988 election of a civilian government was the major breakthrough that brought the *chao po* to national power. The government of Prime Minister Chatichai Choonhavan was called the "buffet cabinet" because the ministers took an "all you can eat" approach to enjoying the perquisites of office. By 1991 Bangkok and the military had had enough; a bloodless coup ousted Chatichai and installed a caretaker government of well-respected technocrats to clean up the mess.

The generals then tried to reclaim power for themselves, but Bangkok was outraged. In May 1992 thousands camped out in the streets to protest the drift toward authoritarianism. A ruthless attempt to disperse the protesters killed hundreds, until the king—intensely revered but usually nonpolitical—called for the bloodshed to stop. In September 1992 a new election pitted the pro-democracy "angels" against the pro-military "devils"; the angels, led by Chuan Leekpai, carried the day. But by 1995 the voting power of the provinces could no longer be denied, and new elections brought a government led by Banharn Silpa-archa—known as the "walking ATM" for his shameless embrace of money politics—and a motley cast of cronies. Endless scandals caused the Banharn government to fall in 1996, but the new government led by General Chavalit Yongchaiyudh was little better.[29]

The financial meltdown of 1997 gave new impetus to political reform. Rule by the provinces was discredited by its complicity in the economic disaster, and Chuan Leekpai and his Democratic party returned to power. More important, a new reformist constitution was able to win passage in Parliament. Among other important structural changes, the constitution calls for the creation of various independent watchdog bodies—an Election Commission, a Human Rights Commission, a Counter-Corruption Commission, and a Constitutional Court—whose purpose is to increase transparency and restrain the corrupting influence of money politics.

So far the new constitution has had mixed results. In the first direct election of Senators in March 2000 (formerly the Senate was an appointed body and stuffed with hacks), the Election Commission tossed out the results in 78 of the 200 races because of vote-buying, and then ordered multiple rounds of polling before all the results were pronounced clean—an impressive flexing of reformist muscle. On the other hand, the Human Rights Commission was effectively neutered when it was placed under executive branch control and staffed with yes-men. And in January 2001, telecom tycoon Thaksin Shinawatra led his new Thai Rak Thai ("Thais Love Thais") party to an overwhelming victory in parliamentary elections on a populist platform—despite the fact that Thaksin was under indictment from the Counter-Corruption Commission for failure to meet financial disclosure requirements. Thaksin was later cleared of the charges against him in an intensely controversial court decision.

Anand Panyarachun, a highly respected former prime minister and principal architect of the new constitution, is philosophical about Thailand's messy political evolution. "We have been progressing well over the past nine years," he told me in January 2000. "We have now had several successions of power in a constitutional context"—that is, without a coup. Looking ahead, he is optimistic that the new constitution will succeed in cleaning up Thai politics, "but we'll need two more general election cycles, perhaps another seven or eight years," before the effects are really visible. "Sometimes, when you're flushing a toilet," he said with a laugh, "you need to do it two or three times." [30]

It must be understood, though, that merely getting rid of the most vulgar forms of political corruption does not dispense with the threat that narrow interests pose to democratic governance—and to the liberal market order. That threat—what James Madison in the *Federalist Papers* called the problem of "faction"—is ineradicable; at best it can be contained. "The friend of popular governments," Madison wrote, "never finds himself so much alarmed for their character and fate as when he contemplates their propensity to this dangerous vice." [31] What was true over two centuries ago remains true today. Although democratic government aspires to policies that reflect a broad public interest, it is always highly vulnerable to the usurpations of narrow groups—what Madison called "factions," and we call "special interests"—whose superior organizational ability allows them to bend public power to their own private ends.

In today's developed democracies we see that vulnerability exploited to the nth degree. The mad proliferation of organized lobbies, their dominance of a now incomprehensibly arcane policymaking process, and the resulting alienation of ordinary citizens from what transpires supposedly in their name—all of these dreary commonplaces of contemporary political life are too familiar to require elaboration here. Their combined effect is to rob democracy of its highest promise, and degrade the public good of market competition with a thousand encrustations, great and small, of narrow-interest privilege.[32]

If this malady is ever to be remedied, the lost wisdom of James Madison and his fellow framers of the U.S. Constitution must first be recovered. Over two centuries ago they saw clearly what today is all but forgotten: The best hope for containing the problem of faction lies in constitutional limits on government power. With their elaborate system of checks and balances, the restriction of government powers to those specifically enumerated, and reservation of rights to the people on which no government can intrude, they sought to craft a constitution that would act as a series of institutional filters—through which would pass the rambunctious, faction-ridden rough-and-tumble of political activity and from which would emerge only those policies that bear a plausible relation to some broadly shared and relatively stable public good.

In the United States, much of the framers' constitutional vision was swept aside during the 1930s to clear the way for the lunge toward centralization. Meanwhile, none of the other industrialized democracies ever did more than dabble with constitutional limits on government power. In recent decades, the pioneering work of Nobel Prize-winning economist James Buchanan has reawakened academic interest in constitutional design.[33] But the project of liberal political reform—of bringing popular government within the discipline of constitutional limits—remains in its infancy. For many years to come, therefore, the market order's political foundation will always be shaky at best.

9

Unpeaceful Coexistence

Over the past three chapters I have endeavored to show that the supposedly worldwide ascendancy of market forces, claimed with equal vigor by both friends and foes of globalization, is nothing more than wild hyperbole. State-owned enterprises, the classic instrumentalities of the command economy, loom large in the economic lives of most of the world's population. Price controls are rampant in dozens of countries. Around the planet, particular sectors—energy, transportation, agriculture, and telecommunications—bear the heavy imprint of centralization and monopoly. Trade barriers seriously impede the flow of goods in developing countries and in important sectors of the advanced nations. At the heart of economic life, top-down controls and an absence of well-developed markets hideously distort the core function of capital allocation in most of the world. And, outside a relatively few rich countries, the basic underpinnings of the market economy—the legal infrastructure of property and contract rules—are pitifully underdeveloped after decades of malign neglect.

This gloomy picture, though accurate so far as it goes, is nonetheless incomplete. While the dead hand of collectivism remains a major force in economic affairs, the past couple of decades have witnessed dramatic changes. The Soviet Empire has fallen and its economic system has been wiped irretrievably from the face of the earth. China is now communist in name only. India, which for decades followed Soviet-style central planning, has turned to the path of liberal reform. The populist corporatism of Latin America was dealt a crushing blow by the debt crises of the 1980s. Privatization has swept the mixed economies of Western Europe. And economic deregulation in the United States has blown open a host of key industries that were previously encased in restrictive controls.

What then is a fair characterization of the world's present situation? Not the triumph of markets, to be sure, but it is fair to say that we are experiencing the collapse of collectivism—the demise of the Industrial Counterrevolution. On the wreckage of this collapse we may one day succeed in building a truly liberal international economic order. That happy outcome is imaginable today in a way that it most assuredly was not just a few years ago. But imagining and achieving are two different things, and the latter remains on the distant horizon.

The current situation then is at best a transitional phase—a twilight era juxtaposed between the statist past and a liberal future. In this in-between time, elements of past and future jostle uneasily alongside each other. And thus far, coexistence has proved anything but peaceful.

During the past several years the tensions between market and anti-market forces have erupted repeatedly in spectacular upheavals in what had been called, somewhat precipitously in some cases, "emerging markets." These economic temblors—first in Mexico in December 1994, followed by East Asia over the course of 1997–98, and then in Russia in August 1998—produced shock waves that were felt around the world. Other, lesser disturbances have occurred more recently in Brazil, Ecuador, Argentina, and Turkey, and future shakeups, great and small, are virtually a certainty.

The critics of globalization have seized upon these episodes as proof of the perils of unregulated markets. Financier George Soros makes that case in *The Crisis of Global Capitalism:*

> Financial markets are inherently unstable and there are social needs that cannot be met by giving market forces free rein. Unfortunately these defects are not recognized. Instead there is a widespread belief that markets are self-correcting and a global economy can flourish without any need for a global society. . . . This idea was called laissez faire in the nineteenth century but . . . I have found a better name for it: market fundamentalism. . . .
>
> [T]he ideology of market fundamentalism is profoundly and irredeemably flawed. To put the matter simply, market forces, if they are given complete authority even in the purely economic and financial arenas, produce chaos and could ultimately lead to the downfall of the global capitalist system.[1]

Anthony Giddens, director of the London School of Economics and widely acclaimed guru of the "third way" movement in Great Britain and elsewhere, echoes Soros' charge—to the point of using the same locution to disparage free markets. "Market fundamentalism has been forced into retreat in domestic politics because of its limited and contradictory nature," he writes. "Yet it still continues to reign at a global level, in spite of the fact that the same problems appear there as more locally." The results of this state of affairs, he contends, can be seen in the recent financial turmoil in Mexico and East Asia: "Crises, erratic fluctuations, the sudden rush of capital into and out of particular countries and regions—these are not marginal but core features of untamed markets."[2]

Such thinking has seeped deeply into the conventional wisdom. Consider, for example, a November 2000 cover story in *Business Week* entitled "Global Capitalism: Can it be made to work better?" "The downside of global capitalism," its authors state, "is the disruption of whole societies, from financial meltdowns to practices by multinationals that would never be tolerated in the West. . . . [T]he global economy is pretty much still in the robber-baron age."[3]

The facts are plain enough: The world economy today is prone to wild swings in financial flows and consequent crippling dislocations. But is it true, as market critics contend, that such volatility is due to, in the words of Soros and Giddens, "market fundamentalism"? Absolutely not. The evidence of the prior three chapters in this book makes abundantly clear that "market fundamentalism" is a straw man: It is a faith practiced nowhere on this earth. At present and for the foreseeable future, the influence of market forces on world economic affairs is deeply compromised by overweening interventionism on the one hand and underdeveloped institutions on the other.

As I explore in further detail for the remainder of this chapter, the recent turbulence in international finance is due not to markets run amok but to collisions between markets and their antithesis. It may be conceded, therefore, that the partial liberalization of the world economy over the past couple of decades is responsible for recent outbreaks of instability. My difference with the critics of globalization, though, is that they blame the liberalization, while I blame its partial nature.

Before reviewing the specific facts of individual financial crises, it is worth stepping back and trying to place the scapegoating of "market fundamentalism" in broader context. In their repudiation of liberal reform, both Soros and Giddens take pains to disavow any allegiance to old-style central planning. "Individual decision making as expressed through the market mechanism," writes Soros, "is much more efficient than collective decision making as practiced in politics."[4] Giddens, meanwhile, concedes that "[s]ocialism . . . failed to grasp the significance of markets as informational devices, providing essential data for buyers and sellers."[5]

Notwithstanding such disclaimers, the mindset that gave rise to the faith in comprehensive central planning still dominates the perspective of globalization's critics. After all, if—as is perfectly obvious—the world today is a jumble of market-oriented and anti-market elements, and if markets are recognized as efficient and useful while full-blown collectivism is counted a failure, why blame markets and not the remnants of discredited collectivism for the fact that the current jumble is sometimes volatile? The answer lies in patterns of thought deeply engrained during the century-long eclipse of economic liberalism. Still in thrall to those thought patterns, even thinkers as sophisticated as Soros and Giddens cannot shed their belief that markets are inherently suspect because no central authority is in charge of them. Order, in their view, is primarily something imposed from the top down; they do not fully grasp the creative power of the complex order that can emerge from bottom-up coordination.

Thus, both Soros and Giddens portray markets as tending naturally toward chaos. How can any system without central direction operate otherwise? With their abiding trust in top-down control, they see as the major threat to international economic order, not national-level mismanagement and dysfunction, but the absence of direction at the top. "To stabilize and regulate a truly global economy," Soros argues, "we need some global system of political decision making. In short, we need a global society to support our global economy."[6] Giddens expresses precisely the same sentiment when he writes, "Global problems respond to local initiatives but they also demand global solutions. We can't leave such problems to the erratic swirl of global markets. . . ."[7]

The prevailing diagnosis of recent international financial crises as a product of "untamed" markets is thus a testament to the continuing power of the dead hand. We have learned through a century's bitter experience that central planning in its ideal form is utterly unworkable, that collectivism in practice is disastrously dysfunctional, that the apparent chaos of market competition is actually a richly complex and dynamic order, and indeed that market competition is only one species of the larger phenomenon of complex "emergent" orders—and still there is a widespread intellectual reflex to long for orders from above. That reflex leads even highly serious students of world affairs to mistake the messy collapse of collectivism for a market phenomenon, and to prescribe as the cure for vestigial collectivism at the national level a new dose of collectivism on a global scale.

<hr />

For all their underlying differences, the recent financial crises in Latin America, East Asia, and Russia shared the same proximate cause: unsustainable monetary policies. Specifically, all of the crisis-affected countries had "pegged" the exchange value of their currencies to the U.S. dollar; in other words, they had promised that holders of those currencies could redeem them for dollars at a more-or-less fixed rate. By making such promises about the exchange value of their currencies, these countries were, in effect, pledging that their central banks would conduct monetary policy in a way that maintained those currencies' values relative to the dollar at the prescribed levels. As it happened, though, the central banks did not keep up their end of the bargain. In the end the gap between promise and reality grew unbridgeable, and the countries ultimately were forced to renege. Currency values nosedived, and economic devastation ensued.

Monetary policy stands out as perhaps the most perilous minefield in all of contemporary economic life. The importance of getting monetary policy right cannot really be overstated: Over the past century, monetary mistakes have rivaled warfare in their capacity for unleashing economic destruction. At the same time, however, knowing what is right is all too seldom clear.

The root of the problem lies in the nature of contemporary money. All money in the world today is fiat money: It has no anchor in underlying tangible assets, but exists instead purely as a creation of governments. Moreover, virtually all money in the world today is, at least with respect to domestic transactions, monopoly money. Within a given monetary area (usually a single nation-state, but sometimes a union of states), there is only a single issuer of currency, the central bank, and that currency is the only legal tender for the fulfillment of monetary claims within that territory. In international transactions parties can choose among currencies (and the U.S. dollar is their leading choice), but at home the local currency enjoys a legally privileged status.

Under these conditions, the task of supplying liquidity—in other words, a serviceable medium of exchange—must be undertaken without benefit of the marketplace's decentralized discovery process. A growing number of economists have hypothesized that money could be supplied competitively by private issuers, with much better results than central banks have typically managed.[8] However intriguing such possibilities might be, they are presently of academic interest only. In the world as it exists today, money is not a product of the marketplace, but part of the centralized institutional framework within which the marketplace exists.

Consequently, it is unsurprising that monetary policy is bedeviled by uncertainty. In the realm of goods and services, the competitive marketplace—with its widespread and incessant experimentation and clear feedback signals of profit and loss—wrests from the fog of uncertainty an increasingly complex and prosperous economic order. But in the realm of money, the central banks that operate now as monetary monopolies do not lose business if they supply too much or too little liquidity; they do not gain market share if their currency is sounder than those of their competitors. And with nowhere but barter or the black market to turn to when central banks err, whole countries are hostage to their guesswork. Monetary order—compared to the economic order that rests upon it—is therefore of necessity a crude and hit-or-miss affair.

Nothing better illustrates the terrifying fragility of the current system than its utter dependence in recent years on one individual: Alan Greenspan. As he managed, year after year, to dodge the twin perils of inflation and recession, he acquired a reputation as a kind of superhuman economic shaman. Recently, the falling stock market and slowing economy that began in 2000 have prompted suggestions that he might actually be fallible. But as Greenspan himself admits in his signature Delphic style, his job of directing monetary policy has always boiled down to playing hunches. "Although we have learned much about managing the financial backdrop to accelerating economic activity," Greenspan warned in a speech at my workplace, the Cato Institute, "it is essential that we not be deluded into believing that we have somehow discovered the Rosetta Stone of monetary policy. . . . [A]ll policy rests, at least implicitly, on a forecast of a future that we can know only in probabilistic terms."[9] What an absurdly precarious state of affairs: the mind-boggling complexity of the contemporary world economy, with its untold billions of interdependent plans and expectations, all riding on the continued sound judgment of a single man!

Historically, the great nemesis of fiat money has been inflation. In the decades after World War II, central bankers under the spell of Keynes purposefully pursued easy money policies in hopes of attaining full employment and spurring higher economic growth. In that particular variant of the Industrial Counterrevolution, an elite cadre of macroeconomic forecasters would be able to guide the "fine tuning" of the economy to optimal performance levels. The long-term consequences of this approach were uniformly dismal: stagflation in the advanced economies and hyperinflation in the developing world. Bitter experience has now forged a new consensus in favor of a much more modest monetary policy; today price stability is generally understood as the overriding mission of the central bank. Though there has been dramatic progress toward this goal over the past 20 years or so, many countries still find it elusive.

The currency meltdowns that have roiled world markets of late represent another species of monetary dysfunction—one that arises from the interaction between national currencies and international capital flows. It is fashionable nowadays to regard those capital flows as a kind of curse visited upon developing countries by profit-hungry Western speculators. But why then don't poorer countries move to lift the curse? They surely know how to do it: A generation ago, the trend in the Third World was to denounce the inflow of foreign capital as "neocolonialism" and then nationalize foreign investments. Why today do they act so differently? Why do most of the countries that have been rocked by crises persist in exposing their economies to the ebb and flow of foreign investor sentiment? Why has Malaysia, which did institute limited capital controls in response to the crisis, reversed course and begun to dismantle those controls? Why does China, whose existing capital controls spared it from the traumas of 1997–98, still maintain full liberalization of its capital account as a long-term policy goal?

The fact is that most developing countries today recognize that foreign capital is not a curse, but a blessing—albeit one with strings attached. Without access to financing from abroad, poor countries would be forced to fund their economic development exclusively from domestic savings—just as Great Britain did, more or less, at the outset of the Industrial Revolution. With only that limited pool of savings from which to draw, financing costs would be high, and, consequently, only the very most profitable investment projects would receive funding. Expanding the pool of savings to include foreign capital reduces financing costs and thereby increases the number of profitable ventures that can be funded. Openness to foreign capital thus gives struggling economies a shortcut to affluence by allowing them to tap into the resources of advanced, capital-rich nations. And foreign investment brings not only additional financial resources but also foreign technology and foreign know-how.

But can't a distinction be drawn between stable, long-term "direct" investment on the one hand and fickle, mercurial "portfolio" investment on

the other? Direct investment consists of establishing or acquiring foreign operations, whether factories or accounting firm offices or retail shops, in the
host country; such investments entail significant sunk costs and are thus unlikely to be uprooted because of temporarily unfavorable conditions in the
host country. Portfolio investment, by contrast, consists of bond purchases
and noncontrolling equity stakes, which can be abandoned with the click of
a mouse when bad news hits. A similar distinction can be made between
short-term and long-term bank loans. Many critics of free capital flows recognize the benefits of direct investment and long-term lending but advocate
restrictions on volatile short-term capital movements.

But the distinction between short-term and long-term investment is not
a valid one. Openness to portfolio investment confers significant benefits on
recipient countries that cannot be replaced by more direct investment.[10] Direct investment allows foreign companies to expand operations in developing countries, but if indigenous companies in developing countries want to
tap into foreign capital, portfolio investment is their only option. Controls
on portfolio investment therefore stunt the growth of domestic enterprises
in poorer countries. Many studies in recent years confirm that openness to
portfolio investment increases the depth, breadth, and liquidity of local
financial markets, reduces the cost of capital, boosts the level of private
investment, and raises per capita GDP.[11]

But to reap the advantages of financial openness, countries must make
appropriate and sustainable monetary arrangements. There are only three
available alternatives. First, countries can choose to pursue domestic macroeconomic stability through discretionary monetary policy, in which case
they must allow the value of their currency to fluctuate relative to other currencies. Second, countries can choose to fix the value of their national currency in relation to some foreign reserve currency, in which case they must
forsake independent monetary policy and instead allow the domestic money
supply to fluctuate with foreign reserve balances. Finally, countries may dispense with a national currency altogether and conduct transactions entirely
in a foreign reserve currency. All of these regimes submit to this basic constraint: It is impossible, in a country open to international capital flows, to
control both the internal and external value of money. If a country seeks to
control the internal value (that is, the domestic price level) it must give
up control over the external value or exchange rate. If, on the other hand,
it wants to control the external value of money (whether through a fixed ex-

change rate or adoption of a foreign currency as domestic money) it must abandon attempts to stabilize the domestic price level.

The recent financial crises in Mexico, East Asia, and Russia all took place in countries that tried to have their cake and eat it, too. They sought to control their exchange rate by pegging to the dollar while at the same time pursuing an independent monetary policy. In each case, the pegged rate system created pent-up imbalances in financial flows and then frustrated the adjustments needed to correct them. During good times the system appeared to operate well, but actually good times sowed the seeds of eventual self-destruction. Sooner or later, the arrival of economic bad news triggered the grim endgame: Foreign reserves dwindled, the credibility of the pegs came into question, speculators probed and then attacked, domestic investors began a run on their own currency, and ultimately the peg collapsed.

To understand the perverse dynamics of the pegged rate system, consider first how bona fide fixed and floating regimes respond to international capital movements. In a fixed regime, the monetary authority—often referred to as a currency board rather than a central bank—expands and contracts the local money supply automatically in response to capital flows. When foreign money flows in to invest locally, the monetary authority buys it in exchange for local currency, thus boosting the local money supply. When foreign investors want to take their dollars out of the country, the monetary authority obliges by selling dollars in exchange for local currency, thereby contracting the local money supply.

These fluctuations in the money supply serve to uphold the exchange rate parity by maintaining the full backing of the local currency by foreign reserves. Moreover, they also work to equilibrate capital movements. Capital inflows trigger a looser money supply, which causes interest rates to fall and local prices to rise. These consequences, in turn, dampen foreign demand for the local currency, because returns are now lower and asset prices have risen. By the same token, a reduction or reversal of capital inflows prompts a tightening of the money supply, with higher interest rates and lower prices. These changes serve to lure foreign investment back into the country.

In a floating rate system, the adjustment to foreign capital flows occurs, not in local prices and interest rates, but in the exchange rate. As capital flows in and investors demand more local currency, they bid up the price of that currency and the exchange rate appreciates. This appreciation, in turn, puts a brake on further inflows. When foreign capital leaves the country, the selling of local currency leads to a depreciation of the exchange rate. As the exchange rate falls, asset prices in that country begin to look cheaper in foreign currency terms, and investors are drawn back.

The pegged rate system, by contrast, attempts to serve two masters simultaneously, and as a result betrays both in the end. In response to capital inflows, the central bank buys up dollars, just as a currency board would, to prevent appreciation of the exchange rate. But then, to squelch any resulting inflation, the central bank "sterilizes" its purchases with a corresponding tightening of domestic credit. As a result, no equilibrating adjustment—neither appreciation nor inflation—is allowed to occur. The market signals to foreign investors are thus distorted, and returns on further investment appear better than they actually are. In other words, during periods of capital inflows, the pegged rate system subsidizes further inflows. The pegged rate system creates a disequilibrating positive feedback loop, the consequence of which is a euphoric boom in foreign investment.

For every boom, however, there is eventually a bust. Sooner or later, some manifestation of economic weakness, whether created by the excesses of the boom or otherwise, will cause investor sentiment to turn unfavorable. As foreign capital exits the country, the central bank buys up its own currency to defend the peg, while at the same time "sterilizing" its actions with looser domestic credit. Once again, this combination of maneuvers blocks any equilibrating adjustment—whether a depreciating currency or deflation and higher interest rates—that would push back against the capital exodus. A new positive feedback loop is generated: The more some foreign investors pull up stakes and leave, the more the rest of them want to follow. Thus, during periods of capital outflow, the pegged rate system subsidizes a stampede for the exits. Unless some nonmonetary adjustment—for example, rising prices for the country's major exports or a new round of privatization or deregulation—breaks the cycle and restores investor confidence, the peg will not survive.

The final adjustment, when it comes, is frequently brutal. If the peg is abandoned only after a long defense by the central bank, the resulting depreciation, having been so long delayed, can be dramatic. And if the boom featured large-scale, unhedged borrowing in foreign currencies, the exchange-rate shock can precipitate a wave of defaults as debts expressed in local currency terms skyrocket.

All of the spectacular currency crashes of the past several years have followed this basic pattern. Each of the crisis-affected countries enjoyed, for a time, a rollicking investment boom. In Mexico, the Salinas administration embarked upon an ambitious program of structural reforms in the wake of the Latin American debt crisis—including privatizations, deregulation, slashing of trade barriers, and an end to fiscal and monetary profligacy—that made the country attractive once again to foreign investors. At the same time, in an effort to add credibility to its anti-inflation campaign, Mexico pegged the peso to the U.S. dollar. As capital flowed in, the Banco de México bought dollars and issued pesos to defend the peg against appreciation; it then sterilized its interventions by tightening domestic credit. With equilibrating forces thus squelched, foreign capital surged into Mexico. Between 1990 and 1993, net capital inflows reached $91 billion, or about one fifth of all net inflows to developing countries. [12]

In East Asia, liberalization of international financial transactions over the course of the 1990s greatly facilitated foreign portfolio investment and bank lending and triggered an upsurge in capital inflows. Monetary authorities responded by defending their preexisting exchange rate pegs and pursuing an aggressive policy of sterilization, thereby connecting the positive feedback loop to which pegged regimes are prone. Monetary tightening drove up domestic interest rates, which in turn attracted more foreign capital, which then prompted more monetary tightening, which resulted in yet higher interest rates, and so on. Between 1993 and 1996, net private inflows into East Asia averaged 5.8 percent of GDP; in Malaysia and Thailand, accumulated inflows over that period exceeded 30 percent of GDP. [13]

After the chaotic collapse of the communist economic system, Russian authorities pegged the ruble to the dollar in July 1995 in a bid to achieve macroeconomic stability. And indeed, tight money policies did succeed in bringing the rate of inflation, which had stood at 131 percent in 1995, down to 11 percent by 1997. [14] The combination of an exchange rate peg and tight money, though, brought on the usual perversities. Capital, attracted by rising interest rates, flooded into the country: Net inflows jumped from 1.1 percent of GDP in 1994 to 7.6 percent in 1997. [15]

Three booms in three very different settings, yet in each case it was internally contradictory monetary policy that worked to inflate a foreign investment bubble. Over time, the vulnerability to a currency crash (and with it, the bursting of the bubble) grew increasingly severe. That vulnerability manifested itself primarily in the form of mounting short-term debt. Short-term capital is typically the most sensitive to interest rate differentials, flitting around the globe in search of the temporarily highest returns. Consequently, as sterilization policies in Mexico, East Asia, and Russia opened up big differentials between domestic and foreign interest rates, it was only natural that the composition of capital inflows shifted decisively toward the short term. In Mexico, short-term inflows from the beginning of 1990 to the third quarter of 1994 totaled at least $40 billion, while international reserves—which would be called upon to discharge that liability—grew only $10 billion.[16] In Korea, Indonesia, and Thailand, the ratio of short-term debt to foreign reserves ranged from 150 percent to over 200 percent by mid-1997.[17] And in Russia, foreign purchases of short-term government debt totaled $21 billion in 1997, while hard currency reserves rose only $1.6 billion.[18] The economic euphoria was thus growing increasingly precarious; all that was required was a spate of bad news to provoke a dramatic reversal of fortune.

Bad news came in different forms to trigger the three resulting crises, but once it came the consequences were grimly similar. Mexico's woes began on January 1, 1994 (the day that the North American Free Trade Agreement took effect) when the Zapatista Army for National Liberation initiated an armed uprising in the poor southern region of Chiapas. Investor fears in the face of ongoing violence in Chiapas were soon compounded by the assassination, in March, of presidential candidate Luis Donaldo Colosio. Meanwhile, a string of interest rate hikes in the United States reduced the relative attractiveness of investing in Mexico. East Asia ran into a similar patch of difficulties in 1996–97. A downturn in the electronics market, among other factors, precipitated a regional export slump: from 20 percent growth in 1995 to a 1 percent contraction in 1996.[19] Real estate and stock market prices began to deteriorate. In Thailand, the fraud-plagued Bangkok Bank of Commerce collapsed in mid-1996, the major developer Somprasong Land defaulted on a Eurobond issue in October, and the largest finance company, Finance One, went down early in 1997. In Korea, 1997 saw the bankruptcies of Hanbo Steel, Kia Motors, and Sammi Steel. Russia, meanwhile, lost favor with investors in late 1997 and into 1998 as drops in oil prices undermined exports, the federal budget continued to hemorrhage red ink, and the shock of the widening Asian crisis bred a newfound appreciation for the riskiness of emerging markets.

As capital inflows began to drop, fidelity to the pegged rate system started the positive feedback loop spinning in reverse. In each case, monetary authorities sold off dollar reserves to defend the peg and then compensated for the resulting demonetization by expanding domestic credit. Between December 1993 and November 1994, the Banco de México boosted domestic credit by 35.4 billion pesos, nearly entirely erasing the equilibrating effects that would have resulted from 36.2 billion pesos in exchange sales over the same period.[20] In the East Asian economies that were soon to be broadsided, monetary aggregates remained stable or grew, even as foreign reserves steadily dwindled.[21] The same occurred in Russia: Foreign reserves plummeted nearly 50 percent between June 1997 and May 1998 as the Russian Central Bank sold dollars and took rubles out of circulation; yet over that same period, base money remained extremely stable, declining a mere 2 percent.[22] By attempting to prevent both depreciation and deflation, the monetary authorities blocked the market signals that ordinarily would have dampened capital outflow. In other words, monetary policy was subsidizing panic. Nowhere were the consequences more spectacular than in East Asia. Net private inflows into Thailand, Korea, Malaysia, Indonesia, and the Philippines went from $97.1 billion in 1996 to negative $11.9 billion in 1997—a one-year swing of nearly $110 billion, or more than 10 percent of those countries' combined GDP.[23]

Without the *deus ex machina* of nonmonetary developments (such as new economic conditions or policies) that would restore investor confidence, the exchange rate pegs were doomed to self-destruct. And that is precisely what occurred. The combination of spontaneous capital flight and concerted speculative attacks accelerated into full-fledged runs on the embattled currencies. Faced with the imminent exhaustion of foreign reserves, central banks resigned themselves to the inevitable and allowed their currencies to "float"— or, rather, sink like a stone. The Mexican peso fell from 3.44 to the dollar in December 1994 to 6.55 by the middle of 1995. From July 2, 1997 (the day the Thai baht slipped from its peg) until the end of that year, the baht, the Korean won, and the Malaysian ringgit lost 40 to 50 percent of their exchange value; by August (one month later), the Indonesian rupiah had dropped by 80 percent. After Russia's default and devaluation on August 17, 1998, the ruble nosedived more than 60 percent in a single month.

Serious structural flaws in domestic economic policies and institutions greatly magnified the economic devastation unleashed by these currency crashes. Before turning to those national-level issues, however, there were additional policy distortions affecting the international flow of capital that played an important role in the meltdowns of recent years.

First of all, protection of domestic financial institutions from foreign competition renders small economies dramatically more vulnerable to international capital shocks. Even when the exchange rate regime and monetary policy are aligned properly so as to not make matters worse, sudden shifts in international capital flows can prove destabilizing simply because of their size relative to the domestic economy. In a floating-rate country, an inrush of foreign capital can produce a steep appreciation in the exchange rate that is highly disruptive for exporting firms. If the rate is fixed or a foreign currency is used, the injection of additional liquidity can overheat the economy through inflation. When foreign capital floods out of a country, deflation and recession can afflict a fixed-rate country, while a floating-rate regime will have to contend with the problems caused by a sudden spike in import prices. Indeed, so many countries have pursued the false lure of pegged rate systems not out of sheer perversity but precisely to avoid (or so they think) the fits and starts caused by the lurches of shifting investor sentiment.

It has become painfully clear that the peg cure is worse than the disease. But what remains almost totally unacknowledged is the extent to which the disease is itself the result of misguided government policies. It is not the small size of less developed markets that makes them vulnerable to the vagaries of international capital flows; the culprit, rather, is the lack of integration between those small economies and the ambient pool of global capital. In particular, restrictions on international banking have given us a balkanized world of national banking systems, in which national financial markets are dominated by domestic financial institutions. This state of affairs is accepted unthinkingly as entirely natural, when in fact it is grotesquely artificial: It is as absurd for most countries to have their own banks as it is to have their own automobile producers. We have come to recognize the absurdity in the latter case, but take the former for granted. Meanwhile, even countries with relatively open access to foreign banks still generally require those foreign entrants to segregate their domestic and international operations (for example, by separately balancing their local currency and U.S. dollar accounts).

The segmentation of financial markets along national lines is a potent source of instability, especially for small economies. If banking were fully internationalized, adjustments to excess supply of or demand for funds in a particular country could be made smoothly within the financial system. Banks could easily shift excess liquidity out of the country to lend in some other market where opportunities are more promising; likewise, when capital is suddenly tight, it would be easy for banks to increase their foreign liabilities to supply needed liquidity. But when markets are segmented, banks are hindered in their ability to make such adjustments. Consequently, the burden of adjustment falls on monetary policy, through fluctuations either in the domestic price level or the exchange rate, with all the attendant disruptions that such fluctuations entail. Macroeconomic adjustment, in other words, must substitute for microeconomic adjustment, and the substitution is frequently awkward.

Furthermore, national banking systems with all or most of their assets in the domestic economy are flying in the face of the first rule of portfolio management: Thou shalt diversify. When so many eggs are in such a small basket, a downturn in a single sector can trigger nationwide bank failures and, thus, a macroeconomic crisis. In a world of truly globalized banking, by contrast, the inevitable ups and downs of particular industries could be absorbed by the financial system without difficulty.

The experience of Panama gives a real-world example of how eliminating segmentation promotes stability. Despite its fair share of woeful misrule, Panama has avoided the kind of boom-and-bust turbulence that often afflicts developing countries exposed to large international capital movements. It has done so through a combination of "dollarization" and financial integration. The U.S. dollar has been legal tender in Panama since 1904, and in 1970 a new banking law threw open the door to foreign entrants; it even allowed them to finance local lending with external funds.

The result has been an exceptional record of macroeconomic calm, notwithstanding political crises, coups, and even a war with the United States in 1989. Inflation averaged only 3 percent from 1961 to 1997 and exceeded 10 percent only twice—in the oil-shock years of 1974 and 1980. Elsewhere in Latin America during this period, double-digit inflation was more the rule than the exception, and triple- and even quadruple-digit inflation was not unheard of. Meanwhile, the real (that is, inflation-adjusted) exchange rate has been extremely stable, with year-to-year fluctuations of less than 4 percentage points since 1961. By contrast, real exchange rate swings of 30 to 50 percent in a single year have occurred with some frequency throughout the rest of Latin America. And, notwithstanding poor regulatory supervision and no deposit insurance, Panama has suffered no systemic banking crises.

Especially noteworthy for present purposes is the fact that Panama's smooth sailing has been undisturbed by major shifts in capital flows. As a result of the new banking law, outstanding loans to the private sector more than doubled from 1968 to 1972, yet consumer prices in Panama grew more slowly than in the United States. Net capital inflows averaged 17 percent of GDP during 1973–75, while outflows averaged 9.2 percent of GDP in 1985–86; on both occasions, though, the real exchange rate barely budged. And after the 1988–89 showdown with the United States, bank deposits grew 80 percent in three years, but no overheating of the economy resulted.[24]

Unfortunately, Panama's story is both highly unusual and almost totally unknown. Most developing countries that have opened themselves to foreign capital have done so without fully internationalizing their financial sectors; consequently, they are put to a choice between exchange rate volatility and domestic price volatility. Many, in turn, have sought to evade that choice through a pegged exchange rate system. What follows is a particularly nasty interplay of monetary dysfunctions: The combination of increased capital flows and continued market segmentation heightens the need for monetary adjustment, but the adjustment process is stifled by attempts to maintain the peg. In the end, both external and internal volatility erupt with a vengeance.

Adding to the woes caused by pegged rates and financial segmentation is yet another policy distortion of international capital movements: the phenomenon known as "moral hazard." The term comes from the insurance industry: When you insure against any risky event, you decrease the cost of that bad outcome to the insured and thereby reduce his incentives to guard against it. Moral hazard, then, is the increased risk that the insured event will occur as a result of the very act of insurance.

The international capital marketplace of recent years has been positively toxic with moral hazard. And no institution has done more to bring about that sad state of affairs than the International Monetary Fund. The IMF—which was created to support the Bretton Woods system of pegged exchange rates after World War II (a system that, unsurprisingly, could not survive in the face of steady capital liberalization)—now busies itself by providing emergency financial assistance to cash-strapped developing countries that have balance-of-payments difficulties. Accordingly, when exchange rate pegs implode, as in Mexico, East Asia, and Russia, the IMF is now expected to mop up the mess and prevent the spread of financial "contagion." Specifically, the IMF is tasked with trying to prevent defaults by lending distressed countries the money they need to repay foreign banks and investors. These "bailouts" can assume staggering proportions. After the Mexican crisis hit, the IMF offered an assistance package of $17.8 billion;

in East Asia, the IMF promised loans of more than $100 billion; in Russia, the IMF announced a rescue package of over $20 billion in an ultimately vain attempt to prevent default.[25]

Enormous controversy has blown up around the IMF's role in responding to financial crises. Much of the attention has focused on the quality of the advice the IMF gave beforehand to countries that later hit the wall, as well as the strings that it placed on its aid through so-called "conditionality." While those issues are serious matters, my focus here is on the effect of IMF intercession, not on the borrowing countries, but rather on the creditors. By bailing out those creditors, admittedly for the laudable goal of containing financial panic, IMF policy worked to create a state of affairs that has been humorously described as "laissez welfare"—in which risky, high-yield investments still pay off for the investor even when they fail.[26] The effect of IMF intervention was thus to subsidize risky behavior by reducing its costs—in other words, to generate moral hazard.

In retrospect it is clear that the Mexican bailout (co-managed by the IMF and the U.S. Treasury's Exchange Stabilization Fund) helped to set the stage for the future crises in East Asia and Russia. In this regard, it was not necessary for investors to calculate consciously that the IMF would step in to cover any downside risk. But consider what would have happened had the Mexican government and banks been allowed to sink or swim on their own: either to default or else strike some accommodation with their creditors. It is virtually unthinkable that banks and investors would not have exercised more caution in other potentially risky markets.

What happened instead was that foreign banks and investors remained blithely indifferent to the dangers that lurked in East Asia, Russia, and elsewhere. For example, according to a study published by the Institute of International Finance, the spread between yields on bonds issued by 14 emerging-market governments and bonds issued by high-rated corporations in advanced countries actually fell in the aftermath of the Mexican crisis. The authors calculated that the average spread was only 130 basis points in the second quarter of 1997—compared to about 245 basis points had the relationship between spreads and economic performance stayed the same as during 1992–1996.[27] As to corporate debt, spreads for East Asian borrowers in late 1996 and early 1997 were only slightly above those for long-term loans to U.S. corporations.[28] Can anyone seriously contend that investors would have been so recklessly bullish if many of them were still smarting from losses in Mexico?

Meanwhile, in Russia, the IMF extended funds again and again, regardless of the government's repeated failures to live up to agreed-upon conditions for assistance. It was obvious to everyone that aid was being extended to Russia on political, not economic, grounds. The IMF's forbearance served only to help Russia dig a deeper hole for itself. In particular, throughout the spring and summer of 1998 the government moved aggressively to replace ruble debt with more attractive foreign currency–denominated debt. During the first eight months of 1998, Russia's foreign debt increased by $18.5 billion—as all the while its fiscal situation became increasingly and obviously grave.[29] Even the IMF now admits that investors purchased this debt in the expectation that the IMF would ensure its repayment.[30] This time, though, they bet wrong.

The meltdowns in Mexico, East Asia, and Russia were triggered by the perverse logic of exchange rate pegs and compounded by the interventionist ills of financial segmentation and moral hazard. But the real roots of these crises go even deeper than this trio of policy errors. After all, Taiwan and Singapore also had exchange rate pegs; furthermore, neither of those economies enjoyed Panama's level of financial integration (though Singapore came much closer than Taiwan), and both faced the same moral hazard–addled investors that plunged heedlessly into the rest of the region.[31] Yet despite being forced off their pegs in the general melee of 1997, and despite experiencing thereafter the sharp depreciation of their currencies, neither Taiwan nor Singapore suffered anything like the hardship that some of their neighbors had to endure.

When we examine the individual circumstances of the crisis-affected countries of East Asia, and also those of Mexico and Russia, what we find is that the distortions in the international capital marketplace addressed in the previous section were not operating in a vacuum. Rather, they interacted with underlying structural defects in particular countries' domestic policies and institutions. It was the interaction between those domestic economic distortions and the distortions in international capital flows that wrought the havoc we have experienced in recent years.

Specifically, it is impossible to understand the dynamics that drove all three crises without examining the role the domestic financial systems played in the affected countries. As I addressed previously, in the run-up to disaster all the central banks concerned pursued the perverse logic of exchange rate pegs by loosening monetary policy in the face of capital outflows. That logic, however, was not their only motivation. In each of these three episodes, the central banks felt compelled to pump liquidity into the domestic economy in order to shore up tottering financial institutions.

In Mexico, East Asia, and Russia, the unfavorable turn in economic conditions that prompted capital outflows simultaneously exposed serious weaknesses in the banking system. Problems with the banks' loan portfolios became increasingly apparent; meanwhile, on the liability side, the banks were growing ever more dependent on short-term, foreign currency-denominated debt. This combination of circumstances put central bankers in a no-win situation. On the one hand, devaluation of the exchange rate would spell catastrophe for the banks, since their foreign currency debts would skyrocket in local currency terms; on the other hand, a full-fledged defense of the currency through higher interest rates would likely prove ruinous for the banks as well, since slamming on the macroeconomic brakes would surely worsen their mounting bad-loan problems.

Thus, as the investment booms faded, the central banks were trapped. They could not shield the banks from calamity on the liability side without increasing the dangers on the asset side, and vice versa. With nowhere to go, they chased their own tails: propping up the exchange rate pegs by selling foreign exchange and then turning around and undermining them by increasing domestic liquidity. In the end they only made matters worse—the currency crashes and steep recessions that followed wrought devastation on both sides of the balance sheet.

But what had caused the banking systems to become so vulnerable? In Mexico and East Asia, the banking slump was a direct consequence of the preceding boom: Good times bred excesses, the consequences of which were ultimately disastrous. Exchange rate pegs and moral hazard combined to subsidize capital inflows; financial segmentation then kept those inflows captive there and put them in the hands of relatively backward and uncompetitive domestic financial institutions.

In Chapter 7, I describe the kinds of policy distortions that afflict banking systems around the world: Political interference with lending decisions shifts capital away from its most profitable uses, while deposit insurance and "too big to fail" policies create another layer of moral hazard on the domestic level. The flaws of over-centralized, bank-dependent finance can remain hidden so long as uncertainty about allocating capital remains within certain limits. But when formerly scarce capital suddenly becomes readily available, and when "catch-up" growth begins to yield diminishing returns, uncertainties about how best to deploy resources start to multiply—and the latent flaws of top-down financial systems begin to make themselves known. Such was the case in Mexico and East Asia. In both of those economies, a surge in liquidity propelled banking systems toward the shoals. And in East Asia, the continued progress of the economic "miracle" made gross misallocations of capital increasingly likely.

In the late 1980s and early '90s, Mexico experienced a dramatic wave of financial reforms: The commercial banks, virtually all of which had been nationalized in 1982 in the depths of the debt crisis, were privatized; interest rate controls were eliminated; directed credit mandates were scuttled; and high reserve requirements were lifted. What followed was an explosive monetization of the economy: The ratio of broad money (M_2) to GDP shot up from 7.1 percent in 1988 to 30 percent in 1994.[32] Bank credit expanded by leaps and bounds: From December 1988 to November 1994, lending from commercial banks to the private sector increased by 277 percent in real terms, or 25 percent a year.[33] The newly privatized banks—often poorly capitalized, poorly staffed, and poorly supervised—were simply overwhelmed by the pace of growth. Meanwhile, the promise of full insurance for almost all depositors reduced the banks' incentives to lend prudently. It is unsurprising, then, that Mexico's credit expansion was marked by increasingly questionable lending: Declared nonperforming loans jumped from 3.9 percent at the end of 1991 to 5.5 percent only a year later, and then to 8.3 percent by September 1994.[34]

In East Asia, the influx of foreign capital combined with domestic financial liberalization to spark a credit boom. Growth in bank lending to the private sector raced far ahead of GDP growth in Indonesia, the Philippines, and Thailand.[35] Exposure to the property sector grew high, with real estate loans approaching 20 percent of total loans outstanding in Indonesia, Thailand, and Malaysia by 1997. In Korea and Indonesia, bonds and other securities climbed toward 20 percent of total bank assets.[36]

Furthermore, unlike the situation in Mexico, this boom was coming after years or even decades of sustained high growth. Thus, the region was now awash with liquidity after many of the most obviously profitable investment opportunities in the region had already been exploited. As the 1990s progressed, therefore, East Asian financial systems were forced to cope with unprecedented levels of uncertainty regarding how best to allocate capital. It should come as no surprise that, under these circumstances, centralized financial systems that had previously been perfectly serviceable quickly became acutely dysfunctional. Nor should it be a surprise that the more competitive, more market-oriented financial systems of the region weathered the challenges of uncertainty far better than their more crudely top-down counterparts.

A clear distinction can be drawn between the financial systems of Thailand, Korea, and Indonesia—the economies hardest hit by the Asian crisis—and those of Hong Kong, Singapore, and Taiwan, which came through the storm with much less damage. The former were noteworthy for their heavy reliance on bank lending, their poor legal infrastructure, and the limited access granted to foreign financial institutions. By contrast, Hong Kong and Singapore were highly open to foreign banks and had better developed capital markets; their legal protections for investors, a legacy of British rule, were far superior to the Asian norm. Taiwan, meanwhile, did labor under a tightly controlled formal financial system; on the other hand, its highly active, informal "curb market" served to democratize the availability of financing, and was later supplemented by a thriving venture capital market.

Over the course of the 1990s, a variety of indicators showed a growing divergence in economic performance between East Asian economies with highly centralized financial systems and those in which market principles held greater sway. A survey covering the period between 1992 and 1996 found that, on average, corporations in Thailand, Korea, and Indonesia were failing to create net economic value added; in other words, their returns on assets were less than their cost of capital. By contrast, corporations in Hong Kong and Singapore succeeded in creating wealth.[37] As performance flagged, debts mounted: By 1996 debt-equity ratios for corporations stood at 188 percent in Indonesia, 236 percent in Thailand, and a whopping 355 percent in Korea; by contrast, the corresponding ratios for Taiwan, Singapore, and Hong Kong were 80 percent, 105 percent, and 156 percent, respectively (for purposes of comparison, the average U.S. ratio that year was 113 percent).[38] The debt buildup left corporations that utilized the more centralized financial systems in an increasingly precarious position: In Thailand, the ratio of operating cash flow to annual interest expenses dropped from 460 percent at the end of 1992 to a mere 192 percent at the end of 1996; on the latter date, the ratio for Hong Kong stood at a comfortable 1,107 percent.[39]

In Russia, meanwhile, the troubles of the banking sector arose from an altogether different set of circumstances. Sadly, Russian banks were too abysmally dysfunctional to be able to translate foreign capital inflows into a credit boom for the private sector. As I briefly addressed in Chapter 7, Russian banks in the aftermath of communism's demise did not really embrace the normal task of banks everywhere (namely, using depositors' savings to finance lending). Instead, they scavenged for quick profit-making opportunities presented by the prevailing economic chaos. The taming of hyperinflation during the mid-1990s, however, eliminated many of their most lucrative rackets; caught in a squeeze, banks turned increasingly to borrowing heavily from abroad to finance purchases of the Russian government's ballooning and high-interest-paying debt. It was a good ride while it lasted, but it didn't last long. Russia's public debt was soaring on an unsustainable trajectory, and when default and devaluation came on August 17, 1998, the Russian banking system was doubly wiped out: Its assets lost their value just as its liabilities exploded in ruble terms.

Russia's ruinous fiscal profligacy was driven by a fundamental contradiction in its postcommunist economic policies. Beginning in 1995, Russia attempted to restore macroeconomic order by tightening monetary policy and subduing runaway inflation. It pursued that laudable path, though, while at the same time maintaining the old "soft budget constraint" that allowed Soviet-era enterprises to stay in business regardless of hemorrhaging losses. The combination of hard money and soft budgets was untenable, and initiated a spiraling sequence of mutually reinforcing maladies that led ultimately to the breakdown of August 17.

Russia's earlier hyperinflation had reflected the underlying problem of the zombie economy, as the central bank simply monetized the costs of propping up moribund enterprises. By attacking inflation without addressing that underlying problem, Russia's "reform" efforts amounted really to suppressing symptoms while ignoring the disease. Soon, other equally troubling symptoms manifested themselves: specifically, rising public debt and the bizarre spread of payment arrears and barter arrangements. Continued subsidies—mainly in the form of free energy and toleration of tax delinquency—produced rising budget deficits, which now had to be financed through borrowing rather than inflation. Increased borrowing pushed up interest rates; the resulting liquidity problems in the enterprise sector prompted resort to nonpayments and barter and increasing need for subsidies. Those higher subsidies exacerbated the budget deficit and increased the debt burden, putting further upward pressure on interest rates and thus perpetuating the cycle. Such a dynamic had only one logical endpoint: macroeconomic collapse.[40]

〰〰〰

Globalization is undeniably a messy and uncertain process. Most spectacularly, it has resulted in the repeated eruption of major international financial crises. Less visibly, it generates incessant turmoil and dislocation within national economies, as long-established economic structures totter and fall and the people whose lives depended upon those structures find their worlds upended.

That said, the critics of globalization who blame all the tumult on "market fundamentalism" are viewing the world through ideological blinkers. Only by willfully ignoring the facts can anyone maintain that the upheavals of recent years are due solely and simply to the perversities of unfettered market forces. Yes, markets do enjoy a much wider scope of operation today than they did 20 years ago, but they remain enmeshed in a dense matrix of government policies that both suppress and undermine the institutions of market competition. It is not markets alone, but the interactions of market forces with that pre-existing, anti-market matrix, that have wrought such havoc on the reemergent world economy.

Those interactions and their destructive potential were plainly evident in globalization's greatest catastrophes to date—the crises in Mexico, East Asia, and Russia. Without a doubt, market-oriented liberalization—the fall of communism in Russia, deep structural reforms in Mexico, gradual financial opening in East Asia—played an important role in these episodes. This liberalization allowed large sums of foreign money to flow in—and, later on, to flow out. Unfortunately, liberalization left untouched many anti-market policies whose effect was to distort the new flows of capital in ultimately calamitous ways. The self-defeating overburdening of monetary policy through pegged exchange rate systems, the segmentation of financial markets through restrictions on foreign banks, the subsidization of reckless investments through moral hazard, the overloading of backward domestic financial sectors, the fiscal chaos caused by the postcommunist zombie economy—none of this can be confused in any way with economic liberalism. And when these anti-market policies operated on newly liberalized capital movements, the results were disastrous.

But don't market excesses deserve at least some of the blame? After all, it is commonly said that financial markets are powered alternately by greed and fear—two of the less attractive components of the human emotional repertoire. Didn't greed-addled shortsightedness cause investors to ignore obvious risks during the good times, just as fearful panic led them to over-state problems during the bust? Isn't at least part of the amplitude of the boom-and-bust wave attributable to witless "herd instinct"?

Of course investors have made many foolish choices—and paid dearly for them (at least when the IMF didn't intervene). Markets are human in-stitutions, and thus are prey to human failings. Investors were excessively sanguine about the prospects of "emerging markets," and once burned many will doubtless be slow to recognize real opportunities there when they present themselves. Nevertheless—and the point is of crucial signifi-cance—markets contain self-correcting mechanisms that compensate for the inevitable shortcomings of their participants. Specifically, when greed or fear causes markets to overshoot, it becomes highly profitable to go against the herd—to short overvalued assets, or scoop up undervalued ones. The market order thus creates strong incentives for mistakes and misjudg-ments to be corrected.

It shouldn't be too surprising, therefore, that academic studies have found little evidence of herding behavior in international capital markets.[41] In the Asian crisis, in which "contagion" effects were widely asserted, it is clear now that the judgments of investors proved relatively discriminat-ing. The countries that were hardest hit (Korea, Indonesia, Thailand, and Malaysia) turned out to have the most seriously defective policies and insti-tutions, while better-managed economies like Hong Kong, Singapore, and Taiwan weathered the ordeal in relatively good order.

Critics of liberalization raise a more serious issue when they question the wisdom of opening financial markets before other, more urgently needed reforms have been made. As we have seen, partial liberalization can be a risky proposition, and the proper sequencing of reforms can spell the difference between prosperity and penury. All deregulation is not created equal: Whether a particular reform proposal is actually pro-market or anti-market depends on whether, in the context of the rest of the policy mix, it facilitates the transmission of market signals or instead merely exacerbates distortions created by other interventions.

But to argue that capital liberalization should have awaited more fundamental reforms is to make the perfect the enemy of the good. Before financial crises revealed the dangers of pegged-rate regimes and top-down, politicized financial systems, there was no constituency for fixing those problems or undertaking other needed structural reforms. In East Asia, for example, as long as economic growth rolled along at 7 or 8 percent a year, the prevailing mentality was "if it ain't broke, don't fix it." Indeed, it was stoutly argued and widely accepted that the over-centralization of Asian finance was not a weakness but a strength. Only the shock of a violent economic reversal was capable of shaking that complacency and creating momentum for further reforms.

I do not wish to be so Panglossian as to argue that the crises were all for the best: They were terrible tragedies and their human costs were staggering. But it must be remembered that the far greater tragedy is the humdrum, everyday deprivation suffered by the billions of human beings who are born, live, and die in conditions of economic underdevelopment. We know now how to lift that curse: All the best in economic theory and analysis, and all the accumulated disillusionment of a century of collectivist experimentation, tell us that market competition is the surest path to affluence. The global tragedy of mass deprivation and suffering and wasted human potential can be relieved most quickly and thoroughly by the full embrace of economic liberalism—of the principles and institutions that support and sustain the discovery process of market competition.

And so from this perspective, the silver lining of these financial crises is that they taught a valuable, if painful, lesson: that partial liberalization is not enough, that basic structural reforms are needed around the world, even in those star performers of the Asian "miracle" that before seemed unable to do wrong. Openness to capital flows has thus proved to have an historic, systemic significance that goes far beyond the incremental contribution of foreign capital to economic development. And going forward, the fluctuating ups and downs of foreign-investor sentiment give to policymakers in borrower countries rapid and unambiguous feedback about the perceived market-friendliness of their policies. The feedback is far from perfect—investors are often operating with incomplete facts and wrongheaded theories—but it is precise enough to warn against at least some clear mistakes and reward at least some right moves. Capital liberalization thus offers more than its direct economic benefits; it offers some measure of guidance along the often treacherous path of liberal reform.

In this twilight era of unpeaceful coexistence, it is unrealistic to expect that the transition from the collectivist past to a liberal future will always be navigated smoothly. Horrendous mistakes were made in that past, and their inertia carries forward: The sins of the fathers are visited upon the sons. Mistakes on such a massive scale are virtually impossible to correct without disruption and dislocation. And thus far, at least, the progress of liberalism's renaissance has been propelled by upheaval: the collapse of the communist system, the travails of stagflation in the advanced countries, the debt crisis of the 1980s, and now the financial crises of the 1990s. It has not been a smooth path, but the ultimate destination has been and is still worth the struggle. In the final analysis, any suggestion that we should flinch from attempting further progress until we receive some impossible guarantee that everything will be neat and tidy must be rejected as the counsel of reaction.

10

Recasting the Safety Net

Opponents of liberal reform are fond of declaring that theirs is the cause of "social cohesion." Globalization's heedless progress, they claim, is fraying the bonds that hold communities together: the connections that lift us above our narrower interests and embrace all of us, rich and poor alike, in a greater whole. The frenzy of unchecked competition, the argument goes, has set one group against another while leaving the neediest and most vulnerable to fend for themselves.

Such sentiments can be found on both ends of the political spectrum. "The social question—how does a society sustain equable relations among its own people?—has been brushed aside by the economic sphere," according to left-wing author William Greider. "Social cohesion and consent, even the minimal standards of human decency, are irrelevant to free markets."[1] Meanwhile, John Gray, coming from a right-wing perspective, draws a similar conclusion. "[T]he economic argument for unregulated global free trade involves a wild abstraction from social realities," he writes in *False Dawn: The Delusions of Global Capitalism*. "[M]aximal productivity achieved at the cost of social desolation and human misery is an anomalous and dangerous social ideal."[2]

French politicians have a particular knack for expressing these sentiments pithily. Socialist Prime Minister Lionel Jospin has famously remarked that he favors a "market economy but not a market society." His Gaullist predecessor, Edouard Balladur, took a rather more pugnacious line. "What is the market?" he asked in an angry dissent from the course of world trade talks back in 1993. "It is the law of the jungle, the law of nature. And what is civilization? It is the struggle against nature."[3]

There is nothing new about such attitudes: The belief that market competition alienates and atomizes was from the beginning a driving impulse of the Industrial Counterrevolution. Nowhere was the thought expressed with more passionate ferocity than in Marx and Engels' *The Communist Manifesto*. Only two years after the Corn Laws were repealed, Karl Marx was already proclaiming the socially corrosive effects of then nascent globalization:

> The bourgeoisie . . . has left remaining no other nexus between man and man than naked self-interest, than callous "cash payment." It has drowned the most heavenly ecstasies of religious fervour, of chivalrous enthusiasm, of philistine sentimentalism, in the icy water of egoistical calculation. It has resolved personal worth into exchange value, and in place of the numberless indefeasible chartered freedoms, has set up that single, unconscionable freedom—Free Trade.[4]

Marx, of course, had no use for the old feudal ties that capitalism was severing; he hailed the bourgeoisie's role in their demise as progressive. His allegiance was to the new and all-embracing community that supposedly would emerge once private property and competition were eradicated. In other words, his program was one of "back to the future": to recreate the bygone *Gemeinschaft* of old on a new and progressive basis. By thus recasting atavistic longing for traditional society into a prophetic vision of history's unfolding destiny, Marx defined the terms that would carry the Industrial Counterrevolution to worldwide power.

But how does such thinking fit into today's historical context—now that the future has come and gone? For a century, the collectivist, centralizing impulse worked to shape the goals and instrumentalities of social policy. Now, with the general disillusionment with top-down controls, much of that work is coming into question. And so, for partisans of social cohesion, the shoe is now on the other foot: Where once they fought in the name of alluring, untested possibilities, today they must defend existing and increasingly dilapidated structures from criticism and reform. By dint of their own success, the partisans of anti-market social cohesion have transformed themselves from reformers and revolutionaries into conservatives and reactionaries.

The rearguard defense is occurring along two fronts. First, it has become increasingly apparent that traditional social insurance policies are doomed by their misdesign to inevitable collapse, and thus are in need of fundamental rethinking. Rather than acknowledge the need for reform, anti-liberal forces have chosen instead to blame globalization for social insurance's fiscal distress. And second, those same forces are fighting in the name of social co-hesion to preserve a motley mix of interventionist policies whose common theme is protection of the economic status quo against the dynamic forces of marketplace adaptation.

The collectivist cause of social cohesion is a mirage—worse, a cruel hoax. Yes, the pace and complexity of modern life do put strains on the human psyche; it was true a hundred years ago and it remains true today. But there is nothing in the ills of modernity that collectivist nostrums can cure. On the contrary, blind resistance to needed reforms will only further rend the social fabric. Behind the appealing rhetoric of unity, the contem-porary anti-liberal agenda stands revealed as deeply divisive: It pits the privileged beneficiaries of current policies against their more numerous but less visible victims. It sets current pensioners against the young and middle-aged whose hopes for retirement security are imperiled by the de-fects of current pension systems. It sets the unemployed and underem-ployed against those whose jobs are now treated as entitlements. And it sets those propped up in declining industries against all who have a stake in the fledgling or unborn industries of the future. In the promotion of these ster-ile, zero-sum conflicts, the embattled rearguard of the Industrial Counter-revolution makes its sad, final stand—the one-time would-be liberators reduced to rancorous obstructionism.

There is no inherent conflict between the principles of economic liber-alism and a decent provision for the needy and unfortunate. First of all, a free society will invariably complement its commercial sphere with a rich and thriving independent sector. Civil society includes, not just profit-seeking enterprises, but also nonprofit institutions and initiatives dedicated to sup-plying public goods—including assistance for those in need. Furthermore, it is perfectly consistent with liberal precepts for government to supplement the charitable efforts of civil society with a more comprehensive and sys-tematic social safety net. Whether provided privately or by government, so-cial assistance lies outside the market, in the realm of public goods. That realm is not in conflict with the market; it is in addition to the market.

F. A. Hayek, widely regarded as the premier theorist of economic lib-eralism in the 20th century, was quite clear on this point. "What we now know as public assistance or relief," he wrote in *The Constitution of Liberty,* "which in various forms is provided in all countries, is merely the old poor law adapted to modern conditions. The necessity of some such arrangement in an industrial society is unquestioned. . . ."[5] Hayek went on to acknowledge the propriety of compulsory insurance programs as one element of social policy: "Once it becomes the recognized duty of the public to provide for the extreme needs of old age, unemployment, sickness, etc., irrespective of whether the individuals could and ought to have made provision themselves, . . . it seems an obvious corollary to compel them to insure (or otherwise provide) against those common hazards of life."[6]

Nevertheless, market critics contend that the practical effect of liberalism's progress has been to unstring the social safety net—especially in the advanced countries that enjoy more elaborate social protections. William Greider summarizes the argument:

> In military terms, the free-running market has mounted a pincer movement against the modern welfare state and is advancing to disable it. One flank of the attack is formed by debt, the accumulated indebtedness of the wealthiest governments as they are unable to keep up with the costs of long-established social commitments. The other flank is capital exit—the flight of firms and investors to other locations when nations fail to shrink the overhead costs that the welfare state imposes on enterprise and labor markets. As these two flanks tighten, each makes the situation worse for the societies under attack, swelling the ranks of dependent citizens and the cost of resistance.[7]

Let's start with the second flank, which is merely a variation on the more general fear that increasing economic ties between rich and poor countries threaten to drag the former down to the latter's level. The basis of that fear is set forth in typical fashion in a 1994 publication of the World Economic Forum, host of the famed annual conclaves in Davos:

> Today, the so-called industrialized nations employ 350 million people who are paid an average hourly wage of $18. However, during the past 10 years, the world economy has gained access to large and populated countries, such as China, the former Soviet Union, India, Mexico, etc. Altogether, it can be estimated that a labour force of some 1,200 million people has thus become reachable, at an average hourly cost of $2, and in many regions, under $1. . . . There is no doubt that many industries will be tempted to relocate in countries with low-cost labour. . . Thus, the question of wealth creation in industrialized countries becomes more and more acute.[8]

The presumed threat, then, is that the massive infusion of low-wage workers into the global labor pool is rendering the high cost of labor in advanced countries (including not only wages but also payroll taxes to fund social insurance programs) increasingly uncompetitive. Market forces, if left to their own devices, will supposedly move jobs from high-cost to low-cost regions until all unsustainable differentials are eliminated—that is, until compensation costs in different countries are more or less equalized. International competition, in this view, acts to arbitrage living standards across countries; under unchecked globalization, therefore, high wages and high social protections in the currently rich countries are being steadily arbitraged away.

Such thinking is very popular. In an April 2000 Business Week/Harris poll, 68 percent of Americans said that trade agreements with low-wage countries like China and Mexico lead to lower wages in the United States, while only 19 percent thought that more open trade increased wages at home.[9] Moreover, such thinking has been around for a very long time. "The first and great disadvantage [of high wages] is that of being undersold by the French and Dutch in our principal manufactured goods," warned the English author of *Propositions for Improving the Manufactures, Agriculture, and Commerce of Great Britain* back in 1763. "The high price of labour is a fatal stab to the trade and manufactures of this country; and without the greatest care taken, it will in time be attended with very dreadful consequences."[10]

Despite its popularity and pedigree, the fear of low-wage countries is completely wrongheaded. It is based on the simplistic notion that people are affluent because they have well-paying jobs; on that assumption, anything that threatens existing well-paying jobs is therefore a threat to the overall standard of living. But those jobs are not simply given; they did not descend like manna from heaven. In a market economy, employee compensation—including wages and other benefits—is a function of productivity. When an economy is rich (that is, when the process of capital accumulation is advanced) the productivity of workers is higher than in a capital-poor economy; the price of labor is consequently higher in capital-rich countries because market competition for labor bids up its price to reflect its superior productivity. High wages and generous benefits are therefore not a cause of wealth; they are a consequence of wealth.

And increasing economic integration across political borders fosters the process of wealth creation on both sides of the border. In the face of intensified competition, industries strive to increase their productivity; the more successful expand, while the less successful contract. Accordingly, international trade pushes economies to specialize in what they do best—in other words, their relatively most productive sectors. With rising productivity comes rising living standards. The internationalization of economic life, far from promoting an immiserizing race to the bottom, spurs instead a race to the top.

The empirical evidence explodes the myth that globalization is causing an exodus of jobs and capital from rich to poor countries. Industrialized countries accounted for 82.8 percent of world industrial output in 1980; fifteen years later, notwithstanding the spectacular rise of China and Southeast Asia, the advanced nations' share of total industrial output was still 80.3 percent.[11] In the United States, despite all the hand-wringing about "deindustrialization," manufacturing output rose by more than 40 percent over the course of the 1990s. Meanwhile, the primary destination of cross-border direct investment in new factories and businesses remains the industrialized world. According to a Deloitte & Touche study, 80 percent of foreign direct investment by U.S. manufacturers in 1998 was in other advanced countries—the top five recipients were the United Kingdom, Canada, the Netherlands, Germany, and Singapore. The United States is itself a leading haven for foreign direct investment capital. Indeed, it has been a net importer of manufacturing investment: Between 1994 and 1998, inbound manufacturing FDI exceeded outbound by an average of $12 billion a year.[12]

Accordingly, the second flank of Greider's pincer movement is a phantom. International trade is a positive-sum game: The more economic contact there is between poor and rich countries, the richer both will become. In the advanced countries, increased productivity leads to even higher compensation for workers, including fringe benefits and payroll taxes that pay for social insurance programs. Far from putting the squeeze on compensation in the advanced countries, globalization creates additional room for compensation to grow.

What about Greider's first flank? The argument here is that the market forces unleashed by globalization compromise national governments' ability to tax (and thereby to fund) the social safety net. In other words, even if globalization does increase wealth, at the same time it makes that wealth harder for governments to get their hands on. "[T]he increasing mobility of capital has rendered an important segment of the tax base footloose, leaving governments with the unappetizing option of increasing tax rates disproportionately on labor income," according to Harvard University economist Dani Rodrik in *Has Globalization Gone Too Far?* "Yet the need for social insurance for the vast majority of the population that remains internationally immobile has not diminished. If anything, this need has become greater as a consequence of increased integration."[13]

It is difficult even to take seriously the proposition that, whether because of globalization or otherwise, the governments of industrialized countries are hurting for tax revenue. Between 1965 and 1998, while globalization was supposedly eroding rich countries' tax bases, average total tax revenues as a percentage of GDP rose for OECD-member countries from just over 25 percent to well over 35 percent.[14] In the United States, federal tax revenues climbed to over 20 percent in 1999—the highest level since World War II.[15] There is, in short, no evidence whatsoever that national governments lack the resources to fund appropriate social policies.

It is true that the taxation of capital is constrained to a degree by international competition. But since most international capital movements occur within and among the rich, relatively high-tax countries, the intensity of tax competition is fairly modest. Furthermore, personal income taxes and payroll taxes, which in the United States account for the vast bulk of federal revenues, are virtually immune from such competitive forces. "Tax exile," after all, is a realistic option only for a tiny minority of the individuals on whom those taxes fall.

Meanwhile, the notion that globalization has increased the need for social insurance does not square with the facts. The theory behind the notion is that international integration increases the risk of dislocation (and thus the need for the safety net) in those sectors of the economy exposed to international competition. But the majority of social spending goes to senior citizens who are retired from the work force; their exposure to the slings and arrows of foreign competition is nil.[16] Furthermore, while competition in tradable sectors has grown more intense, the percentage of people working in those sectors is not rising, but declining—and declining faster thanks to globalization.

In the United States, for example, manufacturing workers have fallen from 35 percent of the work force in 1953 to only 14 percent today.[17] This fact has nothing to do with "deindustrialization": Real U.S. manufacturing output continues to grow briskly, and manufacturing's share of GDP has held steady for decades at between 20 and 25 percent. The decline in employment share is a testament to manufacturing prowess, not failure. Because increases in manufacturing productivity have outpaced increases in the service sector, it takes relatively fewer workers to make the goods we need and want. The same dynamic explains the fall of U.S. agricultural employment from around 40 percent of the total work force in 1900 to only 3 percent a century later.[18] Globalization, by accelerating productivity growth in tradable sectors, thus quickens the pace at which employment in tradable sectors shrinks.

It is undeniably the case that the welfare states of the advanced countries are now under severe fiscal strain. But if globalization is not the culprit, what is? The social safety net, like the commercial sphere it complements, has been badly distorted by the centralizing imperatives of the Industrial Counterrevolution. Over time, the collectivized, top-down systems that prevail around the world have grown increasingly dysfunctional and now face eventual or even imminent collapse. In a crowning irony, the unreconstructed welfare state, established and defended in the name of social cohesion, now poses an enormous and growing threat to social security, especially for the middling and lower ranks of society.

There are obvious differences between the for-profit and nonprofit sectors, but there are underlying similarities as well. Both spheres may be seen as discovery processes: complex phenomena driven by the search for and application of socially useful knowledge. The differences between them arise from the fact that, in the nonprofit sector, provision of goods is divorced, at least in part, from the ability or willingness to pay. Because of this divorce, private nonprofit enterprises can face serious free-riding problems in securing funding for their operations or otherwise achieving their goals. Consequently, under certain circumstances—namely, when the need for comprehensive provision of the public benefit outweighs the advantages of decentralized experimentation—government can assume a useful role in providing public benefits. Specifically, government coercion can be used to overcome free-riding problems.

But even when government does step in, it does not follow that a headlong rush toward centralization is warranted. If government's role in providing social benefits is to be constructive, it must be structured so as to maximize openness to new ideas and to offer clear feedback about the effectiveness of those ideas. In other words, even when government asserts itself to advance some public goal, it should seek, wherever possible, to harness competitive market processes in service of its objectives. Top-down, monopolistic approaches should be shunned.

In the area of the social safety net, government involvement can promote more comprehensive protection against various risks that threaten destitution: old age, disability, sickness, unemployment, and so forth. In particular, it can supplement private insurance markets with "social insurance"—a pooling of risk in which all are required to participate. It can also subsidize consumption of certain vital goods and services—housing and health care, for example.

But under the sway of the Industrial Counterrevolution, the government's role in providing a social safety net went far beyond merely compelling or subsidizing participation in markets. Instead of supplementing markets in a manner consistent with liberal principles, governments often supplanted them altogether with top-down, bureaucratic regimes. Rather than subsidizing participation in private housing and health care markets through voucher schemes, governments established public housing authorities and national health services. Programs to help the unemployed failed to guard against creating perverse incentives, and so ended up subsidizing dependency rather than encouraging a return to gainful work. And with respect to social insurance against the hazards of old age, governments created enormous, monolithic systems that violated basic precepts of actuarial soundness.

A full discussion of the dysfunctions of collectivist social policy is well beyond the scope of this book. Here I focus only on the largest and most fiscally explosive element of the modern welfare state: state-run pensions for retired workers. It is this particular brand of social insurance that is primarily responsible for the welfare state's mounting financial woes.

The founding father of collectivized social insurance, Bismarck, was brutally candid about the political benefits of centralization. As ambassador to Paris in 1861 he had seen how Napoleon III had used state pensions to buy support for the regime. "I have lived in France long enough to know that the faithfulness of most of the French to their government . . . is largely connected with the fact that most of the French receive a state pension," he recalled later.[19] For Bismarck, then, the appeal of social insurance was that it bred dependency on, and consequently allegiance to, the state. "Whoever has a pension for his old age," he stated, "is far more content and far easier to handle than one who has no such prospect."[20]

Social insurance was thus born of contemptuous disregard for liberal principles: What mattered was not the well-being of the workers but the well-being of the state. With that animating principle, social insurance necessarily assumed a collectivist character. In particular, it would clearly not do simply to compel workers to provide for their own retirement; funded pensions that actually belonged to the workers would not inspire the proper feelings of dependency and subservience. Far better was the "pay as you go" system in which the government, acting as intermediary and benefactor, would transfer funds directly from current taxpayers to current retirees.

The pay-as-you-go system flies flagrantly in the face of market logic. Indeed, when such ventures are attempted in the private sector, they go by the name of pyramid or Ponzi schemes and constitute criminal fraud. The essence of a pyramid scheme is that investors' money is never put to productive use; instead, it is simply diverted to pay off earlier investors. As long as new victims can be found, everything seems to work fine; eventually, though, the promoters of the scheme run out of new investors, and the whole house of cards collapses.

Pay-as-you-go public pension systems operate in precisely the same way. As long as the contributions of active workers are sufficient to defray payments to current retirees, the system is fiscally healthy. Indeed, in the early decades of such programs, it appears that the market has been outfoxed. Consider economist Paul Samuelson's smug optimism back in 1967:

> The beauty of social insurance is that it is actuarially unsound. Everyone who reaches retirement age is given benefit privileges that far exceed anything he has paid in. . . . How is this possible? It stems from the fact that the national product is growing at compound interest. . . Always there are more youths than old folks in a growing population. . . . A growing nation is the greatest Ponzi game ever contrived.[21]

Sooner or later, though, such hubris must receive its grim comeuppance. Shifting demographics impose the ultimate constraint. As populations age, the number of retirees begins to grow faster than the number of new workers; the former become a progressively heavier burden on the latter, until at last the burden is unsustainable.

Meanwhile, the perverse incentive structure of collectivized social insurance works to accelerate the system's ultimate breakdown. "The fundamental problem with pay-as-you-go systems," according to José Piñera, the world's foremost advocate of privatizing public pension systems, "is that they divorce effort from reward. Wherever that divorce occurs on a large scale over a long enough period of time, disaster is inevitable."[22] In particular, workers have strong incentives to minimize or evade their contributions to the system, while retirees have an obvious stake in campaigning for higher benefits. Such dynamics steadily worsen the relationship between revenues and obligations and thereby hasten the eventual day of reckoning.

Today, with a global pension crisis that affects rich, developing, and postcommunist nations alike, the reckoning is at hand. Around the world, the ratio of active workers to retirees is shrinking. Promised benefits have spiraled out of control, while either demographic changes or widespread evasion reduce the relative size of the contribution base. Consequently, the hopes for retirement security of hundreds of millions of workers are now in serious jeopardy.

The inevitable Ponzi endgame is now obvious in the rich countries of the industrialized world. In the United States, for example, average life expectancy at birth was only 61.7 years in 1935 when Social Security was established—in other words, lower than the original minimum retirement age. Today, U.S. life expectancy stands at 76.5 years, and it is expected to climb to around 80 over the next 20 years. For most other industrialized countries, current and projected life expectancies are even higher. Meanwhile, fertility has dropped sharply. With the single exception of Ireland, birth rates in all the advanced countries are now below the "replacement rate" of 2.1 children per woman. In Japan, the fertility rate is only 1.68; in Austria, 1.45; in Italy, a mere 1.33. Continued declines in fertility are expected.[23]

The upshot of these demographic trends is a steady erosion in the funding base for social insurance benefits. In 1950, there were 16 workers in the United States for every retiree; today the ratio is only three to one, and in 20 years it will have fallen to two to one. Elsewhere the outlook is even bleaker: By 2020, worker-to-retiree ratios are expected to fall to 1.8 in France and Germany, and 1.4 in Italy and Japan.[24]

Social insurance in the advanced countries is indeed caught in a pincer movement, but not the one that Greider imagined. It is caught in a squeeze between rising life expectancy on one flank and falling fertility on the other. In that tightening vise, what once seemed so clever is now a catastrophe in the making. "When population growth slows down, so that we no longer have the comfortable Ponzi rate of growth or we even begin to register a decline in total numbers," a chastened Paul Samuelson wrote in 1985, "then the thorns along the primrose path reveal themselves with a vengeance."[25]

Already today, public pension spending in the rich member countries of the OECD averages 24 percent of the total government budget, or 8 percent of GDP. To fund these enormous outlays, the tax burden imposed on current employees has reached punishing levels: In Italy, Germany, and Sweden, for example, the combination of employer and employee contributions and personal income taxes now averages around 50 percent of gross labor costs.[26] And while workers put more and more into the system, they can expect to receive less and less. In Sweden, the average rate of return for the generation retiring 25 years after the establishment of the public pension system approached 10 percent per year; for the generation retiring 20 years later, the rate of return had dropped to 3 percent.[27] In the United States, real rates of return for two-earner couples now range from –0.45 percent to 2.13 percent, depending on income.[28]

Even with rising tax rates and declining returns, pay-as-you-go systems throughout the advanced nations are heading toward financial collapse. In the United States, Social Security revenues currently exceed expenses, but the system is expected to begin running deficits in 2016. The annual shortfall is projected to be $1.3 trillion by 2030, a figure that represents more than two-thirds of the entire federal budget for 2001. Over the next 75 years, Social Security's total unfunded liabilities have an estimated present value of $9 trillion—as compared to the current national debt of $5.7 trillion. In Germany and Japan, the current unfunded liabilities of the public pension system are well over 100 percent of GDP; in France and Italy, they exceed 200 percent.[29]

Since developing countries still have relatively young populations, one might expect that the problems with their pension systems remain in the distant future. One would be wrong. First of all, the availability of accelerated catch-up growth also extends to demographics. Developing countries are making the transition from high birth and death rates to low fertility and mortality much faster than did the advanced nations. It took France 140 years to double the share of the population over 60 years of age (from 9 to 18 percent), while Belgium needed nearly 120 years; China, on the other hand, will repeat the feat in 34 years, and Venezuela will do it in 22.[30] Between 1990 and 2030, the percentage of the world's population over 60 years of age is expected to increase from 9 percent to 16 percent, and most of that growth will occur in poorer countries.[31]

Furthermore, demographic changes are amplified by the maturation of public pension systems. When such systems are first established, they frequently do not extend benefits to people already retired or about to retire. Consequently, as those systems reach maturity over their first decades, they experience a rapid rise in the "dependency ratio" of beneficiaries to current workers as the initial retired cohort dies off and is replaced by people who qualify for benefits. In Mexico, for example, the ratio of old to working-age people actually declined from 1960 to 1992, but the public pension system's dependency ratio nearly tripled from 4 percent to 11 percent over that same period.[32]

In addition, administering public pension systems in poor countries is severely complicated by the large informal sectors endemic to those societies.[33] A vicious circle is often triggered. Because many people work in the informal sector, payroll taxes (collected only in the formal sector) have to be higher than would otherwise be necessary. High payroll taxes, though, create incentives for even more people to retreat into the informal sector, thus necessitating even higher rates, which push more people into tax evasion, and so forth. Rising payroll tax rates in Uruguay, for example, caused the proportion of workers contributing to the system to fall from 81 percent in 1975 to 67 percent in 1989.[34] In Brazil, evasion cut contribution revenues by more than a third during the 1980s.[35]

The transitional economies of the former Soviet Empire have inherited no end of problems from the Communist era, including tottering public pension systems. During Soviet rule, dependence on pay-as-you-go systems was nearly total, since occupational pensions and private saving were virtually nonexistent. With communism's collapse, the folly of that dependence has become abundantly clear. To begin with, the countries in question have populations that are nearly as old as those in the advanced nations: As of 1990, over 15 percent of people in former Communist-bloc countries were over 60, as compared to 18 percent in the OECD.[36] Like developing nations, though, they also have large informal sectors that erode the contribution base.

The trauma of ending the old command economy added further complications. The sudden drop in economic output and rise in unemployment dealt additional blows to system revenues. But just as contributions were squeezed, obligations ballooned: Early retirement and liberal approval of disability pensions were widely used to encourage Communist-era enterprises to shed unneeded workers. In Hungary, for example, the number of pensioners grew by 3.1 percent a year from 1989 to 1995, while the number of contributors fell at an annual rate of 5.3 percent; in Latvia pensioners increased at a similar rate, while the number of contributors plummeted by 50 percent between 1991 and 1995.[37]

By the mid-1990s the pension systems of the transitional economies were saddled with cripplingly high dependency ratios. In Poland, pensioners totaled 61 percent of active workers by 1996; in Ukraine the figure was 68 percent; in Bulgaria, 79 percent. To cope with this crushing burden, contribution rates were forced to remain at the punitive levels that had been set during Communist rule: 26 percent in the Czech Republic, 30.5 percent in

Hungary, and 42 percent in Bulgaria.[38] With the demise of the command economy, though, such high rates only accelerated workers' flight into the informal sector, aggravating dependency ratios even further.

Government-provided social insurance is defended on the ground that it shields retirees from the market risks that attend private pension plans. Indeed it does, but only at the cost of subjecting current and future retirees to a far greater risk—the risk of living until the Ponzi scheme of pay-as-you-go pensions begins to break down. Over the past couple of decades retirees around the world have discovered, much to their chagrin, that substituting political risk for market risk has been a poor bargain indeed, as governments have been forced to renege on promises and slash benefits in order to stave off financial collapse.

The breach of faith has been especially severe in developing and transition countries. Failure to adjust benefits for inflation was a favorite strategy in Latin America. The average real pension dropped 80 percent in Venezuela between 1974 and 1992 because of inflation; benefits fell 30 percent in Argentina between 1985 and 1992 for the same reason.[39] In the transition economies, a combination of inflation, explicit benefit cuts, and accumulation of arrears kept pension expenditures as a percentage of GDP more or less constant despite rapid growth in the number of pensioners. Consequently, in Romania, retirees' real per capita income fell 23 percent between 1987 and 1994; in Hungary, the fall was 26 percent; in Latvia, 42 percent.[40] In 1999, some four million elderly Russians were expected to survive on the minimum pension of 234 rubles (less than ten dollars) a month. Millions more received nothing as the government simply failed to honor its obligations to its most vulnerable citizens.[41]

On a less dramatic scale, chiseling has been occurring in rich countries as well. In the United States, a 1983 patch-job for Social Security included making benefits taxable for high-income recipients, skipping inflation indexation for one year, and gradually raising the retirement age from 65 to 67. Belgium shored up its system's ailing financing with a number of "index skips" in the 1980s. Germany has scheduled an increase in the retirement age and reduced benefit levels by basing them on post-tax rather than pre-tax wages. Japan cut benefits back in 1986. Iceland shifted to a means-tested benefit in 1992, thereby eliminating payments altogether for thousands of retirees.[42] While such moves and others like them may have been necessary under the circumstances, the fact remains that promises have been broken, repeatedly, and more infidelity is in store. The well-meaning but misguided attempt to eliminate retirement risk has blown up in the faces of its intended beneficiaries. "Defined benefit" pension plans, it turns out, are anything but.

※※※※

As the gap between promise and reality grows ever wider, countries around the world have begun to experiment with alternatives to the collectivized status quo. Leading the way was Chile, which in 1981 moved to phase out its pay-as-you-go system and replace it with privately owned individual retirement accounts. Instead of the old 26 percent payroll tax, workers are now required to deposit 10 percent of their wages into special savings accounts. Private companies, known as *administradoras de fondos de pensiones,* or AFPs, manage the accounts. Workers are free to choose their AFP and switch their savings from one to another. Upon retirement, workers can either use their accumulated savings to purchase a lifetime annuity from an insurance company, or else leave the money in the account and make programmed withdrawals. Any money remaining in the account when the retiree dies is inheritable.

Workers who entered the labor force after the new system was in place were required to participate in the new system, while those who had already retired had their benefits under the old system guaranteed. Transitional workers were given the choice between sticking with the old system or switching to the new; if they switched, they were given a "recognition bond" to credit them for their prior contributions. The bond was placed in the worker's account and its amount was set so that, at retirement, it would be equal to the worker's accrued benefits under the old system.

Finally, the Chilean pension reform maintains a safety net in the form of a minimum pension guarantee. If for any reason a retiree's private benefits do not meet a minimum threshold, the government will supplement those benefits to bring them up to that threshold. Such supplemental payments are funded from general tax revenues, not a payroll tax.

Chile's pension reforms have been a spectacular success. Some 5.9 million workers owned private savings accounts by the end of 1998—up from 1.4 million at the end of 1981. More than 95 percent of the transition workers who were given a choice have decided to join the new system. Assets under management have grown to over 40 percent of GDP and are projected to reach 134 percent of GDP by 2020. The real rate of return on those assets averaged a gaudy 11.3 percent a year through 1999. A 1995 study found that pension benefits averaged 78 percent of a retiree's average salary over the last ten years of his working life.[43]

Meanwhile, the reforms have generated an impressive array of ancillary benefits. In conjunction with other market-oriented reforms, pension privatization has helped to raise Chile's national savings rate from around 10 percent in the late 1970s to over 25 percent at the beginning of the 21st century. Capital markets have deepened dramatically thanks to the accumulation of large private pension funds. Financial markets have grown in sophistication as well as size: Stock market liquidity has increased; new financial instruments like indexed annuities and mortgage-backed bonds have been developed; and transparency has improved with better disclosure and the emergence of credit-rating institutions. One econometric analysis credits the development of financial markets promoted by pension reform and related factors with increasing total factor productivity in Chile by 1 percentage point per year, or half the overall rate of increase.[44]

Perhaps most important, pension reform has helped to end the class warfare that so convulsed Chile during the 1970s. "We recognized that when workers do not have property, they are vulnerable to demagogues," recalls José Piñera, who as Minister of Labor was the architect of Chile's pension privatization. "The key insight of our pension reform was that, by allowing workers to acquire property in the form of financial capital, we could strengthen their commitment to the free market by aligning their interests with the health of the economy." Piñera and his fellow reformers turned the tables on Marx: Workers became owners of the means of production, but through the expansion of the market system rather than its overthrow. In the process, Marxist-style collectivism lost much of its appeal. "Since our reforms we have had three center-left governments," observes Piñera, "and none of them has touched the core of our major free-market policies. And one reason for this is that nobody dares to threaten the value of the workers' retirement accounts."[45]

A host of other countries have followed Chile's example in recent years. Argentina, Australia, Bolivia, Colombia, El Salvador, Hungary, Kazakhstan, Mexico, Peru, Poland, Sweden, Switzerland, the United Kingdom, and Uruguay have all instituted mandatory private savings plans that, to a greater or lesser extent, substitute for the old pay-as-you-go approach. In most of these countries the new private system only partially replaces the pay-as-you-go system. In Hungary, for example, workers contribute 6 percent to private accounts while a 24 percent payroll tax continues to support the old system.[46] In Sweden, a 16 percent payroll tax goes to maintain the old system, while 2.5 percent of a worker's salary now goes into a private account.[47] The Bush administration is now considering a similar partial privatization for the United States.

Partial reforms, although a step in the right direction, are still only a partial solution. Private accounts will help to generate higher returns for future generations of retirees, but those generations will still be saddled with a dysfunctional, if somewhat shrunken, pay-as-you-go Ponzi scheme. And the longer that thoroughgoing reform is delayed, the more unfavorable the demographic situation becomes and the more onerous the burdens of maintaining the old system are.

It must be acknowledged, though, that the path toward full-scale privatization—with government-provided benefits limited to ensuring some guaranteed minimum—is both arduous and lined with hazards. The most obvious hurdle to overcome is financing the transition from the old to the new system. Phasing out the traditional system does not create any new costs; on the contrary, by preventing future unfunded liabilities from accruing, reform contains and ultimately cuts off the flow of red ink. But there is a temporary cash-flow problem: Benefits under the old system must be paid out to current retirees, but the contributions that formerly funded those benefits are now being directed into private accounts. Other sources of funds must be tapped to pay off the remaining liabilities—which can be staggeringly large.

The Chilean experience shows that this obstacle, though daunting, is not insuperable. The implicit debt of its pay-as-you-go system had grown in excess of 100 percent of GDP—in other words, the country had dug itself into an impressively deep hole. But shifting most current workers out of the old system quickly slashed that figure. To deal with what remained, Chile availed itself of a variety of methods. It continued a portion of the payroll tax for a number of years, sold off state-owned enterprises to raise revenue, cut other government expenditures, issued new government bonds, and painlessly reaped the benefits of the additional tax revenues that came from a faster-growing economy. Together, these measures have sufficed to cover the transition's financing requirements, which have ranged from 1.4 to 4.4 percent of GDP per year.[48]

Other risks lurk in designing this new system. While some measure of prudential regulation may be necessary, especially in countries with under-developed financial markets, excessive government meddling in how private accounts are to be invested can reduce returns for savers—possibly cata-strophically. Chile, for example, still requires AFPs to guarantee a minimum return relative to other AFPs. Consequently there is little difference in the portfolios of the various AFPs, therefore denying savers the opportunity to choose different mixes of risk and return. Also, Chile has rigid restrictions on the commissions charged by AFPs that prevent discounts based on maintain-ing a specific balance or keeping an account for some specified amount of time. Thus prevented from competing effectively on product or price, the AFPs attempt to lure customers through marketing ploys—just as American banks in the days of interest rate controls offered toasters for new accounts. Such empty competition drives up administrative costs.[49]

In Mexico, meanwhile, fund managers are required to invest a mini-mum of 65 percent of assets in government securities—a grievously wrong-headed mandate that risks turning the system into a dumping ground for government debt. A fiscal crisis, not a remote contingency in Mexico by any means, could wipe out the retirement savings of a generation. The Mexican system also prohibits investments in equities or any foreign assets. Such re-strictions stifle the financial deepening that is an enormous side benefit of privatization, as well as prevent prudent portfolio diversification. In poorer countries with underdeveloped financial markets, it is especially important that savers be allowed to invest in high-quality foreign assets.[50]

In Kazakhstan, the new private system features a guaranteed government-run State Accumulation Fund in addition to private pension funds. Because of the miserable state of the legal infrastructure on which financial markets depend, distrust of the private alternatives was understandably widespread. When the new system was established in 1998, some 85 percent of Kazakh employees chose to put their money in the State Accumulation Fund.[51]

Whether in the form of regulation or market participation, overween-ing government control over investments in a "privatized" system merely substitutes one form of hyper-centralization for another. Indeed, for decades a number of developing countries have pursued this variation on top-down control in a pure and explicit form. Rather than adopting pay-as-you-go systems, these countries, including India, Malaysia, Singapore, and a number of African nations, created retirement plans in which there is a single retirement fund or "provident fund" and the government manages all the investment assets.

These provident fund systems do avoid the perverse Ponzi-scheme dynamics of conventionally collectivized social insurance—but only to fall prey to other dysfunctions. Specifically, the government as investment-fund monopolist is immune from competitive pressure to earn a decent return; consequently, it is not constrained from investing in ways that are politically advantageous but economically dubious. Unsurprisingly, the performance of provident fund systems has ranged from lackluster to disastrous. In the latter category, Kenya's system averaged a −3.8 percent rate of return during the 1980s, while returns in Zambia averaged −23.4 percent.[52]

So much then for the charge that social insurance is menaced by excessive reliance on markets. On the contrary, it is the systematic suppression of market principles that has put the retirement security of millions in jeopardy. Undoing past mistakes will require formidable resolve, as will resisting the continuing temptation to attempt control from above. But if the resolve can be found, the proper direction is clear: For the sake of retirement security, for the sake of true social cohesion, the growing movement in favor of market-based reform is the one best hope there is.

〜〜〜〜〜

In a liberal social order, a nonprofit sector dedicated to providing public benefits complements and coexists with the private wealth-creating activities of the for-profit commercial sphere. There is a role for government in the realm of public benefits, namely, to extend and systematize the efforts of voluntary initiatives through regulation or tax-based funding. However, that role must be to supplement, rather than supplant, the decentralized experimentation of commercial markets and private noncommercial activity.

The collectivist error is to assume that, because some measure of government centralization can prove useful, it therefore follows that centralization carried to its most extreme limits works best. Under the influence of that error, monopoly and bureaucracy plague the provision of public goods around the world. The dysfunctions of collectivized social insurance, reviewed in detail in the previous section, are a case in point.

Much of what goes on in the name of social cohesion, though, goes beyond the malprovision of public benefits and extends to intervention in the commercial sphere. The purpose of social safety nets, properly conceived, is to help people cope with the disruptions and dislocations that economic change sometimes brings. The interventionist policies in question, on the other hand, seek instead to prevent change from happening. Such policies are the utter perversion of social assistance: Rather than helping the few who fall behind to share in the general bounty, they sacrifice the future of the bounty itself. Consequently, they produce, not cohesion, but division and conflict.

In earlier chapters I surveyed the persistence of various kinds of interventionist controls. Chapter 6 examines government domination of markets for goods and services, while Chapter 7 addresses the ongoing suppression of capital markets. These controls are maintained today, among other reasons, because they provide a kind of safety net. They maintain people in jobs (and thus with income and benefits) that would disappear if competitive forces were unleashed. Economic policy and social policy thus become fused.

The blurring of commerce and social welfare is most obvious in the struggling enterprises left over from communist command economies. In China, for example, state-owned enterprises act as mini-welfare states, shouldering a wide variety of social functions. As of the mid-1990s, state-owned firms ran more than 18,000 schools that had over six million students enrolled, and they operated hospitals that accounted for one-third of all hospital beds in the country. They also continued to build nearly half of all new housing in urban areas. But perhaps their heaviest burden consists of their unfunded pension liabilities. China's pay-as-you-go pension system has been run at the enterprise level and has an implicit debt of around 50 percent of GDP.[53]

In Russia, the Magnitogorsk steel mill (discussed in Chapter 6) provides electricity for the city and builds local roads in lieu of tax payments. According to a study by the consulting firm McKinsey, some 20 percent of workers in a typical Russian steel plant perform social welfare duties—staffing kindergartens, concert halls, sports arenas, and so forth.[54]

More important than any ancillary services these firms provide, their mere existence is itself a social welfare function. Here I refer to those moribund firms that actually destroy wealth, whose output is worth less than the sum of their inputs. But though these zombie enterprises serve no economic purpose, they are at present all that stands between millions of people and destitution. Take the 100 or so small steel mills in Russia, virtually all of which are beyond redemption. Some 40 percent of them, though, provide more than 15 percent of total employment in their communities.

And the persistence of elements of the Soviet *propiska* system of required residence permits makes it difficult for laid-off workers to make a new start elsewhere.[55] In China, the scale of the problem is mind-boggling: Some 80 million people work in the state-owned sector, and a significant fraction of those workers are redundant. If these workers and their dependents were suddenly cut loose, the potential for social and political upheaval is difficult to overstate.

Yet continuing to prop up the zombie economy just for the sake of the jobs it provides is a devil's bargain. Unless unproductive enterprises are allowed to die, productive ones cannot thrive—and cannot create new jobs and new opportunities, real opportunities, for the future. Of course it is necessary—morally as well as politically—to ease the burdens of those whose livelihoods depend upon the old and unsustainable system. But one does not rescue shipwreck victims by attaching floats to the ruined vessel and then leaving the ill-fated passengers to drift; the proper course is to transfer those passengers to a seaworthy ship and continue the journey. In the same way, perpetuating the economic waste of the communist system is not only contrary to the general interest in a vital and thriving economy; it is also a disservice to the workers in those doomed enterprises to leave them trapped in a failed past.

But the temptation to use restrictions on competition as a surrogate for social policy is difficult to resist—and not just in the postcommunist world. In both developing and advanced countries, it is all too common for established interests to claim that the human toll of this or that competitive challenge is unbearable, ignoring all the while the human toll of throwing sand into the engines of growth. Pandering to such claims, meanwhile, is almost always the path of least resistance for politicians—a path with which they are intimately familiar.

In Japan, the failure to resist this temptation has been a major contributor to the economic doldrums of the past decade. Japan is now infamous for its "dual economy"—a world-beating export sector on the one hand, and a backward and stagnant domestic sector on the other. Export industries, Japan's public face, still exceed the productivity of their closest rivals by 20 percent; meanwhile, those industries that do not face international competition are nearly 40 percent less productive, on average, than world-best practice. Unfortunately for the country's overall vitality, the Toyotas and Sonys employ only about 10 percent of the work force, while the rest are stuck in the vast underachieving stretches of the economy.[56]

Retailing, for example, accounts for about 12 percent of employment. Some 55 percent of those workers, though, are still in traditional "mom and pop" stores (as compared to 19 percent in the United States and 26 percent in France). Interventionist policies designed explicitly to preserve small shopkeepers are a major cause of the disparity. The notorious Large Retail Store Law required big retailers to get the permission of their smaller rivals before they could open a new store—needless to say, permission was seldom forthcoming. The law was finally phased out in 2000, only to be replaced by a new statute that continues to restrict large stores, though now in the name of environmental and urban planning concerns. Obstacles for new entrants are matched by barriers to exit. Since 1998, the government has provided retailers with some $40 billion in loan guarantees with virtually no assessment of the borrowers' creditworthiness.[57]

Construction, meanwhile, occupies another 10 percent of the Japanese work force. By contrast, only 5 percent of U.S. employment is in the construction industry. This featherbedding is made possible by, among other things, lavish budgets for public works. Government contracts account for an estimated half of total construction output. And for most of those contracts, competition is effectively suppressed by the officially illegal but nonetheless pervasive *dango* system of bid rigging.[58]

Restrictions on competition in product markets are buttressed by Japan's over-centralized system of finance. While Japanese multinationals have access to world capital markets, small and medium-sized enterprises remain heavily dependent on banks to finance their ventures. The banks, however, have tended to favor incumbents and established ways of doing things. Consequently, upstarts who threaten the status quo in Japan's sleepy, stagnant domestic sectors have found it difficult, if not impossible, to raise the capital they need. Meanwhile, existing firms have, until recently at least, felt little or no pressure from capital markets to maximize shareholder returns. Without this prod to shake things up, it has been that much easier to maintain the lazy calm that characterizes too many of Japan's domestic industries.

In sum, it is estimated that thoroughgoing elimination of competitive barriers in Japan would cost ten million jobs, or some 15 percent of the current work force. By the same estimate, such reform would create an additional 11 million jobs. Opponents of liberal reform, within Japan and outside, claim that the country would be torn apart by such an intense bout of creative destruction. "If Japan's policy-makers yield to the demands of the Washington consensus," warns John Gray, "Japan will join all those Western societies in which mass unemployment, epidemic crime and the collapse of social cohesion are problems without solutions."[59]

Yet the assumption that economic vibrancy and social cohesion are incompatible is flatly belied by Japan's own experience. During its golden years of rapid growth, Japan underwent a dizzying transformation in the deployment of its work force. In 1950, 45 percent of employed workers were still in agriculture; by 1975, farm workers amounted to only 13 percent of the labor force. Over the same period, the share of employment held by manufacturing, construction, and utilities soared from 29 percent to 42 percent.[60] Here is a country whose social and cultural structures are rooted in long-standing feudal traditions, a country for which rice growing holds a quasi-religious significance, but which nonetheless staged a breakneck flight from agriculture to manufacturing in less than a generation—without social upheaval or loss of its distinctive cultural identity. In the light of that history, are we really to believe that "Japaneseness" cannot survive the restructuring of the service sector?

If Japan occupies one end of the spectrum of advanced nations regarding its restrictions on competition, the United States, generally speaking, is situated on the other. Nevertheless, important obstacles to competition do remain, and they are staunchly defended for the social values they allegedly preserve. Take, for example, protectionist barriers against imports: They are still formidable for textiles, clothing, steel, and many farm goods.

The defenders of residual protectionism argue that they are trying to save jobs and ways of life. But their interest in saving jobs is curiously selective. The annual toll of "displaced workers" in the United States (ones who have been cut or laid off after more than three years on the job) exceeded 2.5 million in 1995–97. But of these, 75 percent were employed in service sector jobs that do not face foreign competition. As to the remaining quarter, only a fraction of those who were displaced from manufacturing, agriculture, or mining (the so-called "tradable" sector) lost their jobs to imports.[61] It is always painful to lose one's job, whatever the cause; a pink slip is a pink slip regardless of whether it occurs because of a domestic competitor, or a merger, or automation, or corporate restructuring—or competition from abroad.

In particular, no serious voice in the United States proclaims that technological progress should be halted because it threatens existing jobs. We hear no protests on behalf of bank employees displaced by automatic teller machines, or receptionists who lost their jobs to voice mail. Yet if a company seeks to make its operations more productive by moving an assembly plant overseas, that is somehow supposed to be intolerable. Both trade and technology help enterprises to improve their productivity, and one inescapable byproduct of rising productivity is that old jobs are eliminated and new ones created.

In particular, demand for low-skilled workers is now on the decline in all the more advanced economies. Critics of globalization blame this fact on increased trade; friends of open markets counter that technology is the primary cause. The apportionment of responsibility is doubtless of academic interest, but otherwise why should it matter? Is the current trend one that anybody in good conscience could actually oppose? Would it really be preferable if demand for low-skilled labor were rising—if our economies were growing ever more dependent on brute muscle and rote clerical work? Chaplin's vision of "Modern Times" should not provoke nostalgia; on the contrary, we should celebrate the fact that the new knowledge-based economy increasingly requires us to stretch our minds, not break our bodies. Of course we should strive to help those who lack the skills to take advantage of the new opportunities; but it ought to be unthinkable for us to wish upon the next generation the same narrow horizons that now confine too many of its parents.

※※※

There is another species of interventionism that I have not yet addressed, but that is especially implicated in the blurring of economic and social policy. Specifically, the Industrial Counterrevolution led governments to overrun, not just product and capital markets, but labor markets as well.

The very concept of labor markets strikes collectivists as repellent: The "commodification" of human beings, in their view, is inherently degrading and exploitative. Such thinking gained currency at a time when, by current standards, the world was desperately poor. Most work was dirty and hard, and the market price for it paid for little more than subsistence. Today, when mass affluence is a reality in the advanced countries and a realizable goal for many developing ones, the vision of deep-seated class conflict between capital and labor has faded considerably.

Still, though, the exchange of work for wages continues to rankle. There is, admittedly, an inevitable harshness about a system that treats human beings as abstract inputs. But ironically, it is precisely because labor markets are coldly impersonal that their operation is so beneficent. By subjecting the valuation of human effort to the impersonal coordination of untold millions of personal decisions, labor markets generate incredibly rich information about the relative usefulness and attractiveness of various occupations. The market signals of job openings and layoffs, of wages and benefits and other terms of employment, guide people to different lines of work with much greater sensitivity to social needs and wants than any centralized process for allocating labor could ever hope to accomplish.

But around the world, labor markets are to a greater or lesser degree hampered and distorted by centralizing interventions. Wages are sometimes fixed by statute or administratively without regard for market realities. Compulsory unionization and various corporatist arrangements over-centralize and politicize the wage bargaining process. Restrictive work rules imposed by labor cartels undermine productivity. And restrictions on layoffs and plant closings frustrate adjustments to changing conditions and sap the forces of economic dynamism.[62]

Consider the situation in Western Europe, where highly restrictive labor policies are widely heralded as safeguards of social cohesion. Compulsory labor unions dominate wage bargaining in most countries there. In Germany and France, for example, union contracts cover 95 percent of workers, while in Italy coverage is 92 percent. By comparison, only 18 percent of the U.S. labor force works under union contracts. Strong national unions and employers' associations that represent the whole country are also prevalent in Europe, as are arrangements that give the government an explicit and regular role in the negotiating process. Austria, Belgium, Finland, and Norway have carried such centralization the farthest. Even when bargaining occurs mainly on the sectoral (or even enterprise) level, "pattern bargaining" and other forms of coordination among leading employers and unions work to reduce differences in negotiating outcomes. Germany and Austria stand out for their highly developed coordination mechanisms.[63]

European labor regulations exert influence over not only the terms of employment but the termination of it as well. Dismissal of employees is subject to all manner of onerous rules and requirements: Employers must jump through a variety of procedural hoops (previous warnings, written statements of reasons, prior notification of the union, etc.) before they are permitted to dismiss an employee. In addition, employees are entitled to lengthy notice periods (up to seven months in Germany) and often severance pay as well (one month's pay per year of service in Portugal, with a legal minimum of three month's pay). Strict rules regarding "unfair" dismissals are also common. In Germany and elsewhere, it is considered unfair to lay off a worker if it was possible to retain him in another capacity; in Denmark layoffs because of a corporate takeover are deemed unfair. Compensation for unfair dismissals can range up to 12 month's pay in Germany; in Norway, reinstatements of the dismissed workers are frequently ordered.[64]

Two decades of unusually high unemployment have brought Europe's web of labor regulations under considerable critical scrutiny. Throughout the 1960s and '70s, European unemployment rates were consistently lower than the U.S. rate, often by a substantial margin. They caught up during the severe recession that wracked both sides of the Atlantic in the early 1980s; then, as U.S. unemployment gradually subsided, joblessness in Europe persisted and even worsened. Although improving job performance has brought the average unemployment rate for the European Union back into single digits, that figure is still roughly double the U.S. rate. Meanwhile, long-term joblessness is dramatically more prevalent in Europe: As of 1999, 47.5 percent of the unemployed in the European Union had been out of work for a year or more, compared with only 6.8 percent in the United States.[65]

Perhaps more troubling than the statistics on unemployment are those on job creation and employment. After all, unemployment figures are expressed as a percentage of the active labor force, and thus can vary significantly depending on whether certain people without jobs—students, homemakers, the late middle-aged, or recipients of social assistance—are classified as in or out of the job market. The real bottom line is the capacity of the economy to generate work, and on that score, European performance over the past two decades has been nothing less than dismal. From 1980 to 1997, there was no net private-sector job creation in the European Union— none at all. By contrast, the United States added some 30 million new private-sector jobs over that same period. The percentage of Europeans between the ages of 15 to 64 who had jobs declined from 65 percent in the mid-1970s to 60 percent in the mid-'90s; in the United States, even with strong population growth due to immigration, the employment rate for working-age people rose from 63 to 73 percent.[66]

The burdens of joblessness are not distributed evenly through European society—far from it. Rather, they fall with punishing severity on people who are at the start and end of their working lives. For people aged 15 to 24, unemployment in 1999 stood at 17.2 percent, while the employment rate was only 39.5 percent. In the United States, by contrast, the unemployment rate was only 9.9 percent, while the employment rate was 59 percent. Among European men aged 55 to 64, the employment rate was a low 48.3

percent, compared to 66.1 percent in the United States.[67] These dry figures speak of a massive waste of human talent. In an underpowered economy that cannot provide enough work, the most experienced members of society are shunted aside while the promise of the new generation is squandered.

It is difficult to assess the extent to which labor market regulations are responsible for Europe's grim employment picture. Many other factors have doubtless played a role. Excessively generous unemployment benefits offer a direct subsidy to joblessness. High tax rates discourage participation in the labor force and deter job creation. Restrictive regulation of product and capital markets inhibits entrepreneurs from starting new businesses and hiring workers.

Empirical studies do reveal, however, that labor controls bear at least some of the blame. Although results are mixed, there is evidence that union strength and dismissal restrictions are associated with poor overall job creation.[68] Also, there is a clear connection between dismissal restrictions and the length of unemployment. Although the purpose of such laws is to prevent workers from being fired, they also make it harder for workers that are let go to be rehired later.[69]

The link between labor regulations and the lack of job growth comes into clearer focus when examining the effect on particular types of jobs. There is a strong correlation between centralized bargaining and wage compression—that is, the squeezing of the wage scale to eliminate especially low-paying and high-paying jobs. In conjunction with minimum wage laws, the effect is to deter creation of both low-skill and high-skill jobs.[70] Dismissal restrictions, unsurprisingly, reduce labor turnover; consequently, they tend to slow job growth in industries with fluctuating employment needs and high levels of job-hopping.[71]

The upshot is that the industries in which job creation is deterred by labor controls are precisely the ones that would otherwise be experiencing the fastest job growth—namely, the industries of the service sector. In all the advanced countries, there is a steady and inevitable employment shift underway from manufacturing to services. But while factory jobs steadily disappear on both sides of the Atlantic, Europe lags behind the United States in compensating for those losses with job creation in the service sector. Some 54.9 percent of working-age Americans have jobs in the service sector; the corresponding figure for the E.U. is only 40 percent.[72] Labor restrictions are at least partly responsible for this predicament. Empirical research shows a connection between the restrictiveness of dismissal regulations and underdevelopment of the service sector. The job-destroying effects of wage compression, meanwhile, are visible in particular service industries—namely high-end jobs in business and professional services and lower-end jobs in hotels and restaurants.[73]

Opponents of labor reform often dismiss the shift to service jobs as a blight—a proliferation of low-paying, dead-end "McJobs." In particular, they take aim at the U.S. record of job creation: The quantity of new jobs is so impressive, they say, only because the quality is so poor. In fact, though, the service sector considered as a whole is considerably more skill-intensive than the goods-producing industries. Throughout the OECD, the ratio of low-skill jobs to medium- and high-skill jobs in the service sector is less than 1 in 2, whereas the ratio for goods-producing jobs is 1.25 to 1. Likewise, the proportion of university-trained workers in service industries is over three times higher than in the goods sector.[74] In the United States, contrary to the "McJobs" canard, job creation has been most brisk at the top of the skill and pay ladder. From 1990 to 1995, the fastest growing service occupations were found in the categories "executive, administrative, managerial," and "professional specialty," with a combined 8.6 new jobs per 1,000 working-age people.[75]

Yes, the U.S. economy has also created large numbers of lower-paying jobs in retail, hotels and restaurants, and other personal services. But this is nothing to apologize for. These positions offer opportunities for immigrants, experience for younger workers, and flexibility for mothers who want to contribute a second income to the family. Does anyone really think that these people would be better off unemployed? The American service sector, in its dizzying variety, creates work for every skill level, every taste, every level of commitment—from part-time and temporary work to demanding professional careers, from customer assistance and clerical work to high-powered analytical positions. It therefore draws more people into the work force because its diversity offers something for nearly everyone.

European countries, on the other hand, have actually been trying to shrink their work forces. They encourage early retirement to hasten the exit of older workers, and subsidize endless years of postsecondary schooling to stall job-seeking by the young. France, notoriously, has legislated a 35-hour work week in the pathetic pursuit of "work sharing." These quack cures treat the symptoms of high unemployment, but worsen the underlying disease of falling employment. On the brighter side, some countries have adopted measures to loosen restrictions on part-time and temporary work, encourage greater wage restraint in the bargaining process, reduce the tax wedge, and limit the anti-work incentives of unemployment benefits. Real progress has been made, especially in the Netherlands, Ireland, and, more recently, Spain. On the whole, though, the continued posture of Western Europe leans more toward hanging on to the past than embracing the future.

European joblessness is a complex phenomenon with many contributing causes—not only labor regulations, but also high taxes, incentive-skewing social assistance, and stultifying restrictions on product and capital markets. Divvying up guilt is really beside the point, since all of these causes are merely facets of a single, fundamental problem—the ongoing inertia of the Industrial Counterrevolution. In the name of social cohesion, the opponents of liberal reform struggle to preserve the industries and economic structures that were built during collectivism's heyday. And yes, their rearguard action is slowing job declines in waning sectors. But at what cost?

At the cost, I would argue, of true social cohesion. Without dynamism, without confidence in the future, modern society cannot sustain any sense of an all-embracing common interest. When the positive-sum game of continuing growth gives way to the zero-sum game of stagnation and sclerosis, every group and faction comes to see all others as the enemy—as threats to its share of limited and dwindling spoils. Conflicts deepen and multiply when every gain is someone else's loss. Europe's backward-looking labor restrictions have sought to tame the unruly process of creative destruction as it applies to employment. But the destruction continues, if more slowly; creation, meanwhile, has ground to a halt—and with it, so has any basis for durable solidarity. The ugly resentment of immigrants so prevalent in Europe today is one obvious example of how lack of economic opportunity breeds division and rancor.

Furthermore, the means by which most people develop a sense of social belonging and inclusion is participation in the great, shared enterprise of productive work. In Europe, however, the levels of participation are falling as anti-market policies throttle the engines of job creation. As a consequence, growing numbers of people, especially younger and older people, are educated, able-bodied—and useless. Consider the Netherlands, widely and properly praised for bringing unemployment down to a mere 3 percent; yet even there, an astounding 12 percent of working-age people are officially classified as permanently disabled.[76] In other countries the situation is much worse. Such a waste of human ability is more than an economic loss; it is a social tragedy.

11

Liberalization by Fits and Starts

On May Day, 2000, thousands of protesters gathered in London to rage against the perceived injustices and indignities of global capitalism. The event marked yet another in a cycle of anti-globalization demonstrations in the United States and Europe—a cycle that began with the riots in Seattle in late 1999 that disrupted the ministerial meeting of the World Trade Organization. Most of the marchers in London that day were peaceful, but an unruly few broke into and looted a McDonald's, defaced a statue of Winston Churchill, and spraypainted graffiti on the Cenotaph, the monument to the British dead of the two world wars. This last act of vandalism was especially offensive, prompting widespread public condemnation of the protesters. Tony Blair, in particular, referred to them as "idiots." [1]

But however idiotic, the choice to desecrate the Cenotaph was also fitting in a strange sort of way. For there is a link, obscure but vital, that connects the current anti-globalization protest movement with the dead whose memories were dishonored. The protest movement, ragtag and feeble, represents the last shudder of a once-mighty and world-upending convulsion—a convulsion whose first great blasts transformed Europe from the center of the new world economy into the central battleground of two world wars. The tragic marching of yesteryear, and the farcical marching of today, share the same driving beat: confusion in the face of modernity's dizzying and messy complexities, and longing for utopian simplicity and certainty.

It seems incomprehensible to us today, but the outbreak of World War I was greeted across Europe with wild and rapturous euphoria. Now Western politicians dread the public reaction to even the slightest trickle of military casualties. Witness the recent NATO bombing campaign in the Kosovo conflict, in which all other strategic and tactical considerations were subordinated to the single and overriding goal of minimizing loss of life on the allied side. But then, back in August 1914, the prospect of wholesale slaughter led young men to queue up in droves at recruiting posts, and mothers to urge their reluctant sons to put duty and glory above personal safety.

Intellectuals in particular swooned with war fever. Ever since Vietnam, we have typically associated intellectuals with pacifism and even contempt for things military. But back then, writers and thinkers and poets on both sides embraced the war ecstatically, and many backed their words with action and volunteered to fight and die in the trenches. "In this hour it was generally felt that a special national destiny reached into everybody's hearts, the greatest and smallest alike, and decided what each of us is and is worth," wrote philosopher Max Scheler in *The Genius of War*. "We were no longer what we had been—alone!"[2] Among other notables who hailed the coming of hostilities: Henri Bergson, Émile Durkheim, Anatole France, Sigmund Freud, Stefan George, André Gide, Thomas Hardy, Thomas Mann, Marcel Proust, Rainer Maria Rilke, Max Weber, and H. G. Wells. Even Gandhi recruited for the British in India.[3]

What made Europe so hungry for war? It had been a century since the last general war—a century that had witnessed an explosion of economic and technological progress, of social and cultural dynamism, unparalleled in all of history. How could Europe turn its back on that century and descend, willingly, into bottomless savagery? What hole existed in its soul that demanded to be filled with young men's corpses?

In Chapter 4, I made the argument that the rise of the Industrial Counterrevolution created an intellectual climate in which war seemed rational and even inevitable. The liberal ideals of cosmopolitanism and free trade had given way to a new collectivist vision of protectionist imperial blocs, clashing incessantly for control of markets and resources. That vision helped to spur the arms races and multiplying alliances that ultimately converted the spark of Sarajevo into full-scale conflagration.

My current question, though, goes deeper—not why war seemed

necessary, but why it seemed wonderful. What explains the widespread jubilation on both sides as armies mobilized and clashed, or the amazing endurance of suffering as the war dragged on so pitilessly and pointlessly? The historian A. J. P. Taylor pointed the way toward an answer when he wrote, "Men's minds seem to have been on edge in the last two or three years before the war . . . as though they had become unconsciously weary of peace and security. . . ." According to Taylor, "Men wanted violence for its own sake; they welcomed war as a relief from materialism."[4]

In his fascinating book *Redemption by War: The Intellectuals and 1914,* Roland Stromberg explores this theme in depth. In great and convincing detail he documents the increasing bellicosity of European culture up to and through the Great War—the mood summed up in Rupert Brooke's famous line, "Come and die. It'll be great fun." What Freud struggled to explain as a "death wish," Stromberg attributes to profound disorientation in the face of industrial society's emergence:

> We ought to be able to understand the magnitude of the psychic crisis that confronted human nature when it was first released from primeval group solidarity to face the anomic megalopolitan wilderness, the terrible freedom of total permissiveness. Then, in 1914, as young intellectuals repeatedly testified, the sense of community suddenly reappeared with the shock of war, and struck them with the force of a raw *reality* they could not resist.[5]

In other words, the war fever of August 1914 was yet another expression of the spiritual turmoil stirred up by modernity—the same turmoil that made the fallacies of the Industrial Counterrevolution so irresistibly appealing. Faced with the breakdown of traditional beliefs and social structures, confronted with a strange new world in which, according to Marx, "all that is solid melts into air," people craved the return of certainty and rootedness. War, like collectivism in all its many variations, answered that craving.

And today we see that very same craving, that "quest for community," in the rantings of the anti-globalization protesters. Like their predecessors of a hundred years past, they are groping for some utopian release from a confusing and manifestly imperfect world. And like their predecessors, they long for something higher than mere materialism, and they believe it can be found in political action.

Note, in this regard, what the marchers in Seattle and London and elsewhere are protesting against. Though they hold themselves out as defenders of the world's poor against economic injustice, it is striking how much of their ire is directed, not against poverty, but against affluence. McDonald's restaurants are a favorite target of both verbal and physical assaults, as are Starbucks coffee shops. Why? Their primary sin is that they symbolize middle-class consumerism and plenty.

Consider, along similar lines, a two-page advertisement placed in *The New York Times* by a group called the Turning Point Project. The ad, entitled "Global Monoculture," contains 13 photographs that document the supposed horrors of globalization. The photos show the following: a cloverleaf interchange, a parking lot of new automobiles, people working at computer consoles, an industrial chicken farm, a residential subdivision, pipes spewing runoff, a deforested area, a grocery store aisle, a high-rise apartment building, people leaving an office building, an urban skyline, traffic congestion, and, of course, a McDonald's sign. By my count, that makes three shots of environmental problems and ten of material well-being.

In short, the anti-globalization protesters are motivated as much by cultural hostility toward material prosperity as by any economic grievances. Yes, they rail against markets for failing to deliver the goods, but their bitterest complaint is that markets deliver nothing but the goods. They reject contemporary affluence as shallow and banal, and yearn for authenticity in a world of artifice. In the future, they hope, lies some great political redemption, but in the present they find solace in the simple joys of marching and chanting and renouncing.

A century ago, utopian longings similar to those of today's protesters helped to launch the great historical cataclysm I have called the Industrial Counterrevolution. That cataclysm resulted in wars and revolutions and countless lesser ills, and in the process destroyed the first global economic order just as it was getting underway. Could such things happen again? Are the present expressions of radical discontent the first stirrings of a new cataclysm? And will the current episode of globalization end as badly as the first?

Fortunately, the answer to these questions is almost certainly *no*. The anti-globalization protesters fancy themselves the leaders of some new political movement, but they are really just the straggling rearguard of an old and failed one. For all the media attention they have received, and all their Internet-based organizational savvy, their quest to reawaken the grand utopian passions of the past is virtually hopeless.

Here in the United States, the protest movement is best understood as one small but noisy contingent in a larger anti-globalization political coalition—a crazy-quilt assemblage of labor unions, environmentalist groups, left-wing activists, and far-right xenophobes. Forged initially during the debate over the North American Free Trade Agreement in the early 1990s, the coalition has won some significant victories. Legislation to renew "fast track" procedures for approving new trade agreements, strongly opposed by anti-trade groups, failed twice in Congress in 1997 and 1998. Efforts to negotiate a Multilateral Agreement on Investment under the auspices of the OECD fell apart at the end of 1998, due in part to frenzied lobbying by anti-MAI groups. And in the Seattle debacle of late 1999, the WTO was forced to abort the launch of a new round of worldwide trade talks. Although the protests in the streets were not directly to blame, it is fair to say that key elements of the U.S. negotiating position at Seattle (including a refusal to discuss the reform of particular U.S. trade barriers, and an insistence on extending the WTO mandate to include labor rights issues) reflected a desire to appease domestic anti-trade groups. The U.S. position, flatly unacceptable to many developing countries, proved a major factor in the round's collapse.

Despite its successes, the strength of the anti-globalization movement in the United States should not be overestimated. Events since Seattle have clearly demonstrated that opponents of trade liberalization can still be defeated. In May 2000, in the face of ferocious opposition, the House of Representatives voted to extend permanent normal trade relations to China, thus paving the way for that country's entry into the WTO. The Senate later passed the "PNTR" bill by an overwhelming margin. And in June 2000, the House rejected a resolution to withdraw the United States from the WTO. Supporters of the measure were able to muster only 56 votes—or roughly a third of the votes against joining the WTO in the first place five years earlier.

This last defeat is particularly telling as to the limitations of the U.S. anti-globalization coalition. Its successes have come when it acts as a blocking force—an impediment to further opening of markets. As the vote on withdrawing from the WTO reveals, though, the coalition is basically impotent as a rollback force. Yes, continued progress in reducing trade barriers has become more difficult in the United States because of the emergence of the anti-globalization movement (although not impossible, as the victory on PNTR with China demonstrates). However, there is no indication of any serious political support for reversing prior liberalizing gains. And since most U.S. barriers to foreign competition have already been eliminated, that fact consigns the anti-globalization coalition to the unglamorous task of defending a small and gradually shrinking protectionist fiefdom.

Thus, even on its home turf in the United States, the anti-globalization protest movement is in no position to precipitate a fundamental shift away from the present course of continued international economic integration. It is little more than a sideshow in a motley anti-reform coalition—a coalition that is capable of obstruction, but of little besides.

Meanwhile, in the developing countries, the anti-globalization protesters must confront the embarrassing fact that they are widely condemned by the very people they presume to speak for. Insofar as the protesters have any coherent agenda, their focus is on the need to incorporate protection of labor rights and the environment into new WTO agreements—ostensibly to stop or slow globalization's "race to the bottom" in living standards and social protections. In one alternative, the WTO would require national governments to observe certain "core" labor and environmental standards, with violations punishable by trade sanctions. In another possibility, the WTO could create broad new exceptions to existing agreements that allow national governments to close their markets for social policy reasons (for example, restricting imports from countries that don't guarantee a particular minimum wage or fail to meet certain air-quality standards). Either way, the protesters want to make trade conditional upon the implementation of particular favored social policies.

Developing countries overwhelmingly reject these efforts to attach strings to their access to rich-country markets. A generation ago, most leaders of the old Third World renounced dependence upon foreign markets and capital as neocolonialism; today, however, there is a strong consensus that export-oriented growth, as pioneered in East Asia, is the surest path from poverty to prosperity. Thus, the "Group of 77" coalition of developing countries, which once campaigned for the highly illiberal "new international economic order," now declares its support for "the liberalization of international trade under WTO rules as a powerful and dynamic force for accelerating growth and development."[6] Accordingly, any initiative that might create excuses for blocking exports from poorer countries is now viewed with deepest suspicion.

Most developing-country leaders therefore view the protesters, not as benefactors, but as threats to their people's welfare. According to Mexico's former president Ernesto Zedillo, the aim of the protesters is "to save the people of developing countries from . . . development."[7] And during the Seattle riots, a junior diplomat from Gabon, who was blocked by the crowds from entering the WTO meeting, remarked contemptuously: "They understand nothing, and are as remote from our problems as you'd expect from middle-class whites in Washington state."[8]

Marginalized at home and reviled abroad, the anti-globalization protest movement is a weak and guttering flicker of the old utopian flame—the quest for secular salvation through collectivizing politics. To understand our present era, we must understand what has happened, in just the past 20 years or so, that has brought that quest to such a dwindled and exhausted state.

The answer does not lie, primarily at least, in a shortage of discontents. It is probably true that the psychological trauma associated with the collapse of traditional beliefs and social structures is less acute today than a century or even a generation ago. Raised in it, we are relatively accustomed to the swirling flux of modern life; we believe less in anything solid, and so are less distressed when it melts into air. On the other hand, the complexity and pace of life have increased dramatically in just the past generation, and promise to continue their upward spiral. Under these conditions, a kind of spiritual vertigo remains a relatively common ailment. And this ailment can still turn tragically destructive—witness such events as the Oklahoma City bombing, the Heaven's Gate group suicide, and the Columbine shootings. Indeed, around the world, radical violent movements remain a significant threat: right-wing hate groups, eco-saboteurs, and most serious of all, terrorists claiming to act in the name of Islam.

The fundamental change has occurred not in our emotions, but in our knowledge. In rich and poor countries alike, the prevailing consensus of informed opinion now holds that boundless centralization, as a general principle, is a failure. It has been tried, exuberantly and repeatedly, and found wanting. People have learned that competitive markets with privately-owned enterprises function better than state-owned monopolies. They have learned that money must maintain a relatively stable value if markets are to work. They have learned as well that markets require an underlying infrastructure of fairly enforced property and contract rules. They are beginning to learn that capital markets can allocate resources better than bureaucrats, and that social policies work best when they supplement the market instead of crushing it.

By and large these lessons have been learned, not because of some new ideological enthusiasm, but in spite of emotional or pecuniary attachments to old ways of thinking. Consistent, unswerving allegiance to the principles of economic liberalism (or "market fundamentalism" as its detractors label it) remains a decidedly minority taste. As a result, lessons are often applied grudgingly and incompletely.

Nonetheless, the change in intellectual climate is real, and it is enormously important. The genius of the Industrial Counterrevolution was that its ideas tapped into the deeply felt need for community and rootedness *while at the same time promising greater material abundance*. This was the promise of "back to the future," and it was fundamental to the triumph of the centralizing impulse. A mere renunciation of modernity's stresses, on its own with nothing more, was the voice of reaction; it did have appeal, but in the end could not compete against the tidal power of modernity's scientific and technological progress. The Industrial Counterrevolution, though, rose above simple reaction; it offered a return to archaic values, yes, but in order to complete and perfect modernity, not abandon it. In short, it offered the irresistible temptation of having one's cake and eating it, too.

The popular appeal of various radical alternatives to the liberal path therefore rested crucially on the presumption that collectivism was "progressive," that it was "the wave of the future"—specifically, that it would give the masses a better life. And so Bismarck offered to lift up the workers; the Bolsheviks promised land and bread for the peasants; the Nazis put the jobless back to work; Mussolini made the trains run on time; and the various statist leaders of the Third World held out the prospect of industrialization and modernization and accelerated development.

But in the past couple of decades, collectivism's failure to live up to its promises finally became undeniable. In short, it didn't deliver the goods. The now-crumbling institutions of the collectivist era still have their defenders, but they are on the defensive. The weight of opinion is against them when they argue that theirs is the true path to material abundance. They have lost the mantle of the future, and have become the shrill, bitter voices of reaction.

Hence my characterization of the anti-market forces today as the "dead hand" of the past. They no longer represent a living and vital interpretation of modernity; they no longer offer a plausibly workable vision of the future to guide the reform or overhaul of current policies and institutions. And so anti-market forces today are consigned to clinging to the past: not proposing their own changes, but merely opposing and resisting liberal change. They are now only forces of negation and obstruction; they have lost the capacity to advance a positive agenda. They are still formidable, but they are sterile.

There is at present only one viable vision of economic development: the liberal model of markets and competition. It is neither widely loved nor widely understood, but it is all there is. And so when existing institutions break down so badly that changes become unavoidable, leaders in search of a template for constructive action now turn to the liberal model by default. In this way the dead hand yields, bit by bit, to the invisible hand of the market.

My account of globalization gives the central and decisive role to ideas—ideas about what policies and institutions best serve the public good. Thus, a global division of labor first developed during the 19th century as a consequence of the spread of liberal ideas. But when the diametrically opposed ideas of the Industrial Counterrevolution gained first wide acceptance and then power, that initial episode of globalization came to a tragic end. In recent decades, disillusionment with the ideas of centralization and top-down control has allowed a global division of labor to reassert itself. Globalization's current state lies in the messy transition between disillusionment with failed collectivist ideas and implementation of the liberal alternative.

In this interpretation of events, politics can be seen as a kind of discovery process at least dimly analogous to the discovery process of the competitive marketplace. The purpose of political institutions, after all, is to discern and apply socially useful knowledge—specifically, knowledge about which policies and institutions best serve social needs. Politics, though, is woefully inefficient at performing its task. Any process of discovery requires first experimentation and then feedback mechanisms that interpret and apply the experimental data. Politics suffers from grievous deficiencies on both fronts.

First, its range of experimentation is limited by its necessarily centralized structure. Even highly decentralized governments that devolve power to regional and local authorities are still far more centralized than the marketplace. Such governments are simply nested monopolies: For different matters, the size of the jurisdiction varies, but within that jurisdiction the relevant government institutes a single and exclusive set of policies.

Next, the feedback mechanisms in politics are terribly inexact. Even using the best available methods of social science, empirical analysis of specific policy results seldom delivers a definitive assessment. Isolating the effects of a particular policy from the swarm of other relevant variables is notoriously difficult; more fundamentally, defining what constitutes policy success usually turns on contestable value judgments. And of course, real-life policy debates are never conducted with anything faintly resembling scientific objectivity. The leading participants in those debates generally have an ideological axe to grind or a financial stake in the outcome, or both. So even when dispassionate analysis clearly favors one side of the debate, the other side will do its best to muddy the waters with tortured but plausible-sounding arguments and data. Objective feedback, even when it exists, is often lost in a cacophony of static.

Meanwhile, even feedback regarding subjective preferences is difficult to obtain. In undemocratic regimes, of course, there is no institutional means of registering the preferences of most citizens, and often those preferences are systematically ignored. Yet, even when the broader public is free to participate in politics, the problems are still formidable. Voting is a very crude indicator of preferences, since candidates hold assortments of policy views and voters can only select which overall package they prefer. As to lobbying, the signals it conveys are badly distorted by the differing abilities of various interest groups to organize and apply political pressure. In particular, small, cohesive groups have an enormous advantage over large, diffuse groups when it comes to making their views heard. Accordingly, many vitally important but poorly organized interests (most notably, consumers and taxpayers) are routinely underrepresented in the political process.

It should be unsurprising, then, that the verdicts of politics often go badly awry. All learning proceeds according to trial and error, but in politics errors can be repeated and compounded and institutionalized before they are even detected. The Industrial Counterrevolution demonstrates the point on a colossal scale. The advent of technology-intensive industrial society during the 19th century was a major discontinuity in human history—perhaps *the* major discontinuity since the beginning of recorded history. Political activity around the world strove to adapt to the novel circumstances, but misguided by pervasive and profound error, it yielded instead more or less severe maladaptation—with often incalculably tragic consequences.

Today the world is recovering—slowly, fitfully, and unevenly—from those past mistakes. The progress of globalization reflects the partial and ongoing correction of error. What has made this incomplete recovery possible—and what raises hopes that it will continue? Most basically, the nearly universal desire for higher living standards creates incentives for sound policy. Reactionaries who eschew modernity's riches in favor of other values are a minority in virtually every country on earth; the overwhelming majority of the earth's inhabitants long for more material necessities, comforts, and conveniences. Politicians seeking to gain and hold power are therefore under considerable pressure to increase the public bounty. In democratic regimes, politicians win votes on the basis of their economic records, but even autocratic regimes derive legitimacy and public support (or at least acquiescence) from perceived economic success.

Over the long term, broad-based increases in living standards cannot be maintained except through relatively liberal policies. It is possible to fake prosperity for a time through redistribution or inflationism, and even to achieve solid records of catch-up growth with highly interventionist policies. But sooner or later, dysfunctional policies will yield poor results, and at that point market-oriented reforms offer the possibility of a substantial political payoff.

Furthermore, a growing economy means growing tax receipts, and therefore more resources at politicians' disposal. Accordingly, even political leaders utterly indifferent to the larger public good have an incentive to promote sound policies—at least to a point. The economist Mancur Olson wrote brilliantly on this topic. He compared government to a roving bandit who decides to settle down and occupy a particular stretch of territory. Once the bandit does so, his incentives change dramatically—notwithstanding the fact that his predatory instincts remain unabated:

> [T]he criminal who is only one among many will take 100 percent of the money in any till he robs. By contrast, the stationary bandit with continuing control of an area wants to make sure that the victims have a motive to produce and engage in mutually advantageous trade. The more income the victims of theft generate, the more there is to take.[9]

The bandit's new stake in the territory he pillages Olson referred to as an "encompassing interest." Any government with a reasonably firm grasp on power likewise has an "encompassing interest," that is, a selfish interest in maximizing tax revenue. And when the regime's time horizons are extended sufficiently—when the issue is no longer how much money can be wrung from an economy over one lifetime, but rather how to sustain a steadily growing stream of revenue indefinitely—that interest creates an incentive to pursue pro-growth policies.

Thus, the direct or indirect influence that public opinion exerts over government, plus politicians' selfish desire to maximize the resources under their control, combine to push policy toward benign objectives. But even if their goals are commendable, how do political leaders learn how to realize them? How do they know which policies will actually promote higher growth, rising living standards, and a growing tax haul? They need to be able to choose among realistic alternative courses of action, and for those alternatives they can look abroad for experiences in other countries.

Any discovery process requires experimentation. The nature of politics—namely, the fact that its institutions are monopolies within their respective jurisdictions—tightly circumscribes the extent of experimentation that any government can engage in directly. But at the national level, where economic policymaking authority primarily resides, it is possible at least to examine the successes and failures of other nations' policies and attempt to learn from their example. This international demonstration effect can be a rich source of information to guide (or misguide) the political process.

During the Industrial Counterrevolution, the demonstration effect played a major role in propagating collectivist policies. To reiterate, the centralizing momentum of that counterrevolution did not carry the day simply because it offered a balm for spiritual turmoil; it succeeded, for a time, because it plausibly fulfilled its promise of outperforming the "chaos" of market competition. As particular countries appeared to thrive after turning to collectivism, reformers and revolutionaries in other countries trumpeted these successes as evidence of centralization's promise.

Thus, Bismarck's Germany exerted a powerful influence on Progressives in the United States and "national efficiency" collectivists in Great Britain. A few decades later, Germany's experience with "wartime socialism" quickly became a model for Bolshevik economic policy in the Soviet Union. The Soviet experience in turn had an enormous impact. The Russian Revolution moved socialism out of the realm of dreams and into that of practical possibility; as American journalist Lincoln Steffens declared in 1919, "I have been over to the future—and it works!" The prestige of Soviet central planning was never higher than during the early 1930s, when the juxtaposition of the Great Depression in the West and rapid industrialization under Stalin's Five Year Plans seemed to many to offer conclusive proof of the latter's superiority. Less radically, the "Swedish model" guided generations of social democrats, while the "Japanese miracle" lent prestige to industrial policy and inspired a host of imitation MITIs up and down the Pacific Rim.

In symmetrical fashion, the retreat from collectivism in recent decades has repeatedly sought direction from foreign developments. Most notably, the collapse of communism in the Soviet Empire and its effective abandonment in China were watersheds in the general worldwide disillusionment with centralization. More narrowly, the association of specific countries' liberal policies with favorable results has encouraged copycat liberalization elsewhere. For example, the spectacular economic successes of export-oriented East Asia dealt a major blow to protectionist import-substitution policies, especially in Latin America. Chile's privatization of its public pension system has provided an impetus, if not the exact blueprint, for reform in a host of other nations. And the surging U.S. economy during the 1990s, especially when contrasted with Japanese stagnation and the Asian financial crisis, has strengthened the hand of financial-sector reformers who wish to facilitate the growth of capital markets in previously bank-dependent financial systems.

There is an element of national rivalry that speeds the spread of new ideas. Economic performance is widely assessed in relative terms: Is this country "falling behind" or "catching up with" that one? Both political leaders and the broader public gain much of their sense of domestic economic potential by looking at conditions in other, similarly situated countries. International comparisons thus lend focus both to the public desire for improved material welfare and politicians' pursuit of fiscal strength. As a result, political leaders in laggard countries often find themselves under pressure to match foreign countries' successes by imitating their policies.

The political discovery process is especially messy. Ideological enthusiasm and special pleading by vested interests can lead decision-making deep into the wilderness of error and hold it there for decades at a stretch. Nowhere was such a detour more spectacularly wrongheaded or more doggedly followed than in the Soviet Union. In the final official May Day parade in 1990, one sardonic protest banner said it all: "72 years on the road to nowhere." But despite politics' egregious fallibility, there are reasons not to lose hope. The division of political authority among national units and the relative ease with which new policy ideas cross borders provide a certain openness to experimentation. Furthermore, the nearly universal public preference for rising living standards, combined with the relationship between economic growth and rising tax revenues, ensures that political decisions will be met, sooner or later, with appropriate feedback signals.

With respect to economic policy at least, the political process does feature real mechanisms for experimentation and feedback—weak and imperfect, yes, but real nonetheless. It is clear that those mechanisms have been operating in a wide variety of political settings over the past couple of decades to move policies and institutions into closer alignment with the public interest—that is to say, away from the errors of collectivism and toward the practical superiority of market competition. In my opinion, therefore, it does not require extravagant optimism to expect that those same mechanisms will continue to operate and that, consequently, economic policies and institutions around the world will continue to move in a more or less liberal direction.

An important caveat applies. Unfortunately, there remain a substantial number of countries in which politics is so abysmally disordered that the preconditions of progress do not obtain. The situation is especially bleak in large parts of sub-Saharan Africa. In many countries, only chaos reigns; the transition from roving bandits to a single stationary bandit has not yet been made. Other countries, only slightly less miserable, remain in the kleptocratic stage, where rulers seek only to maximize their own personal plunder—a state of affairs that encourages relapse into Hobbesian civil war. In these benighted places, there is no political order worthy of the name, and thus no discovery process in operation.

It must also be noted that not all political processes are equally conducive to progress toward freedom and prosperity—not by any stretch of the imagination. In the political realm as in the commercial realm, institutional design and performance are crucially important. The bottom line: Better political institutions yield better policy results. Specifically, as I address in Chapter 8, the great challenge for governments is to be able simultaneously to control their citizens and control themselves. While a handful of autocratic regimes have managed this trick at least temporarily, by and large the lack of institutional restraints on government power has been a recipe for disaster. In the long run, the only reliable political foundation for market competition is a stable democracy. But democracy alone is insufficient; constitutional restrictions that curb special-interest power are essential.

⪼⪻

In the interpretation presented here, the grand drama of the world economy today is one in which the discovery process of politics is struggling to unleash the wealth-creating discovery process of the marketplace. Inside the Plato's cave of politics, nations grope unsurely and unevenly toward greater fidelity to the public interest, and thus toward market-oriented reform.

Before going on to examine the further implications of this explanatory model for the world economy's future, let me first address some rival interpretations. For my views are by no means generally accepted. On the contrary, the leading theories today advance a top-down vision of globalization's dynamics. What I mean here is that these theories attempt to explain the trend toward market-based reforms in general, and the loosening of restrictions on international markets in particular, as something imposed from above on national governments by some external force.[10]

The most popular understanding of what drives globalization is one I addressed back in Chapter 1. This is the view that national policy changes are driven by the demands of foreign investors, and it is a view shared by both the critics and the boosters of globalization. According to this oft-repeated analysis, the revolutions in information and communications technologies have liberated capital to flit around the world in search of the highest returns. The existence of this global pool of fickle and footloose capital has put nations into competition with each other; they are forced to do the bidding of international investors if they hope to bring in the resources needed to fund economic development. Critics decry the competition for investment dollars as a "race to the bottom" in which the gutting of living standards and social protections feeds the profits of corporations and financiers. The friends of open markets, on the other hand, celebrate international capital's newfound leverage; the discipline imposed by the "golden straitjacket" (to use Thomas Friedman's turn of phrase) is, in their view, compelling the acceptance and adoption of market-friendly policies.

As I argue earlier, this explanation does not even come close to getting to the heart of the matter. First, it grossly exaggerates the influence wielded by foreign investors. Foreign money poured into Indonesia and Thailand and Korea despite the obvious structural flaws in their financial systems; it likewise poured into Russia notwithstanding egregious economic misrule there. The "golden straitjacket," it seems, is none too snug. As for fears of a "race to the bottom," there is no evidence that foreign investment is drawn to countries with poor environmental protection or abusive labor practices.[11] After all, most cross-border investment goes from one rich country to another; customers with fat wallets, not poverty and squalor, are the primary magnets for foreign capital.

More fundamentally, the "golden straitjacket" and "race to the bottom" schools of thought fail to explain why less developed countries are now so interested in luring international investors. Until relatively recently, most were not. Nationalistic Third World leaders of a generation ago routinely condemned foreign capital as exploitative and insisted upon self-sufficiency as the path to development. It is true today that capital's improved mobility does allow investors, to a limited extent at least, to play countries off each other—assuming they want to play. But that assumption cannot be taken for granted. A viable explanation of the changing face of the world economy must provide reasons for why so many developing-country leaders have changed their minds and decided to enter the foreign-money sweepstakes. The "golden straitjacket" and "race to the bottom" scenarios do not even acknowledge that a change has occurred.

The change has occurred because of a change in ideas at the national level. Policymakers in poorer countries now have a very different view of what constitutes the national economic interest than did their collectivist predecessors. They recognize that access to a global pool of savings, and global technology and know-how, can accelerate the pace of economic growth. They have come to recognize as well that foreign money will not come, or stay, unless certain policy preconditions are met. At a bare minimum, public order and tolerable security of property rights, including freedom of exit, are requisite; beyond that, a number of other policy achievements—including macroeconomic stability, absence of corruption, adequate physical infrastructure, an educational system capable of producing skilled workers, and well-developed financial markets—all improve a country's standing with investors. The conventional view thus mistakes effect for cause: While the demand for footloose global capital does create incentives for further liberalization, it is the initial embrace of liberalization that creates the demand for global capital in the first place.

The role of foreign capital in today's global system is best understood as an additional feedback signal that informs national leaders in their quest for pro-growth policies. It is much less powerful, in the final analysis, than the feedback from domestic public opinion or the state of public finances. But the judgments of international investors do provide exceptionally clear signals, since their reactions are so speedy and unambiguous. And although the signals can occasionally mislead—investors are fallible, especially in an atmosphere of moral hazard—there is at least a rough correspondence between success at attracting investors and broader success in promoting growth.

The opponents of market-oriented reforms often blame their global spread on another external force besides foreign capital—namely, the power and influence of the World Trade Organization, World Bank, and the International Monetary Fund. According to the marchers in Seattle, London, and elsewhere, and all their fellow travelers, the three international economic institutions are guilty of ramming "market fundamentalism" down the throats of an unwilling world. On the other side, many friends of globalization laud these institutions as indispensable to the health of the world economy. Here is another top-down understanding of international economic order: Order exists, for good or ill, because it is bestowed (or inflicted) from above.[12]

In my account, by contrast, international order is something that emerges from the bottom up. It is primarily a byproduct of decisions at the national level, pursued for reasons of national interest. As to the international institutions, their contribution to the spread of liberalization is at best modest. Indeed, contrary to the prevailing view in both the pro- and anti-globalization camps, the net effect of two out of the three institutions has probably been to retard, not advance, the adoption of market-oriented policies.

Let's look first at the World Trade Organization. Its detractors depict it as immensely powerful, but in truth the WTO is exceptionally weak and fragile. Its functions—like those of its predecessor, the General Agreement on Tariffs and Trade—are basically two. First, it serves as a neutral forum in which member countries can agree to change their policies in a concerted manner, that is, to reduce their trade barriers at the same time other countries do the same. After its founding in 1947, the GATT organized eight "rounds" of multilateral tariff cutting and mutual reductions in other trade barriers; the WTO, which came into existence in 1995, has thus far brokered some sectoral trade deals in the areas of information-technology products, telecommunications, and financial services.

But the GATT could not and the WTO cannot impose these agreements by force: They are struck only if all members agree, and they apply only to those members that do agree. Furthermore, WTO agreements are not self-executing; if they include a change in some country's national legislation, that country's legislature must act before the change is effected. Despite the vocal complaints about the WTO's threat to U.S. sovereignty, the fact is that the United States has veto power over every WTO agreement, and no WTO agreement alters any U.S. law until Congress passes and the president signs the necessary implementing legislation.

The WTO's second function is to serve as a neutral forum for resolving disputes about previously signed agreements. A country that suspects another WTO member of failing to honor its obligations under an agreement can invoke dispute settlement procedures. Under the old GATT's toothless arrangements, the defendant country had to give its permission before an adverse verdict could be announced; WTO rules do not extend that courtesy to rule breakers. But once the WTO announces its decision, it has no coercive powers to force members to comply. Its last resort is to authorize aggrieved countries to impose trade sanctions against recalcitrant violators—but countries have always had the power on their own to close their markets to each other. Here again the WTO is accused of undermining national sovereignty—this time by striking down national laws left and right like some rogue judicial tribunal. In reality, though, the only power the WTO wields lies in the moral authority of its reputation for fairness. If countries don't voluntarily mend their ways in compliance with adverse rulings, the WTO is powerless to press the issue.

The past couple of decades have witnessed dramatic reductions in trade barriers around the world, but these developments owe comparatively little to the GATT and WTO. The boldest moves toward opening markets have occurred outside the context of negotiations: Countries as diverse as Australia, New Zealand, Argentina, Bolivia, Peru, Chile, the Philippines, Thailand, Indonesia, and India decided unilaterally to forsake the old import-substitution model in favor of greater integration with the global economy. The driving force for sweeping change in those countries was not tough bargaining or the prospect of a quid pro quo, but rather the realization that protectionism was causing economic stagnation.

Even when liberalization has occurred under GATT or WTO auspices, it has often deviated from the predicted path. Trade negotiations are thought to work on the principle of reciprocity: One country "gives up" trade barriers at home in order to "get" improved access to foreign markets. Official WTO parlance reflects this thinking. Offers to open one's own market are referred to as "concessions," while other countries' offers to liberalize are called "benefits." The underlying assumption is that countries have no real interest in cutting their own trade barriers; they do so only to gain new markets for their exports.

But an examination of some of the WTO's recent successes in reducing trade barriers reveals the shakiness of that assumption. For example, dozens of developing countries agreed to participate in recent agreements on telecommunications and financial services—despite the fact that their own industries are in no real position to export such services or otherwise expand abroad. These countries were motivated not by reciprocity but by the recognition that more open domestic markets would promote economic development at home. Likewise, consider China's bold offer of market-opening commitments in its bid for WTO membership. China had first sought membership in the GATT back in 1986, but talks went nowhere until 1999, when suddenly China began to agree to sweeping liberalization of its market. Why the change of heart? It seems clear that China's leadership came to the conclusion that a new burst of market reforms was necessary to reverse the country's flagging economic performance. Wrapping those reforms in a package of international obligations, it judged, would make them easier to get past domestic political opposition and then insulate them from subsequent reversal.

These examples show that while the WTO can facilitate trade liberalization, it is not the main engine. Trade negotiations can strengthen the political prospects for dismantling domestic barriers by sweetening the pot. Liberalization always provokes opposition from domestic import-competing interests; trade agreements help to overcome that opposition by adding a new partner to the pro-trade lobbying coalition—namely, exporters eager for better access to foreign markets. Furthermore, trade agreements are especially useful in consolidating and institutionalizing prior liberalizing gains. Once countries decide to open their own markets in their own national interest, those decisions are harder to undo by subsequent protectionist-minded governments if liberalization has been enshrined as an international obligation. Trade agreements can thus "lock in" reforms by imposing additional political constraints on their reversal.

But even if the WTO were wiped from the face of the earth, the ongoing worldwide process of reducing trade barriers would still continue. Progress would be slower and more selective, but it would not come to a halt. That is because the fundamental impetus for market-opening comes, not from international agreements and institutions, but from national-level decisions regarding national economic interests.

Unlike the WTO, the IMF and World Bank exert real, tangible power—the power of the purse. At the end of 1998, the World Bank's outstanding loans to 156 borrowing members totaled $210 billion; IMF credits outstanding to 96 countries amounted to $94 billion.[13] Money from these institutions comes with strings attached (the official term is "conditionality") to encourage aid recipients to adopt particular policies. And since the 1980s at least, the general thrust of the institutions' policy preferences has been market-friendly: Fiscal balance, low inflation, reduction of trade barriers, openness to foreign investment, and privatization of state-owned enterprises are the major elements of what has come to be known as the "Washington consensus."

Anti-globalization activists have demonized the World Bank and the IMF for their complicity in the spread of free-market reforms. The two organizations are "the chief instruments used by political and corporate elites to create today's unjust, destructive global economic order," according to organizers of April 2000 protests in Washington, D.C. "The IMF and World Bank are in many ways the 'parents' of the WTO," the protesters charge; "they operate together to preserve corporate power and constrain the rights and opportunities of the majority of the world's people."[14]

The IMF and the World Bank are deeply flawed institutions, but not in the ways the enemies of economic liberalism imagine. Despite their obvious clout and apparent pro-market tendencies, the international financial institutions deserve little credit for the advance of liberal reforms. On the whole, in fact, they have probably been responsible for slowing down, not accelerating, the pace of liberalization.

It must be remembered that the IMF and World Bank are survivors from a long gone era. The two "Bretton Woods" organizations were created at the end of World War II to support an international order that today is virtually unrecognizable. The Bank was designed to operate in a world where poor countries lacked any real access to private foreign capital. Yet by the 1990s, total World Bank lending averaged only 2 percent of private-sector financial flows to developing countries.[15] As for the IMF, it was established to support a global regime of fixed exchange rates anchored by the U.S. dollar. That regime, and hence the IMF's *raison d'être,* collapsed more than a quarter-century ago.

But the two institutions have persisted—indeed, flourished—in spite of changing conditions. The World Bank, which originally concentrated on infrastructure projects, expanded its mission and its budgets under Robert McNamara's leadership in the 1970s to promote all manner of ambitious, and doomed, central planning schemes. In the 1980s it reversed course and began making "structural adjustment loans" to assist countries in undoing their earlier collectivist mistakes. The IMF, meanwhile, took advantage of the oil-price shocks of the 1970s to begin lending to oil-importing countries. In the early 1980s, the Latin American debt crisis provided the occasion for a new IMF role in managing developing-country financial crises— a role significantly expanded during the rolling turmoil of the 1990s.

Through all their transformations and ideological opportunism, the two organizations have remained unswervingly faithful to one guiding principle: Keep finding reasons to lend money. Supporting market-oriented reform is the current reason of choice, but it is a means to an end. The end is bureaucratic self-preservation.

Consequently, the IMF and World Bank are incapable of wielding their leverage effectively in the liberal cause. However market-friendly the terms of lending "conditionality," when the chips are down both institutions have an overwhelming incentive to continue disbursing funds regardless of whether the client state in question has met the stipulated conditions. If they are too stringent, they will exclude themselves from too many potential clients. Even worse, if they cut off aid to a country and it then reforms and prospers on its own, they have ended up demonstrating their own irrelevance. And so both the IMF and the World Bank routinely extend financial assistance to governments that either have no interest in reform or are unable to pull it off. In so doing, they provide those governments with additional financial breathing space and thus reduce the incentives for making needed changes. Consequently, the end result of their interventions is, all too often, to subvert the spread of pro-market policies.

The history of IMF lending demonstrates the hollowness of the "conditionality" threat. Out of 124 countries that borrowed from the Fund between 1949 and 1999, nearly 70 percent borrowed in at least three-quarters of all the years after the year of their first loan; 44 percent borrowed every single year after becoming an IMF client. Dependence can stretch on for decades: 56 percent of those 124 countries have stayed on the IMF dole for 20 or more years.[16] In recent times, Russia provided an especially notorious example of conditionality's fecklessness. The Fund persisted in pumping money into Russia despite a consistent record of noncompliance with IMF agreements. In July 1999, former Russian Deputy Prime Minister Boris Fedorov wrote to the IMF in opposition to a further loan, which was eventually granted anyway. "I strongly believe that IMF money injections in 1994–1998 *were detrimental to the Russian economy* and interests of the Russian people," Fedorov wrote. "Instead of speeding up reforms, they slowed them."[17]

The perverse effects of IMF lending can be especially pernicious because of the problem of moral hazard. Not only does the IMF lending dull the incentives for reform in the borrowing country, but it also signals to private investors that their downside risk is covered. Booming investment inflows create the impression that all is well and further undermine the case for needed policy shifts. In addition, the country's problems are later compounded by the consequences of the eventual bust.

The World Bank's record is equally dismal. According to its own internal evaluations, 59 percent of all lending projects between 1990 and 1999 failed to achieve satisfactory sustained results; in Africa the failure rate was 73 percent.[18] A World Bank working paper found that borrowers are rarely held to the terms of their agreements. "[A]lmost all adjustment loans disburse fully," the analysis concluded, "even if policy conditions are not met."[19] A broader survey of official development assistance that included World Bank loans reveals that policy failure is all too often rewarded. Specifically, of 20 countries whose overall ratings for pro-market policies in the *Economic Freedom of the World* report declined or remained the same from 1985 to 1990, 19 saw an increase in aid flows as a percentage of GDP.[20]

The IMF and the World Bank are not without their redeeming features. They are staffed by bright and capable people who have considerable intellectual influence in foreign capitals around the world. The consensus of these organizations in favor of market-oriented policies has doubtless had an impact on the climate of public (or at least elite) opinion in many developing countries. Furthermore, their technical assistance with the devilish details of policy reform and economic management has been of value to reform-minded governments.

That said, the core function of these organizations today—to facilitate reforms by doling out money—is fundamentally misconceived. It is premised on a simplistic top-down worldview in which enlightened international technocrats can use their financial resources to mold national policies to their liking. But for those countries whose governments have not yet committed to market-based reform, bribes from international agencies will seldom be the decisive factor in their conversion. What is much more likely is that governments still wedded to statist policies will take advantage of the IMF and World Bank's need to lend in order to obtain resources that allow them to maintain those policies at least a while longer. More often than not, then, instead of the backward client state's bending to the will of the far-sighted international technocrats, the technocrats are manipulated into serving the retrograde purposes of the client.

Many defenders of globalization still regard institutions like the Fund and the Bank as essential to the maintenance of international economic order. Such a view is rooted in a deeply held but wrongheaded belief that international order is impossible without international authority. According to this thinking, a global economy requires global governance; consequently, any suggestion to curtail or eliminate existing international institutions is dismissed as benighted isolationism or else naïve "market fundamentalism."

Robert Gilpin, a leading scholar of international relations, epitomizes this top-down vision of globalization. In his book *The Challenge of Global Capitalism,* he warns that the lack of sufficiently muscular international governance poses a major threat to the future health of the world economy. "The international capitalist system could not possibly survive without strong and wise leadership," he writes. "International leadership must promote international cooperation to establish and enforce rules regulating trade, foreign investment, and international monetary affairs." He looks back in nostalgia at the heyday of the Bretton Woods system in the first decades after World War II, and fears that "the underpinning of the post–World War II global economy has steadily eroded since the end of the Soviet threat."[21]

In reality, though, it was only after the collapse of the Bretton Woods system that a truly global economy came into being. The historically unprecedented level of international economic integration enjoyed today does not rely on top-heavy international structures. It is, instead, primarily a bottom-up phenomenon: It reflects changing perceptions of national economic interest on the part of national governments, one upshot of which is a marked decline in barriers to commerce between nations. Trade agreements struck internationally have lent modest encouragement to this turn of events; international lending and aid policies, on the other hand, have done more to frustrate than help it along. Up to this point and into the foreseeable future, the main action in the globalization drama has been and will continue to be found in the maddeningly fallible discovery process of national political life.

⚬⚬⚬⚬⚬⚬⚬

In this chapter I have made a case for liberal optimism. The old and dying faith in centralization is unlikely to be rekindled. The political process is capable of recognizing and learning from mistakes, and it is currently doing so with respect to the grievous mistakes of the Industrial Counterrevolution. The worldwide correction of collectivist error now underway is not dependent on the *deus ex machina* of global governance; it is proceeding, as do all discovery processes, by decentralized trial and error. It is therefore more robust than many (even many of those who wish it well) would have us believe.

But optimism, though well founded, must be tempered. Although further progress toward a more securely liberal future seems highly likely, it will not come easily. It will be frustratingly slow and uneven and messy. In many countries, grandly trumpeted reform initiatives will come to nothing; in other nations it will become clear only years later that decisive changes have occurred. Liberalization, or what passes for it, will frequently be blamed for making things worse than before—and sometimes with good reason. Backsliding will occur; some countries that showed promise will squander it. Meanwhile, others deemed hopeless will suddenly flare up as star performers.

None of this should come as a surprise: The exact course of any discovery process is always unpredictable. Beyond that basic truth, there are firm and specific reasons for supporters of economic liberalism to avoid even the faintest whiff of triumphalism. They should instead be girding themselves for a long and nasty slog.

First of all, understanding of and commitment to liberal economic principles remain patchy at best. Free-market partisans sometimes talk as if they have already won the war of ideas, but the self-congratulations are dangerously premature. They have confused passing a turning point with bringing the campaign to completion; they should recall, as a useful analogy, that the fighting between Gettysburg and Appomattox was some of the bloodiest of the Civil War.

Consider the situation in the United States, where pro-market opinion is on firmer footing than just about anywhere else. But even in that nation, many relatively straightforward proposals for market-based reforms continue to be marginalized as "extreme" and "out of the mainstream"—for example, the wholesale substitution of taxes and tradable permits for command-and-control environmental regulations, the replacement of Medicare with private health insurance vouchers, the repeal of compulsory labor union membership, the phase-out of federal deposit insurance for banks, and the elimination of the antidumping law, which penalizes imports that are deemed too inexpensive. Other reform ideas now receive serious attention, but remain bitterly controversial—including privatization of Social Security, educational voucher or tax credit programs, and defunding of the IMF, to name a few.

The fundamental problem is that equating order with top-down control retains a powerful intuitive appeal. Despite the obvious successes of unplanned markets, despite the spectacular rise of the Internet's decentralized order, and despite the well-publicized new science of "complexity" and its study of self-organizing systems, it is still widely assumed that the only alternative to central authority is chaos. In other words, if "somebody" isn't "in charge" of a given process, that process can succeed only by a stroke of blind luck. The idea that decentralized experimentation and feedback can outperform centralized direction—even if nobody can predict exactly how—still strikes many people as speculative and unconvincing. They learn to accept various specific applications of the general principle, but the principle itself has yet to carry the day. Consequently, whenever some issue becomes a matter of public concern, there is inevitably strong pressure to impose some top-down mandate or create a new bureaucracy to manage the problem. Meanwhile, those who resist such centralized policy responses are routinely castigated for their callous disregard of the issue.

Furthermore, progress in achieving new liberal reforms is complicated, ironically enough, by the sheer productivity of markets and their resilience in the face of interference. Adam Smith put the point succinctly over two centuries ago:

> The natural effort of every individual to better his own condition, when suffered to exert itself with freedom and security, is so powerful a principle, that it is alone, and without any assistance, not only capable of carrying on the society to wealth and prosperity, but of surmounting a hundred impertinent obstructions with which the folly of human laws too often incumbers its operations. . . .[22]

The creative power of market competition can cover a multitude of policy sins—thereby weakening the feedback that might alert leaders to their mistakes. In particular, in developing countries the availability of accelerated catch-up growth allows even badly distorted economies to post impressive numbers for sustained periods of time. And in the rich countries, the lavish abundance generated by private enterprise can support a heavy load of incentive-squelching redistribution.

The relative weakness of liberal ideas and the overwhelming strength of liberal practice combine to bolster the influence of those narrow interests that benefit from anti-market policies. Even when interventionist policies are clearly failing, their defenders are able to take advantage of public skepticism about decentralization. They claim that the liberal approach amounts to "doing nothing," and their arguments usually find a large, receptive audience. Meanwhile, strong overall economic performance can mask any number of specific policy failures—often for many years, and sometimes indefinitely. The partisans of those policies dismiss all objections as theoretical, and critics are hard pressed to justify the inevitable disruptions caused by change. "If it ain't broke, don't fix it" is a formidable obstacle to liberal reforms.

Consequently, those reforms—when they do finally come—are all too often shot through with compromise. Either flawed in original conception or watered down in implementation, many "reforms" are pro-market in name only. Too often, weak half-measures work less to improve the transmission of market signals than to amplify the distortions caused by other bad policies. As reviewed at length in Chapter 9, the interplay between expanding markets and persistent interventionism can be highly volatile, and the resulting explosions are often seized upon as evidence of free markets' inherent untrustworthiness. The Asian financial crisis, for example, has strengthened the pressure for renewed capital controls, while, in Russia, the Yeltsin administration's sham liberalization has given free markets a bad name in many quarters.

On balance, though, economic crisis is the midwife of liberal change. Sharp reverses in economic performance make the political situation much more fluid than in normal times, as the status quo falls quickly into disrepute and loses its privileged place. Narrow interests drop their pugnacious defense of existing policies for fear of public backlash; politicians put aside their normal caution and contemplate bold initiatives to stave off economic (and political) collapse. During emergent conditions, sweeping changes in policy thus become possible—but in which direction? Here the larger shift in intellectual climate is decisive. If some change is necessary, what real choice is there but to move, or at least appear to move, along a pro-market course? These days, the alternative—a return to more heavy-handed interventionism—will seldom appear credible in the eyes of policymakers and opinion leaders. By default, if not from conviction, the political process will more often than not lurch toward free markets in response to crisis.

Looking ahead, then, the worldwide advance of liberalization over the past two decades is likely to continue for many years to come. However, as before, progress will be uneven. Some countries will experience a kind of reform cycle: Crisis begets reform; reform begets the euphoria of rising expectations; those expectations are self-fulfilling for a time as they fuel an investment boom; as the boom persists, underlying economic weaknesses gradually come to the surface; the boom eventually turns to bust, and the cycle begins again. Elsewhere, maintaining macroeconomic stability will allow only small, incremental changes—many of which will come to nothing, while others turn out years later to be profoundly consequential.

The outlook presented here is something less than soaring: Half-victories and complete frustration are sure to be in plentiful supply. But I do not want to conclude on such a dour note, for the central message of this book is one of hope.

By presenting the intertwined stories of the rise and fall of the Industrial Counterrevolution, and the fall and rise of the world economy, I have sought to calm some of the fears that presently swirl around the topic of globalization. The fact is that many people today—and not just anti-market zealots—view globalization with considerable anxiety. Familiar if grim realities are breaking down; the pace of change jars and unsettles. With the outlines of the new dispensation still obscured by controversy and misunderstanding, it is only natural that its advent be greeted with a measure of skepticism and even hostility. "Better the devil one knows" is a commonplace reaction under such circumstances. Remember the children of Israel, who longed for the lost certainties of servitude during their desert wanderings.

In the midst of our own desert wanderings, this book serves as a reminder that we left somewhere to get to this place, and we left there for good reason. For a century the world was enthralled by the false promises of the Industrial Counterrevolution; the chains of misplaced faith have now been broken, and globalization is one consequence. The present era, uncertain and trying as it sometimes may be, is thus a time of deliverance. Furthermore, there is good reason to believe that we are on our way to somewhere better. The political discovery process is leading us away from the waste and cruelty of error and toward the greater opportunity and abundance that result from sound policies and institutions. The Promised Land may still be a distant dream, but at least we are heading in the right direction.

Epilogue

This book was already written, and on the verge of being printed, when the terrorist attacks of September 11, 2001 consigned that date to the annals of infamy. In Chapter 11 I noted that radical discontent with modernity still poses significant dangers; in particular, I singled out "terrorists claiming to act in the name of Islam" as an especially serious threat. In light of the recent horrors, that passing mention now seems woefully inadequate. In this epilogue I offer some brief and preliminary elaboration.

It requires little stretch to fit what has happened into the narrative of this book: There is a sad but undeniable continuity between these latest atrocities and all the sordid bloodletting of the century just past. With the sickening clarity of explosions in a clear September sky, we now see all too well that totalitarianism still lives: Osama bin Laden and Al-Qaeda and their co-conspirators are the modern-day successors of Lenin and Stalin, Mussolini and Hitler, Mao and Pol Pot.

In the tragic, broken societies of the Islamic world—where free markets have gained little foothold, and democracy even less—radical hostility to modernity still festers on a large scale. Groaning under the oppressive legacy of the collectivist dead hand, the region has given rise to a distinctive form of totalitarianism: one that uses a perverted form of religious faith, rather than any purely secular ideology, as its reactionary mythos. For the past quarter-century, Islamist fundamentalism has roiled the region in which it arose. Now it has reached out and waged a direct, frontal assault on its antithesis, its "Great Satan"—the United States.

Despite its trappings of religious fervor, Islamist totalitarianism is strikingly similar to its defunct, secular cousins. It is an expression, not of spirituality, but of alienation: in particular, a seething resentment of Western prosperity and strength. And just like its communist and fascist predecessors, Islamist totalitarianism seeks redemption through politics. It is animated by the pursuit of temporal power: the destruction of the "decadent" (that is, liberal) West and creation of a pan-Islamic utopian state featuring unrestrained centralization of authority. Whether the utopian blueprint calls for mullahs or commissars or Gauleiters to wield absolute power is of secondary importance; it is the utopian idea itself—the millennial fantasy of a totalitarian state—that is the fundamental feature and common thread that unites all the radical movements of the Industrial Counterrevolution.

The point bears emphasis. Radical Islamist fundamentalism not does content itself with mere rejection of the West's alleged vices. If that were all there were to it, its program might be simply to stage a retreat from modernity's wickedness—to do, in other words, what the Amish have done. But Islamist totalitarianism, though it claims otherworldly inspiration, is obsessed with worldly power and influence. It does not merely reject the West; it wants to beat the West at its own game of worldly success. Osama bin Laden has claimed that the United States is weak and can be defeated; he and his colleagues lust for power and believe they can attain it. And so, although it attempts to appropriate a particular religious tradition, Islamist totalitarianism is not at bottom a religious movement. It is a political movement; it is a quest for political power.

In Chapter 11 I focused on the anti-globalization protests of recent years as a vestige of the once-mighty Industrial Counterrevolution. It is not unfitting to portray the attacks of September 11 as an obscene escalation of those protests: The primary target, after all, was an icon of the global economy, the appropriately named World Trade Center. Yes, there is an enormous moral gulf that separates the petty hooliganism of the protesters and the mass murder of the terrorists. But in the terrible, simplifying clarity of war, it is apparent who is on one side and who is on the other. In the struggle between civilization and barbarism, those who throw rocks through McDonald's and those who ram airplanes into buildings are expending their destructive energies in a common cause.

Will the terrorist war against globalization succeed? Will the Islamist sectaries of the Industrial Counterrevolution be able to stop and reverse the emergence of a liberal international order? Was my metaphor of a dead hand premature?

I think not. In the first place, the ideology that motivates today's terrorists is far less attractive than the totalitarian creeds of the previous century.

Because it is parasitic upon a specific religious faith, it does not speak to people outside that faith's community; accordingly, Islamism lacks the potentially global appeal of fascism and communism. Perhaps more important, Islamist fundamentalism is purely and unabashedly reactionary. By contrast, as I discussed at length in Chapter 2, fascism and communism offered alternative visions of "back to the future"—marrying reactionary social values with an embrace of technological modernity. Because radical Islamism renounces modernity, it cannot take advantage—as the 20th century ideologies were able to do—of the immense historical momentum of technological progress.

Furthermore, radical Islamism is weaker than its totalitarian predecessors, not only intellectually, but geopolitically as well. Fascism and communism had political bases in militarily formidable great powers; Islamist totalitarianism has no such advantage. In the decades since Islamists won their first and greatest prize in Iran, totalitarian regimes have come to power only in Sudan and Afghanistan—backwaters even by regional standards. It is certainly conceivable that U.S. military responses to the September 11 attacks will precipitate a new wave of radicalization in the Islamic world—one which might topple existing regimes and sweep additional countries into the totalitarian fold. But even under the worst circumstances, there is no possible standard-bearer for the radical Islamist cause that could—as Germany and Japan and the Soviet Union once did—offer serious resistance to the resolute exercise of U.S. military power.

I do not mean to underestimate the threat of further horrors, or of serious shocks to the international economy. In a single attack of diabolical ingenuity, terrorists managed to kill thousands of people, close financial markets for days and then send them into a tailspin upon reopening, and cripple entire industries. Their destructive power is now undeniable. But in the end, I do not believe they can avoid the fate of the other radical movements of the Industrial Counterrevolution: interment in what President Bush so stirringly referred to as "history's unmarked grave of discarded lies."

Notes

Chapter 1   The Weight of the Past

1. The term "globalization" is a slippery one. In this book I use the word in three distinct but interrelated senses: first, to describe the economic phenomenon of increasing integration of markets across political boundaries (whether due to political or technological causes); second, to describe the strictly political phenomenon of falling government-imposed barriers to international flows of goods, services, and capital; and, finally, to describe the much broader political phenomenon of the global spread of market-oriented policies in both the domestic and international spheres. Since I contend that globalization in the first sense is due primarily to globalization in the second sense, and that globalization in the second sense is due primarily to globalization in the third sense, I do not think it is unduly confusing to use the same word to mean three different things.

2. Thomas L. Friedman, *The Lexus and the Olive Tree* (New York: Farrar, Strauss and Giroux, 1999), 62.

3. Arthur Schlesinger Jr., "Has Democracy A Future?", *Foreign Affairs* 76, no. 5 (September/October 1997): 8.

4. For Western European government expenditures as a percentage of gross domestic product, see James Gwartney and Robert Lawson (with Dexter Samida), *Economic Freedom of the World: 2000 Annual Report* (Vancouver: Fraser Institute, 2000); for U.S. federal tax receipts as a percentage of GDP, see *Economic Report of the President* (Washington, D.C.: U.S. Government Printing Office, 2001), 368; for employment in Chinese state-owned enterprises, see *China Statistical Yearbook 2000* (Beijing: China Statistics Press, 2000), 115 (total employment in state-owned enterprises was 85.7 million as of 1999, but there have been further layoffs since then); for estimate of Indian subsidies as a percentage of GDP, see World Trade Organization, *Trade Policy Review: India, Minutes of Meeting,* WTO document no. WT/TPR/M/33, September 22, 1998, 6; Article 27 of the 1917 Constitution of Mexico, as amended, asserts state ownership of all natural resources, including petroleum, and specifically grants to the state exclusive authority to exploit petroleum products.

5. Patrick J. Buchanan, *The Great Betrayal: How American Sovereignty and Social Justice Are Being Sacrificed to the Gods of the Global Economy* (Boston: Little, Brown and Company, 1998), 287, 288.

6. George Soros, *The Crisis of Global Capitalism* (New York: Public Affairs, 1998), xx, xxii.

7. Karl Polanyi, *The Great Transformation: The Political and Economic Origins of Our Time* (Boston: Beacon Press, 1957 [1944]), 29.

8. William Greider, *One World, Ready or Not: The Manic Logic of Global Capitalism* (New York: Simon & Schuster, 1997), 43.

CHAPTER 2   THE INDUSTRIAL COUNTERREVOLUTION

1. The recreation of Bellamy's Boston contains specific descriptions and events of my own invention, but in every essential draws directly from Bellamy's imagination and prose. Thus, Bellamy describes Boston at the millennium as a city with "[m]iles of broad streets, shaded by trees and lined with fine buildings," and states that "[e]very quarter contained large open squares filled with trees, along which statues glistened and fountains flashed in the late-afternoon sun." Elsewhere he writes of "the glorious new Boston with its domes and pinnacles, its gardens and fountains." He identifies Muster Day as falling on October 15 and calls it "the great day of the year with us, whence we reckon all other events, our Olympiad, save that it is annual." Edward Bellamy, *Looking Backward: 2000–1887* (New York: Signet Classic, 1960 [1888]), 43, 204, 59. Other details taken directly from *Looking Backward* include the terms of service in the industrial army (59), the badges of rank (95), and the existence of central kitchens and laundries (91) as well as collective umbrellas (112). That last bit of gadgetry is offered as a metaphor for "the difference between the age of individualism and that of concert" (112).

2. Ibid., 54.

3. Ibid., 165.

4. Ibid., 157.

5. Ibid., 112.

6. Arthur E. Morgan, *Edward Bellamy* (New York: Columbia University Press, 1944), 247, 275. Arthur Morgan, in addition to being Bellamy's adoring biographer, was a prominent New Dealer. As the first chairman of the Tennessee Valley Authority, Morgan attempted to implement Bellamy's vision of social engineering at the regional level. For interesting accounts of Morgan's career, see Thomas P. Hughes, *American Genesis: A Century of Invention and Technological Enthusiasm* (New York: Penguin Books, 1989), 364–81; John M. Jordan, *Machine–Age Ideology: Social Engineering & American Liberalism, 1911–1939* (Chapel Hill, N.C.: University of North Carolina Press, 1994), 243–47.

7. Erich Fromm, foreword to Bellamy, *Looking Backward,* v.

8. The term "Industrial Counterrevolution" is my own, but the idea is not new. For example, Nobel Prize-winning economist Douglass North explains the rise of collectivism as a reaction against the stresses and strains of industrialization. See Douglass C. North, *Structure and Change in Economic History* (New York: W. W. Norton & Company, 1981), 179–84. In similar fashion, historian Theodore von Laue describes fascism and communism as "counterrevolutions" against Western modernization. Theodore H. von Laue, *The World Revolution of Westernization: The Twentieth Century in Global Perspective* (New York: Oxford University Press, 1987), 60–79.

Also, in his great but too-little remembered polemic against the "collectivist counter-revolution," the journalist Walter Lippmann diagnosed the then-reigning faith in centralized control (a faith he once shared fervently) as a rebellion against industrial society's complex division of labor. "[T]he industrial revolution," he wrote, "has instituted a way of life organized on a very large scale, with men and communities no longer autonomous but elaborately interdependent, with change no longer so gradual as to be imperceptible, but highly dynamic within the span of each man's experience. No more profound or pervasive transformation of habits and values and ideas was ever imposed so suddenly on the great mass of mankind." In a later passage, he continued, "[A]s the revolutionary transformation proceeds, it must evoke resistance and rebellion at every stage. It evokes resistance and rebellion on the right and on the left—that is to say, among those who possess power and wealth, and among those who do not. . . . Though these two movements wage a desperate class struggle, they are, with reference to the great industrial revolution of the modern age, two forms of reaction and counter-revolution. For, in the last analysis, these two collectivist movements are efforts to resist, by various kinds of coercion, the consequences of the increasing division of labor." Walter Lippmann, *The Good Society* (Boston: Little, Brown and Company, 1937), 165, 168.

9.   Karl Marx and Friedrich Engels, "Manifesto of the Communist Party," in *The Marx-Engels Reader,* 2nd ed., ed. Robert C. Tucker (New York: W. W. Norton & Company, 1978 [1848]), 476. For a fascinating examination of modernity's disorienting and exhilarating flux, see Marshall Berman, *All That Is Solid Melts Into Air: The Experience of Modernity* (New York: Penguin Books, 1988 [1982]). The book not only borrows its title from the quoted passage, but also includes a highly insightful chapter on Marx's response to modernization.

10.   Robert Nisbet, *The Quest for Community: A Study in the Ethics of Order & Freedom* (San Francisco: Institute for Contemporary Studies Press, 1990 [1953]), 32.

11.   Ibid., 166.

12.   One interesting variation on the counterrevolutionary theme, especially influential in American history, was the support of government centralization to combat business centralization. In the United States, the "trustbusting" strain of the Progressive movement did not share the prevailing collectivist enthusiasm for size and centralization in industry; instead their ideal was a decentralized economy of small, competing firms. But in pursuit of that ideal, they called for sweeping new government authority to dismantle large enterprises and regulate industrial structure on an ongoing basis. In the name of resisting what they feared was excessive centralization by Big Business, they supported dramatic centralization in the hands of Big Government as well as collusion on the part of smaller enterprises. See the chapter on "Louis Brandeis and the Origins of the FTC" in Thomas K. McCraw, *Prophets of Regulation* (Cambridge, Mass.: Belknap Press of the Harvard University Press, 1984), 80–142; see also Ellis W. Hawley, *The New Deal and the Problem of Monopoly: A Study in Economic Ambivalence* (New York: Fordham University Press, 1995 [1966]).

13.   Douglass North refers to the "wedding of science and technology" that occurred at this time as the "second economic revolution"; in his schema the first economic revolution corresponds to the invention of agriculture. North thus sees what is often called the "second industrial revolution" as the truly tranformational event, and views the earlier British industrial revolution as its forerunner. See North, *Structure and*

Change in Economic History, 158–86,159. The story of the rise of the American mass-production economy is masterfully told in Alfred D. Chandler, Jr., *The Visible Hand: The Managerial Revolution in American Business* (Cambridge, Mass.: Belknap Press of Harvard University Press, 1977).

14. See, for example, Charles Ferguson, "From the People who brought you Voodoo Economics," *Harvard Business Review* (May–June 1988): 55–62, 61 ("In semiconductors, a combination of personnel mobility, ineffective intellectual property protection, risk aversion in large companies, and tax subsidies for the formation of new companies contribute to a fragmented, 'chronically entrepreneurial' industry. U.S. semiconductor companies are unable to sustain the large, long-term investments required for continued U.S. competitiveness.").

15. Bellamy, *Looking Backward,* 54.

16. Ibid., 209–10.

17. Thorstein Veblen, *The Theory of Business Enterprise* (New York: Charles Scribner's Sons, 1910), 25, 27.

18. Ibid., 39, 48–49.

19. There is now a voluminous "revisionist" literature that examines the complex mixture of complicity and rivalry between Big Business and Big Government in American history. For a comprehensive account of business lobbying during the Progressive Era, see Robert H. Wiebe, *Businessmen and Reform: A Study of the Progressive Movement* (Chicago: Elephant Paperbacks, 1989 [1962]). An interesting account of Big Business' anti-competitive stance during the interwar years is provided in Butler Shaffer, *In Restraint of Trade: The Business Campaign Against Competition, 1918–1938* (Cranbury, N.J.: Associated University Presses, 1997).

20. Quoted in Wiebe, *Businessmen and Reform,* 83.

21. Quoted in Paul H. Weaver, *The Suicidal Corporation: How Big Business Fails America* (New York: Simon and Schuster, 1988), 125.

22. Quoted in Shaffer, *In Restraint of Trade,* 123 (emphasis in original).

23. Quoted in Hughes, *American Genesis,* 251.

24. Quoted in Robert Kanigel, *The One Best Way: Frederick Winslow Taylor and the Enigma of Efficiency* (New York: Viking Penguin, 1997), 473.

25. Quoted in Dan Clawson, *Bureaucracy and the Labor Process: The Transformation of U.S. Industry, 1860–1920* (New York: Monthly Review Press, 1980), 217–18.

26. Quoted in ibid., 229.

27. Quoted in Hughes, *American Genesis,* 256.

28. Friedrich A. Hayek, *The Road to Serfdom* (Chicago: University of Chicago Press, 1972 [1944]), 21–22.

29. Quoted in Edmund Wilson, *To the Finland Station* (New York: The Noonday Press of Farrar, Strauss and Giroux, 1972 [1940]), 290.

30. Gordon A. Craig, *Germany 1866–1945* (New York: Oxford University Press, 1978), 94–95, 175, 292; see also William H. Dawson, *German Socialism and Ferdinand Lassalle* (New York: Charles Scribner's Sons, 1899).

31. Quoted in Craig, *Germany 1866–1945,* 45.

32. William H. Dawson, *Bismarck and State Socialism* (London: Swan Sonnenschein & Co., 1890), 63.

33. An interesting account of the nationalization of Prussian railroads is provided in Fritz Stern, *Gold and Iron: Bismarck, Bleichröder, and the Building of the German Empire* (New York: Vintage Books, 1979 [1977]), 208–17.

34. Ralf Dahrendorf, *Society and Democracy in Germany* (London: Weidenfeld and Nicolson Ltd., 1968), 39.

35. Quoted in Daniel T. Rodgers, *Atlantic Crossings: Social Politics in a Progressive Age* (Cambridge, Mass.: Belknap Press of Harvard University Press, 1998), 82–83.

36. Evalyn A. Clark, "Adolf Wagner: From National Economist to National Socialist," *Political Science Quarterly* LV, no. 3 (September 1940): 378–411, 397.

37. Quoted in ibid., 378.

38. Quoted in Arthur A. Ekirch Jr., *The Decline of American Liberalism* (New York: Atheneum, 1967 [1955]), 183–84.

39. Quoted in Rodgers, *Atlantic Crossings,* 276.

40. Jagdish Bhagwati, *Protectionism* (Cambridge, Mass.: The MIT Press, 1988), 66–67.

41. G. R. Searle, *The Quest for National Efficiency: A Study in British Politics and Political Thought, 1899–1914* (Atlantic Highlands, N.J.: The Ashfield Press, 1990 [1971]), 13.

42. Ibid., 54.

43. Quoted in ibid., 249.

CHAPTER 3   CENTRALIZATION VERSUS UNCERTAINTY

1. For an engaging introduction to the new sciences of complexity, see M. Mitchell Waldrop, *Complexity: The Emerging Science at the Edge of Order and Chaos* (New York: Touchstone, 1992).

2. Bellamy, *Looking Backward,* 55–56.

3. Quoted in Jordan, *Machine-Age Ideology,* 34–35.

4. Quoted in ibid., 209, 214.

5. F. A. Hayek, "The Use of Knowledge in Society," in *Individualism and Economic Order* (South Bend, Ind.: Gateway Editions, 1948), 85–86.

6. Ibid., 86.

7. Ibid., 80.

8. For a comprehensive analysis of the "economic calculation" problem, see David Ramsay Steele, *From Marx to Mises: Post-Capitalist Society and the Challenge of Economic Calculation* (La Salle, Ill.: Open Court, 1992).

9. For an overview of the early Soviet experience that explicitly addresses its implications for economic calculation in the absence of markets, see Peter J. Boettke, *The Political Economy of Soviet Socialism: The Formative Years, 1918–1928* (Boston: Kluwer Academic Publishers, 1990).

10. Quoted in Mikhail Heller and Aleksandr M. Nekrich, *Utopia in Power: The History of the Soviet Union from 1917 to the Present* (New York: Summit Books, 1986), 59.

11. Report quoted and summarized in Michael Polanyi, "The Span of Central Direction," in *The Logic of Liberty* (Chicago: University of Chicago Press, 1951), 127–28.

12. Heller and Nekrich, *Utopia in Power,* 108.

13. Ibid., 120.

14. Quoted in M. Polanyi, "The Span of Central Direction," 129–30.

15. For a good, accessible overview of the Soviet system as it actually worked, see Paul Craig Roberts and Karen LaFollette, *Meltdown: Inside the Soviet Economy* (Washington: Cato Institute, 1990).

16. Hayek, "The Use of Knowledge in Society," 81–82.

17. Vladimir I. Lenin, *The State and Revolution,* trans. Robert Service (New York: Penguin Books, 1992 [1918]), 91 (emphasis in original) (quotations are from Friedrich Engels).

18. Quoted in Shaffer, *In Restraint of Trade,* 36–37.

19. William H. Whyte Jr., *The Organization Man* (Garden City, N.Y.: Doubleday Anchor Books, 1956), 152.

20. Joseph A. Schumpeter, *Capitalism, Socialism and Democracy* (New York: Harper Torchbooks, Harper & Row, 1976 [1942]), 61.

21. Ibid., 134.

22. Ibid., 132.

23. Quoted in Joseph A. Schumpeter, *History of Economic Analysis* (New York: Oxford University Press, 1954), 1173, n. 3.

24. See a representative presentation of this view by one of its more prominent adherents in Alvin H. Hansen, "Economic Progress and Declining Population Growth," *American Economic Review* XXIX, no. 1, Part I (March 1939): 1–15.

25. John Maynard Keynes, *The General Theory of Employment, Interest, and Money* (New York: A Harvest Book by Harcourt Brace & Company, 1964 [1936]), 378.

26. John Kenneth Galbraith, *The New Industrial State,* 4th ed. (New York: Mentor, published by the Penguin Group, 1986 [1967]), 30–31.

27. F. A. Hayek, *The Constitution of Liberty* (Chicago: University of Chicago Press, 1960), 24.

28. F. A. Hayek, "Competition as a Discovery Procedure," in *New Studies in Philosophy, Politics, Economics and the History of Ideas* (Chicago: University of Chicago Press, 1978), 179–80 (emphasis in original).

29. Ibid., 188.

30. Nathan Rosenberg and L. E. Birdzell, Jr., *How the West Grew Rich: The Economic Transformation of the Industrial World* (New York: Basic Books, 1986), 258.

31. Ronald H. Coase, "The Nature of the Firm," in *The Nature of the Firm: Origins, Evolution, and Development,* ed. Oliver E. Williamson and Sidney G. Winter (New York: Oxford University Press, 1991 [1937]), 21.

32. Inspired by Coase's seminal article, a whole branch of transaction costs economics has developed. See, for example, Oliver E. Williamson, *Markets and Hierarchies: Analysis and Antitrust Implications* (New York: Free Press, 1975).

33. Let me make a brief clarification concerning terminology. I use "uncertainty" to mean unpredictability, or the impossibility of knowing in advance which of various rival approaches will turn out best. When such uncertainty is present, competition among rival approaches is indicated. On the other hand, it is also possible to use "uncertainty" to refer to the costliness or impossibility of obtaining additional knowledge—for example, because of the presence of high transaction costs. Using uncertainty in that

sense, Oliver Williamson argues that the centralized organization of the business firm is a response to uncertainty—that is, a method for economizing transaction costs. See Williamson, *Markets and Hierarchies*, 9, 21–26. Thus, depending on how the word uncertainty is used, the presence of uncertainty can be either a justification for competition or a spur to centralization. Despite this confusing state of affairs, the basic point remains the same, regardless of the terminology employed. That point, to reiterate, is that the fundamental tradeoff between centralization and competition is between using available knowledge effectively (particularly attractive when, because of high transaction costs, additional knowledge is too difficult to obtain) and openness to new information (which competitive markets can utilize best when transaction costs are relatively low).

34. Chandler, *The Visible Hand*, 485.

35. Ibid., 285—86.

36. See James R. Beniger, *The Control Revolution: Technological and Economic Origins of the Information Society* (Cambridge, Mass.: Harvard University Press, 1986). Beniger provides a detailed account of how the complexity of the new industrial economy precipitated a "crisis of control," the foremost response to which was the growth of formal bureaucratic administration.

37. Chandler, *The Visible Hand*, 8.

38. Hayek, *The Road to Serfdom*, 36.

CHAPTER 4   FROM WORLD ECONOMY TO WORLD WAR

1. John Keegan, *The Face of Battle* (New York: Penguin Books, 1978 [1976]), 234.

2. Ibid., 249; Martin Gilbert, *The First World War: A Complete History* (New York: Henry Holt and Company, 1994), 259.

3. Modris Eksteins, *Rites of Spring: The Great War and the Birth of the Modern Age* (New York: Anchor Books, 1990 [1989]), 144.

4. Paul Krugman, "Growing World Trade: Causes and Consequences," *Brookings Papers on Economic Activity 1* (Washington, D.C.: Brookings Institution, 1995), 327–62, 331; Michael D. Bordo, Barry Eichengreen, and Douglas A. Irwin, "Is Globalization Today Really Different Than Globalization a Hundred Years Ago?", National Bureau of Economic Research Working Paper 7195, June 1999, 28; see also Kevin H. O'Rourke and Jeffrey G. Williamson, *Globalization and History: The Evolution of a Nineteenth-Century Atlantic Economy* (Cambridge, Mass.: MIT Press, 1999).

5. Chandler, *The Visible Hand*, 83–86; O'Rourke and Williamson, *Globalization and History*, 34.

6. O'Rourke and Williamson, *Globalization and History*, 33–36.

7. J. Bradford DeLong, *Slouching Towards Utopia? 20th Century Economic History*, unpublished manuscript, available online at http://www.j-bradford-delong.net/TCEH/Slouch_Old.html, chapter VIII, 11–17.

8. Ibid., chapter VIII, 13–16; O'Rourke and Williamson, *Globalization and History*, 54.

9. Adam Smith, *An Inquiry into the Nature and Causes of the Wealth of Nations*, (New York, Modern Library, 1937 [1776]), 437–38.

10. O'Rourke and Williamson, *Globalization and History,* 38–39.

11. Speech at Manchester, January 15, 1846, in *Speeches on Questions of Public Policy by Richard Cobden, M.P.,* ed. John Bright and James E. Thorold Rogers (London: Macmillan and Co., 1870), 362–63.

12. The great statement of the interconnections between collectivism and protectionism, and between protectionism and war, is to be found in Lionel Robbins, *Economic Planning and International Economic Order* (London: Macmillan, 1937).

13. Quoted in Abraham Ascher, "Professors as Propagandists: The Politics of the Kathedersozialisten," in *Gustav Schmoller (1838–1917) and Werner Sombart (1863–1941),* ed. Mark Blaug (Brookfield, Vt.: Edward Elgar, 1992), 77.

14. Bellamy, *Looking Backward,* 105.

15. Quoted in Bernard Semmel, *Imperialism and Social Reform: English Social-Imperial Thought 1895–1914* (London: George Allen & Unwin Ltd., 1960), 130.

16. O'Rourke and Williamson, *Globalization and History,* 95–96, 116–17.

17. Jeffrey D. Sachs and Andrew Warner, "Economic Reform and the Process of Globalization," *Brookings Papers on Economic Activity 1,* 6–7, n. 6.

18. As Lionel Robbins wrote, "Once national areas are treated as if they were the private property of the state, their markets preserved for its citizens only, their resources open to development only by national labour and national capital, then territorial possession does matter very much indeed. . . . The claim for a place in the sun ceases to be empty bombast. It becomes the fateful expression of an urgent and insistent need.... If it can be justly said by the leaders of a hungry people, 'Your poverty is the result of *their* policy. *Your* deprivation is the result of *their* possession'—then there is grave risk of war. There is a real danger of a combination of the 'have-nots' to plunder the 'haves'. . . . In a liberal world the theory that the main causes of war are economic is a malignant invention. Independent national planning creates the conditions which make it true." Robbins, *Economic Planning and International Order,* 94–96 (emphasis in original).

19. Let me be clear: I do not believe that the actual protectionist policies of the prewar decades, modest as they were, contributed significantly to the outbreak of hostilities. What was crucially important, however, was the change in general expectations about the likely future course of international economic relations. Until the 1870s, the clear trend had been toward progressive liberalization; afterwards, the overall trend was in the opposite direction. It was therefore plausible to extrapolate that barriers to trade would continue to grow, and indeed that extrapolation became the conventional wisdom throughout Europe. The simultaneous rush for colonies by all the major powers made for a convincing case that the emerging world order was one of rival autarkic blocs. As the historian Wolfgang Mommsen writes of the mood in Germany, "During the final decade before 1914 many journalists and academics, and some industrialists, became exercised by a fear that the system of virtually barrier-free world trade which had evolved since the 1860s—and which, broadly speaking, had functioned well despite the protectionist policies pursued by certain countries—might not have much life left in it. They foresaw a division of the world into a number of economic spheres of influence, each more or less well shielded against external competition by means of high tariff walls." Wolfgang J. Mommsen, *Imperial Germany 1867–1918: Politics, Culture, and Society in an Authoritarian State,* trans. Richard Deveson (New York: Arnold, 1997), 91. This world-

view was a powerful inducement to the arms buildup and increasing bellicosity that ultimately resulted in war.

20.   It may be objected that the distinction between a liberal period of cosmopolitan peace and a subsequent collectivist period of increasing international tension (culminating in World War I) is overblown. After all, during the supposed liberal ascendancy, European wars were by no means uncommon: for example, the Crimean War (1853–56), the Franco-Austrian War (1858–60), the Prusso-Danish War (1864), the Austro-Prussian War (1866), and the Franco-Prussian war (1870–71). Without a doubt it must be conceded that, even during their heyday, liberal principles of international affairs were—like those of domestic affairs—too often honored in the breach. That fact, however, should not obscure the real sea change that occurred on the international scene around 1880. Beforehand, those who carried the banners of reform and progress looked toward a world in which the causes of war were gradually extinguished; afterwards, the leading shapers of public opinion marched in precisely the opposite direction, toward a world increasingly riven by intractable and never-ending conflict. Beforehand, political leaders were at least, to some extent, constrained by anti-war sentiment; afterward, the pressure of nationalistic sentiment increasingly goaded them into provocative actions they might not otherwise have taken. Here is the bottom line: Between 1815 and 1914 Europe experienced no general wars, in sharp contrast to the record of the 17th and 18th centuries and even sharper contrast to that of the 20th. It is no coincidence that this century of relative peace coincided with the rise and decline of the liberal worldview.

21.   William H. Dawson, *Bismarck and State Socialism,* 14.

22.   Quoted in Ascher, "Professors as Propagandists," 83.

23.   Quoted in ibid., p. 86; quoted in Clark, "Adolf Wagner," 386.

24.   See Kenneth Barkin, "Adolf Wagner and German Industrial Development," *Journal of Modern History* 41, no. 2 (June 1969): 144–59, 153.

25.   Quoted in Ludwig von Mises, *Omnipotent Government: The Rise of the Total State and Total War* (Spring Mills, Penn.: Libertarian Press, 1985 [1944]), 136; Ascher, "Professors as Propagandists," 88.

26.   Quoted in Ascher, "Professors as Propagandists," 81; quoted in Clark, "Adolf Wagner," 405, 403.

27.   In the two decades before the war, German public opinion followed the *Kathedersozialisten* toward ever more strident jingoism. Virulently nationalistic organizations like the Pan-German League, the Naval League, and Colonial Union rallied popular support for a projection of German power that "increasingly lost any sense of what could and could not be achieved by foreign and colonial policy within the constraints of the international situation." Mommsen, *Imperial Germany,* 84. These organizations actually used articles by Wagner, Schmoller, and other intellectuals in their propaganda. Craig, *Germany 1866–1945,* 119. After the Agadir crisis of 1911, writes Mommsen, "Public opinion (or, at any rate, the publicly voiced opinions of those sections of German society that were politically active) began to push the government into adopting an aggressive foreign policy quite contrary to its own inclinations." Mommsen, *Imperial Germany,* 93. It is fair to say that the *Kathedersozialisten*—with their noxious brew of collectivism, protectionism, and nationalism—seduced a whole nation, and with it the world, onto the battlefield.

28. Quoted in Semmel, *Imperialism and Social Reform,* 62, 85.

29. Quoted in William Manchester, *The Last Lion, William Spencer Churchill: Visions of Glory, 1874–1932* (Boston: Little, Brown and Company, 1983), 407.

30. Let me anticipate an obvious objection: I do not mean in any way to suggest that the growth of collectivist ideology was "the" root cause of World War I. Events of that magnitude have innumerable causes, and the historical explorations of why the world exploded into war at that time will doubtless continue forever. My point is to say that the rise of the Industrial Counterrevolution contributed significantly to the conditions that made a general war possible and even likely. Or to put it more strongly, it is impossible to make any sense of the outbreak of World War I without reference to the rise of collectivism generally—and, specifically, to Bismarck's fateful decision to turn against liberalism and embrace instead collectivism and protectionism.

31. Quoted in Mommsen, *Imperial Germany,* 211.

32. Quoted in Hayek, *The Road to Serfdom,* 175.

33. Quoted in Mommsen, *Imperial Germany,* 212.

34. Vladimir I. Lenin, "The Impending Catastrophe and How to Combat It," in *Lenin's Economic Writings,* ed. Meghnad Desai (Atlantic Highlands, N.J.: Humanities Press International, Inc., 1989 [1917]), 212.

35. Quoted in Boettke, *The Political Economy of Soviet Socialism,* 99, n. 49.

36. Quoted in Manchester, *The Last Lion,* 680.

37. William E. Leuchtenburg, "The New Deal and the Analogue of War," in *Change and Continuity in Twentieth-Century America,* ed. John Braeman, Robert Bremner, and Everett Walters (Columbus, Ohio: Ohio State University Press, 1964), 81–143, 109.

38. Quoted in Eksteins, *Rites of Spring,* 309; quoted in Mommsen, *Imperial Germany,* 215.

39. Quoted in Robert Higgs, *Crisis and Leviathan: Critical Episodes in the Growth of American Government* (New York: Oxford University Press, 1987), 171.

40. Quoted in John A. Garraty, *The Great Depression* (New York: Harcourt Brace Jovanovich, 1986), 203.

41. Gilbert, *The First World War,* 391, 395.

42. Barry Eichengreen, *Golden Fetters: The Gold Standard and the Great Depression, 1919–1939* (New York: Oxford University Press, 1992), 79, Fig. 3.4.

43. De Long, *Slouching Towards Utopia?,* chapter XII, 233–34.

44. Forrest Capie, *Depression and Protectionism: Britain between the Wars* (London: George Allen & Unwin, 1983), 26.

45. See Eichengreen, *Golden Fetters,* for the definitive account of the interrelationship between the gold standard and the coming of the Great Depression.

46. See Richard H. Timberlake, *Monetary Policy in the United States: An Intellectual and Institutional History* (Chicago: University of Chicago Press, 1993), 263–73. Figures derived from Table 17.1.

47. See Higgs, *Crisis and Leviathan,* 161; Lionel Robbins, *The Great Depression* (Freeport, N.Y.: Books for Libraries Press, 1971 [1934]), 204, 210; Timberlake, *Monetary Policy in the United States,* 267.

48. See Barry Eichengreen and Jeffrey Sachs, "Exchange Rates and Economic Recovery in the 1930s," *Journal of Economic History* 45, no. 4 (December 1985): 925–46.

49. Quotation from Labour Party publication, "Labour and the New Social Order," 1918, quoted in Rodgers, *Atlantic Crossings,* 293.

50. Quoted in Shaffer, *In Restraint of Trade,* 109.

51. Quoted in Jordan, *Machine-Age Ideology,* 250. Of fascist Italy Tugwell wrote in 1934, "It's the cleanest, neatest, and most effectively operating piece of social machinery I've ever seen; it makes me envious." Quoted in Rodgers, *Atlantic Crossings,* 420. With respect to Soviet central planning, he concluded in the 1930 edition of his economics textbook that "judged as an economic mechanism, it shows an amazing power to produce and distribute goods." Rexford G. Tugwell, Thomas Munro, and Roy E. Stryker, *American Economic Life and the Means of Its Improvement,* 3rd ed. (New York: Harcourt, Brace and Company, 1930 [1925]), 711.

52. A useful survey of trade policy in the interwar period is provided in League of Nations, *Commercial Policy in the Interwar Period: International Proposals and National Policies* (Geneva: League of Nations, 1942).

53. League of Nations, *Review of World Trade 1936* (Geneva: League of Nations, 1937), 10.

54. Quoted in Clark, "Adolf Wagner," 401.

55. Von Mises, *Omnipotent Government,* 1.

56. James Burnham, *The Managerial Revolution* (London: Putnam, 1942 [1941]), 168.

57. Ibid., 69–70.

58. Ibid., 165.

59. Ibid., 167.

60. Ibid., 250 (emphasis in original).

CHAPTER 5   TWILIGHT OF THE IDOLS

1. Hayek, *The Road to Serfdom,* 135.

2. Ibid., 137, 135.

3. Hawley, *The New Deal and the Problem of Monopoly,* 17–146; Higgs, *Crisis and Leviathan,* 177–80.

4. Higgs, *Crisis and Leviathan,* 225–27.

5. John Jewkes, *The New Ordeal by Planning: The Experience of the Forties and the Sixties* (New York: St. Martin's Press, 1968 [1948]), 81. Jewkes' book, published originally in 1948, is a must for readers interested in a detailed and factually specific account of how planning corrupts democracy and other liberal values.

6. Ibid., 139–41, 175–216.

7. Jim Tomlinson, *Democratic Socialism and Economic Policy: The Attlee Years, 1945–1951* (Cambridge: Cambridge University Press, 1997), 79–85, 124–46, 227–232; A. Cairncross, "Reconversion, 1945–51" in *The British Economy since 1945,* ed. N. F. R. Crafts and N. W. C. Woodward (New York: Oxford University Press, 1991), 25–51; N. F. R. Crafts, "'You've never had it so good?': British economic policy and performance, 1945–60," in *Europe's Post-war Recovery,* ed. Barry Eichengreen (Cambridge: Cambridge University Press, 1995), 255.

8. A good overview of ordoliberal thought is provided in Razeen Sally, *Classical Liberalism and International Economic Order: Studies in Theory and Intellectual History* (London: Routledge, 1998), 105–30.

9. The story of Erhard, ordoliberalism, and the birth of the social market economy is well told (if briefly) in Daniel Yergin and Joseph Stanislaw, *The Commanding Heights: The Battle between Government and the Marketplace That Is Remaking the Modern World* (New York: Simon and Schuster, 1998), 32–38.

10. For insightful analysis of the U.S. conversion from Smoot-Hawley protectionism to leadership of a renewed liberal trading system, see I. M. Destler, *American Trade Politics,* 3rd ed. (New York: Twentieth Century Fund, 1995 [1986]), 3–38. A good account of the GATT's early years can be found in Douglas A. Irwin, "The GATT's contribution to economic recovery in post-war Western Europe," in *Europe's Post-war Recovery,* 127–50. A thorough overview of the GATT (and now WTO) system is provided by John Jackson, *The World Trading System: Law and Policy of International Economic Relations,* 2nd ed. (Cambridge, Mass.: MIT Press, 1997 [1989]).

11. Crafts, "'You've never had it so good?'," 255; Barry Eichengreen, *Globalizing Capital: A History of the International Monetary System* (Princeton, N.J.: Princeton University Press), 93–114.

12. A clear-eyed assessment of the Bretton Woods system's inherent instability is provided by Francis J. Gavin, "Bretton Woods: A Golden Era?" in *Global Fortune: The Stumble and Rise of World Capitalism,* ed. Ian Vásquez (Washington, D.C.: Cato Institute, 2000), 213–24.

13. Paul Krugman, "Growing World Trade," 331.

14. Cordell Hull, *The Memoirs of Cordell Hull,* vol. 1 (New York: Macmillan, 1948), 363–64.

15. For a brilliant interpretation of the tragic symbiosis between collectivism and underdevelopment, see von Laue, *The World Revolution of Westernization.*

16. Ibid., 46.

17. Quoted in Yergin and Stanislaw, *The Commanding Heights,* 71.

18. Kwame Nkrumah, *The Autobiography of Kwame Nkrumah* (Edinburgh, Scotland: Thomas Nelson and Sons, 1957), x.

19. Ibid., x.

20. Quoted in von Laue, *The World Revolution of Westernization,* 63–64.

21. Quoted in P. T. Bauer, *Dissent on Development* (Cambridge, Mass.: Harvard University Press, 1976 [1971]), 32–33.

22. Gunnar Myrdal, *Asian Drama: An Inquiry into the Poverty of Nations,* vol. 2 (New York: Pantheon, 1968), 715.

23. Ibid., 710.

24. Myrdal, *Asian Drama,* vol. 1, p. 73.

25. P. T. Bauer, "Subsistence, Trade, and Exchange: Understanding Developing Economies," in *The Revolution in Development Economics,* ed. James Dorn, Steve Hanke, and Alan A. Walters (Washington, D.C.: Cato Institute, 1998), 279.

26. Ibid., 278–79.

27. Vladimir Lenin, "Imperialism, The Highest Stage of Capitalism," in *The Lenin Anthology,* ed. Robert C. Tucker (New York: W. W. Norton & Company, 1975 [1917]), 255.

28. Bauer, *Dissent on Development,* 165.

29. Economic Commission for Latin America, *The Economic Development of Latin America and Its Principal Problems* (New York: United Nations, 1950), 1. Prebisch was the author of this U.N. report.

30. Ibid., 1.

31. Quoted in Albert O. Hirschman, "The Political Economy of Import-Substitution in Latin America," *Quarterly Journal of Economics* LXXXII, no. 1 (February 1968): 1–32, 2.

32. For a thorough and thoughtful analysis of the Latin American dependency movement, see Robert A. Packenham, *The Dependency Movement: Scholarship and Politics in Development Studies* (Cambridge, Mass.: Harvard University Press, 1992).

33. Fernando Henrique Cardoso and Enzo Faletto, *Dependency and Development in Latin America,* trans. Marjory Mattingly Urquidi (Berkeley: University of California Press, 1979), p. viii.

34. Samir Amin, *Unequal Development: An Essay on the Social Formations of Peripheral Capitalism,* trans. Brian Pearce (New York: Monthly Review Press, 1976), 383.

35. Charles Lipson, *Standing Guard: Protecting Foreign Capital in the Nineteenth and Twentieth Centuries* (Berkeley, Calif.: University of California Press, 1985), 98.

36. Quoted in Peter T. Bauer and Basil S. Yamey, "World Wealth Redistribution: Anatomy of the New Order," in *The First World & the Third World: Essays on the New International Economic Order,* ed. Karl Brunner (Rochester, N.Y.: University of Rochester Policy Center Publications, 1978), 193.

37. For a good overview of the development of pro-trade policies in Korea, Taiwan, Thailand, Malaysia, and Indonesia, see World Bank, *The East Asian Miracle: Economic Growth and Public Policy* (New York: Oxford University Press, 1993), 123–56.

38. James Fallows, *Looking at the Sun: The Rise of the New East Asian Economic and Political System* (New York: Pantheon Books, 1994), 208.

39. For a highly informative account of Japan, Inc.'s transition from miracle to malaise, see Richard Katz, *Japan: The System that Soured: The Rise and Fall of the Japanese Economic Miracle* (Armonk, N.Y.: M. E. Sharpe, 1998).

40. See Kozo Yamamura, "Success that Soured: Administrative Guidance and Cartels in Japan," in *Policy and Trade Issues of the Japanese Economy: American and Japanese Perspectives,* ed. Kozo Yamamura (Seattle: University of Washington Press, 1982), 77–112.

41. See David E. Weinstein and Yishay Yafeh, "On the Costs of a Bank–Centered Financial System: Evidence from the Changing Main Bank System in Japan," *Journal of Finance* LIII, no. 2 (April 1998): 635–72, 637.

42. Katz, *Japan: The System that Soured,* 5.

43. An analysis of Japanese innovations in automobile production is provided in James P. Womack, Daniel T. Jones, and Daniel Roos, *The Machine that Changed the World* (New York: Macmillan, 1990).

44. For an account of the declining effectiveness of MITI's attempts at industrial targeting, see Scott Callon, *Divided Sun: MITI and the Breakdown of Japanese High-Tech Industrial Policy, 1975–1993* (Stanford, Calif.: Stanford University Press, 1995).

45. A good review of the bubble economy's excesses and final collapse is provided in Christopher Wood, *The Bubble Economy: Japan's Extraordinary Speculative Boom of the '80s and the Dramatic Bust of the '90s* (New York: Atlantic Monthly Press, 1992).

46. For a highly readable account of collectivism's global collapse, see Yergin and Stanislaw, *The Commanding Heights*.

47. Sebastian Edwards, *Crisis and Reform in Latin America: From Despair to Hope* (New York: Oxford University Press, 1995), 17.

48. For a recent statement of the importance of cultural values to economic development, see Lawrence E. Harrison and Samuel P. Huntington, eds., *Culture Matters: How Values Shape Human Progress* (New York: Basic Books, 2001). The contributors to that volume contend that culture, rather than policies or institutions, is the primary determinant of a country's economic prospects—a position that I find wholly unconvincing. Without a doubt, culture is enormously important in influencing economic performance. Look at the disproportionate contributions made by Chinese minorities to economic growth in Southeast Asia, even where they have been systematically discriminated against; in the United States, the success of Jewish and East Asian minorities makes the same point. On the other hand, what is the cultural difference that explains the different economic paths taken by East and West Germany? North and South Korea? Thailand and Cambodia? Chile and Colombia? Great Britain, before and after Thatcher? China, before and after Deng? Yes, within a given set of institutions, results will vary because of cultural differences; and yes, culture can play a role in deciding which sets of institutions are adopted. But in the economic history of the past century, it is emphatically the case that differences in ideology and institutions, not differences in culture, have been the crucial variable. Collectivism cut across all cultural lines in its sweep to power; likewise, market-oriented institutions have been adopted and have worked in all manner of cultural settings. Both the allure of the Industrial Counterrevolution and the subsequent quest for relief from its failures have transcended cultural boundaries.

49. An argument along similar lines is advanced in Jose Edgardo Campos and Hilton L. Root, *The Key to the Asian Miracle: Making Shared Growth Credible* (Washington, D.C.: Brookings Institution, 1996), 76–108.

50. Quoted in Robert Skidelsky, *The Road from Serfdom: The Economic and Political Consequences of the End of Communism* (New York: Penguin Books, 1997 [1995]), 110.

51. Let me take note of another way in which technological growth has undermined collectivism: by improving people's knowledge about goings-on around the world. The growth of instant communications has dramatically increased public awareness of how conditions at home compare with those elsewhere, and thus has sharpened the incentives faced by governments to pursue policies that achieve decent results. Accordingly, the progress of economic development simultaneously increases the difficulty of centralized control and makes the failures of centralization more apparent when they occur.

CHAPTER 6   THE DEAD HAND

1. Friedman, *The Lexus and the Olive Tree*, 40.

2. John Scott, *Behind the Urals: An American Worker in Russia's City of Steel* (Bloomington, Ind: Indiana University Press, 1989 [1942]), 3.

3. Ibid., 5.

4. Ibid., 92.

5. Interview with author, July 26, 1999.

6. Interview with author, July 26, 1999.

7. European Bank for Reconstruction and Development, *Transition Report 1999* (London: EBRD, 1997), 24.

8. Gerhard Pohl, Robert E. Anderson, Stijn Claessens, and Simeon Djankov, "Privatization and Restructuring in Central and Eastern Europe," World Bank Technical Paper no. 368, August 1997, 6, 9.

9. Thane Gustafson, *Capitalism Russian-Style* (Cambridge, U.K.: Cambridge University Press, 1999), 36.

10. McKinsey Global Institute, *Unlocking Economic Growth in Russia* (Washington, D.C.: McKinsey Global Institute, October 1999), Chapter 4.

11. Raj M. Desai and Itzhak Goldberg, "Vicious Circles of Control: Regional Governments and Insiders in Privatized Russian Enterprises," World Bank Policy Research Paper no. 2287, February 2000, 5.

12. Joseph R. Blasi, Maya Kroumova, and Douglas Kruse, *Kremlin Capitalism: The Privatization of the Russian Economy* (Ithaca, N.Y.: ILR Press, 1997), 139–40.

13. Gustafson, *Capitalism Russian-Style,* 205.

14. Brian Pinto, Vladimir Drebentsov, and Alexander Morozov, "Give Growth and Macro Stability in Russia a Chance: Harden Budgets by Dismantling Nonpayments," World Bank Policy Research Paper no. 2324, April 2000.

15. McKinsey Global Institute, *Unlocking Economic Growth in Russia,* Chapter 3, "Steel," Exhibit 9.

16. Ibid., Chapter 4.

17. Mark A. Groombridge, "China's Long March to a Market Economy: The Case for Permanent Normal Trade Relations with the People's Republic of China," Cato Institute Trade Policy Analysis no. 10, April 24, 2000, 3.

18. World Bank, *The East Asian Miracle,* 59.

19. "Keep Spending," Economist Intelligence Unit, March 8, 2001, available on http://www.chinaonline.com.

20. Nicholas R. Lardy, *China's Unfinished Economic Revolution* (Washington, D.C.: Brookings Institution Press, 1998), 25–31.

21. Ibid., 39–43.

22. World Bank, "Special Focus: Financial & Corporate Restructuring," in *East Asia Update* (Washington, D.C.: World Bank, March 2001), 3.

23. Ibid., 8.

24. James Gwartney and Robert Lawson with Dexter Samida, *Economic Freedom of the World: 2000 Annual Report* (Vancouver, B.C.: Fraser Institute, 2000), 231–32.

25. Countries awarded a score of 0 include Albania, Algeria, Bulgaria, Burundi, Central African Republic, Chad, China, Republic of Congo, Croatia, Guyana, Jordan, Madagascar, Malawi, Morocco, Nicaragua, Nigeria, Romania, Sierra Leone, Slovakia, Slovenia, Syria, Togo, Ukraine, and Zambia; countries awarded a score of 2 include Bangladesh, Belize, Benin, Democratic Republic of Congo, Côte d'Ivoire, Egypt, Fiji, India, Iran, Israel, Kenya, Myanmar, Nepal, Oman, Pakistan, Poland, Rwanda, Taiwan, Tanzania, Tunisia, Uganda, Venezuela, and Zimbabwe; countries awarded a score of 4 include Austria, Bahrain, Bolivia, Botswana, Cameroon, Colombia, Dominican Republic, Ecuador, Estonia, France, Gabon, Ghana, Greece, Guinea-Bissau, Hungary,

Indonesia, Kuwait, Latvia, Lithuania, Malaysia, Mali, Niger, Norway, Russia, Spain, Sri Lanka, and Trinidad & Tobago.

26. Gwartney and Lawson, *Economic Freedom of the World: 2000 Annual Report,* 232.

27. Countries awarded a score of 0 include Bangladesh, Cameroon, Central African Republic, Republic of Congo, Madagascar, Myanmar, Rwanda, South Korea, and Syria; countries awarded a score of 2 include Benin, Democratic Republic of Congo, Côte d'Ivoire, Cyprus, Gabon, Haiti, India, Indonesia, Iran, Jordan, Malta, Nepal, Taiwan, Togo, and Zambia; countries awarded a score of 4 include Albania, Algeria, Bahamas, Bahrain, Burundi, Chad, Colombia, Croatia, Ecuador, Egypt, Honduras, Jamaica, Lithuania, Malawi, Malaysia, Mali, Morocco, Namibia, Nicaragua, Niger, Nigeria, Oman, Pakistan, Panama, Senegal, Slovakia, Sri Lanka, Tanzania, Venezuela, and Zimbabwe.

28. Robert Bacon, "A Scorecard for Energy Reform in Developing Countries," World Bank Public Policy for the Private Sector Note no. 175, April 1999.

29. Nicola Tynan, "Private Participation in the Rail Sector—Recent Trends," World Bank Public Policy for the Private Sector Note no. 186, June 1999.

30. Carsten Fink, Aaditya Mattoo, and Ileana Cristina Neagu, "Trade in International Maritime Services: How Much Does Policy Matter?" World Bank Policy Research Working Paper no. 2522, 2000.

31. Organisation for Economic Co-operation and Development, *Agricultural Policies in OECD Countries: Monitoring and Evaluation 1999* (Paris: OECD, 1999), 22, 24, 167, 168.

32. Organisation for Economic Co-operation and Development, *Agricultural Policies in Emerging and Transition Countries: 1999,* vol. 1 (Paris: OECD, 1999), 159–71.

33. Ibid., 69, 187, vol. II, 86.

34. Organisation for Economic Co-operation and Development, *Communications Outlook 1999* (Paris: OECD, 1999), 19, 32–33.

35. Ibid., 30.

36. Ada Karina Izaguirre, "Private Participation in Telecommunications—Recent Trends," World Bank Public Policy for the Private Sector Note no. 204, December 1999.

37. OECD, *Communications Outlook 1999,* 120.

38. Ibid., 110–11, 121.

39. J. Michael Finger and Ludger Schuknecht, "Market Access Advances and Retreats: The Uruguay Round and Beyond" (paper presented at the WTO-World Bank Conference on Developing Countries and the Millennium Round, Geneva, September 20–21, 1999), available online at http://www.itd.org/wb/dc_milpap.htm.

40. These figures were obtained from the World Trade Organization's most recently completed trade policy reviews of these countries.

41. Finger and Schuknecht, "Market Access Advances and Retreats," 65.

42. Ibid., 58.

43. Average tariff rates discussed above were taken from the U.S. International Trade Commission, "The Economic Effects of Significant U.S. Import Restraints," Publication 3201, Investigation No. 332–325, May 1999.

44. Shaffer, *In Restraint of Trade,* 137.

45.   Robert Sobel, *The Age of Giant Corporations: A Microeconomic History of American Business, 1914–1992,* 3rd ed. (Westport, Conn.: Praeger, 1993 [1972]), 11–12, 169–71.

46.   William H. Barringer and Kenneth J. Pierce, *Paying the Price for Big Steel* (Washington, D.C.: American Institute for International Steel, 2000), 38.

47.   Ibid., 36.

48.   Ibid., 42.

Chapter 7   Hollow Capitalism

1.   See Henry Sender, "New Kid in Town," *Far Eastern Economic Review,* February 11, 1999. After on-again, off-again negotiations, the deal finally closed in December 1999. President Kim Dae-Jung himself singled out the sale as a litmus test for the broader success of Korean economic reforms.

2.   Interview with author, March 26, 1999.

3.   Robert B. Reich, *The Next American Frontier* (New York: Times Books, 1983), 171.

4.   Akio Morita and Shintaro Ishihara, *The Japan That Can Say "No": The New United States–Japan Relations Card,* 8. The quotation is taken from an unauthorized translation published in the *Congressional Record,* November 14, 1989, E 3783. The official English translation, published in 1991, did not include Morita's sections.

5.   Chalmers Johnson, *Japan: Who Governs?* (New York: W. W. Norton & Company, 1995), 63.

6.   Clyde Prestowitz, *Trading Places: How We Are Giving Our Future to Japan and How to Reclaim It* (New York: Basic Books, 1993 [1988]), 519.

7.   For a full discussion of the Asian financial crisis, see chapter 9.

8.   A decade after the bubble burst, final resolution of the bad loans from that era remains far from complete. As a result, there is still no precise accounting of total losses. For various estimates of the damage done, see International Monetary Fund, "Japan: Selected Issues," IMF Staff Country Report No. 98/113, October 1998, 111–12.

9.   Bank for International Settlements, *70th Annual Report* (Basel, Switzerland: BIS, June 5, 2000), 49.

10.   Bellamy, *Looking Backward,* 211.

11.   Prestowitz, *Trading Places,* 256.

12.   I am writing at a time when financial markets are in bad odor after the collapse of the "dot com" bubble. The recent bust, though, does not undermine the case for open and decentralized financial markets. That case should never rest on the claim that "markets always know best"; markets are human institutions and therefore prey to human weaknesses, including fallibility. With the advent of the Internet, investors were working in pitch-black uncertainty about how best to exploit this revolutionary new technology; along the way, many bet incorrectly that rapid growth was the key to eventual profits, while others were simply swept up in the hype. The great value of capital markets is that they respond to errors with corrective feedback (in this case, harrowing losses) much more swiftly than more centralized arrangements for allocating capital.

Meanwhile, the openness of the market made possible a dramatic acceleration of the growth of good ideas as well as the ultimate exposure of bad ones.

13. Robert G. King and Ross Levine, "Finance and Growth: Schumpeter Might Be Right," *Quarterly Journal of Economics* 108, no. 3 (August 1993): 717–37.

14. Jeffrey Wurgler, "Financial Markets and the Allocation of Capital," *Journal of Financial Economics* 58, no. 1 (October 2000): 187–214.

15. Asli Demirgüç-Kunt and Vojislav Maksimovic, "Law, Finance, and Firm Growth," *Journal of Finance* LIII, no. 6 (December 1998): 2107–137.

16. Ross Levine and Sarah Zervos, "Stock Markets, Banks, and Economic Growth," *American Economic Review* 88, no. 3 (June 1998): 537–59.

17. Raghuram G. Rajan and Luigi Zingales, "Financial Dependence and Growth," *American Economic Review* 88, no. 3 (June 1998): 559–86.

18. Interview with author, March 26, 1999.

19. Interview with author, March 26, 1999

20. Information on Siam Syntech's restructuring plan was obtained from reports in *The Nation,* an English-language daily newspaper in Thailand.

21. World Bank, "Special Focus: Financial & Corporate Restructuring," 4.

22. Bank for International Settlements, *70th Annual Report,* 47.

23. World Bank, "Regional Overview," in *East Asia Brief* (Washington, D.C.: World Bank, September 2000), 7.

24. World Bank, "Country Brief: Korea," in *East Asia Brief,* 8.

25. Richard Katz, "Bad debt blues," *The Oriental Economist,* September 2000.

26. James R. Barth, Gerard Caprio Jr., and Ross Levine, "Banking Systems around the Globe: Do Regulation and Ownership Affect Performance and Stability?", World Bank Policy Research Working Paper no. 2325, April 2000.

27. Joe Stilwell, "The Savings & Loan Industry: Averting Collapse," Cato Institute Policy Analysis no. 7, February 15, 1982.

28. See James R. Barth, *The Great Savings and Loan Debacle* (Washington, D.C.: American Enterprise Institute, 1991), for a good account of what went wrong.

29. The figure for Microsoft's market capitalization is as of March 2001—dramatically reduced from its historic highs.

30. Sebastian Edwards, *Crisis and Reform in Latin America,* 203–208.

31. For analysis of the interconnection between financial repression and public finance, see Alberto Giovannini and Martha de Melo, "Government Revenue from Financial Repression," *American Economic Review* 83, no. 4 (September 1993): 953–63; Nouriel Roubini and Xavier Sala-i-Martin, "A Growth Model of Inflation, Tax Evasion, and Financial Repression," *Journal of Monetary Economics* 35, no. 2 (April 1995): 275–301.

32. The 40 countries are Albania, Algeria, Bangladesh, Bulgaria, Burundi, Cameroon, Central African Republic, Chad, China, Democratic Republic of Congo, Republic of Congo, Croatia, Czech Republic, Egypt, Fiji, Germany, Iceland, India, Iran, Israel, Madagascar, Malawi, Mali, Malta, Myanmar, Nepal, Pakistan, Poland, Romania, Russia, Rwanda, Senegal, Sierra Leone, Slovakia, Syria, Taiwan, Tanzania, Togo, Uganda, and Ukraine. See Gwartney and Lawson, *Economic Freedom of the World: 2000 Annual Report.*

33. The 40 countries are Algeria, Benin, Bulgaria, Burundi, Cameroon, Central African Republic, Chad, China, Democratic Republic of Congo, Republic of Congo, Côte d'Ivoire, Estonia, Gabon, Guatemala, Guinea-Bissau, Guyana, Haiti, Jamaica, Latvia, Madagascar, Malawi, Mali, Mexico, Myanmar, Niger, Nigeria, Pakistan, Romania, Rwanda, Senegal, Sierra Leone, Somalia, Syria, Tanzania, Togo, Uganda, Ukraine, Uruguay, Venezuela, and Zambia. Of those, the 19 countries in which real interest rates were frequently or persistently negative are Algeria, Benin, Bulgaria, China, Democratic Republic of Congo, Estonia, Guinea-Bissau, Guyana, Haiti, Malawi, Myanmar, Nigeria, Romania, Rwanda, Sierra Leone, Somalia, Syria, Ukraine, and Venezuela. See Gwartney and Lawson, *Economic Freedom of the World: 2000 Annual Report*.

34. These data were obtained from International Monetary Fund, *International Financial Statistics Yearbook 1999* (Washington, D.C.: IMF, 1999), lines 22d and 99b.

35. Nicholas Lardy, "When Will China's Financial System Meet China's Needs?" (paper presented at the Conference on Policy Reform in China, Center for Research on Economic Development and Policy Reform, Stanford University, Stanford, Calif., November 18–20, 1999) (paper revised February 2000).

36. The following discussion of Russia's banking system relies on the analysis in Gustafson, *Capitalism Russian-Style,* 77–107.

37. Maria Maher and Thomas Andersson, *Corporate Governance: Effects on Firm Performance and Economic Growth* (Paris: Organisation for Economic Co-operation and Development, 1999), 26.

38. Ibid., 16.

39. Glen Yago and Juan Montoya, "Capital Access Index: Asia Postcrisis," Milken Institute, Number 11, March 8, 2000, 29.

40. Bank for International Settlements, *67th Annual Report* (Basel, Switzerland: BIS, June 9, 1997), 105.

41. "Boomtown," *The Economist,* January 15, 2000, 75.

42. See Clay Chandler and Akiko Kashiwagi, "'Internet Tsunami' Draws Foreign Cash, Stirs Up Long-Stagnant Venture Climate," *Washington Post,* February 13, 2000.

43. See Edmund L. Andrews, "The Metamorphosis of Germany Inc.," *New York Times,* March 12, 2000; "Europe's New Capitalism: Bidding for the future," *The Economist,* February 12, 2000, 71–74.

44. "Europe's New Capitalism," 72.

45. The following discussion relies on newspaper accounts in the *Wall Street Journal,* especially its Asian edition, as well as the two main English-language daily newspapers in Thailand, the *Bangkok Post* and *The Nation.*

CHAPTER 8 THE RULE OF LAWLESSNESS

1. Hughes, *American Genesis,* 269–71.

2. World Bank, *India: Policies to Reduce Poverty and Accelerate Sustainable Development* (Washington, D.C.: World Bank, 2000), 76–77.

3. World Bank, *Averting the Old Age Crisis: Policies to Protect the Old* and *Promote Growth* (New York: Oxford University Press, 1994), 123.

4. Friedrich Schneider and Dominik H. Enste, "Shadow Economies: Size, Causes, and Consequences," *Journal of Economic Literature* XXXVIII (March 2000): 77–114, 100–01.

5. Hernando de Soto, *The Mystery of Capital: Why Capitalism Triumphs in the West and Fails Everywhere Else* (New York: Basic Books, 2000), 32–33.

6. Ibid., 34–35.

7. There are sizable shadow economies even in the developed world. In Denmark and Germany, for instance, over 20 percent of working-age adults are believed to engage in significant unreported economic activity. In Italy, the figure may be as high as 48 percent. Examining 20 developed countries, Schneider and Enste found an average ratio of informal output to official GDP of 15.1 percent. Schneider and Enste, "Shadow Economies," 102, 105–06.

8. Friedman, *The Lexus and the Olive Tree,* 350.

9. Paulo Mauro, "Corruption and Growth," *Quarterly Journal of Economics* 110 (August 1995): 681–712.

10. Gwartney and Lawson, *Economic Freedom of the World: 2000 Annual Report,* 10, 86.

11. Transparency International, "New Index highlights worldwide corruption crisis," June 27, 2001.

12. World Economic Forum, *Global Competitiveness Report 2000* (New York: Oxford University Press, 2000), 94, 247–252.

13. Pablo T. Spiller and Mariano Tommasi, "The Institutional Foundations of Argentina's Development," preliminary draft, August 27, 1999.

14. Interview with staff of Fundacion del Tucumán, June 6, 2001; interview with Ignacio Colombres Garmendia, June 6, 2001.

15. Pamela Druckerman, "Argentina, Land of Fiscal Loose Cannons," *Wall Street Journal,* March 2, 2001.

16. Ana I. Eiras and Brett D. Schaefer, "Argentina's Economic Crisis: An 'Absence of Capitalism,'" Heritage Foundation Backgrounder no. 1432, April 19, 2001, 3.

17. Joshua Goodman, "Argentina's Provincial Profligates," *Business Week,* January 29, 2001 (International edition).

18. Interview with author, June 6, 2001.

19. Adrián C. Guissarri, "Costos de la Justicia y Eficiencia en la Asignacion de Recursos" ("Costs of Justice and Efficiency in the Allocation of Resources") Proyecto Justicia y Desarrollo Economico (Project on Justice and Economic Development), Buenos Aires, June 1998.

20. This point is central to Douglass North's analysis of economic history. See North, *Structure and Change in Economic History,* especially pp. 33–44; see also Douglass C. North, "Institutions, Ideology, and Economic Performance," in *The Revolution in Development Economics,* 95–107.

21. Mancur Olson, *Power and Prosperity: Outgrowing Communist and Capitalist Dictatorships* (New York: Basic Books, 2000), 173.

22. See George B. N. Ayittey, *Africa Betrayed* (New York: St. Martin's Press, 1992), 120–21.

23. Freedom House, 1999–2000 Freedom in the World survey, available at www.freedomhouse.org.

24. See Ayittey, *Africa Betrayed,* 253–62.

25. Ibid., 103.

26. James Madison, "Federalist No. 51," in Alexander Hamilton, James Madison, and John Jay, *The Federalist Papers* (New York: New American Library, 1961 [1787–88]), 322.

27. Indeed, in Chile's case, the government pursued a program of explicitly liberal economic reform.

28. My point here is that the proliferation of organized interests provoked by economic development helps to promote mature and stable democracies. Olson made a similar point in his last and posthumously published book. Olson, *Power and Prosperity,* 30–34. In an earlier work, however, he attempted a very different argument—namely, that the unchecked growth of organized interests in stable democracies tends, over time, to undermine economic development. Mancur Olson, *The Rise and Decline of Nations* (New Haven, Conn.: Yale University Press, 1982). Writing in the early 1980s, Olson contrasted the lower economic growth of Great Britain and the United States with the more dynamic performance of Japan and West Germany, and ascribed the difference to the fact that economically harmful narrow interests had been wiped out in the latter two countries by their defeat in World War II. In the former pair of countries, on the other hand, narrow interests had continued to accumulate like so many barnacles, gradually and progressively hindering wealth creation with a steady build-up of special-interest privileges.

History has not been kind to Olson's thesis. The United States and Great Britain have staged dramatic restructurings over the past 20 years, while Germany and especially Japan have stumbled off the high-growth path. Although it is true that the interests of narrow groups often conflict with the general interest in market competition, the long-term effect of the steady growth of such groups is ambiguous. As discussed in the text, an increase in the number of groups that are jostling for privileges can make it harder for any one group to succeed; also, democratic stability breeds organized groups with steadily broader interests, which then act as a check on narrow-group lobbying. Furthermore, and perhaps most important, it seems that narrow groups can eventually overreach: Public frustration with poor economic performance can discredit the self-serving claims of narrow interests and allow public-spirited market reforms to carry the day. That is what happened in Great Britain and the United States; in Japan and Germany, on the other hand, the public's patience with declining economic prospects has not yet been exhausted.

29. This account of recent Thai political history up to the Asian crisis relies heavily on Pasuk Phongpaichit and Chris Baker, *Thailand's Boom and Bust* (Chiang Mai, Thailand: Silkworm Books, 1998), 216–43.

30. Interview with author, January 28, 2000.

31. James Madison, "Federalist No. 10," in Hamilton, Madison, and Jay, *The Federalist Papers,* 77.

32. For an interesting commentary on the hypertrophy of organized lobbies, see Jonathan Rauch, *Government's End: Why Washington Stopped Working* (New York: Public Affairs, 1999). Rauch relies heavily on Mancur Olson's work for the theoretical framework of his own reporting and analysis.

33. The literature of "public choice" constitutional economics spawned by Buchanan's work is vast and growing, but a good introduction is James Buchanan, *The Limits of Liberty: Between Anarchy and Leviathan* (Chicago: University of Chicago Press, 1977).

CHAPTER 9   UNPEACEFUL COEXISTENCE

1. Soros, *The Crisis of Global Capitalism*, xx, xxvii.

2. Anthony Giddens, *The Third Way: The Renewal of Social Democracy* (London: Polity Press, 1998), 147–48.

3. Peter Engardio et al., "Global Capitalism: Can it be made to work better?" *Business Week*, November 6, 2000 (Asian edition), 40–68, 43.

4. Soros, *The Crisis of Global Capitalism*, xxiii.

5. Giddens, *The Third Way*, 5.

6. Soros, *The Crisis of Global Capitalism*, xxix.

7. Giddens, *The Third Way*, 153.

8. See, for example, Lawrence H. White, *Competition and Currency: Essays on Free Banking and Money* (New York: New York University Press, 1989); James A. Dorn, ed., *The Future of Money in the Information Age* (Washington, D.C.: Cato Institute, 1997).

9. "Challenges for Monetary Policymakers," remarks by Alan Greenspan, "Monetary Policy in the New Economy," 18th annual monetary conference, Cato Institute, Washington, D.C., October 19, 2000.

10. Indeed, restrictions on portfolio investment actually discourage direct investment. First, such restrictions raise the cost of capital in the host country. When companies determine where to invest abroad, the local cost of capital is an important consideration. A higher cost of capital reduces the projected profitability of possible investments, and thus encourages companies to look elsewhere. Furthermore, the presence of capital controls raises the possibility of further restrictions in the future; heightened risk that an investing company might be hampered in repatriating profits acts as a deterrent against further direct investment. For a discussion of these issues, see Geert Bekaert and Campbell R. Harvey, "Capital Markets: An Engine for Economic Growth," *Brown Journal of World Affairs* V, no. 1 (Winter/Spring 1998): 33–53; see also Robert Krol, "The Case for Open Global Capital Markets," Cato Institute Trade Briefing Paper no. 11, March 15, 2001, 6.

11. See Krol, "The Case for Open Global Capital Markets," 2–4, and cited sources.

12. A. James Meigs, "Mexican Monetary Lessons," *The Cato Journal* 17, no. 1 (Spring/Summer 1997): 35–72, 45–46.

13. Pedro Alba, Amar Bhattacharya, Stijn Claessens, Swati Ghosh, and Leonardo Hernandez, "Volatility and Contagion in a Financially-Integrated World: Lessons from East Asia's Recent Experience," World Bank Policy Research Working Paper no. 2008, December 3, 1998, 3–4.

14. Pinto et al., "Give Growth and Macro Stability in Russia a Chance," 9.

15. Andrei N. Illarionov, "Creating Crises: Russian Economic Policy, 1992–1998," unpublished manuscript, Institute of Economic Analysis, January 1999, 13.

16. Francisco Gil-Díaz, "The Origins of Mexico's 1994 Financial Crisis," *The Cato Journal* 17, no. 3 (Winter 1998): 303–313, 308, n. 12.

17. Alba et al., "Volatility and Contagion in a Financially-Integrated World," 43.

18. Illarionov, "Creating Crises," 13.

19. World Bank, *East Asia: The Road to Recovery* (Washington, D.C.: World Bank, 1998), 9.

20. Meigs, "Mexican Monetary Lessons," 64.

21. Information on monetary aggregates was obtained from International Monetary Fund, *International Financial Statistics Yearbook 1999*.

22. Illarionov, "Creating Crises," 12.

23. World Bank, *East Asia: The Road to Recovery,* 10.

24. The above discussion relies heavily on Juan Luis Moreno-Villalaz, "Lessons from the Monetary Experience of Panama: A Dollar Economy with Financial Integration," *The Cato Journal* 18, no. 3 (Winter 1998): 421–439.

25. *Report of the International Financial Institution Advisory Commission* (better known as the Meltzer Commission report), Washington, D.C., March 8, 2000, 29–34.

26. The term "laissez welfare" comes from Gerald Celente, "Capitalism for Cowards," *New York Times,* October 16, 1998.

27. William R. Cline and Kevin J. S. Barnes, "Spreads and Risks in Emerging Markets Lending," Institute of International Finance Research Papers no. 97–1, December 1997, 2.

28. Alba et al., "Volatility and Contagion in a Financially-Integrated World," 37.

29. Illarionov, "Creating Crises," 9.

30. Meltzer Commission Report, 34.

31. It should be noted, though, that Taiwan is not a member of the IMF—a fact that may have some significance in explaining why it suffered less than other economies in the region.

32. William C. Gruben, "Banking Structures, Market Forces, and Economic Freedom: Lessons from Argentina and Mexico," *The Cato Journal* 18, no. 2 (Fall 1998): 263–74, 268.

33. Gil-Díaz, "The Origins of Mexico's 1994 Financial Crisis," 306–07.

34. Gruben, "Banking Structures, Market Forces, and Economic Freedom," 268.

35. James R. Barth, R. Dan Brumbaugh Jr., Lalita Ramesh, and Glenn Yago, "The Role of Governments and Markets in International Banking Crises," Milken Institute Policy Brief, 1998.

36. Alba et al., "Volatility and Contagion in a Financially-Integrated World," 39.

37. Michael Pomerleano, "The East Asian Crisis and Corporate Finances: The Untold Micro Story," World Bank Working Paper no. 1990, October 1998, 20–21.

38. Stijn Claessens, Simeon Djankov, and Larry Lang, "Corporate Growth, Financing, and Risks in the Decade before East Asia's Financial Crisis," World Bank Policy Research Paper no. 2017, 9.

39. Pomerleano, "The East Asian Crisis and Corporate Finances," 13–14.

40. This analysis relies heavily on Pinto et al., "Give Growth and Macro Stability in Russia A Chance."

41. See Krol, "The Case for Open Global Capital Markets," 5, and cited sources.

CHAPTER 10   RECASTING THE SAFETY NET

1. Greider, *One World, Ready or Not,* 308.

2. John Gray, *False Dawn: The Delusions of Global Capitalism* (New York: The New Press, 1998), 83.

3. Quoted in Buchanan, *The Great Betrayal,* 288.

4. Marx and Engels, "Manifesto of the Communist Party," in *The Marx-Engels Reader,* 475.

5. Hayek, *The Constitution of Liberty,* 285.

6. Ibid., 286.

7. Greider, *One World, Ready or Not,* 332.

8. Quoted in Mauricio Rojas, *Millennium Doom: Fallacies about the End of Work* (London: Social Market Foundation, 1999), 44.

9. "Globalization: What Americans Are Worried About," *Business Week,* April 24, 2000, 44.

10. Quoted in Douglas A. Irwin, *Against the Tide: An Intellectual History of Free Trade* (Princeton, N.J.: Princeton University Press, 1996), 154.

11. Rojas, *Millennium Doom,* 48.

12. Daniel T. Griswold, "WTO Report Card: America's Economic Stake in Open Trade," Cato Institute Trade Briefing Paper no. 8, April 3, 2000, 12.

13. Dani Rodrik, *Has Globalization Gone Too Far?* (Washington, D.C.: Institute for International Economics, 1997), 6.

14. "The Mystery of the Vanishing Taxpayer," *The Economist,* January 29, 2000.

15. See International Monetary Fund, *International Financial Statistics Yearbook 2000* (Washington, D.C.: IMF, 2000), 993.

16. In 1998, Social Security and Medicare expenses alone constituted just over 50 percent of total non-defense, non-interest federal outlays. See U.S. Census Bureau, *Statistical Abstract of the United States: 1999* (Lanham, Maryland: Bernan Press, 2000), Table no. 548.

17. W. Michael Cox and Richard Alm, *Myths of Rich and Poor: Why We're Better Off Than We Think* (New York: Basic Books, 1999), 129.

18. Ibid., 128.

19. Peter A. Koehler, Hans F. Zacher, and Martin Partington, *The Evolution of Social Insurance 1881–1981* (New York: St. Martin's Press, 1982), 13.

20. A. J. P. Taylor, *Bismarck: The Man and the Statesman* (New York: Vintage Books, 1955), 203.

21. Quoted in World Bank, *Averting the Old Age Crisis,* 105.

22. Interview with author, April 12, 2001.

23. Centers for Disease Control and Prevention, *National Vital Statistics Report* 47, no. 28 (December 13, 1999): Table 12; William G. Poortvliet and Thomas P. Laine,

"Privatization and Reform of Social Security Pension Plans as a Global Trend," *Journal of the American Society of CLU and ChFC* (July 1997): 54–62.

24. Peter J. Ferrara and Michael Tanner, *A New Deal for Social Security* (Washington, D.C.: Cato Institute, 1998), 40; Poortvliet and Laine, "Privatization and Reform of Social Security Pension Plans as a Global Trend," 60.

25. Quoted in World Bank, *Averting the Old Age Crisis,* 109.

26. "Privatising Peace of Mind," *The Economist,* October 24, 1998.

27. World Bank, *Averting the Old Age Crisis,* 136.

28. Ferrara and Tanner, *A New Deal for Social Security,* 69.

29. Ibid., 57, 132.

30. World Bank, *Averting the Old Age Crisis,* 34.

31. Ibid., 1, 25.

32. Ibid., 144.

33. See the discussion in Chapter 8.

34. World Bank, *Averting the Old Age Crisis,* 148.

35. Ibid., 27.

36. Ibid., 26.

37. Marco Cangiano, Carlo Cottarelli, and Luis Cubeddu, "Pension Developments and Reforms in Transition Economies," International Monetary Fund Working Paper 98/151, October 1998, 8, 12.

38. Ibid., 19.

39. World Bank, *Averting the Old Age Crisis,* 155.

40. Cangiano et al., "Pension Developments and Reforms in Transition Economies," 16.

41. Ethan B. Kapstein and Branko Milanovic, "Dividing the Spoils: Pensions, Privatization, and Reform in Russia's Transition," World Bank Working Paper no. 2292, March 1, 2000, 2.

42. World Bank, *Averting the Old Age Crisis,* 112–13, 159–60.

43. The above description of the Chilean system relies heavily on L. Jacobo Rodríguez, "Chile's Private Pension Sytem at 18: Its Current State and Future Challenges," Cato Institute Social Security Privatization Paper no. 17, July 30, 1999; see also Ferrara and Tanner, *A New Deal for Social Security,* 132–141.

44. Estelle James, "New Systems for Old Age Security—Theory, Practice and Empirical Evidence," World Bank Policy Research Working Paper no. 1766, May 1997, 21.

45. Interview with author, April 12, 2001.

46. Mitchell A. Orenstein, "How Politics and Institutions Affect Pension Reform in Three Postcommunist Countries," World Bank Policy Research Working Paper no. 2310, March 1, 2000, 69.

47. Göran Normann and Daniel J. Mitchell, "Pension Reform in Sweden: Lessons for American Policymakers," Heritage Foundation Backgrounder no. 1381, June 29, 2000.

48. Rodríguez, "Chile's Private Pension System at 18," 12.

49. Ibid., 7–11.

50. A good overview of Mexico's system is provided by L. Jacobo Rodríguez, "In Praise and Criticism of Mexico's Pension Reform," Cato Institute Policy Analysis no. 340, April 14, 1999.

51.   Orenstein, "How Politics and Institutions Affect Pension Reform in Three Postcommunist Countries," 26.

52.   World Bank, *Averting the Old Age Crisis,* 95.

53.   Lardy, *China's Unfinished Economic Revolution,* 43–47, 50–51.

54.   McKinsey Global Institute, *Unlocking Economic Growth in Russia,* "Steel," Exhibit 41.

55.   Ibid., Chapter 2, Exhibit 48.

56.   McKinsey Global Institute, *Why the Japanese Economy Is Not Growing* (Washington, D.C.: McKinsey Global Institute, July 18, 2000), Chapter 2, 3–4.

57.   Ibid., Executive Summary.

58.   Katz, *Japan: The System that Soured,* 34–35.

59.   Gray, *False Dawn,* 173–74.

60.   Katz, *Japan: The System that Soured,* 132.

61.   Daniel T. Griswold, "Trade, Jobs, and Manufacturing: Why (Almost All) U.S. Workers Should Welcome Imports," Cato Institute Trade Briefing Paper no. 6, September 30, 1999, 11.

62.   For an overview of labor regulations in Korea, Latin America, and India, respectively, see Organisation for Economic Co-operation and Development, *Pushing Ahead with Reform in Korea: Labour Market and Social Safety-Net Policies* (Paris: OECD, 2000); World Bank, *India: Policies to Reduce Poverty and Accelerate Sustainable Development,* chapter 6; Sebastian Edwards and Nora Claudia Lustig, eds., *Labor Markets in Latin America: Combining Social Protection with Market Flexibility* (Washington, D.C.: Brookings Institution Press, 1997).

63.   Organisation for Economic Co-operation and Development, *Employment Outlook* (Paris: OECD, July 1997), 63–92.

64.   Ibid., 49–132.

65.   Assar Lindbeck, "Problems of Unemployment in Europe and the United States" (paper presented at the Stockholm Conference on Job Creation and Labor Market Policy, Stockholm, Sweden, May 29, 1997); Organisation for Economic Co-operation and Development, *Employment Outlook* (Paris: OECD, June 2000), Statistical Annex, Tables A, G.

66.   Lindbeck, "Problems of Unemployment in Europe and the United States." Figures on U.S. private sector job growth were obtained from U.S. Census Bureau, *Statistical Abstract of the United States: 1999,* Tables 649, 678.

67.   OECD, *Employment Outlook,* June 2000, Table C.

68.   See, for example, Pietro Garibaldi and Paulo Mauro, "Deconstructing Job Creation," International Monetary Fund Working Paper 99/109, August 1999, 17–22.

69.   Organisation for Economic Co-operation and Development, *Employment Outlook* (Paris: OECD, June 1999), 82–88.

70.   OECD, *Employment Outlook,* July 1997, 77; see also Stephen J. Davis and Magnus Henrekson, "Wage-Setting Institutions as Industrial Policy," National Bureau of Economic Research Working Paper no. 7502, January 2000.

71.   OECD, *Employment Outlook,* June 1999, 82–88.

72.   Ibid., 106.

73.   Ibid., 100–105.

74.   Ibid., 96.

75. Martin Neil Baily, "Economic Perspectives on Job Creation: Lessons for Europe" (paper presented at the Stockholm Conference on Job Creation and Labor Market Policy, Stockholm, Sweden, May 29, 1997).

76. Olivier Blanchard, "Dutch Lessons for EU Partners," *The Irish Times,* August 11, 2000.

CHAPTER 11   LIBERALIZATION BY FITS AND STARTS

1. Kristin Gazlay, "May Day Rallies Create Tensions," Associated Press Online, May 1, 2000.

2. Quoted in Roland N. Stromberg, *Redemption by War: The Intellectuals and 1914* (Lawrence, Kansas: The Regents Press of Kansas, 1982), 85.

3. Ibid., 2, 52.

4. Quoted in ibid., 181.

5. Ibid., 189.

6. Group of 77, "Ministerial Declaration," 23rd Annual Meeting of the Ministers of Foreign Affairs, New York, September 24, 1999, paragraph 18.

7. Ernesto Zedillo, "Can We Take Open Markets for Granted?" Remarks at the plenary session, World Economic Forum, Davos, Switzerland, January 28, 2000.

8. Quoted in Eugenie L. Evans, "Delegates Disgusted by Seattle Protesters Rather Than Inspired," *Financial Times,* January 7, 2000.

9. Mancur Olson, *Power and Prosperity,* 8.

10. My thinking on "top down" and "bottom up" visions of globalization has been greatly influenced by Sally, *Classical Liberalism and International Economic Order.* Sally distinguishes between liberalism "from above" and "from below."

11. See Håkan Nordström and Scott Vaughan, "Trade and Environment," World Trade Organization Special Studies 4, 1999, 35–46; Organisation for Economic Cooperation and Development, *International Trade and Core Labour Standards* (Paris: OECD, 2000), 31–42.

12. Razeen Sally's distinction between liberalism "from above" and liberalism "from below" pertains specifically to relative roles of national and international institutions in maintaining international economic order. See Sally, *Classical Liberalism and International Economic Order.*

13. World Bank figures from Meltzer Commission Report, 59, Table 3–1; IMF figures available on the IMF's Web site http://www.imf.org.

14. These statements appeared on the Web site http://www.a16.org, under the headline "Mobilization for Global Justice: De-fund the Fund! Break the Bank! Dump the Debt!"

15. Meltzer Commission Report, 58.

16. Ian Vásquez, "The International Monetary Fund: Challenges and Contradictions," Testimony before the International Financial Institution Advisory Commission, U.S. Congress, September 28, 1999.

17. Quoted in ibid. (emphasis in original).

18. Meltzer Commission Report, 81, Table 3–8.

19.   Quoted in Ian Vásquez, "Official Assistance, Economic Freedom, and Policy Change: Is Foreign Aid Like Champagne?" *Cato Journal* 18, no. 2 (Fall 1998): 275–86, 281.

20.   Ibid., 279.

21.   Robert Gilpin, *The Challenge of Global Capitalism: The World Economy in the 21st Century* (Princeton, N.J.: Princeton University Press, 2000), 3–4, 14.

22.   Smith, *Wealth of Nations,* 508.

References

Alba, Pedro, Amar Bhattacharya, Stijn Claessens, Swati Ghosh, and Leonardo Hernandez. "Volatility and Contagion in a Financially-Integrated World: Lessons from East Asia's Recent Experience." World Bank Policy Research Working Paper no. 2008, December 1998.

Amin, Samir. *Unequal Development: An Essay on the Social Formations of Peripheral Capitalism.* Translated by Brian Pearce. New York: Monthly Review Press, 1976.

Ascher, Abraham. "Professors as Propagandists: The Politics of the Kathedersozialisten." In *Gustav Schmoller (1838–1917) and Werner Sombart (1863–1941),* edited by Mark Blaug, 72–92. Brookfield, Vt.: Edward Elgar Pub. Co., 1992.

Ayittey, George B. N. *Africa Betrayed.* New York: St. Martin's Press, 1992.

Bacon, Robert. "A Scorecard for Energy Reform in Developing Countries." World Bank Public Policy for the Private Sector Note no. 175, April 1999.

Baily, Martin Neil. "Economic Perspectives on Job Creation: Lessons for Europe." Paper presented at the Stockholm Conference on Job Creation and Labor Market Policy, Stockholm, 29 May 1997.

Bank for International Settlements (BIS). *67th Annual Report.* Basel, Switzerland: BIS, 1997.

———. *70th Annual Report.* Basel, Switzerland: BIS, 2000.

Barkin, Kenneth. "Adolf Wagner and German Industrial Development." *Journal of Modern History* June 1969: 144–159.

Barringer, William H., and Kenneth J. Pierce. *Paying the Price for Big Steel.* Washington, D.C.: American Institute for International Steel, 2000.

Barth, James R. *The Great Savings and Loan Debacle*. Washington, D.C.: American Enterprise Institute, 1991.

Barth, James R., Gerard Caprio, Jr., and Ross Levine. "Banking Systems around the Globe: Do Regulation and Ownership Affect Performance and Stability?" World Bank Policy Research Working Paper no. 2325, April 2000.

Barth, James R., R. Dan Brumbaugh, Jr., Lalita Ramesh, and Glenn Yago. "The Role of Governments and Markets in International Banking Crises: The Case of East Asia." Milken Institute Policy Brief, 1998.

Bauer, P. T. *Dissent on Development*. Cambridge, Mass.: Harvard University Press, 1976 [1971].

———. "Subsistence, Trade, and Exchange: Understanding Developing Economies." In *The Revolution in Development Economics,* ed. by James Dorn, Steve Hanke, and Alan A. Walters, 275–287. Washington, D.C.: Cato Institute, 1998.

Bauer, P. T., and Basil S. Yamey. "World Wealth Redistribution: Anatomy of the New Order." In *The First World & the Third World: Essays on the New International Economic Order,* edited by Karl Brunner, 191–219. Rochester, N.Y.: University of Rochester Policy Center Publications, 1978.

Bekaert, Geert, and Campbell R. Harvey. "Capital Markets: An Engine for Economic Growth." *Brown Journal of World Affairs* Winter/Spring 1998: 33–53.

Bellamy, Edward. *Looking Backward: 2000–1887*. New York: Signet Classic, 1960 [1888].

Beniger, James R. *The Control Revolution: Technological and Economic Origins of the Information Society*. Cambridge, Mass.: Harvard University Press, 1986.

Berman, Marshall. *All That Is Solid Melts into Air: The Experience of Modernity*. New York: Penguin Books, 1988.

Bhagwati, Jagdish. *Protectionism*. Cambridge, Mass.: MIT Press, 1988.

Blasi, Joseph R., Maya Kroumova, and Douglas Kruse. *Kremlin Capitalism: The Privatization of the Russian Economy*. Ithaca, N.Y.: ILR Press, 1997.

Boettke, Peter J. *The Political Economy of Soviet Socialism: The Formative Years, 1918–1928*. Boston: Kluwer Academic Publishers, 1990.

Bordo, Michael D., Barry Eichengreen, and Douglas A. Irwin. "Is Globalization Today Really Different Than Globalization a Hundred Years Ago?" National Bureau of Economic Research Working Paper no. 7195, June 1999.

Bright, John, and James E. Thorold Rogers, eds. *Speeches on Questions of Public Policy by Richard Cobden, M.P.* London: Macmillan and Co., 1870.

Buchanan, James. *The Limits of Liberty: Between Anarchy and Leviathan.* Chicago: University of Chicago Press, 1977.

Buchanan, Patrick J. *The Great Betrayal: How American Sovereignty and Social Justice Are Being Sacrificed to the Gods of the Global Economy.* Boston: Little, Brown and Co., 1998.

Burnham, James. *The Managerial Revolution.* London: Putnam, 1942 [1941].

Cairncross, A. "Reconversion, 1945–51." In *The British Economy Since 1945,* edited by N. F. R. Crafts and N. W. C. Woodward, 25–51. New York: Oxford University Press, 1991.

Callon, Scott. *Divided Sun: MITI and the Breakdown of Japanese High-Tech Industrial Policy, 1975–1993.* Stanford, Calif.: Stanford University Press, 1995.

Campos, Jose Edgardo, and Hilton L. Root. *The Key to the Asian Miracle: Making Shared Growth Credible.* Washington, D.C.: Brookings Institution Press, 1996.

Cangiano, Marco, Carlo Cottarelli, and Luis Cubeddu. "Pension Developments and Reforms in Transition Economies." International Monetary Fund Working Paper no. 98/151, October 1998.

Capie, Forrest. *Depression and Protectionism: Britain between the Wars.* London: George Allen & Unwin, 1983.

Cardoso, Fernando Henrique, and Enzo Faletto. *Dependency and Development in Latin America.* Translated by Marjory Mattingly Urquidi. Berkeley, Calif.: University of California Press, 1979.

Chandler, Alfred D., Jr. *The Visible Hand: The Managerial Revolution in American Business.* Cambridge, Mass.: Harvard University Press, Belknap Press, 1977.

China Statistical Yearbook 2000. Beijing: China Statistics Press, 2000.

Claessens, Stijn, Simeon Djankov, and Larry Lang. "Corporate Growth, Financing, and Risks in the Decade before East Asia's Financial Crisis." World Bank Policy Research Paper no. 2017, November 1998.

Clark, Evalyn A. "Adolf Wagner: From National Economist to National Socialist." *Political Science Quarterly* September 1940: 378–411.

Clawson, Dan. *Bureaucracy and the Labor Process: The Transformation of U.S. Industry, 1860–1920.* New York: Monthly Review Press, 1980.

Cline, William R., and Kevin J. S. Barnes. "Spreads and Risks in Emerging Markets Lending." Institute of International Finance Research Papers no. 97-1, December 1997.

Coase, Ronald H. "The Nature of the Firm." In *The Nature of the Firm: Origins, Evolution, and Development,* edited by Oliver E. Williamson and Sidney G. Winter, 18–33. New York: Oxford University Press, 1991 [1937].

Cox, W. Michael, and Richard Alm. *Myths of Rich and Poor: Why We're Better Off Than We Think.* New York: Basic Books, 1999.

Crafts, N. F. R. "'You've never had it so good?': British economic policy and performance, 1945–60." In *Europe's Post-war Recovery,* edited by Barry Eichengreen, 246–270. Cambridge: Cambridge University Press, 1995.

Craig, Gordon A. *Germany 1866–1945.* New York: Oxford University Press, 1978.

Dahrendorf, Ralf. *Society and Democracy in Germany.* London: Weidenfeld and Nicolson Ltd., 1968.

Davis, Stephen J., and Magnus Henrekson. "Wage-Setting Institutions as Industrial Policy." National Bureau of Economic Research Working Paper no. 7502, January 2000.

Dawson, William H. *Bismarck and State Socialism.* London: Swan Sonnenschein and Co., 1890.

———. *German Socialism and Ferdinand Lassalle.* New York: Charles Scribner's Sons, 1899.

De Long, J. Bradford. *Slouching Towards Utopia? 20th Century Economic History.* Unpublished manuscript. Available online at http://www.j-bradford-delong.net/TCEH/Slouch_Old.html.

de Soto, Hernando. *The Mystery of Capital: Why Capitalism Triumphs in the West and Fails Everywhere Else.* New York: Basic Books, 2000.

Demirgüç-Kunt, Asli, and Vojislav Maksimovic. "Law, Finance, and Firm Growth." *Journal of Finance* December 1998: 2107–2137.

Desai, Raj M., and Itzhak Goldberg. "Vicious Circles of Control: Regional Governments and Insiders in Privatized Russian Enterprises." World Bank Policy Research Paper no. 2287, February 2000.

Destler, I. M. *American Trade Politics.* 3rd ed. New York: Twentieth Century Fund, 1995 [1986].

Dorn, James A., ed. *The Future of Money in the Information Age.* Washington, D.C.: Cato Institute, 1997.

Edwards, Sebastian. *Crisis and Reform in Latin America: From Despair to Hope.* New York: Oxford University Press, 1995.

Edwards, Sebastian, and Nora Claudia Lustig, eds. *Labor Markets in Latin America: Combining Social Protection with Market Flexibility.* Washington, D.C.: Brookings Institution Press, 1997.

Eichengreen, Barry. *Golden Fetters: The Gold Standard and the Great Depression, 1919–1939.* New York: Oxford University Press, 1992.

———. *Globalizing Capital: A History of the International Monetary System.* Princeton, N.J.: Princeton University Press, 1996.

Eichengreen, Barry, and Jeffrey Sachs. "Exchange Rates and Economic Recovery in the 1930s." *Journal of Economic History* December 1985: 925–946.

Ekirch, Arthur A., Jr. *The Decline of American Liberalism.* New York: Atheneum, 1967 [1955].

Eksteins, Modris. *Rites of Spring: The Great War and the Birth of the Modern Age.* New York: Anchor Books, 1990 [1989].

European Bank for Reconstruction and Development. *Transition Report 1999.* London: EBRD, 1999.

Fallows, James. *Looking at the Sun: The Rise of the New East Asian Economic and Political System.* New York: Pantheon Books, 1994.

Ferguson, Charles. "From the People Who Brought you Voodoo Economics." *Harvard Business Review* May/June 1988: 55–62.

Ferrara, Peter J., and Michael Tanner. *A New Deal for Social Security*. Washington, D.C.: Cato Institute, 1998.

Finger, J. Michael, and Ludger Schuknecht. "Market Access Advances and Retreats: The Uruguay Round and Beyond." Paper presented at the WTO/World Bank Conference on Developing Countries and the Millennium Round, World Trade Organization, Geneva, 20–21 September 1999.

Fink, Carsten, Aaditya Mattoo, and Ileana Cristina Neagu. "Trade in International Maritime Services: How Much Does Policy Matter?" World Bank Policy Research Working Paper no. 2522, 2000.

Friedman, Thomas L. *The Lexus and the Olive Tree*. New York: Farrar, Strauss and Giroux, 1999.

Galbraith, John Kenneth. *The New Industrial State*. 4th ed. New York: Mentor, published by the Penguin Group, 1986 [1967].

Garibaldi, Pietro, and Paulo Mauro. "Deconstructing Job Creation." International Monetary Fund Working Paper no. 99/109, August 1999.

Garraty, John A. *The Great Depression*. New York: Harcourt Brace Jovanovich, 1986.

Gavin, Francis J. "Bretton Woods: A Golden Era?" In *Global Fortune: The Stumble and Rise of World Capitalism,* edited by Ian Vásquez, 213–24. Washington, D.C.: Cato Institute, 2000.

Giddens, Anthony. *The Third Way: The Renewal of Social Democracy*. London: Polity Press, 1998.

Gilbert, Martin. *The First World War: A Complete History*. New York: Henry Holt and Co., 1994.

Gil-Díaz, Francisco. "The Origins of Mexico's 1994 Financial Crisis." *The Cato Journal* Winter 1998: 303–313.

Gilpin, Robert. *The Challenge of Global Capitalism: The World Economy in the 21st Century*. Princeton, N.J.: Princeton University Press, 2000.

Giovannini, Alberto, and Martha de Melo. "Government Revenue from Financial Repression." *American Economic Review* September 1993: 953–963.

Gray, John. *False Dawn: The Delusions of Global Capitalism.* New York: New Press, 1998.

Greenspan, Alan. "Challenges for Monetary Policymakers." Paper presented at the Cato Institute 18th Annual Monetary Conference, Washington, D.C., 19 October 2000.

Greider, William. *One World, Ready or Not: The Manic Logic of Global Capitalism.* New York: Simon and Schuster, 1997.

Griswold, Daniel T. "Trade, Jobs, and Manufacturing: Why (Almost All) U.S. Workers Should Welcome Imports." Cato Institute Trade Briefing Paper no. 6, 30 September 1999.

————. "WTO Report Card: America's Economic Stake in Open Trade." Cato Institute Trade Briefing Paper no. 8, 3 April 2000.

Groombridge, Mark A. "China's Long March to a Market Economy: The Case for Permanent Normal Trade Relations with the People's Republic of China." Cato Institute Trade Policy Analysis no. 10, 24 April 2000.

Gruben, William C. "Banking Structures, Market Forces, and Economic Freedom: Lessons from Argentina and Mexico." *The Cato Journal* Fall 1998: 263–274.

Gustafson, Thane. *Capitalism Russian-Style.* Cambridge, U.K.: Cambridge University Press, 1999.

Gwartney, James, and Robert Lawson, with Dexter Samida. *Economic Freedom of the World: 2000 Annual Report.* Vancouver: Fraser Institute, 2000.

Hamilton, Alexander, James Madison, and John Jay. *The Federalist Papers.* New York: New American Library, 1961 [1787-88].

Hansen, Alvin H. "Economic Progress and Declining Population Growth." *American Economic Review* March 1939: 1–15.

Harrison, Lawrence E., and Samuel Huntington, eds. *Culture Matters: How Values Shape Human Progress.* New York: Basic Books, 2001.

Hawley, Ellis W. *The New Deal and the Problem of Monopoly: A Study in Economic Ambivalence.* Princeton, N.J.: Princeton University Press, 1995 [1966].

Hayek, F. A. "The Use of Knowledge in Society." In *Individualism and Economic Order.* South Bend, Ind.: Gateway Editions, 1948, 77–91.

———. *The Constitution of Liberty.* Chicago: University of Chicago Press, 1960.

———. *The Road to Serfdom.* Chicago: University of Chicago Press, 1972 [1944].

———. "Competition as a Discovery Procedure." In *New Studies in Philosophy, Politics, Economics and the History of Ideas,* 179–190. Chicago: University of Chicago Press, 1978.

Heller, Mikhail, and Aleksandr M. Nekrich. *Utopia in Power: The History of the Soviet Union from 1917 to the Present.* New York: Summit Books, 1986.

Higgs, Robert. *Crisis and Leviathan: Critical Episodes in the Growth of American Government.* New York: Oxford University Press, 1987.

Hirschman, Albert O. "The Political Economy of Import-Substitution in Latin America." *Quarterly Journal of Economics* February 1968: 1–32.

Hughes, Thomas. *American Genesis: A Century of Invention and Technological Enthusiasm.* New York: Penguin Books, 1989.

Hull, Cordell. *The Memoirs of Cordell Hull.* New York: Macmillan, 1948.

Illarionov, Andrei N. "Creating Crises: Russian Economic Policy, 1992–1998." Unpublished manuscript. Institute of Economic Analysis, January 1999.

International Monetary Fund. "Japan: Selected Issues." IMF Staff Country Report no. 98/113, October 1998.

Irwin, Douglas A. "The GATT's contribution to economic recovery in postwar Western Europe." In *Europe's Post-war Recovery,* edited by Barry Eichengreen, 127–150. Cambridge: Cambridge University Press, 1995.

———. *Against the Tide: An Intellectual History of Free Trade.* Princeton, N. J.: Princeton University Press, 1996.

Izaguirre, Ada Karina. "Private Participation in Telecommunications—Recent Trends." World Bank Public Policy for the Private Sector Note no. 204, December 1999.

Jackson, John. *The World Trading System: Law and Policy of International Economic Relations.* 2nd ed. Cambridge, Mass.: MIT Press, 1997 [1989].

James, Estelle. "New Systems for Old Age Security—Theory, Practice and Empirical Evidence." World Bank Policy Research Working Paper no. 1766, May 1997.

Jewkes, John. *The New Ordeal by Planning: The Experience of the Forties and the Sixties.* New York: St. Martin's Press, 1968 [1948].

Johnson, Chalmers. *Japan: Who Governs?* New York: W. W. Norton and Co., 1995.

Jordan, John M. *Machine-Age Ideology: Social Engineering & American Liberalism, 1911–1939.* Chapel Hill, N.C.: University of North Carolina Press, 1994.

Kanigel, Robert. *The One Best Way: Frederick Winslow Taylor and the Enigma of Efficiency.* New York: Viking Penguin, 1997.

Kapstein, Ethan B., and Branko Milanovic. "Dividing the Spoils: Pensions, Privatization, and Reform in Russia's Transition." World Bank Working Paper no. 2292, March 2000.

Katz, Richard. *Japan: The System that Soured—The Rise and Fall of the Japanese Economic Miracle.* Armonk, N.Y.: M. E. Sharpe, 1998.

Keegan, John. *The Face of Battle.* New York: Penguin Books, 1978 [1976].

Keynes, John Maynard. *The General Theory of Employment, Interest, and Money.* New York: Harcourt Brace and Co., 1964 [1936].

King, Robert G., and Ross Levine. "Finance and Growth: Schumpeter Might Be Right." *Quarterly Journal of Economics* August 1993: 717–737.

Koehler, Peter A., Hans F. Zacher, and Martin Partington. *The Evolution of Social Insurance 1881–1981.* New York: St. Martin's Press, 1982.

Krol, Robert. "The Case for Open Global Capital Markets." Cato Institute Trade Briefing Paper no. 11, 15 March 2001.

Krugman, Paul. "Growing World Trade: Causes and Consequences." In *Brookings Papers on Economic Activity* Issue no. 1: 327–362. Washington, D.C.: Brookings Institution Press, 1995.

Lardy, Nicholas R. *China's Unfinished Economic Revolution*. Washington, D.C.: Brookings Institution Press, 1998.

————. "When Will China's Financial System Meet China's Needs?" Paper presented at the Conference on Policy Reform in China, Center for Research on Economic Development and Policy Reform, Stanford University, Stanford, California, 18–20 November 1999.

League of Nations. *Review of World Trade 1936*. Geneva: League of Nations, 1937.

————. *Commercial Policy in the Interwar Period: International Proposals and National Policies*. Geneva: League of Nations, 1942.

Lenin, Vladimir I. "Imperialism, The Highest Stage of Capitalism." In *The Lenin Anthology,* edited by Robert C. Tucker, 204–274. New York: W. W. Norton and Co., 1975 [1917].

————. "The Impending Catastrophe and How to Combat It." In *Lenin's Economic Writings,* edited by Meghnad Desai, 177–220. Atlantic Highlands, N.J.: Humanities Press International, 1989 [1917].

————. *The State and Revolution*. Translated by Robert Service. New York: Penguin Books, 1992 [1918].

Leuchtenburg, William E. "The New Deal and the Analogue of War." In *Change and Continuity in Twentieth-Century America,* edited by John Braeman, Robert H. Bremner, and Everett Walters, 81–143. Columbus, Ohio: Ohio State University Press, 1964.

Levine, Ross, and Sarah Zervos. "Stock Markets, Banks, and Economic Growth." *American Economic Review* June 1998: 537–559.

Lindbeck, Assar. "Problems of Unemployment in Europe and the United States." Paper presented at the Stockholm Conference on Job Creation and Labor Market Policy, Stockholm, 29 May 1997.

Lippmann, Walter. *The Good Society*. Boston: Little, Brown and Co., 1937.

Lipson, Charles. *Standing Guard: Protecting Foreign Capital in the Nineteenth and Twentieth Centuries*. Berkeley, Calif.: University of California Press, 1985.

Maher, Maria, and Thomas Andersson. *Corporate Governance: Effects on Firm Performance and Economic Growth.* Paris: Organisation for Economic Co-operation and Development, 1999.

Manchester, William. *The Last Lion, William Spencer Churchill: Visions of Glory, 1874–1932.* Boston: Little, Brown and Co., 1983.

Marx, Karl, and Friedrich Engels. "Manifesto of the Communist Party." In *The Marx-Engels Reader.* 2nd ed. Edited by Robert C. Tucker, 469–500. New York: W. W. Norton and Co., 1978.

Mauro, Paulo. "Corruption and Growth." *Quarterly Journal of Economics* August 1995: 681–712.

McCraw, Thomas K. *Prophets of Regulation.* Cambridge, Mass.: Harvard University Press, Belknap Press, 1984.

McKinsey Global Institute. *Unlocking Economic Growth in Russia.* Washington, D.C.: McKinsey Global Institute, October 1999.

———. *Why the Japanese Economy Is Not Growing.* Washington, D.C.: McKinsey Global Institute, 18 July 2000.

Meigs, A. James. "Mexican Monetary Lessons." *The Cato Journal* Spring/Summer 1997: 35–72.

Mommsen, Wolfgang J. *Imperial Germany 1867–1918: Politics, Culture, and Society in an Authoritarian State.* Translated by Richard Deveson. New York: Arnold, 1997.

Moreno-Villalaz, Juan Luis. "Lessons from the Monetary Experience of Panama: A Dollar Economy with Financial Integration." *The Cato Journal* Winter 1998: 421–439.

Morgan, Arthur E. *Edward Bellamy.* New York: Columbia University Press, 1944.

Morita, Akio, and Shintaro Ishihara. *The Japan That Can Say "No": The New United States–Japan Relations Card.* Unauthorized translation published in the *Congressional Record,* 14 November 1989, E 3783.

Myrdal, Gunnar. *Asian Drama: An Inquiry into the Poverty of Nations.* New York: Pantheon, 1968.

Nisbet, Robert. *The Quest for Community: A Study in the Ethics of Order and Freedom.* San Francisco: Institute for Contemporary Studies Press, 1990 [1953].

Nkrumah, Kwame. *The Autobiography of Kwame Nkrumah*. Edinburgh, Scotland: Thomas Nelson and Sons, 1957.

Nordström, Håkan, and Scott Vaughan. "Trade and Environment." World Trade Organization Special Studies no. 4, November 1999.

Normann, Göran, and Daniel J. Mitchell. "Pension Reform in Sweden: Lessons for American Policymakers." Heritage Foundation Backgrounder no. 1381, 29 June 2000.

North, Douglass C. *Structure and Change in Economic History*. New York: W. W. Norton and Co., 1981.

———. "Institutions, Ideology, and Economic Performance." In *The Revolution in Development Economics,* edited by James Dorn, Steve Hanke, and Alan A. Walters, 95–107. Washington, D.C.: Cato Institute, 1998.

Olson, Mancur. *The Rise and Decline of Nations*. New Haven: Yale University Press, 1982.

———. *Power and Prosperity: Outgrowing Communist and Capitalist Dictatorships*. New York: Basic Books, 2000.

Orenstein, Mitchell A. "How Politics and Institutions Affect Pension Reform in Three Postcommunist Countries." World Bank Policy Research Working Paper no. 2310, March 2000.

Organisation for Economic Co-operation and Development (OECD). *Employment Outlook*. Paris: OECD, July 1997.

———. *Employment Outlook*. Paris: OECD, June 1999.

———. *Agricultural Policies in Emerging and Transition Countries: 1999*. Paris: OECD, 1999.

———. *Agricultural Policies in OECD Countries: Monitoring and Evaluation 1999*. Paris: OECD, 1999.

———. *Communications Outlook 1999*. Paris: OECD, 1999.

———. *Employment Outlook*. Paris: OECD, July 1997.

———. *Employment Outlook*. Paris: OECD, June 1999.

———. *Employment Outlook*. Paris: OECD, June 2000.

———. *International Trade and Core Labour Standards*. Paris: OECD, 2000.

————. *Pushing Ahead with Reform in Korea: Labour Market and Social Safety-Net Policies.* Paris: OECD, 2000.

O'Rourke, Kevin H., and Jeffrey G. Williamson. *Globalization and History: The Evolution of a Nineteenth-Century Atlantic Economy.* Cambridge, Mass.: MIT Press, 1999.

Packenham, Robert A. *The Dependency Movement: Scholarship and Politics in Development Studies.* Cambridge, Mass.: Harvard University Press, 1992.

Phongpaichit, Pasuk, and Chris Baker. *Thailand's Boom and Bust.* Chiang Mai, Thailand: Silkworm Books, 1998.

Pinto, Brian, Vladimir Drebentsov, and Alexander Morozov. "Give Growth and Macro Stability in Russia a Chance: Harden Budgets by Dismantling Nonpayments." World Bank Policy Research Paper no. 2324. April 2000.

Pohl, Gerhard, Robert E. Anderson, Stijn Claessens, and Simeon Djankov. "Privatization and Restructuring in Central and Eastern Europe." World Bank Technical Paper no. 368, August 1997.

Polanyi, Karl. *The Great Transformation: The Political and Economic Origins of Our Time.* Boston: Beacon Press, 1957 [1944].

Polanyi, Michael. "The Span of Central Direction." in *The Logic of Liberty.* Chicago: University of Chicago Press, 1951.

Pomerleano, Michael. "The East Asian Crisis and Corporate Finances: The Untold Micro Story." World Bank Working Paper no. 1990, October 1998.

Poortvliet, William G., and Thomas Laine. "Privatization and Reform of Social Security Pension Plans as a Global Trend." *Journal of the American Society of CLU and ChFC* July 1997: 54–62.

Prebisch, Raúl. *The Economic Development of Latin America and Its Principal Problems.* New York: United Nations, 1950.

Prestowitz, Clyde. *Trading Places: How We Are Giving Our Future to Japan and How to Reclaim It.* New York: Basic Books, 1993 [1988].

Rajan, Raghuram G., and Luigi Zingales. "Financial Dependence and Growth." *American Economic Review* June 1998: 559–586.

Rauch, Jonathan. *Government's End: Why Washington Stopped Working.* New York: Public Affairs, 1999.

Reich, Robert B. *The Next American Frontier*. New York: Times Books, 1983.

Report of the International Financial Institution Advisory Commission. Washington, D.C., 8 March 2000.

Robbins, Lionel. *Economic Planning and International Economic Order*. London: Macmillan, 1937.

————. *The Great Depression*. Freeport, N.Y.: Books for Libraries Press, 1971 [1934].

Roberts, Paul Craig, and Karen LaFollette. *Meltdown: Inside the Soviet Economy*. Washington, D.C.: Cato Institute, 1990.

Rodgers, Daniel T. *Atlantic Crossings: Social Politics in a Progressive Age*. Cambridge, Mass.: Harvard University Press, Belknap Press, 1998.

Rodríguez, L. Jacobo. "In Praise and Criticism of Mexico's Pension Reform." Cato Institute Policy Analysis no. 340, 14 April 1999.

————. "Chile's Private Pension Sytem at 18: Its Current State and Future Challenges." Cato Institute Social Security Privatization Paper no. 17, 30 July 1999.

Rodrik, Dani. *Has Globalization Gone Too Far?* Washington, D.C.: Institute for International Economics, 1997.

Rojas, Mauricio. *Millennium Doom: Fallacies about the End of Work*. London: Social Market Foundation, 1999.

Rosenberg, Nathan, and L. E. Birdzell, Jr. *How the West Grew Rich: The Economic Transformation of the Industrial World*. New York: Basic Books, 1986.

Roubini, Nouriel, and Xavier Sala-i-Martin. "A Growth Model of Inflation, Tax Evasion, and Financial Repression." *Journal of Monetary Economics* April 1995: 275–301.

Sachs, Jeffrey D., and Andrew Warner. "Economic Reform and the Process of Globalization." *Brookings Papers on Economic Activity* Issue no. 1. Washington, DC: Brookings Institution Press, 1995.

Sally, Razeen. *Classical Liberalism and International Economic Order: Studies in Theory and Intellectual History*. London: Routledge, 1998.

Schlesinger, Arthur, Jr. "Has Democracy A Future?" *Foreign Affairs* September/October 1997: 8.

Schneider, Friedrich, and Dominik H. Enste. "Shadow Economies: Size, Causes, and Consequences." *Journal of Economic Literature* March 2000: 77–114.

Schumpeter, Joseph A. *History of Economic Analysis.* New York: Oxford University Press, 1954.

———. *Capitalism, Socialism and Democracy.* New York: Harper Torchbooks, Harper and Row, 1976 [1942].

Scott, John. *Behind the Urals: An American Worker in Russia's City of Steel.* Bloomington, Ind.: Indiana University Press, 1989 [1942].

Searle, G. R. *The Quest for National Efficiency: A Study in British Politics and Political Thought, 1899–1914.* Atlantic Highlands, N.J.: Ashfield Press, 1990 [1971].

Semmel, Bernard. *Imperialism and Social Reform: English Social-Imperial Thought 1895–1914.* London: George Allen & Unwin Ltd., 1960.

Shaffer, Butler. *In Restraint of Trade: The Business Campaign Against Competition, 1918–1938.* Cranbury, N.J.: Associated University Presses, 1997.

Skidelsky, Robert. *The Road from Serfdom: The Economic and Political Consequences of the End of Communism.* New York: Penguin Books, 1997 [1995].

Smith, Adam. *An Inquiry into the Nature and Causes of the Wealth of Nations.* New York: Modern Library, 1937 [1776].

Sobel, Robert. *The Age of Giant Corporations: A Microeconomic History of American Business, 1914–1992.* 3rd ed. Westport, Conn.: Praeger, 1993 [1972].

Soros, George. *The Crisis of Global Capitalism: Open Society Endangered.* New York: Public Affairs Books, 1998.

Steele, David Ramsay. *From Marx to Mises: Post-Capitalist Society and the Challenge of Economic Calculation.* La Salle, Ill.: Open Court, 1992.

Stern, Fritz. *Gold and Iron: Bismarck, Bleichröder, and the Building of the German Empire.* New York: Vintage Books, 1979 [1977].

Stilwell, Joe. "The Savings & Loan Industry: Averting Collapse." Cato Institute Policy Analysis no. 7, 15 February 1982.

Stromberg, Roland N. *Redemption by War: The Intellectuals and 1914.* Lawrence, Kan.: Regents Press of Kansas, 1982.

Taylor, A. J. P. *Bismarck: The Man and the Statesman.* New York: Vintage Books, 1955.

Timberlake, Richard H. *Monetary Policy in the United States: An Intellectual and Institutional History.* Chicago: University of Chicago Press, 1993.

Tomlinson, Jim. *Democratic Socialism and Economic Policy: The Attlee Years, 1945–1951.* Cambridge: Cambridge University Press, 1997.

Tugwell, Rexford G., Thomas Munro, and Roy E. Stryker. *American Economic Life and the Means of Its Improvement.* 3rd ed. New York: Harcourt, Brace and Company, 1930 [1925].

Tynan, Nicola. "Private Participation in the Rail Sector—Recent Trends." World Bank Public Policy for the Private Sector Note no. 186, June 1999.

Vásquez, Ian. "Official Assistance, Economic Freedom, and Policy Change: Is Foreign Aid Like Champagne?" *Cato Journal* Fall 1998: 275–286.

———. "The International Monetary Fund: Challenges and Contradictions." Testimony before the International Financial Institution Advisory Commission, U.S. Congress, 28 September 1999.

Veblen, Thorstein. *The Theory of Business Enterprise.* New York: Charles Scribner's Sons, 1910.

von Laue, Theodore H. *The World Revolution of Westernization: The Twentieth Century in Global Perspective.* New York: Oxford University Press, 1987.

von Mises, Ludwig. *Omnipotent Government: The Rise of the Total State and Total War.* Spring Mills, Penn.: Libertarian Press, 1985 [1944].

Waldrop, M. Mitchell. *Complexity: The Emerging Science at the Edge of Order and Chaos.* New York: Touchstone, 1992.

Weaver, Paul H. *The Suicidal Corporation: How Big Business Fails America.* New York: Simon and Schuster, 1988.

Weinstein, David E., and Yishay Yafeh. "On the Costs of a Bank-Centered Financial System: Evidence from the Changing Main Bank System in Japan." *Journal of Finance* April 1998: 635–672.

White, Lawrence H. *Competition and Currency: Essays on Free Banking and Money.* New York: New York University Press, 1989.

Whyte, William H., Jr. *The Organization Man.* Garden City, N.Y.: Doubleday Anchor Books, 1956.

Wiebe, Robert H. *Businessmen and Reform: A Study of the Progressive Movement.* Chicago: Elephant Paperbacks, 1989 [1962].

Williamson, Oliver E. *Markets and Hierarchies: Analysis and Antitrust Implications.* New York: Free Press, 1975.

Wilson, Edmund. *To the Finland Station.* New York: The Noonday Press of Farrar, Strauss and Giroux, 1972 [1940].

Womack, James P., Daniel T. Jones, and Daniel Roos. *The Machine that Changed the World.* New York: Macmillan, 1990.

Wood, Christopher. *The Bubble Economy: Japan's Extraordinary Speculative Boom of the '80s and the Dramatic Bust of the '90s.* New York: Atlantic Monthly Press, 1992.

World Bank. *The East Asian Miracle: Economic Growth and Public Policy.* New York: Oxford University Press, 1993.

————. *Averting the Old Age Crisis: Policies to Protect the Old and Promote Growth.* New York: Oxford University Press, 1994.

————. *East Asia: The Road to Recovery.* Washington, D.C.: World Bank, 1998.

————. *East Asia Brief.* Washington, D.C.: World Bank, 2000.

————. *India: Policies to Reduce Poverty and Accelerate Sustainable Development.* Washington, D.C.: World Bank, 2000.

————. *East Asia Update.* Washington, D.C.: World Bank, 2001.

Wurgler, Jeffrey. "Financial Markets and the Allocation of Capital." *Journal of Financial Economics* October 2000: 187–214.

Yago, Glenn and Juan Montoya. "Capital Access Index: Asia Postcrisis." Milken Institute Policy Brief no. 11, 8 March 2000.

Yamamura, Kozo. "Success that Soured: Administrative Guidance and Cartels in Japan." In *Policy and Trade Issues of the Japanese Economy: American and Japanese Perspectives,* edited by Kozo Yamamura, 77–112. Seattle: University of Washington Press, 1982.

Yergin, Daniel and Joseph Stanislaw. *The Commanding Heights: The Battle between Government and the Marketplace That Is Remaking the Modern World.* New York: Simon and Schuster, 1998.

Index

Administradoras de fondos de pensiones (AFPs) (Chile), 229, 232
Africa:
  insecurity of rights in, 177–179
  pension system in, 233
  political system in, 169, 182, 257
Agriculture, 12, 128–129
Albania, 122
Alreja, Adarsh, 165, 166
American Economics Association, 35
Amin, Idi, 177
Amin, Samir, 105
Andean Pact, 104
Anti-Corn Law League, 65
Anti-globalization movement, 4–5, 6–7, 190–193, 215–216, 218–221, 244–250. *See also* Protest movements
Anti-Semitism, 84
Argentina:
  financial system in, 152, 157
  legal system in, 170–174
  pension system in, 228, 230
Armenia, 122
Asian model:
  of economic development, 106–110
  of politics, 181

Asquith, Herbert, 37
Association for Social Policy (Germany), 34, 35
Attlee, Clement, 91
Australia, 230
Austria, 225, 239
Autocracies:
  appeal of, 22–23, 97–98
  economic growth and, 180–183
  rhetoric of democracy and, 182–183
Automobile industry:
  in India, 162–165
  as model of central planning, 162
Ayittey, George, 178
Azerbaijan, 122

Bad loans:
  in Asia, 137, 142, 145–149
  in other countries, 149–150
  in U.S. savings-and-loan crisis, 150–151
Balladur, Edouard, 215–216
Bangladesh, 131
Bank of Japan, 110
Banks:
  bad loans and, 145–151

Banks *(continued)*
   capital markets and, 138, 156
   central (*see* Monetary policy)
   dominant in Asian financial system, 137–145
   financial crises and, 206–211
   political interference with, 12–13, 150–155
Barter, in Russia, 121–122, 124, 210
Baruch, Bernard, 133
Bauer, Peter, 101, 102
Beard, Charles, 19
Bebel, August, 32
Belarus, 122, 129
Belgium, 226, 228, 239
Bellamy, Edward, 16–20, 27, 39, 68, 276*n*1
   finance and, 143
   Germany and, 34–35
   protectionism and, 69
Berlin, 86–88
Bernstein, Eduard, 68
bin Laden, Osama, 271, 272
Birdzell, L. E., Jr., 51–52
Bismarck, Otto von, 23, 32–34, 37, 68, 72, 83, 223, 251, 255
Blair, Tony, 244
Bohm, Franz, 92
Bolivia, 152, 230
Borderless World, The (Ohmae), 4
Bosnia, 122
"Brain work," centralization of, 30, 38–39
Brazil:
   financial sector in, 152, 153, 157
   pension system in, 227

   shadow economy in, 166
Bretton Woods system, 94–95, 204, 263, 266
Bright, John, 65, 66–67
Britain. *See* Great Britain
Broadcasting industry, 130
Brooke, Rupert, 246
Buchanan, James, 188
Buchanan, Patrick, 6
Bulgaria, 122, 227, 228
Burnham, James, 84–85, 88–89
Business enterprises:
   centralization within, 52–56
   consolidation of during Industrial Revolution, 26–27
   hostility to competition, 28, 82
   as inspiration for collectivists, 29–30
   tendency toward conservatism, 47, 48–49

Capitalism, Socialism and Democracy (Schumpeter), 49
Capitalist developmental state, in East Asia, 106–110
Capital markets:
   benefits of well-developed, 155–156
   underdevelopment of, 12, 156–158
Cardoso, Fernando Henrique, 104, 105
Cellular telephony, 129–130
Central banks. *See* Monetary policy
Centralization. *See also* Collectivism
   and businesses enterprises, 52–56
   role of government in providing social benefits, 57–58, 217–218, 222–223

Centralization *(continued)*
  role of government in supporting
    market competition, 56–57,
    168–170
  tradeoffs between competition
    and, 54, 55–56, 58, 115, 208–
    209, 280–281*n*33
Chaebol, 139, 148
Challenge of Global Capitalism, The
    (Gilpin), 266
Chamberlain, Joseph, 74–75
Chandler, Alfred, 55–56, 85
Change. *See* Uncertainty, as justifi-
    cation for competition
Chao po, 185, 186
Chase, Stuart, 40
Chiang Kai-Shek, 181
Chile:
  capital markets in, 157
  liberalization in, 126
  pension system in, 229–232, 256
  political system in, 181
China:
  capital controls in, 195
  central planning in, 96
  financial system in, 153–154
  in first world economy, 65
  liberalization in, 2, 7, 111–112,
    124–125, 189, 255
  pension system in, 226
  state-owned sector in, 5, 125–126,
    234, 235
  in World Trade Organization,
    248, 261–262
Choonhavan, Chatichai, 186
Churchill, Winston S., 37, 75, 77
Clay, Lucius, 92

Coase, Ronald, 53–54
Cobden-Chevalier Treaty, 66
Cobden, Richard, 65, 66–67
Collectivism. *See also* Industrial
    Counterrevolution; *specific countries*
  as allegedly progressive movement,
    23–24, 251
  appeal of, 267–268
  collapse of, 2–3
  continuing influence of, 11–14
  contrasted to markets, 38–43
  demonstration effect and spread of,
    255
  in Germany, 30–35
  in Great Britain, 35–37
  as reaction against Industrial Rev-
    olution, 16–37
  vs. uncertainty, 47–52, 58, 115,
    208–209, 280–281*n*33
Colombia, 152, 230
Colombres Garmendia, Ignacio, 173
Colosio, Luis Donaldo, 200
Common Market, 95
Communism, threat of, 181
Communist Manifesto, The (Marx and
    Engels), 22, 216
Community, sense of loss of. *See*
    Modernity
Competition:
  business leaders' discouragement
    of, 28
  as discovery process, 46–52
  Industrial Counterrevolution's re-
    jection of, 20, 40
  tradeoffs between centralization
    and, 54, 55–56, 58, 115, 208–
    209, 280–281*n*33

Complexity theory, 39, 267
Complex systems, markets as, 39
Computer manufacturing, in India,
 165–166
Constitution of Liberty, The (Hayek),
 217–218
Contract rights, markets' reliance on,
 57, 169. *See also* Legal systems
Corn laws, repeal of, 25, 65
Costa Rica, 166
Crisis of Global Capitalism, The
 (Soros), 6, 7, 190
Croatia, 122
Cultural values, 114–115, 288n48
Czech Republic, 122, 227

Daewoo, 148
Dahrendorf, Ralf, 33–34
Dawson, William, 72–73
Debt. *See* Bad loans; Financial crises
Demirgüç-Kunt, Asli, 145
Democracy:
 dictatorships and rhetoric of, 182–
 183
 economic growth and, 183–184
 special interests in, 187–188,
 295n28
 in Thailand, 185–187
 transition to, 184–185, 257
Deng Xiaoping, 2, 7, 111, 181
Denmark, 239–240, 294n7
Dependency theory, 101, 104–105
De Soto, Hernando, 167–168
Developing countries:
 American protectionism and, 132–
 133
 collectivism in, 96–99
 dependency theory, 101, 104–105

foreign investment and, 8, 195,
 249, 258–259
 legal systems in, 168, 176–177
 pension systems in, 226–227
 protectionism and, 131–132
 shadow economy in, 166–168
 spiritual trauma of modernization
 in, 23, 97–98
 telephony in, 130
 "vicious circle" and, 100–101
Dewey, John, 19
Dialectical materialism, 31–32
Dictatorship. *See* Autocracies
Direct investment. *See* Foreign
 investment

East Asia. *See also specific countries*
 financial systems in, 137–139,
 208–209
 international flow of capital and,
 201–206
Economic efficiency, 43–44
Economic Freedom of the World report,
 126–127, 152, 170
Economic growth:
 autocracies and, 180–183
 democracy and, 183–184
 legal systems and, 174–177
 political systems and, 179–180
Economic liberalism. *See* Liberalism
Economics, reduced to engineering,
 43
Ecuador, 152
EDP Aids, 165–166
Egypt, 131, 167, 168
Electricity consumption, as economic
 measure, 167. *See also*
 Energy/utilities

El Salvador, 230

"Encompassing interest," 254

End of the Nation State, The (Ohmae), 4

Energy/utilities:

    nonpayment of, in Russia, 122, 124

    regulation of, 12, 127–128

    as shadow economy measure, 167

Engels, Friedrich, 22, 216

England. *See* Great Britain

Enste, Dominik, 167

Equatorial Guinea, 177

Equity markets. *See* Capital markets

Erhard, Ludwig, 92

Eucken, Walter, 92

European Union, labor policies in, 239–243. *See also specific countries*

Exchange controls. *See* Protectionism

Exchange rate policies. *See also* Financial crises

    fixed rate systems, 80, 197

    floating rate systems, 95, 197–198, 202

    pegged rate systems, 94–95, 193, 196–201, 202, 204, 207

Fabianism and the Fiscal Question (Shaw), 69

Fabians, 68–69

Faletto, Enzo, 104

Fallows, James, 108

False Dawn: The Delusions of Global Capitalism (Gray), 7, 215

Feder, Gottfried, 78

Federalist Papers (Madison, Hamilton, and Jay), 179–180, 187–188

Federal Reserve Board, 80–81, 194

Federov, Boris, 264

Feedback. *See* Information

Financial crises, 189–214

    Asian crisis of 1997–98, 2, 110, 137–139, 142, 147–148, 198–201, 205, 208–209

    debt crisis of 1980s, 2, 111, 113

    domestic banking policies and, 206–211

    exchange rate pegs and, 196–201

    financial market segmentation and, 202–204

    international capital flows and, 195–196, 212

    liberalization encouraged by, 213, 269

    Mexican crisis of 1994, 198–201, 205, 208

    moral hazard and, 204–206

    Russian crisis of 1998, 155, 198–201, 206, 210–211

    transition from collectivism to free markets and, 189–193, 211–214

Financial markets. *See also* Banks; Capital markets; Monetary policy

    Asian contrasted to U.S., 137–149

    functions of, 144–145, 291n12

    hostility to, 143–144

    segmentation of, 202–204

Financial repression, 152–153

Finland, 239

Fixed exchange rates, 80, 197

Floating exchange rates, 95, 197–198, 202

Ford, Henry, 162

Fordney-McCumber Tariff, 80, 95

Foreign investment:

    in Argentina, 173

    in China, 125

Foreign investment *(continued)*
  in developing countries, 8, 258–259
  exchange rate policy and, 196–201, 258
  short-term vs. long-term, 195–196, 296*n*10
  in United States, 220
France:
  aftermath of World War I in, 80
  financial system in, 156–157
  labor policies in, 239, 242
  pension system in, 225, 226
  protectionism during 19th century in, 70
Freedom House, 177
Friedman, Thomas, 4, 5, 120, 168–169
  Africa and, 169, 177, 179
Fujimori, Alberto, 7

Gaidar, Yegor, 117
Galbraith, John Kenneth, 20, 50
Gary, Elbert, 28, 133
General Agreement on Tariffs and Trade (GATT), 94, 95
  WTO contrasted, 260–261
General Agreement on Trade in Services (GATS), 131
General Theory (Keynes), 50
Genius of War, The (Scheler), 245
Germany:
  aftermath of World War I in, 78, 79–80
  collectivism in, 25, 30–35, 255
  financial system in, 156–157, 158
  influence as a model, 34–37, 255
  Great Depression in, 82
  labor policies in, 239, 240

late 19th, early 20th century economy of, 36, 63, 66
  liberalism in, 34, 66, 92, 284*n*30
  militarism of, 36, 72–74, 75–77
  National Socialism and, 78, 83–84
  pension system in, 225, 226, 228
  protectionism during first world economy in, 69, 70, 83
  shadow economy in, 294*n*7
  state socialism and, 32–34, 72–77, 83, 255, 283*n*27
Giddens, Anthony, 190–192
Gifford, Walter S., 48–49
Gilpin, Robert, 266
Global Competitiveness Report, 171
Globalization. *See also* Liberalism
  definitions of, 275*n*1
  Industrial Revolution and first world economy, 63–65
  as political event, 9
  popular misinterpretations of, 3–9
  protests against, 244–250
  "Golden straitjacket," 4, 5, 8, 258–259
Gorbachev, Mikhail, 112
Governments. *See also* Legal systems; Subsidies, government
  alleged liberal hostility toward, 168–169, 176
  needed to support markets, 56–57, 168–170
  role in providing social benefits, 57–58, 217–218, 222–223
Gray, John, 7, 215, 236–237
Great Britain:
  aftermath of World War I in, 79, 80
  collectivism in, 35–37, 91–92, 93
  Great Depression in, 82, 83

Great Britain *(continued)*
 late 19th, early 20th century economy of, 63–64
 liberalism in, 25, 65–66
 liberalism revived after World War II in, 91–92, 94
 nationalism and, 68–69, 74–75
 pension system in, 230
 protectionist movement before World War I in, 74–75
 relative decline of, 35–36
Great Depression, 80–83
Great Transformation, The (Polanyi), 6
Greenspan, Alan, 194
Greider, William, 6–7, 215, 218
Group of 77, 249
Guatemala, 166

Haiti, 168
Harriman, Henry, 82
Has Globalization Gone Too Far? (Rodrik), 7, 220
Hayek, F. A., 31, 43, 55, 91, 92, 100
 on broad role for government, 58
 on competition, 51
 on markets' use of dispersed information, 40–41, 42
 on planning vs. freedom, 89–90
 on social safety net, 217–218
 on uncertainty, 48, 54
Heine, Heinrich, 86
Hierarchy costs, 54–56
Hitler, Adolf, 83
Honduras, 152, 166
Hong Kong:
 and "Asian miracle," 95, 106–107
 financial system in, 138, 157, 209
 political system in, 181

Hoover, Herbert, 40, 77–78, 82
Horton, Tom, 139
Hull, Cordell, 94, 95
Hungary, 227–228, 230, 231
Hyundai, 148

Iceland, 228
Import substitution, 8, 11, 103–104, 111, 112, 116, 256
Independent (nonprofit) sector, 57, 217, 222
India:
 agriculture policy, 128
 collapse of collectivism in, 7, 111, 189
 collectivism in, 96, 99
 financial system in, 157
 in first world economy, 65
 pension system in, 232–233
 protectionism in, 131
 shadow economy in, 162–166
Indonesia:
 and "Asian miracle," 106
 catch-up growth in, 116
 financial crisis in, 142, 148, 200–201
 financial system in, 208, 209
 in first world economy, 65
 political system in, 181, 182
 shadow economy in, 166–167
Industrial Counterrevolution, 10, 16–37, 276n8. *See also* Collectivism
 as family of movements, 20–21, 67
 globalization and collapse of, 2–3, 9, 11, 112, 252, 270
 reactionary social values of, 21–24, 71–72, 96–97, 244–246
 reasons for endurance of, 113–118

Industrial Counterrevolution *(continued)*
   World War I and, 11, 62, 65–79,
     245–246
Industrial Revolution. *See also* Indus-
    trial Counterrevolution
   and first world economy, 63–65
   misinterpretation of, 10
   as new form of economic order,
     25–26, 277*n*13
   spiritual trauma caused by, 21–22
Inflation, 79, 113, 194–195
Informal sector. *See* Shadow
   economies
Information. *See also* Knowledge
   markets' efficient use of, 40–43
   and political process, 252–257
Innovation, promoted by competi-
   tion, 46–52, 144
International Monetary Fund (IMF),
    94, 204–206, 259–260, 262–266
Internet, 130–131, 174–175
Intrinsic value, concept of, 44
Ireland, 243
Ishihara, Shintaro, 140–141
Islamist fundamentalism, 271–273
Italy:
   pension system in, 225, 226
   rise of fascism in, 82, 84
   shadow economy in, 294*n*7

Japan:
   "bubble economy" and aftermath
    in, 2, 110, 142, 149
   as capitalist developmental state,
    106–110
   catch-up growth in, 115–116
   financial system in, 2, 140–141,
    142, 156–158, 236

   in first world economy, 63, 65
   pension system in, 225, 226, 228
   restrictions on competition in,
    235–237
Japan That Can Say "No," The
    (Morito and Ishihara), 140–141

Johnson, Chalmers, 141
Johnson, Hugh, 77, 78–79
Jospin, Lionel, 215
Jünger, Ernst, 62

Kaset Thai Sugar Company, 158–161
Kathedersozialisten. See State socialism
   (Germany)
Kazakhstan, 122, 129
   pension system in, 230, 232
Keegan, John, 61–62
Kenya, 233
Keynes, John Maynard, 20, 50, 111,
   152, 194
Kim Dae-Jung, 182
King, Robert, 144
Knowledge. *See also* Information
   competition's contribution to
    new, 46–52, 144
   political process and discovery of
    new, 252–257
Korea:
   and "Asian miracle," 95, 106
   financial crisis in, 142, 148, 200–
    201
   financial system in, 137, 139, 157,
    208, 209
   political system in, 181–182
Korea First Bank, 137, 139
Korean War, 134
Kyrgyzstan, 122

Labor markets:
    effect of globalization on, 218–220
    regulation of, 238–243
    World Trade Organization and,
        248, 249
Lamont, Robert, 133
Lassalle, Ferdinand, 32
Latin America:
    catch-up growth in, 116
    collapse of collectivism in, 2, 111,
        189, 256
    financial repression in, 152–153
    import-substitution policies in,
        103
    pension systems in, 228
    political systems in, 182
    protectionism during first world
        economy in, 70
    shadow economy in, 166–168
Latvia, 122, 227, 228
Leekpai, Chuan, 186
Legal systems. *See also specific*
        countries
    consequences of poor, 13, 169–174
    economic growth and, 174–179
    political systems and, 179–188,
        295*n*28
    shadow economies and, 162–168
Lenin, Vladimir, 77, 98–99
    central planning and, 44, 45, 48
    Taylor and, 30
    theory of imperialism, 101–102
Lensch, Paul, 76
Leuchtenburg, William, 78
Levine, Ross, 144, 145
Lexus and the Olive Tree, The (Fried-
        man), 4, 120, 169
LG (Korean *chaebol*), 148

Liberalism:
    ascendancy during 19th century,
        65–67
    eclipsed by Industrial Counter-
        revolution, 24, 25, 34
    revival of, 88–95, 250–257, 266–
        270
    revival of, other interpretations,
        257–266
    and role of government, 56–60,
        168–169, 176
Liebknecht, Wilhelm, 32
Lippmann, Walter, 276–277*n*8
Lithuania, 122
Living standards, desire for higher,
        253–255
Lloyd George, David, 37
Lobbying, 253
Looking Backward: 2000–1887
        (Bellamy), 16–20, 27, 39,
        276*n*1
Losses, as market signals, 52

Macedonia, 122
Madison, James, 179–180, 187–188
Magnitogorsk steel mill, 120–122,
        124
Maksimovic, Vojislav, 145
Malaysia:
    and "Asian miracle," 106
    capital controls in, 195
    financial crisis in, 142, 148, 201
    financial system in, 153, 199, 208
    pension system in, 232–233
    political system in, 181, 182
    shadow economy in, 167
Managerial revolution, 84–85, 88–89
Market competition. *See* Competition

"Market fundamentalism," 6–7, 169, 190–193, 211, 250

Markets:
as complex systems, 39
contrasted to central planning, 43–46
resilience of, 268–269
use of dispersed information by, 40–43

Marx, Karl, 22, 97, 216, 246
and socialism's inevitability, 31–32, 68

Material affluence:
anti-globalization protests as reaction against, 246–247
radical Islamist hostility toward, 271–273
World War I as relief from, 245–246

Mauro, Paulo, 170

McNamara, Robert, 263

Menem, Carlos, 7, 171–172

Mexico:
banking system and, 207–208
collapse of collectivism in, 111
financial repression in, 152, 153
International Monetary Fund and, 204–205
pegged exchange rate policy in, 199–201
pension system in, 226, 230, 232
shadow economy in, 167

"Microchip Immune Deficiency Syndrome," 4

Militarism:
in Germany, 72–74, 75–78
in Great Britain, 74–75

Ministry of International Trade and Industry (Japan), 108–110

Mobutu Sese Seko, 178

Modernity. *See also* Technological progress
anti-globalization protests and hostility to, 246–247, 250–251
in developing countries, 23, 97–98
Industrial Counterrevolution as reaction against, 21–24, 71–72, 96–97, 245–246
radical Islamist hostility toward, 271–273
World War I and reaction against, 245–246

Moldova, 122

Mommsen, Wolfgang, 282n19, 283n27

Monetary policy:
inflation and, 194–195
nature of money and, 193–194

Moral hazard, 150–151, 204–206, 264

Morgan, Arthur E., 276n6

Morita, Akio, 140–141

Moscow, 1–2

"Most favored nation" principle, 94

Mukhametzianov, Faik, 122

Mussolini, Benito, 82, 84

My Life and Work (Ford), 162

Myrdal, Gunnar, 100

Mystery of Capital, The (de Soto), 167–168

"National efficiency" movement (Great Britain), 36–37, 74, 255

National Industrial Recovery Act, 77, 78–79, 90–91, 133

Nationalism, protectionism and, 70–75, 282nn18,19

National Recovery Administration, 77, 78–79, 90–91, 133

National Socialism, 78, 83–84

"National treatment" principle, 94

Nehru, Jawaharlal, 99

Netherlands, 243

Newbridge Capital, 137, 139

New Deal, 77–78, 90–91

New Economic Policy (NEP) (Soviet Union), 45–46

New Industrial State, The (Galbraith), 50

New international economic order (NIEO) movement, 105, 110

New Zealand, 126

Nguema, Francisco Marcias, 177

Nietzsche, Friedrich, 22

Nigeria, 131, 167

1984 (Orwell), 92

Nisbet, Robert, 22–23

Nkrumah, Kwame, 99

North, Douglass, 276*n*8, 277*n*13

Norway, 239, 240

Nurske, Ragnar, 100

Nyerere, Julius, 105

Obote, Milton, 177

Ohmae, Kenichi, 4

Oil industry, 127–128

Okello, Tito, 177

Olson, Mancur:
  on democracy and special interests, 184, 295*n*28
  on "encompassing interests," 254
  on "spontaneous" vs. "socially contrived" markets, 175, 176

One World, Ready or Not (Greider), 6

Ordoliberal movement, 92

Organisation for Economic Co-operation and Development (OECD), 128, 129, 130

"Organization Man," 49–51

Orwell, George, 92

Other Path, The (de Soto), 167

Pacific Rim. *See specific countries*

Pakistan, 157

Panama, 166, 203–204

Panyarachun, Anand, 187

Park Chung-Hee, 181

Pay-as-you-go public pension systems, 223–229

Peek, George, 78

Pegged exchange rates, 94–95, 193, 196–201, 202, 204, 207

Pension systems, 222–233
  pay-as-you go systems, 223–229
  privatized systems, 229–232
  provident fund systems, 232–233

Perkins, George W., 28

Perón, Juan, 170, 171

Peru, 167, 168, 230

Philbro, 173

Philippines:
  banking system in, 208
  international capital flows and, 201
  shadow economy in, 167, 168

Piñera, José, 224, 230

Plenge, Johann, 76

Poland, 227, 230

Polanyi, Karl, 6–7

Political systems, economic growth and, 179–188
  autocracies, 180–183
  democracies, 183–188

Politics:
    as discovery process, 252–257
    globalization as political event, 9
Portfolio investment, 195–196,
    296*n*10
Poverty:
    dependency theory and Third
        World, 101–105
    underdevelopment of markets and,
        175–176
    "vicious circle" of, 100–101
Prebisch, Raúl, 103–104, 152
Prestowitz, Clyde, 141, 143
Price controls, 12, 46, 127
Privatization, 126–130
    in Central and Eastern Europe,
        122
    in Russia, 121, 122–124
Productivity, compensation as func-
    tion of, 218–220
Profits, as market signals, 52
Progressive Era, 19, 28, 35, 255,
    277*n*12
Property rights, markets' reliance on,
    57, 169–179. *See also* Contract
    rights, markets' reliance on; Le-
    gal systems; Political systems,
    economic growth and
*Propositions for Improving the Manufac-
    tures, Agriculture, and Commerce
    of Great Britain,* 219
Protectionism:
    continuing influence of, 12, 131–
        136
    developing countries and, 131–132
    and Industrial Counterrevolution,
        69–75, 80–84

during interwar years, 80, 82–83
    during 19th century, 70
    and origins of World War I, 11,
        65, 71–72, 282*nn*18,19
    in United States, 132
    U.S. steel industry and, 134–136
Protest movements, anti-
    globalization, 244–250
    developing countries and, 249–
        250
    hostility to material affluence,
        246–247
    political strength in United States,
        247–249
    terrorism and, 272
Provident fund systems, 232–233
Pyramid schemes. *See* Pay-as-you-go
    public pension systems

Quest for Community, The (Nisbet),
    22

"Race to the bottom," 5, 8, 218–219,
    249, 258–259
Railroad industry, 63–64, 128
Rajan, Raghuram, 145
Rao, P.V. Narashima, 7, 111
Real estate. *See* Agriculture; Legal
    systems; Property rights, mar-
    kets' reliance on; Shadow
    economies
Recession cartels, 108, 109
Reciprocal Trade Agreements Act,
    93–94
*Redemption by War: The Intellectuals
    and 1914* (Stromberg), 246
Reich, Robert, 140

Retirement benefits. *See* Pension systems

Road to Serfdom, The (Hayek), 89–90

Robbins, Lionel, 282*n*18

Rodrik, Dani, 7, 220

Romania, 122, 228

Roosevelt, Franklin, 78, 81, 82

Roosevelt, Theodore, 35

Röpke, Wilhelm, 92

Rosebery, Lord (Archibald Philip Primrose), 74

Rosenberg, Nathan, 51–52

Russia. *See also* Soviet Union
  agriculture policy in, 129
  financial system in, 153, 154–155, 207, 210–211
  International Monetary Fund and, 204–206, 264
  pegged exchange rate policy in, 199–201
  pension system in, 228
  privatization in, 121, 122–124
  protectionism during 19th century in, 70
  shadow economy in, 167
  steel industry in, 120–122, 124, 135–136, 234–235

Rüstow, Alexander, 92

Rwanda, 177

Safety net. *See* Social policy

Samsung, 148

Samuelson, Paul, 224, 225

Scheler, Max, 245

Schlesinger, Arthur, Jr., 5

Schmoller, Gustav, 34, 35, 69, 73–74

Schneider, Friedrich, 167

Schumpeter, Joseph, 49–50

Scientific management, 29–30, 48

Scott, John, 120

Searle, G. R., 36

1789 and 1914: The Symbolic Years in the History of the Political Mind (Plenge), 76

Shadow economies:
  in developed world, 294*n*7
  in developing and postcommunist countries, 166–168
  in India, 162–166
  payroll taxes and, 227–228

Shaw, George Bernard, 69

Sherbakova, Yelena, 121

Shinawatra, Thaksin, 187

Siam Syntech, 146–147

Sierra Leone, 177

Silpa-archa, Banharn, 186

Singapore:
  and "Asian miracle," 95, 106
  financial system in, 138, 157, 209
  pension system in, 232–233
  political system in, 181

Siriviriyakul, Pradit, 159

Siriviriyakul family, 159–161

Smith, Adam, 66, 268

Smoot-Hawley Tariff, 83

Social Democratic Party (Germany), 32, 68

Social engineering, 39–40

Socialism:
  German "state," 32–34, 72–77, 83, 255, 283*n*27
  Marx and inevitability of, 31–32, 68
  National, 78, 83–84

Social policy, 13–14, 215–243
  alleged loss of tax base and, 220–221
  dependence on state encouraged
    by collectivist, 223–224
  government role in, 57–58, 217–
    218, 222–223, 233–234
  labor policies, 233–243
  pension systems, 222–233
Social Security. *See* Pension systems
Somalia, 177
Sombart, Werner, 76
Somme, Battle of the, 61–62
Soros, George, 6, 7, 190–192
Soviet Union. *See also* Russia
  attempt at central planning in,
    44–46
  catch-up growth in, 116–117
  collapse of, 2, 111–112, 255
  as collectivist model, 96, 98–99,
    255
  Henry Ford and, 162
  importance of ideological enthusi-
    asm in, 114–115
  inspired by American example,
    29–30
  inspired by German war economy,
    77
Spain, 80, 243
Stagnationists, 49–50
Stalin, Joseph, 29, 45–46, 98–99,
  116–117
State and Revolution, The (Lenin), 48
State-owned enterprises (SOEs), 122,
  124–130
State socialism (Germany), 32–34,
  72–77, 83, 255, 283*n*27
Steamships, and first world economy,
  64

Steel industry:
  in Russia, 120–122, 124, 135–136,
    234–235
  in United States, 28, 133–136
Steffens, Lincoln, 255
Stromberg, Roland, 246
Subsidies, government:
  agriculture, 128–129
  in China, 125–126, 153
  in Russia, 123–124, 129
Sudan, 177
Suffrage, 33, 253
Sweden, 225–226, 230, 231
Switzerland, 128, 230

Taiwan:
  and "Asian miracle," 95, 106
  financial system in, 138, 157, 209,
    297*n*31
  political system in, 181–182
Tajikistan, 122
Tariffs. *See* Protectionism
Tax revenues:
  and "encompassing interests," 254
  and social policy, 220–221
Taylor, Frederick Winslow, 29–30,
  38, 48, 133
Technocracy, Inc., 40
Technological progress. *See also*
  Modernity
  globalization and, 8–9
  undermines collectivism, 117–118,
    288*n*51
Telecommunications industry, 129–
  131
Thailand:
  and "Asian miracle," 106
  catch-up growth in, 116

Thailand *(continued)*
  financial crisis in, 142, 146–148,
    200–201
  financial system in, 142, 151, 153,
    157, 208, 209
  in first world economy, 65
  legal system in, 158–161
  political system in, 181–182, 185–
    187
  protectionism in, 131
  shadow economy in, 166–167
Theory of the Business Enterprise, The
    (Veblen), 27–28
"Theory of the Firm, The" (Coase),
    53
Third World. *See* Developing coun-
    tries
Three Years of World Revolution
    (Lensch), 76
Totalitarianism. *See* Autocracies
Transaction costs, 53–56, 174–175,
    280–281*n*33
Transparency International, 171
Transportation industries, regulation
    of, 12, 128
Treaty of Rome, 95
Trotsky, Leon, 44, 45, 46
Truman, Harry S., 91, 134
Tugwell, Rexford, 82, 285*n*51
Turkmenistan, 122
Turning Point Project, 247

Uganda, 177
Ukraine, 122, 227
Uncertainty, as justification for com-
    petition, 47–52, 58, 115, 208–
    209, 280*n*33
Unemployment, 240–243

United Nations Economic Commis-
    sion for Latin America (ECLA),
    103, 104
United States:
  collectivism in, 77–78, 82, 90–91,
    93, 188
  as collectivist model, 25–30
  deregulation in, 126, 190
  federal tax revenues in, 5, 221
  financial system in, 139–140, 141–
    142, 156–157
  in first world economy, 63–64, 70
  foreign direct investment in, 220
  in Great Depression, 80–83
  influenced by Germany, 34–35
  job creation and losses in, 237–
    238, 240–241, 242
  liberalism revived in, 90–91, 93–
    94
  manufacturing and, 220, 221
  protectionism in, 132–133, 134–
    135
  protest movement in, 247–249
  savings-and-loan crisis in, 150–
    151, 156
  Social Security system in, 225,
    226, 228, 231
  steel industry in, 28, 133–136
  terrorist attacks against, 271–273
  World Trade Organization
    (WTO) and, 248, 260
Uruguay, 227
Uzbekistan, 122

Veblen, Thorstein, 27–28, 143
Venezuela, 166, 226, 228
Visible Hand, The (Chandler), 55, 85
Vollmar, Georg, 68

von Laue, Theodore, 98–99, 276*n*8
von Mises, Ludwig, 43, 84
von Tirpitz, Alfred, 36
Voting, 33, 253

Wagner, Adolf, 34, 73–74, 84
Wagner's law, 34, 83
Wansley, Michael, 158–161
Wealth of Nations, The (Smith), 66
Webb, Eric, 147
Whyte, William, 49
Wild, Jack, 146
Williamson, Oliver, 280–281*n*33
Wilson, Harold, 92
World Bank, 259, 262–266
World Economic Forum, 218
World Trade Organization (WTO),
    259–262
  China and, 248, 261–262
  GATT contrasted, 260–261

protests and, 244, 248, 249
United States and, 248, 260
World War I:
  Battle of the Somme, 61–62
  consequences of, 76–80
  origins of, 11, 62, 65–76,
    282*nn*18,19, 283*nn*20,27, 284*n*30
  steel industry and, 133
  war fever at outset of, 245–246
World War II, 85
  consequences of, 88–89
  steel industry and, 133
Wurgler, Jeffrey, 144–145

Yongchaiyudh, Chavalit, 186

Zambia, 233
Zedillo, Ernesto, 249
Zervos, Sarah, 145
Zingales, Luigi, 145